Statute Rolls of the Irish Parliament
Richard III – Henry VIII

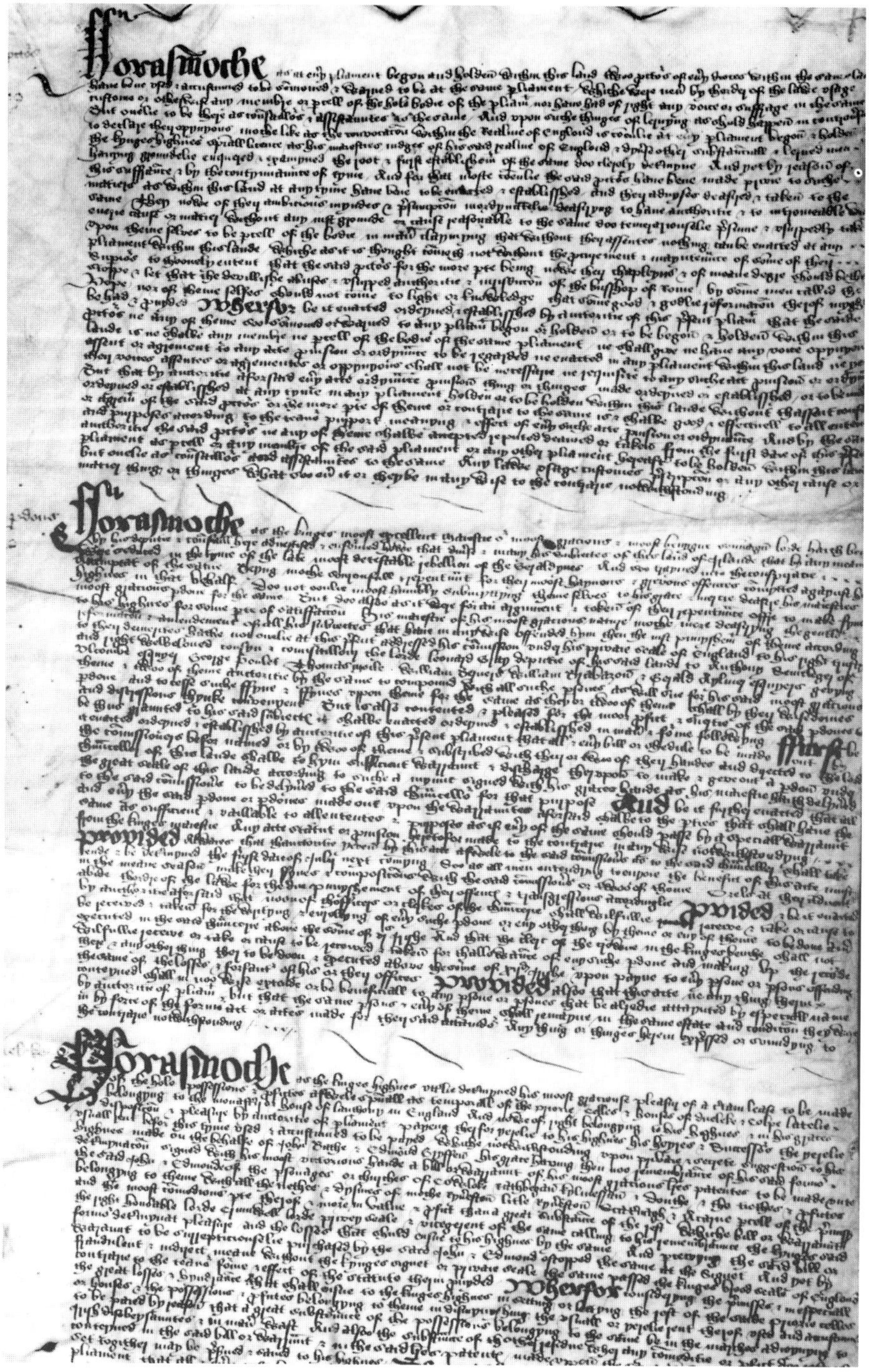

A detail from Statute Roll 28–29 Henry VIII, chapters 19–21 (NAI, CH 1/1 m. 20).

Statute Rolls of the Irish Parliament

Richard III – Henry VIII

Philomena Connolly

Editor

FOUR COURTS PRESS

for

THE NATIONAL ARCHIVES OF IRELAND

Set in 10.5 on 13 point Ehrhardt for
Four Courts Press Ltd
Fumbally Lane, Dublin 8, Ireland
e-mail: info@four-courts-press.ie
and in North America
Four Courts Press
c/o ISBS, 5824 N.E. Hassalo Street, Portland, OR 97213

A catalogue record for this title
is available from the British Library

ISBN 1–85182–682–3

Printed in Great Britain
by MPG Books, Bodmin, Cornwall

In memory of Margaret C. Griffith, M.A., B.Litt.,
Deputy Keeper of the Public Records of Ireland, 1956–1971

Contents

Preface

The publication of the present volume marks the culmination of a project begun in 1811 by the Irish Record Commission, continued by the Public Record Office of Ireland, and now completed by the National Archives. As with other long-term projects, each new generation of editors has relied heavily on the work of their predecessors, and it is fitting that the names of those involved at various stages should be recorded here:

> Irish Record Commission: William Shaw Mason, secretary of the Commission, William Ball, Bartholomew Duhigg, Edward Lawson, Henry J. Mason and Roderick Connor, all sub-commissioners on the statutes, and the Reverend E. Groves.
>
> Public Record Office of Ireland: James Digges La Touche (Deputy Keeper, 1886–99), James Mills (Deputy Keeper, 1899–1914), Henry F. Berry, Albert E. Langman, T.J. Morrissey, James F. Morrissey, Charles McGarry, Margaret C. Griffith (Deputy Keeper, 1956–71) and Breandán Mac Giolla Choille (Deputy Keeper, 1971–85). The present volume has benefited particularly from the work of the two last-named – Margaret Griffith's work on the Irish Record Commission and its records, and the transcript of the statute roll for 28–29 Henry VIII prepared by Breandán Mac Giolla Choille.

Many people have assisted with and provided information for the present volume and we particularly wish to thank the following: Aideen Ireland, Frances McGee and Lorcan Farrell, National Archives; Mary Clark, Dublin City Archives; Dr Noel Kissane, Manuscripts Department, National Library of Ireland; Dr Raymond Refaussé, Representative Church Body Library; Dr Jean-Michel Picard, Department of French, University College, Dublin; Dr Seán Duffy and Dr Katharine Simms, Department of Medieval History, Trinity College, Dublin; Professor James Lydon, Trinity College, Dublin; Dr Brendan Smith, Department of Historical Studies, University of Bristol; Dr Mario Sughi and Dr Ciarán Parker.

Abbreviations

BL	British Library
Bryan, *Great earl of Kildare*	Donough Bryan, *Gerald FitzGerald, the great earl of Kildare* (Dublin, 1933)
Cal. Ormond Deeds	*Calendar of Ormond Deeds*, ed. E. Curtis, 6 vols (Irish Manuscripts Commission, 1932–42)
Cal. Pat. Rolls	*Calendar of the patent rolls* (London, 1906–)
Chartul. St Mary's, Dublin	*Chartularies of St Mary's abbey, Dublin ... and annals of Ireland, 1162–1370*, ed. J.T. Gilbert (2 vols, 1884-6)
E.H.R.	*English Historical Review*
Facs nat. MSS Ire.	*Facsimiles of the national manuscripts of Ireland*, ed. J.T. Gilbert (4 vols, Dublin, 1874–84)
I.H.S.	*Irish Historical Studies*
IRC	Irish Record Commission
NAI	National Archives, Ireland
NLI	National Library of Ireland
O.E.D.	*The Oxford English Dictionary* (2nd ed., 1989)
P.R.I. rep. D.K. 20	*Twentieth report of the deputy keeper of the public records in Ireland* (Dublin, 1888)
PRO	Public Record Office
PROI	Public Record Office of Ireland
PRONI	Public Record Office of Northern Ireland
Quinn, 'Bills and statutes'	D.B. Quinn, 'The bills and statutes of the Irish parliaments of Henry VII and Henry VIII', *Analecta Hibernica* 10 (1942) pp 71-169
R.I.A. Proc	*Proceedings of the Royal Irish Academy* (Dublin, 1836–)
Rec. comm. Ire. rep., 1811-15 [etc.]	*Reports of the commissioners appointed by his majesty to execute the measures recommended in an address of the house of commons respecting the public records of Ireland, with supplement and appendixes* (3 vols, [London, 1815–25]: i, rep. 1–5, 1811–15; ii, rep. 6-10, 1816–20; iii, rep. 11–15, 1821–5)

Richardson & Sayles, *Ir. parl. in middle ages*	H.G. Richardson and G.O. Sayles, *The Irish parliament in the middle ages* (Philadelphia, 1952)
Richardson & Sayles, *Rot. parl. hact.*	H.G. Richardson and G.O. Sayles, *Rotuli parliamentorum Anglie hactenus inediti* (R. Hist. Soc. London, 1935)
Rot. Pat. Hib.	*Rotulorum patentium et clausorum cancellariae Hiberniae calendarium*, ed. Edward Tresham (Dublin, 1828)
Stat. Ire., 1–12 Edw. IV,	*Statute rolls of the parliament of Ireland, 1st to 12th years of the reign of King Edward IV*, ed. H.F. Berry (Dublin, 1914)
Stat. Ire., 12–22 Edw. IV	*Statute rolls of the parliament of Ireland, 12th and 13th to the 21st and 22nd years of the reign of King Edward IV*, ed. James F. Morrissey (Dublin, 1939)
Stat. Ire., Hen. VI	*Statute rolls of the parliament of Ireland, reign of King Henry VI*, ed. H.F. Berry (Dublin, 1910)
Stat. Ire., John–Hen. V	*Statutes and ordinances, and acts of the parliament of Ireland, King John to Henry V*, ed. H.F. Berry, (Dublin, 1907)
Statutes at large	*The statutes at large passed in the parliaments held in Ireland* ... 20 vols (Dublin, 1786–1801)
Statutes of the realm	*The statutes of the realm ... to 1713*, 9 vols (London, 1810–18)
Wood, *Guide*	Herbert Wood, *A guide to the records deposited in the Public Record Office of Ireland* (Dublin, 1919)

Introduction

This volume, the fifth in the series,[1] marks the completion of a project begun in 1811 to publish the enactments of the medieval Irish parliament. It contains the full text of the statute rolls for 1 Richard III (1484), 2–3 Richard III (1485), 8 Henry VII (1493) and 28–29 Henry VIII (1536–7), together with individual acts passed in the reign of Edward IV which were not enrolled on the statute rolls at the time of their enactment and so were not included in volumes 3 and 4 of the present series. No attempt has been made to include acts passed in other parliaments of the reigns of these monarchs, the statute rolls of which did not survive in 1811.[2]

HISTORY OF THE PROJECT

The idea of publishing the medieval Irish statutes in their entirety originated with the Irish Record Commission, a body established in 1810.[3] Although several collections of Irish statutes had been printed, none of these was complete for the medieval period.[4] On 18 February 1811 the Commission ordered that

> ... a complete and authentic edition of the statutes and ordinances of Ireland be prepared and printed, including every law, as well those repealed or expired as those now in force; with a chronological list of them, and tables of the principal matters, and that for the purpose of ascertaining and preserving a memorial of the correct and entire text of the statute law of Ireland, copies be distributed throughout the United

1 The earlier volumes in the series are: *Statutes and ordinances, and acts of the parliament of Ireland, King John to Henry V*, ed. H.F. Berry (Dublin, 1907); *Statute rolls of the parliament of Ireland, reign of King Henry VI*, ed. H.F. Berry (Dublin, 1910); *Statute rolls of the parliament of Ireland, 1st to 12th years of the reign of King Edward IV*, ed. H.F. Berry (Dublin, 1914); *Statute rolls of the parliament of Ireland, 12th and 13th to the 21st and 22nd years of the reign of King Edward IV*, ed. James F. Morrissey (Dublin, 1939). 2 For a reconstruction of these missing rolls from other sources, see D.B. Quinn, 'The bills and statutes of the Irish parliaments of Henry VII and Henry VIII', *Analecta Hibernica* 10 (1941), pp 71–169, and S.G. Ellis, 'Parliaments and great councils, 1483–99: addenda and corrigenda', *Analecta Hibernica* 29 (1980), pp 96–111. 3 For an account of the work of the Irish Record Commission see Margaret Griffith, 'The Irish Record Commission, 1810–30', *I.H.S.*, vii (1950–1), pp 17–38. 4 For a list of printed collections of Irish statutes from 1572 onwards, see Quinn, 'Bills and statutes', pp 76–7.

Kingdom, for custody and public inspection, in such manner as may be determined by the Board.[5]

Four barristers at law – William Ball, Bartholomew Duhigg, Edward Lawson and Henry J. Mason – were appointed sub-commissioners to put this into effect. William Shaw Mason, the secretary of the Commission, was associated with them in this work, and an additional sub-commissioner, Roderick Connor, was appointed in 1812. They saw 1494–5 (10 Henry VII) as a clear dividing line and intended that the first volume, containing a definitive text of the statutes in their original French, together with an English translation, should end at this date. This was partly because the enactment of Poynings' Law in the parliament of that year changed the whole procedure of legislative enactment in Ireland, but also because the records after that date were in English, rather than in Norman-French, and so were easier to consult.

Work on the project continued until 1824 but no volumes were published. In that year, the project is described as 'suspended',[6] probably for financial reasons, and the publication was still in abeyance when the Record Commission was wound up in 1830. Its papers, including the transcripts and translations prepared by the sub-commissioners on the statutes, were deposited in the State Paper Office in Dublin Castle, and, after the establishment of the Public Record Office of Ireland (PROI) in 1867, were transferred to that Office's repository at the Four Courts.[7]

Sir Samuel Ferguson, the first Deputy Keeper of Public Records, proposed the revision of the Record Commission texts and translations with a view to publication, but, due to the pressure of other business, nothing was done. His successor, James Digges La Touche, had the Record Commission material compared with the original rolls, which had also been transferred to the Public Record Office, and in 1901, James Mills, La Touche's successor, got the Lord Lieutenant's approval for the completion of the work of publication.[8] The first volume, covering the period to 1422, appeared in 1907, and was followed by volume 2 (Henry VI) in 1910 and volume 3 (1–12 Edward IV) in 1914; all were edited by Henry F. Berry, an assistant keeper in PROI.

The Four Courts fire in 1922 resulted in the loss of the original statute rolls except that for 28–29 Henry VIII, and also of the Record Commission's volumes of transcripts and translations, except one volume of exemplifications (or certified copies) of statutes of the reign of Edward IV. However, much of the work for the next two volumes had already been done before 1922 and some of this material survived. Henry F. Berry and T.J. Morrissey had prepared

5 *Rec. Comm. Ire. rep. 1811–15*, p. 11. 6 *Rec. Comm. Ire. rep. 1821–5*, p. 20. 7 Wood, *Guide*, pp 268–71. 8 *Stat. Ire., John–Hen. V*, vii.

revised editions of the Record Commission transcripts for publication, and these survived to form the basis of volume 4 (12–22 Edward IV), edited by J.F. Morrissey, which appeared in 1941.[9] The Record Commission's translation had been destroyed so a new translation was made for this volume by Charles McGarry. A further disaster occurred while printing was in progress. A fire at the printing works in August 1935 destroyed the type, but fortunately it was possible to use the proof for publication by means of photo-lithography.[10]

Berry's revised versions of the Record Commission's transcripts of the statute rolls for 1 and 2–3 Richard III and 8 Henry VII also survived the fire of 1922, and it was decided that these, together with the text of the only surviving original roll, that for 28–29 Henry VIII which had never been published in full, should form the basis of the final volume of this series. It was also decided to include the Record Commission's translations of exemplifications of statutes for the reign of Edward IV, which had been omitted from volumes 3 and 4. Further work was done on this volume by James F. Morrissey, Breandán Mac Giolla Choille and the present editor, but on each occasion pressure of other work in an understaffed Record Office prevented the project from being brought to completion until now.

NATURE OF THE ROLLS

The proceedings of the medieval English parliament were enrolled on two series of rolls, parliament rolls and statute rolls.[11] In Ireland, however, there was only one series of rolls, beginning in 1427. These have generally been referred to in modern times as statute rolls, but this terminology was challenged by H.G. Richardson, who suggested that 'parliament rolls' was a more appropriate term.[12] They were referred to in the medieval period as 'rolls of parliament' and contained material other than enactments, such as the election and protestation of the speaker of the commons, and the letter of the earl of Kildare, printed in the present volume, authorising the chancellor to prorogue parliament. It is true too, that many of the enactments are of an administrative nature. However, all enactments, whether 'statutes of public utility', or for the benefit of named individuals, or of an administrative nature, resulted from

9 Although the volume bears the publication date of 1939, it was not in fact published until two years later. **10** *Stat. Ire., 12–22 Edw. IV*, lxxvi–lxxvii. **11** For a discussion of the records of the English parliament, see Richardson & Sayles, *Rot. parl. hact.*, xiii–xxii. **12** H.G. Richardson, 'The Irish parliament rolls of the fifteenth century', *E.H.R.* lviii (1943), pp 448–50. For a short discussion of the records of the medieval Irish parliament see Philomena Connolly, 'The enactments of the 1297 parliament' in James Lydon (ed.), *Law and disorder in thirteenth century Ireland* (Dublin, 1997), pp 139–46.

the same legislative process, and fall into the category of statutes. Furthermore, there was much non-legislative business that was not enrolled on these rolls, and so they cannot be described as a complete record of the proceedings of parliament. Apart from two instances, there is no record of the election of the speaker of the commons,[13] or of any speech made on the opening of parliament. Grants of taxation and the text of messages and statements of grievances sent to the king and council in England were enrolled only occasionally. The text of petitions presented in parliament was not enrolled, although the legislation resulting from successful petitions was, and we do not have any record of judicial proceedings in parliament during this period. These limitations, together with the fact that the heading of each roll begins with the words *Statuta acta et ordinaciones*, justify the application of the term 'statute rolls' to this class of records, which is how the records will be referred to here.

FORMAT OF THE ROLLS

The statute rolls were composed of several parchment membranes sewn together end to end, and in general, only the front of the roll was used. Although there were minor variations between rolls, they all used the same basic format.

Headings

Each roll was usually headed with details of where, when and before whom the parliament had begun, the date and place of any subsequent sessions resulting from prorogations and adjournments (which appear to have been synonymous in this period[14]) and the date of termination of the parliament. This means that it is not possible to determine from the format of the roll which acts were passed at each session, and recourse must be had to other evidence. The rolls for 1 Richard III and 28–29 Henry VIII printed here have this format. However, some rolls, like those for 2–3 Richard III and 8 Henry VII, had an initial heading recording the details of the first session of the parliament, followed by the text of the acts passed in that session. Each subsequent session had a separate sub-heading giving the place and date, followed by the acts passed in that session.

13 1449 and 1450 (*Stat. Ire.. Hen. VI*, pp 110–13, 178–9). 14 D.B. Quinn, 'Parliaments and great councils in Ireland, 1461–1586', *I.H.S.* iii (1941), p. 62.

Customary acts

The heading was immediately followed by the text of the three acts which were customarily enacted at the beginning of each parliament – confirming the liberties of the church, the land of Ireland and the cities and corporate towns. This practice continued until the 16th century, the parliament of 1516 being the last known occasion on which these acts were enrolled on the statute roll.[15] The roll for 8 Henry VII, as it survives in the Record Commission transcript, does not contain the three acts, but it is possible that the first membrane of this roll may have been lost.[16]

Number of rolls kept

It appears that one roll was kept for each parliament, though there may have been drafts. There were two rolls for the parliament of 3 Edward IV (1463), which are partly duplicates of each other, but each of which contains unique material.[17] The reason for this is not clear.

Order of enrolment

The acts were enrolled chronologically by session, probably at the end of each session.[18] However, there is no evidence as to whether the order of enrolment reflects the order in which the acts were passed within each session. In cases where all the sessions were to be listed in one heading at the beginning of the roll, a sizeable blank space was left for the insertion of details of further sessions before proceeding with the enrolment of the first act, as can be seen in the roll for 28–29 Henry VIII. The acts were numbered on the roll, but, in the case of the fifteenth century rolls, it is not clear whether this numbering was contemporary or added at a later date. From 1494–5 onwards, the title of each act appears in the margin of the roll.[19]

15 Quinn, 'Bills and statutes', pp 113, 123, 134–5, 137. 16 See Appendix 2 below. 17 *Stat. Ire., 1–12 Edw. IV*, pp 40–271. In other cases where more than one roll existed for a parliament, it is clear from their contents that they were actually detached portions of the same roll (*Stat. Ire., 12–22 Edw. IV*, pp 584–646). 18 In the 1536–7 parliament the wrong date for the payment of a subsidy was included in the enrolment of c.9, passed in the first session, 'through the misprision and negligence of the clerk', and it was necessary to rectify this by the enactment of a declaratory act (c.41) in the final session. The use of the expression 'the late king' in the heading of the roll for 2–3 Richard III, might be taken to imply that the roll was written after the accession of Henry VII, but if so, there is no reason for the use of sub-headings for each session. It is possible that the word *nuper* (late) was a later insertion, although this is not indicated in the Record Commission transcript. 19 For facsimiles of parts of other statute rolls of this period, see *Facs. nat. MSS Ire.*, part 3, plates xlii (1460), xlviii (1463–4), and liii (1494–5).

Language

Apart from the headings, which were written in Latin, the usual language up to 1494–5 was Norman French, which has been described by H.G. Richardson as 'a lifeless, conventional, ungrammatical French, rendering the English vernacular word for word, innocent of the idiom of France'.[20] Occasionally, English words might be included for clarification of a concept (as in *cotage dez porks ou stye*),[21] or where a suitable French equivalent did not exist. The earl of Kildare's letter to the chancellor, authorising him to prorogue parliament in 1485, was written in English and no attempt was made to translate it for the record. Two acts of the 1493 parliament are in Latin,[22] perhaps reflecting the language of the original petition, but these are the exception. The parliament of 1494–5 was the first one to have the record of its enactments enrolled in English,[23] and this became the standard practice, the only exception being the three customary acts, which continued to be enrolled in French until they disappeared from the rolls. The use of Latin for headings continued even after the body of the roll was in English, as in the case of the roll for 1536–7 printed here.

COMPILATION AND CUSTODY OF THE RECORDS OF PARLIAMENT

The records of the Irish parliament in the fifteenth and early sixteenth centuries frequently suffered from carelessness on the part of their compilers and of the custodians of the rolls.

For the parliament of 3 Edward IV (1463), there were two rolls containing some duplicate material – one roll contains 105 acts; the other contains 28 of these 105 acts, together with three items not included in the first roll.[24] There is no obvious reason for this. Two rolls are known to have contained unfinished items.[25] Not every act passed in a parliament made its way on to the statute roll. The text of some enactments is known to us from exemplifications, while others are known only from references to them in subsequent legislation. There does not seem to be any obvious reason why some acts should have been enrolled and others omitted. Conversely, the same act might be enrolled twice by mistake.[26] Carelessness might also manifest itself by errors in names of per-

20 H.G. Richardson, 'The Irish parliament rolls of the fifteenth century', p. 460. **21** 8 Henry VII c.5. **22** 8 Henry VII c.7 and 8. **23** For the possiblity of enactments in English before Poynings' parliament, see Appendix 2 below. **24** *Stat. Ire., 1–12 Edw. IV*, pp 40–271. **25** In the record of the enactments of the parliament held in 1479–80, chapters 27 and 60 are unfinished, while the record of Kildare's parliament in 1478 contains 12 unfinished items (*Stat. Ire., 12–22 Edw. IV*, pp 584–646, 740–6, 828–30). **26** *Stat. Ire., 12–22 Edw. IV*, pp 420, 456.

sons and places,[27] mistakes such as writing the wrong word (e.g. *commune place* in error for *chief place*),[28] and the repetition and omission of individual words.[29]

The rolls were in the custody of the master of the rolls, and kept with the chancery records in Dublin castle. The buildings in which these records were stored were unsatisfactory for the purpose, and payments were made regularly in the first half of the fifteenth century to make them weatherproof.[30] The rolls themselves were not kept very securely, judging by the ease with which they were interfered with and embezzled in the early 16th century. The roll for 1516 was found to be mutilated in 1520,[31] and chapters 7 and 8 of the enactments of Grey's parliament in 1478 appear to have been deliberately defaced.[32] Chapters 12–15 of the 1465 parliament, were mutilated, possibly by accident, to such an extent that a copy of the enactments from another source was later annexed to the roll with the heading 'here follows the true content of the chapters defaced in this roll, by accident as it appears'.[33] The roll for 1499 was embezzled before 1527 by persons opposed to the earl of Kildare,[34] that for 1531 had disappeared before 1543[35] and a further 6 rolls for the pre-1543 period had disappeared by 1617.[36] There were frequent complaints about the lack of good custody of the statute rolls. An act of the parliament held in 1443 could not be found seven years later 'by negligence of those who had them in their custody and governance', and in 1454 it was enacted that the master of the rolls should be summoned to appear in parliament 'to be examined touching certain records of parliament that should be in his custody'.[37]

The situation relating to parliamentary records was so bad that in the 1521–2 parliament it was proposed that all acts passed in any parliament since 20 Edward IV which could not be shown or found of record should be annulled, and that all the documented acts should be attested by the king's lieutenant, chancellor, treasurer, chief justices of both benches, chief baron of the exchequer, master of the rolls and under treasurer. Furthermore, 'from hense forth noo actis of parliament be effectual within this land but suche as shalbe conteyned in the roll or rolls of parliament subscribed after the end of the parliament with the names aforesaid'. The reason was given that although many acts had been passed in parliament in Ireland, 'a greater part cannot be showed or found of record, so that the effects of many of the said acts cannot now be had in remembrance' and it was alleged that the acts were being 'concealed and

27 e.g. *Skyn* instead of *Skryn* (ibid., p. 248). The parliament of 1474 ordered changes to be made in the parliament roll for 1472–3 in order that the spelling of the names would agree with the versions contained in an exchequer inquisition (ibid., p. 241). 28 Ibid., p. 253. 29 For instances of repetition and omission, see the footnotes to the texts printed in this volume. 30 PRO, E 101/248/8; E 364/7 m.B; E 364/75 m.I; E 364/79 m.A. 31 Quinn, 'Bills and statutes', p. 115. 32 *Stat. Ire., 12–22 Edw. IV*, p. 654. 33 *Stat. Ire., 1–12 Edw. IV*, p. 288. 34 Quinn, 'Bills and statutes', p. 100. 35 Ibid., p. 134 n.1. 36 See Appendix 3 below. 37 *Stat. Ire. Hen. VI*, pp 231, 293.

embezzled purposely by sinister ministers having the guard and keeping of the same; so that such provisoes and articles as should be beneficial for our said sovereign lord or his said subjects might be utterlie put owte of the said acts and the remainder stand in force when the parties for whom the said acts did pass may see their convenient time'.[38]

PARLIAMENTARY PROCEDURE AND RECORDS

The changes in parliamentary procedure resulting from Poynings' Act brought with them changes in the nature of the records relating to parliamentary legislation.

Before 1494–5[39]

Before Poynings' Act, legislation was initiated by petition presented to the chief governor and lords in parliament. The petition might originate with a private individual or group of individuals, a corporation, or the commons as a whole. When it had been discussed, the petition was endorsed with a note of the decision as to whether it had been granted or not, and if granted, the enactment, which usually embodied the wording of the petition, could be enrolled. The files of endorsed petitions appear to have been retained after the statute roll had been compiled, as seen by the fact that copies and exemplifications were made of unenrolled statutes, sometimes many years after their enactment. No original petitions for this period have survived.

After 1494–5[40]

Under the system which existed after the passing of Poynings' Act, a copy of the proposed legislation was sent to the king and council in England, usually in the form of a parchment copy of the text of each proposed act sealed with the Irish great seal,[41] together with a request for licence to hold the parliament. Once the royal approval had been given, the bill was forwarded to the English chancery with a warrant authorising the issue of letters in the king's name granting licence for the holding of the parliament and for the royal assent to be

38 Quinn, 'Bills and statutes', pp 118–20. 39 See Richardson & Sayles, *Ir. parl. in middle ages*, especially pp 196–226. 40 See R.D. Edwards and T.W. Moody,'The history of Poynings' Law, part 1, 1494–1615', *I.H.S.* ii (1940–41), pp 415–24. 41 A sealed copy of a proposed bill for the suspension of Poynings' Act in 1536 (later replaced by c.4) is in the Huntingdon Library, San Marino, California (MS EL 2564) and is printed in R. Dudley Edwards, 'The Irish Reformation parliament of Henry VIII, 1536–7', *Historical Studies* vi (1968), pp 82–4.

given when the bills were passed by the Irish parliament. This took the form of letters under the English great seal, in which the text of the proposed legislation was written out in full. This document, known as a transmiss, was sent to the Irish council, and further transmisses, containing additional legislation, might be sent during the lifetime of the parliament. The transmisses were usually enrolled on the patent rolls of the English chancery, which are our only source of the text, as approved, since the original transmisses were destroyed in the Four Courts fire in 1922. It appears that the 1531 parliament was the last one for which such enrolments were made but the reason for this is not evident.

When parliament had commenced individual bills were presented and the various stages of the legislative procedure were recorded on them – the sending of the bill to the lords, the lords' assent, the formal assent by the Lord Deputy (*le seignur depute le voet*), and the order for the enrolment of the act on the statute roll (*irrotulatur*). A small number of these original annotated bills existed in 1820[42] but none survives to-day. There may also have been unannotated copies of individual acts.

Copies of records

In both the pre- and post-Poynings periods, copies of individual statutes might be made for administrative purposes and circulated to the courts or retained for reference in the chancery or exchequer. Exemplifications, or certified copies, of acts were frequently issued, usually at the request of someone benefiting from the legislation, and enrolled on the patent rolls in the chancery, or, if the crown's financial interests were involved, on the exchequer memoranda rolls.[43] The exemplification took the form of letters in the king's name addressed to all to whom they might come, and stated that the king had inspected a certain act passed in a certain parliament, giving the date, place and the name of the lieutenant or deputy before whom it was held, and going on to quote the text of the act as passed.

THE CONTENT OF THE STATUTE ROLLS, 1484–1537

The rolls contained in this volume reflect the changing political scene in Ireland in the late 15th and early 16th centuries.[44] The two parliaments of

42 They are noted by Shaw Mason in TCD MS 1739, but are not recorded in Wood's *Guide*. It is possible, however, that they were transferred to PROI but were included in the collection of transmisses. 43 See Appendix 1 below. 44 For political developments during this period, see

Richard III show the supremacy of the eighth earl of Kildare and his adherents, with acts being passed to benefit not only Kildare himself, but also Sir Roland FitzEustace, his father-in-law, Sir Thomas FitzGerald, his brother, and Sir Alexander Plunket, one of his leading supporters. Subsidies, materials and labour are procured for building works on the manor of Kildare and the new castle of Castledermot, both belonging to the earl, and for the castle of Lackagh, which belonged to his brother, and Kildare, his wife and other members of his family are among those receiving a licence to found a chantry in the church of St Nicholas in Dundalk.

By 1493, the political situation had changed. Henry VII had become king after the battle of Bosworth, and an attempt to place Lambert Simnel, a Yorkist claimant, on the English throne in 1487 had failed. Kildare had been replaced as Deputy by Walter FitzSimons, archbishop of Dublin, and the acts of the parliament held in 1493 clearly shows those who had grievances against the Kildare administration using parliament to obtain redress. Many of Kildare's actions were annulled, Sir Roland FitzEustace, who had been treasurer of Ireland for more than forty years without accounting, was to be compelled to render his account, and a wide-ranging act of resumption, going back to 1422, was passed with a large number of exemptions.

Forty-three years later, in 1536–7, the situation had again changed radically. The Kildare supremacy was at an end: in fact the first act of this parliament was the attainder of the principal people involved in the rebellion of Silken Thomas, son of the ninth earl. The medieval concept of parliament as a place for redress of what were very often private grievances had given way to the concept of the public or common good, while the procedural changes resulting from Poynings' Act meant a higher degree of control over the actions of parliament. The language used has changed from French to English, and the words and phrases used in the legislation, and especially the way in which the king is referred to, show a shift in the attitude to the monarchy and in the way in which the monarchy saw itself. This is reflected in the sheer length of the acts, in comparison to the pre-Poynings ones. Another striking feature of this parliament is the way in which English legislation is used as a basis for acts passed in Ireland, either by directly quoting the English act and re-enacting it

volumes ii and iii of *A new history of Ireland;* S.G. Ellis, *Tudor Ireland, 1470–1603* (London, 1985), *Reform and revival; English government in Ireland, 1470–1534* (Royal Historical Society, 1986), and *Tudor frontiers and noble power* (Oxford, 1995); Brendan Bradshaw, *The dissolution of the religious orders in Ireland under Henry VIII* (Cambridge, 1974), and *The Irish constitutional revolution of the sixteenth century* (Cambridge, 1979); Mary Ann Lyons, *Gearóid Óg Fitzgerald* (Historical Association of Ireland, 1998).

for Ireland, or by enacting legislation based very closely in wording on the corresponding English act.

Richard III and Henry VII

Acts in the Irish parliament of this period were initiated by petition presented either by individuals, or by the commons, although it is obvious from the contents of some commons petitions that they were for the benefit of individuals. The variety of subjects dealt with is extensive. Private petitions usually related to an individual's claim to land or office, or for redress in connection with legal actions.

The first of Richard III's parliaments saw a major reform of the Irish coinage. The standard and design of the new coinage was laid down and as were provisions for its acceptance throughout the land. At the same time action was taken against Germyn Lynch, the former master of the mint, and against counterfeiters, and it was ordained that the Deputy was to henceforth receive the profits of the mint.

In ecclesiastical affairs, the English-born archbishop of Dublin, John Walton, resigned in favour of Walter FitzSimons, an Anglo-Irishman, with a view to ensuring that future holders of the office would also be natives of Ireland. The new archbishop received licence to appoint Irish clergy to benefices in his gift, in cases where English clergy could not or would not go to minister among the Irish. The lack of respect for church buildings, which were being treated as if they were no more than pig sties, was dealt with by confirming all liberties and privileges granted to the church in the past and enacting that anyone interfering with these liberties was to be an attainted felon. The earl of Kildare and others founded a chantry in Dundalk, and licence was given for several people to go abroad on pilgrimage – the abbot of St Thomas the martyr, Dublin, to Canterbury, and the mayor and bailiffs of Waterford to Santiago de Compostela. Two prebendaries of St Patrick's cathedral, Dublin, received licences to pursue their studies at Oxford. The action of a previous prior of the Dominican house at Trim in making grants without the consent of his convent was referred to parliament by his successor, while another religious house, that of Holmpatrick in north county Dublin, is seen in a more positive light, receiving the grant of a custom on fishing, for the purpose of completing construction work on a harbour there.

The use of parliament as an instrument in enforcing law and order is seen in the passing of acts summoning specified disturbers of the peace to surrender themselves to official custody on a prescribed day – James Bath of Meath in 1484, 28 named wrongdoers from cos. Meath and Louth in 1485 and George Nettervill and 183 other named individuals in 1493.

Relations with the Irish in Louth and Meath are reflected in the provisions made for the payment of wages to Cahir O Connor and his men in 1485, and in the same year, in the problem arising from the non-payment of wages to Irish kerns in co. Louth – they captured several local tenants and held them to ransom, and parliament then had to provide for the reimbursement of those who had paid the ransom. Elsewhere, castles were built and fortified against the Irish, and it appears that the building of the new castle at Castledermot was to be followed by the introduction of English settlers to the recovered lands in co. Carlow. The Deputy also received financial support in the form of taxation for defence against the Irish, In 1485 he was granted £100 from the four counties of Dublin, Meath, Louth and Kildare, and later in the same parliament received a subsidy of 13*s*. 4*d*. from each ploughland in the same counties.

On the constitutional side, the 1485 parliament is noteworthy for the confirmation of the so-called Statute of FitzEmpress, providing for the election of a chief governor when a vacancy occurred in that office,[45] and for the act enabling the chief governor to prorogue parliament by deputy, and the subsequent letter of the earl of Kildare appointing his brother and three others to act as his deputy for that purpose.

Other legislation is of a more miscellaneous kind, but includes the provisions made at the petition of the dean and chapter of St Patrick's to prevent the flooding of the river Poddle near the cathedral, the confirmation of an arbitration made by the sovereign of Galway in a dispute between merchants there, and proceedings against James Collynge, who forged the great seal of Ireland and used it to issue a charter of pardon in favour of the treasurer of Limerick cathedral.

28–29 Henry VIII[46]

The 1536–7 parliament, known as the Reformation parliament, concentrated to a great extent on the establishment of the theoretical and practical basis of the Reformation in Ireland. The king was to replace the pope as supreme head of the church, and resulting from this, acts were passed regulating faculties, probate of wills and testaments, appeals, and the payment of annates and first fruits to the king. The first wave of monasteries, including Bective and the convent of nuns at Timolin, were suppressed and their property transferred to the crown. The succession to the throne was regulated at the beginning of the parliament by the act settling the succession on the children of the king and his

45 For the Statute of FitzEmpress see Richardson & Sayles, *Ir. parl. in middle ages*, pp 324–31.
46 See R. Dudley Edwards, 'The Irish Reformation parliament of Henry VIII, 1536–7', *Historical Studies* vi (1968) pp 59–84.

queen, Anne Boleyn. By the final session in October 1537, Anne had been replaced as queen by Jane Seymour and a new act of succession was necessary. The act of slander provided against persons slandering the king or committing other treasonable acts.

Politically, the attainder of Silken Thomas and his associates marked the end of the supremacy of the house of Kildare. Poynings' Act was temporarily suspended and this suspension had to be explained by a further declaratory act. The age-old problem of maintaining a distinction between the colonists and the Gaelic Irish was dealt with in an act forbidding marriage between members of the two communities, and another prescribing the use of the English order, habit and language. The paying of tribute to Irishmen was prohibited, and there was yet another attempt to deal with the problem of absentees.

The composition of the Irish parliament was permanently changed by an act providing that the proctors of the lower clergy, who had attended since the fourteenth century, should no longer form part of parliament. Commissioners were appointed whose orders relating to bills introduced into the parliament but not passed could have temporary legislative effect until the next parliament. Other acts dealt with the improvement of navigation on the Barrow and other rivers in co. Kilkenny, and on the Boyne, and banned the export of wool and fleeces from Ireland.

Editorial note

SOURCES USED

The description of the original rolls which follows is taken, in the case of those which no longer exist, from the list published by the Irish Record Commission.[1] The description of the roll for 28–29 Henry VIII is based on an examination of the roll which is held in the National Archives. Details of the transcripts on which the present edition is based are also given.

1 Richard III

The original roll consisted of 4 membranes, part of the 26th act and all the 27th being written on the back of the last membrane. In 1819 it was described as 'very much damaged (particularly the sides of the three first membranes) and a considerable portion of the writing destroyed'.

The one surviving transcript of the whole roll is NAI, RC 13/8, a draft made for the Record Commission by Henry J. Mason and compared with the original roll by an unidentified person, presumably a fellow sub-commissioner on the statutes. A further comparison with the original was done in PROI by Henry F. Berry, who annotated the transcript.

The English translation made by the Record Commission no longer exists, but chapters 7–9, 13 and part of 23 were printed by Aquilla Smith from the Record Commission translation in the *Numismatic Chronicle* (1881), pp 314–20.

2–3 Richard III

The original roll consisted of 3 membranes and was described in 1819 as being 'in good preservation'.

There are two surviving transcripts of this roll:

(a) NAI, PRO 7/1, a transcript made in PROI by Henry F. Berry from the Record Commission fair copy (volume 86) and compared with the original roll.

(b) NLI MS 8008 (ii). This is the draft Record Commission transcript made

1 *Rec. comm. Ire. rep., 1816–20*, p. 354.

from the original roll by Roderick Connor and compared with the roll by Edward Lawson, Henry J. Mason, William Ball and Bartholomew T. Duhigg, who, like Connor, were sub-commissioners on the statutes. The first page of this transcript is missing, but its contents can be supplied from NAI, Co. 501, a transcript of the NLI manuscript made when the latter was in the Genealogical Office.

The two transcripts differ in a number of minor readings. The text printed here is taken from the Berry transcript, but in three cases a variant reading from the NLI manuscript is preferred as making more sense. Chapter 13 in the text was unnumbered on the roll; consequently chapters 14–18 in the text correspond to the original chapters 13–17.

The English translation made by the Record Commission survives in the form of a draft (NLI MS 8008 (iii)) which was made and checked against the original roll by Roderick Connor and Henry J. Mason, and compared with the Record Commission transcript by William Ball.

8 Henry VII

The original roll consisted of 10 membranes and was described in 1819 as being 'in tolerable preservation except the 5th membrane which received damp and on which the writing is weak'.

The only surviving transcript of the whole roll is NAI, RC 13/9, a draft made for the Record Commission by Edward Lawson and compared with the original by his fellow sub-commissioners on the statutes, Henry J. Mason and Roderick Connor. A further comparison with the original was done in PROI by Henry F. Berry who annotated the transcript.

The English translation of this roll prepared by the Record Commission is no longer extant.

28–29 Henry VIII

The original roll (NAI, CH 1/1) survived the fire of 1922 because it was temporarily stored in the strongroom adjoining the reading room, rather than in its normal place in the record repository. It consists of 46 parchment membranes approximately 280mm wide and of varying lengths, sewn together end to end with indigo dyed linen thread, and is protected by a parchment wrapper sewn to the top of the first membrane. A vertical line has been drawn approximately 45mm from the left edge to create a space for the title and number of each act and to align the left hand margin of the text. The writing extends to the edge of the parchment on the right hand side, where it is worn away on several

membranes. Apart from this damage, which was noted in the Record Commission list, and several cases where the scribe wrote around existing holes in the parchment, the roll is in good condition. Where each membrane is joined to the preceding or following membranes, a large capital letter or letters or a symbol has been written in the left hand margin, spanning the join, presumably as a security measure.[2] In addition to the modern membrane numbers, the roll has evidence of an earlier numbering system, using arabic numerals. It appears that the present membranes 1–7 did not form part of this system. Membrane 8, although unnumbered, was probably the original m.1, and the consecutive numbering begins on the present m. 9, which was numbered as m. 2, and extends to the last membrane on the roll (now m. 46), which is numbered as m. 39. The reason for this numbering is not clear, as all of the present 46 membranes have the security lettering where they are joined to preceding and/or following membranes and obviously formed part of the same roll.

Although there are several changes of ink, the roll appears to be the work of one scribe, presumably the negligent clerk referred to in c.41, but his name is not known. The regular use of ornate capitals, extending into the left hand margin,at the beginning of each act from c.17 onwards supports the theory that the acts were enrolled by session, as c.17 to c.41 inclusive were all enacted in the final session of the parliament. There are several errors which have been corrected by striking through, and omitted words have been inserted with a caret. The blank spaces between each act are filled in with diagonal strokes, presumably to prevent additional words being inserted. The numbers and titles of the acts, written in the left hand margin, are in the hand of the same scribe, while other marginal annotations are contemporary but in a different hand.

The heading, giving details of the different sessions, appears to have been written at one time, rather than added to on the occasion of each adjournment or prorogation. The existence of a blank space between the end of the heading and the first act implies that a large space was left for the heading, which was added at the end of the parliament.

EDITORIAL PRACTICE

In general, the guidelines laid down by R.F. Hunnisett in *Editing records for publication*[3] have been adopted. Abbreviations have been silently extended where the complete form of the word is obvious. The original spelling has been

2 The letters used are the 23 letters of the alphabet from A to Z, but omitting J, U and W, followed by ampersand, another symbol, then double capitals from AA to TT (omitting JJ), and finally another X. 3 British Records Association (1977).

retained, with the use of u/v and i/j standardised in accordance with modern usage. The use of capitals has been kept to a minimum and punctuation has been added sparingly, usually in order to make the sense more clear. Discrepancies in grammar have been left as they appear in the text, with footnotes showing their occurrence. Where words or letters are missing or illegible in the original, due to damage, they have been supplied where possible and placed in square brackets.

If an act is already in print, either in *Statutes at large* or in a modern historical work, details are given in a footnote. No attempt has been made to give references to earlier printed collections of statutes. Footnotes are also used, in the case of the roll for 28–29 Henry VIII, to give details of related draft bills, certified bills and exemplifications, where they exist, and to provide the date of transmiss (if any), given by Shaw Mason in TCD MS 1739.[4]

Richard III and Henry VII

In the absence of the originals, one has to rely on the Irish Record Commission transcripts which were compared with the original rolls by H.F. Berry. Differences between the IRC draft transcript of the roll for 2–3 Richard III (NLI MS 8008 (ii)) and Berry's revision of the IRC fair copy (NAI, PRO 7/1) are noted in footnotes, though minor differences in spelling (such as -s or -z at the end of a plural in French) have not been noted. All footnotes are the work of the present editor except those by Berry, which are differentiated by being prefixed with the words 'Berry's note'. These usually relate to the condition or legibility of the original roll. In general, footnotes to the French or Latin text of the enactments relate to textual matters; other comments are given as footnotes to the translation.

The translation of the text of the rolls is based on that prepared by Berry and his colleagues. Placenames, but not personal names, have been modernised. English words which occur in the French text have been retained in their original form in the translation, but have been printed in italics.

Titles of acts

The titles of the individual enactments given in the margin of the roll for 28–29 Henry VIII are reproduced here as they appear in the original. In the case of the other rolls, no such marginal titles were given, but they have been supplied here for ease of reference and, like other editorial additions, have been denoted by the use of square brackets.

4 TCD MS 1739: Collation of the Irish public general statutes by William Shaw Mason. This is the manuscript referred to as TCD Add. MS (shelf mark W. 8) in Quinn, 'Bills and statutes'.

List of parliamentary sessions

1 RICHARD III (1484)

19 March 1484	Dublin
28 June or 30 August 1484	Naas

Note: The uncertainty about the date of the second session is caused by the fact that the roll was torn at this point and the date appears as the Monday after the feast of the [...] of St John the Baptist. This feast is either the Nativity (24 June) or the Decollation (29 August) which gives either 28 June 1484 or 30 August 1484 as the date to which the parliament was adjourned. The Record Commission transcript suggests the latter date, which is accepted by Richardson and Sayles (*Ir. parl. in middle ages*, p. 363). A date in late August would be unusual for the holding of a parliament, if one goes by the list of parliaments printed in Richardson and Sayles.

From internal evidence, chapters 1–23 were enacted in the first session; chapters 24–26 could have been enacted at either session. Chapter 27, relating to an incident on 26 March 1484 could have been enacted in the first session, if that session lasted for a week or more; otherwise it must be assigned to the second session. The offender was ordered to surrender himself at Dublin castle on the Monday after the feast of St Ambrose following. If the act was passed at the end of March 1484, this would be 5 April 1484, which allows a very short time for the act to be published and the surrender to take place. On the other hand, in c.4, which was obviously passed in the first session, the sheriffs of Dublin and Meath were given only until 1 April 1484 to send in their returns of workers selected for the works on the manor of Kildare, indicating that a short time-scale was not unusual. In the parliament held the following year, (2–3 Richard III c.6), an act passed on 18 March 1485 at the earliest called for offenders to surrender at Trim castle on or before 17 April following. If the 1484 act was passed in June or August, the offenders would have until 11 April 1485 to surrender, which seems to be an inordinately long interval.

2–3 RICHARD III (1485)

18 March 1485	Dublin
6 June 1485	Trim
8 August 1485	Trim
24 October 1485	Dublin

Note: It is significant that the final session of this parliament was held in the name of Richard III two months after his defeat and death at the battle of Bosworth. For other evidence of the Dublin administration's delay in recognising Henry VII see S.G. Ellis, 'The struggle for control of the Irish mint, 1460 - c.1506', *R.I.A. Proc.* lxxviii (1978) C, p. 20.

Chapters 1–6 were enacted in the first session and chapters 7–16 in the second session. No acts were passed in the third session, and the deputy did not attend in person, but the keeper of the rolls of chancery adjourned the parliament on authority of c.4 and a letter of the deputy dated 21 July 1485. Chapters 16–19 were passed during the fourth session.

---

8 HENRY VII (1493)

Dublin	28 June 1493
Dublin	5 August 1493

Note: Chapters 1–24 were enacted in the first session and chapters 25–32 in the second session.

28–29 HENRY VIII (1536–7)

Dublin	1–31 May 1536
Kilkenny	25–26 July 1536
Cashel	28 July 1536
Limerick	2–19 August 1536

Dublin	15–28 September 1536
Dublin	20 January - 5 or 6 February 1537[1]
Dublin	1–8 May 1537
Dublin	20–21 July 1537
Dublin	13 October - 20 December 1537

Note: The first four sessions are described as having been adjourned; the remainder were prorogued. D.B. Quinn's suggestion[2] that the period 13 October - 20 December 1537 was broken up by several unrecorded prorogations must be rejected as it is based on a misreading of the date given in c.42 for the enactment of c.39 (20 October instead of the correct reading of 13 October).

Chapters 1–11 were enacted in the first session (May 1536); chapters 12–16 in the fifth session (September 1536) and the remainder in the final session.

1 The date is wrongly given in the heading of the roll as Tuesday, 5 February, but the correct date is either Monday, 5 February or Tuesday, 6 February. 2 'Parliaments and great councils in Ireland, 1461–1586', *I.H.S.* iii (1942–3), p. 75 n.11.

Table of enactments

I RICHARD III (1484)

2–3 RICHARD III (1485)

8 HENRY VII (1493)

28–29 HENRY VIII (1536–7)

EDWARD IV (APPENDIX I)

1 Richard III

Statuta ordinaciones et actus in quodam parliamento domini regis apud Dubliniam die veneris proximo post festum Sancti Patricii episcopi anno regni regis Ricardi tercii primo[1] coram predilecto consanguineo ipsius regis Geraldo comite Kildarie deputato Edwardi filii ipsius domini regis primogeniti locumtenentis ipsius domini regis terre sue Hibernie tento edita et abinde ad villam de Naas ibidem die lune proximo post festum [...][2] Sancti Johannis Baptiste proxime sequens tenendo adjornato in hec verba:

c.1

[Imprimis][3] ordeine est et establie que Seint Esglis soit franqe et eit et enjoye toutz sez libertees sicome il ad este devaunt cestz hoeurs.

c.2

[Item ordeine est] et accorde que la terre Dirland soit franqe et eit et enjoye toutz sez privileges et libertees sicome il ad este use devaunt cests hoeurs.

c.3

[Item ord]eine est et assentue que les cittees de Divelyn et Waterford et la vile de Drogheda et touts lez aultres cittees et bones viles dedeins la [terre] Dirland eient et enjoient toutz lour bones usuages et custumes franchesies et privileges sicome ils ount ewez et usez devaunt cest hoeurs.

c.4

[Item al] requisicion dez communes que come le trespuissaunt et gracieux seignur Gerot count de Kildare depute lieutenaunt Dirland ad fait de estre jettez ove[...] bien intende de faire de estre jette graundez et fortez fortresses et fosses a son manere de Kildare al aide et succour des foialx sub[git]ez le roy et restriccion de sez irrois ennemiez et englois rebels; en consideracion ent ordeine est graunte et enacte par auctorite dicest parliament que iiij^{xx} overers hors del barony de Castelknok deins le counte de Divelyn iiij^{xx} overers hors del barony de Dunboyng et aultres iiij^{xx} overers hors del barony de Rathtouth

1 19 March 1484. 2 Berry's note: roll torn. 3 In this and similar cases, the material in square brackets has been supplied by the transcriber as the original roll was torn or the writing obliterated at the time at which the transcript was made.

Statutes, ordinances and acts in a parliament of the lord king held at Dublin on the Friday after the feast of St Patrick the bishop in the first year of the reign of king Richard the third [19 March 1484] before same king's dearly beloved cousin, Gerald, earl of Kildare, deputy of Edward the first-born son of the same lord king, lieutenant of the same lord the king of his land of Ireland and from there adjourned to the town of Naas to be held there on the Monday after the feast of the [...] of St John the Baptist following [28 June or 30 August 1484][1], published in these words:

c.1 [Confirmation of the liberties of the church]
First, it is ordained and established that Holy Church be free and have and enjoy all her liberties as has been customary before now.

c.2 [Confirmation of the privileges and liberties of the land of Ireland]
Also, it is ordained and agreed that the land of Ireland be free and have and enjoy all its privileges and liberties as has been customary before now.

c.3 [Confirmation of the liberties and franchises of cities and towns]
Also, it is ordained and assented that the cities of Dublin and Waterford and the town of Drogheda and all the other cities and good towns within the land of Ireland have and enjoy all their good usages and customs, franchises and privileges as they have had and used before now.

c.4 [Provision of labourers for works on the earl of Kildare's manor of Kildare]
Also, at the request of the commons, that whereas the very powerful and gracious lord, Gerald, earl of Kildare, deputy lieutenant of Ireland, has caused to be built with [...] fully intends to cause to be built large and strong fortresses and ditches at his manor of Kildare for the help and succour of the king's faithful subjects and the restraint of his Irish enemies and English rebels; in consideration of which it is ordained, granted and enacted by authority of this parliament that eighty workmen be provided from the barony of Castleknock

1 The feast is either the Nativity (24 June) or the Decollation (29 August), which gives either 28 June or 30 August 1484 as the date to which the parliament was adjourned. For a discussion of the dates of this parliament, see above p. xxxi.

deins le counte de Mithe une de chescun de lez ditz laborers ove une vange et le aultre ov une tribule potentez et fortez en lour corpsez de laborer jetter et faire fosses a Kildare avauntdit et que lez ditz overers et chescun de eaux en lour propre persons soient a Kildare avauntdit ove lour instrumentz avauntditz le maresdie proschien devaunt le fest de Dymenche dez Palmes[4] et ove vitailx pur v jours cestassever [le p]rimer de aller a Kildare et illeosqes i[ij] jours de overer et le v jour de venire a son hostell et cestez overers de estre garnisez et summonez hors dez sufficientz et plenteuous mea[sons] et chescun overer garnise ou summone fesaunt defaulte forfaita xl s. de estre emploiez sur lez ditz fosses; et par la dit auctorite si ascun [viscount] ou serjeaunt empanella garnisa ou summona ascun overer forsque luy qest sufficient et hors del une plenteuous meason ou preigna ascun [. . .] regarde de empaneller une et de lesser hors une aultre qil forfaita pur chescun defaulte xx [s.] de estre emploie come desuis [et que chescun] de lez ditz overers preigna pur le jour de lez resceauntez de lez ditz baronies sibien artificeres [comme] gavillers et cattallers vj d. d[e estre] levez sur et de eaux par la discrecion de ij de chescun paroche deins chescun de lez ditz baronies ceux queux plerra le dit depute de [nosmer et si] ascun de le ditz persons issint nosme par le dit depute soit negligent ou remisse en cesse ou leve fesaunt ou paiement d[el dit somme aux ditz] overers ou a ascun de eaux quil forfaita vj s. viij d. de estre emploiez come desuis et que bien luist al dit depute [de cesser et faire lever] lez ditz summez si le case issint requiert et que chescun viscount et serjeaunt mitta eins son retourne al [. . . le] joesdie proschien apres le fest del Annunciacion de Nostre Dame proschien avenaunt[5] sur peine avauntdit.

c.5

Item al requision de communes que come lez nobles auncestres del trespuissaunt et gracieux seignur Gerot count de [Kildare] ont ewez et del auncient temps avoient usez une marche deins la vile de Maynoth' de semmayne en s[emmayne en droit de] lour seignurie de Maynoth'; en consideracion ent ordeine est establie graunte et enacte par auctorite dicest parliament [que le dit count et sez] heirs counts de Kildare eient exercisent usent et enjoient annuelment et del semmayne en semmayne deins la dit [vile la dite marche] chescun joesdie et qil eit use et enjoie a lui et a sez heirs lour franque warenne deins tout le dit manere issint que [nuls persons ne] person enterent en ceo saunz licence et volunte du dit count et sez heirs; et auxi est ordeine graunte et enacte [par

4 6 April 1484. 5 1 April 1484.

in the county of Dublin, eighty workmen from the barony of Dunboyne and a further eighty workmen from the barony of Ratoath in the county of Meath, one of each of the said labourers with a spade and the other with a barrow, powerful and strong in their bodies, to labour, build and make ditches at Kildare aforesaid, and that the said workmen and each one of them be in person at Kildare aforesaid with their aforesaid implements on the Tuesday before the feast of Palm Sunday [6 April 1484] with victuals for five days, that is to say, to go to Kildare on the first day, to work there for three days and to return home on the fifth day, and these workmen are to be warned and summoned out of sufficient and plentiful houses, and each workman who has been warned or summoned and makes default shall forfeit 40 pence to be employed on the said ditches; and by the said authority, if any sheriff or serjeant empanels, warns or summonses any workman except one who is sufficient and out of a plentiful house or takes any [...] reward for empanelling one and leaving out another, he shall forfeit for each default 20 shillings to be employed as above; and that each of the said workmen shall receive six pence a day from the residents of the said baronies, artificers as well as gavellers and catallers, to be levied on and from them by the discretion of two men of each parish in each of the said baronies, to be named by the said deputy; and if any of the said persons so named by the said deputy is negligent or remiss in assessing or levying or in paying the said sum to the said workmen or to any of them, he shall forfeit six shillings and eight pence, to be employed as above, and that it shall be lawful for the said deputy to assess and levy the said sums if necessary, and that each sheriff and serjeant shall send in his return to the [...] the Thursday after the feast of the Annunciation of Our Lady next coming [1 April 1484] under the aforesaid penalty.

c.5 [Confirmation to the earl of Kildare of a market, customs and free warren at Maynooth]

Also, at the request of the commons, that whereas the noble ancestors of the very powerful and gracious lord, Gerald, earl of Kildare, have had and from ancient times used a market in the town of Maynooth from week to week in right of their lordship of Maynooth; in consideration of which it is ordained, established, granted and enacted by authority of this parliament that the said earl and his heirs, earls of Kildare, shall have, exercise, use and enjoy the said market in the said town, yearly and from week to week on each Thursday, and that he shall have, use and enjoy to him and to his heirs their free warren in all the said manor so that no persons or person enter it without the permission and against the will of the said earl and his heirs; and it is also ordained, granted and enacted by authority of this parliament that it shall be lawful for

auctorite dicest] parlement que bien luist al dit count quorest et a sez heires de prendre et poient prenderer et recevier del temps [en temps ...] custumes de touts maneres dez marchauntdisez deins la dit vile vendiblez sicome lez meire et baillives del cit[e de Divelyn deins la] dit cite usent de prendre et receivere a avere et a teignire exerciser user et enjoyer lez ditz marchee et warenne a luy et a se[z heirs ...] nient obstaunt que lez auncestres del dit count ou ascun de eaux ou ascun aultre lez ditz marchee ou warenne ou as[cun de eaux] avoient my usez ou misusez et ceo saunz ascun empechement ou empediment molestaunce ou grevaunce de nostre souveraine seignur [le roy sez heirs] successours officers ou ministres queuxconqez en temps avenire ascun estatute acte ordenaunce use custume privilege ou ascun aultre [matier] ou chose au contrarie fait ewe ou provide nient obstaunt et ceo saunz ascun fine ent de estre fait ou fee de estre paie a nostre soveraine seignur le roy en son hanapier de sa chauncerie Dirland pur son graund seall illeosqes; purvieu que cest acte ne soit prejudiciale al citte de Divelyn ne [al] vile de Drogheda ne a nule de lez franqes hommes de ascun de eaux.

c.6

Item al requisicion de communes que come lez deux parties de lez prise vines dicest terre Dirland apparteignount al tresnoble seignur Gerot count de Kildare depute lieutenant Dirland come en droite de nostre soveraine seignur le roy par reison de absente del count de Ormond accordaunt al acte en cele parte deins la dit terre lez queux prisez sount reteignez en la citte de Lymerik par une William Comyn et Thomas Comyn del mesme saunz ascun cause resonable; sur que lez premissez considerez ordeine est enacte et establie par auctorite dicest parliament que lez ditz William [et Thomas] facent duhe satisfaccion ou component ove le dit depute pur lez ditz prise vines parentre cy et le fest de Seint Petre [appelle] ad vincula proschien avenaunt[6] ou aultrement de estre felons atteintez et si lez ditz prise vines ne soient my paiez al dit depute ou se[z assignez] accordaunt al estatute en cele parte use desore enavaunt de touts maneres niefs veignauntez al dit citte lez queux de droite soient prisab[lez que adonqes] il bien luist al dit depute ou a sez assignes de prendre lez biens et corpses de lez ditz William et Thomas lour aidours et mainten[ours et chescun] de eaux demurauntez deins la dit citte laou ils purrount estre trosvez deins la terre Dirland et lez biens et corpses issint prisez reteig[nire jusque] al temps que le dit depute soit duhement satisfie et paie de toute qui de droite appartient a luy par reison de lez ditz prise vines.

6 1 August 1484.

the said earl that now is and his heirs to take, and that they may take and receive from time to time, [...] customs of all kinds of merchandise to be sold in the said town in the same way as the mayor and bailiffs of the city of Dublin are accustomed to take and receive in the said city, to have and to hold, exercise, use and enjoy the said market and warren to him and to his heirs [...], notwithstanding the fact that the ancestors of the said earl or any of them or any other person had not used or had misused the said market or warren or either of them, and this without any hindrance or impediment, molestation or grievance by our sovereign lord the king, his heirs, successors, officers or ministers whomsoever in time to come, notwithstanding any statute, act, ordinance, use, custom, privilege, or any other matter or thing made, had or provided to the contrary, and without any making any fine or paying any fee to our sovereign lord the king in his hanaper of his chancery of Ireland for his great seal there; provided that this act is not prejudicial to the city of Dublin or to the town of Drogheda or to any of the freemen of either of them.

c.6 [William and Thomas Comyn to account for the prise wines at Limerick]

Also, at the request of the commons, that whereas two parts of the prise wines of this land of Ireland belong to the very noble lord, Gerald, earl of Kildare, deputy lieutenant of Ireland, as in right of our sovereign lord the king by reason of the absence of the earl of Ormond according to the act made in that behalf in the said land[2], and these prises are detained in the city of Limerick by one William Comyn and Thomas Comyn of the same, without any reasonable cause; upon which, considering the premises, it is ordained, enacted and established by authority of this parliament that the said William and Thomas make due satisfaction or compound with the said deputy for the said prise wines between this and the feast of St Peter called ad Vincula next coming [1 August 1484] or otherwise be attainted felons; and if the said prise wines are not henceforth paid to the said deputy or his assigns from all manner of vessels coming to the said city which of right are prisable, according to the statute used in that behalf, that then it shall be lawful for the said deputy or for his assigns to take the goods and bodies of the said William and Thomas, their aiders and maintainers and each one of them dwelling in the said city, wherever they can be found in the land of Ireland, and to retain the goods and bodies so taken until the said deputy is duly satisfied of and paid all that of right belongs to him by reason of the said prise wines.

2 19–20 Edward IV c.53. *Stat.Ire., 12–22 Edw. IV*, pp 816–18.

c.7

Item al requisicion des communes que come le cune le roy de estre fait et cune deins sa terre Dirland sibien par commaundement [du roy come par ordenaunce] du parliament establie et ordeine desouth une certeine prente et fourme en difference del prente de son cune de son roy[aume Dengleterre eiaunt] les armes Dengleterre en le une parte ove une croys trefoill en chescun fine et iij corons en la aultre parte ove une semi [. . .] come pluis pleinement est especifie en le dit commaundement acte et ordenaunce al entent qil deveit remainere et demurer deins [la dite terre pur le profite] et bone de sez subjectes en la mesme; en consideracion ent ordeine est enacte et establie par auctorite dicest parliament que [le cune le roy] deins le chastell de Divelin et aillours en ascun aultre lieu[7] que serra loialment appointe de estre fait et overe par lez loialx officers ou [ascun de eaux] desouth cele prente de estre prise et passa entre touts lez subjectez le roy; et par mesme le auctorite est ordeine et establie [que si ascun ou ascuns] person ou persons de quelconqe degree ou condicion il ou ils soient refusent ou serrount trosvez refusauntez de prender en paiement [le dit cune] loialment fait et de estre fait et cune en fourme avauntdit en ascun manere citte vile ou marchee lieu ou aillours deins cest terre [Dirland de] perdire pur le valore de chescun demi denier del dit argent issint refuse xij d. moite au roy et le aultre moite al partie qui voet s[uer pue lez] mesmez et sil fortunera que ascun manere person de lez ditz persons de estre trosvez ou provez refusauntez le dit cune pur paiement come est avauntdit deins ascun de lez ditz citees ou viles que adonqes lez ditz penaltees et forfaitours de chescun xij d. en fourme avauntdit de estre perceivez et levez moite ent au roy et le aultre moite pur murage et pavage de cele citte ou vile lou ascun tiell offense ou offensez fortunerount de estre faitz et le corps ou corpses de chescun de eaux issint trosvez offendauntez de estre arrestez et mittez al garde et prison illeosqes a demurer saunz baill ou mainprise tanque que lez dits penaltees et chescun parcell de eaux soient loialment contentez et paiez ou pur icelx aggrement fait; et que par mesme lauctorite si ascun manere person ou persons dez enhabitauntez ou cittezeines ou burgeisez en ascun de lez cittees ou viles de Waterford Weysford Rosse Kilkenny Dongarvan Yoghill Cork Kynsale Killmallok Lymerik Gal[way] et Athnery et aillours deins ceaux parties dicest terre en fourme avauntdit serrount trosvez ou duhement par credible testmoig[nes] prove refusauntez le dit loiall argent qils ou il de eaux qissint serrount trosvez offendauntez de forfaiter ou perdire a[l summe de] xx li. ceaux de estre levez et perceivez de toutz sez biens et chateux laou ils serrount trosvez moite au roy et le aultre moite [a ceulx] queux suerrount ou voudrount suer pur lez mesmez en le enterest le roy et son ou lour enterest; et sil fortunera ascun

7 Berry's note: *lieu* interlined in roll.

c.7 [The king's coin minted in Dublin castle and elsewhere to be accepted throughout the land of Ireland][3]

Also, at the request of the commons, that whereas the king's coin to be made and coined in his land of Ireland both by mandate of the king[4] and by ordinance of parliament is established and ordained under a certain impression and form different from the impression of his coin of his kingdom of England, having the arms of England on one side with a cross trefoil at each end and three crowns on the other side with a half [cross trefoil at each end], as is more fully specified in the said mandate, act and ordinance, to the intent that it should remain and stay within the said land for the profit and good of his subjects there; in consideration of which it is ordained, enacted and established by authority of this parliament that the king's coin to be made and wrought under that impression by the lawful officers or any of them in the castle of Dublin and elsewhere in any other place that shall be lawfully appointed, shall be taken and pass among all the king's subjects; and by the same authority, it is ordained and established that if any person or persons, of whatever degree or condition he or they may be, refuse or are found refusing to take in payment the said coin lawfully made and to be made and coined in form aforesaid, in any manner of city, town or market place or elsewhere in this land of Ireland, he shall lose twelve pence for the value of each halfpenny of the said silver so refused, half to the king and the other half to the party that will sue for the same; and if it happens that any manner of person of the said persons is found or proved refusing the said coin for payment as is aforesaid in any of the said cities or towns, that then the said penalties and forfeitures of every twelve pence in form aforesaid shall be collected and levied, half thereof to the king and the other half for murage and pavage of the city or town where any such offence or offences shall happen to be committed, and the body or bodies of every person so found offending shall be arrested and committed to custody and prison, to remain there without bail or mainprise until the said penalties and every part of them are lawfully satisfied and paid or agreement made for the same; and that by the same authority, if any manner of person or persons of the inhabitants or citizens or burgesses in any of the cities or towns of Waterford, Wexford, New Ross, Kilkenny, Dungarvan, Youghal, Cork, Kinsale, Kilmallock, Limerick, Galway and Athenry and elsewhere in these parts of this land shall be found or duly proved by credible witnesses refusing the said lawful money in form aforesaid, that they or he who shall be found so offending shall forfeit or lose the sum of twenty pounds, to be levied and collected from

3 Irish Record Commission translation of this chapter (destroyed in 1922) printed by Aquilla Smith in *Numismatic Chronicle* (1881), pp 314–5. 4 *Letters and papers illustrative of the reigns of Richard III and Henry VII*, ed. J. Gairdner (Rolls Series, 1863), ii, 286–7.

de lez di[tz persons] et habitauntz ou cittezeins ou burgeises de ascun de lez ditz cittees ou viles pur le temps esteauntz de repugner [encontre] cest present acte et ordenaunce ou refusent et ne voilent my sufferer le dit loiall cune en fourme come il est ordei[ne] en paiement et passe entre eaux que sur duhe prove ent fait par duhe examinacion et sufficientes crediblez testm[oignes] devaunt le roy en sa chauncery en Irland que tielx cittezeins et burgeises de eaux queux issint serrount prov[e offendauntez de] forfaiter et perdire lour fraunchesie jesqes al temps qils avoient faitz fine ove le roy pur tielx contemptes al [volunte et] consideracion del dit courte; et que par mesme lauctorite est ordeine que cest acte et ordenaunce ne extende my en ascun manere [en prejudice] a lez cittezeins de Divelin ne a lez burgeises de vile de Drogheda.

c.8

Item al requisicion des communes que come le bone publique dicest terre ore de tarde deins cestez iij anes passez ad este grevousment [lesse en taunt] que le minte le roy devaunt cele temps ewe et use en cest terre pur forgement et ferrer del argent le money curraunt adonqez ord[eine pur le] commune profite dez liegez le roy en le mesme par lespace et temps avauntditz fuist surcesse et nient excercise en cest terre par quele toutz manere[s estraungiers] come Portingales Spaynardes Brittons gents de Fraunce et Flemmyngges usauntez cestez parties en cours dez marchauntdisez qui [usoient] de amesner sibien le cune de argent use en lour parties come aultre bullion de estre ferrue en le minte le roy isshie et par icele en subst[ituaunt] lour escheanges en marchauntdise par quele le commune profite dicest terre fuit graundement encresse et en especiale en ceo par le[8] money curraunt dices[t terre] convenientment ewe et courte entre eaux lez foials lieges le roy en le mesme et coment par la surcessir du dit minte et restriccion del amesner de tiell argent et bullion par lez ditz estraungiers duraunt le temps avauntdit tiell chierte et defaulte del cune et money le roy et en curraunce avauntdit ad et est fortune entre le commune people en la mesme qil ne poet my estre ewez ne pur achatement ne pur vendaunce en marchees ne pur escheaunge de ore saunz tresgraundez deperdes pur lescheaunge ne de paier petites parcels as servauntez labourers ne artificers par le quele diverses et plusours dez lieges du roy avoient departez et de jour en aultre ount departez dicest terre et lessount lour habitacions desolatez et gastez et coment la enconvenience[9] et lesion del bone publique est ne poet nule chose estre remedie par le ordre de cele maner minte

8 Berry's note: *le* repeated in roll. 9 Berry's note: *Enconvenice* in roll.

all his goods and chattels wherever they shall be found, half to the king and the other half to those who sue or will sue for the same on the king's behalf and his or their own behalf; and if it happens that any of the said persons and inhabitants or citizens or burgesses of any of the said cities or towns for the time being resist this present act and ordinance or refuse and will not allow the said lawful coin, in the form in which it is ordained, to be received in payment and to pass among them, that upon due proof thereof made by due examination and sufficient credible witnesses before the king in his chancery in Ireland, such citizens and burgesses who shall be proved offending in this way shall forfeit and lose their franchise until they make fine with the king for such contempt at the will and judgment of the said court; and that by the same authority it is ordained that this act and ordinance shall not extend in any manner in prejudice to the citizens of Dublin or to the burgesses of the town of Drogheda.

c.8 [Coinage of groats, half-groats, pennies and halfpennies to be made by the master of the mint according to instructions][5]

Also, at the request of the commons, that whereas the public good of this land recently in the past three years has been grievously injured because the king's mint had and used in this land before that time for working and striking from silver the current money then ordained for the common profit of the king's lieges in the same during the time aforesaid was neglected and not exercised in this land, whereby all manner of strangers, such as Portuguese, Spaniards, Bretons, Frenchmen and Flemings, frequenting these parts in the course of trade who used to bring both the silver coin used in their parts and other bullion to be struck in the king's mint here and thereby substituting their exchanges in merchandise, by which the common profit of this land was greatly increased and especially in regard to the current money of this land conveniently had and circulating amongst the king's faithful lieges in the same, and how by the cessation of the said mint and the restriction of the bringing of such money and bullion by the said strangers during the aforesaid time, such scarcity and lack of the king's coin and money in currency aforesaid amongst the common people in the same has occurred that it cannot be had, either for buying or selling in markets or in exchange for gold, without very great losses on the exchange or to pay small sums to servants, labourers or artificers, whereby many of the king's lieges had departed and from day to day have departed from this land and leave their habitations desolate and waste, and how

5 Irish Record Commission translation of this chapter printed by Aquilla Smith in *Numismatic Chronicle* (1881), pp 315–19.

qui fuist mise hors Dengleterre et limite en pois de xxxvij s. et vj d. a chescun livre pois del Toure de London de estre issint exercise en cest terre et lez causez pur quoy par une certeine ordenaunce de tarde fait en le graunde counseill darreine tenuz en cest terre devaunt cest dit parliament pluis pleinement appiert et coment pur ceo auxi que pur la reformacion ent par vertue del dit ordenaunce est establie et ordeine que le poys de chescun tiell livre serroit ferre et [cune] en le nombre de CCCC et l peces queux sount en chescun unce xxx peces et chescun tiell pece de currer et de estre prise entre le [liege] people pur ij d. unqore la dit enconvenience nest pas pleinement remedie ne le bone publique par icele nule chose encresse pur c[eo que nule] manere bullion amesnez al dit minte en ciphes coclears et aultre argente overez en overe de goldsmyth' ne puissoient my estre receive [de estre] coignez accordaunt al dit ordenaunce mes que le amesner de tiell bullion fuit mise a tresgraundez deperdez a demurer le fynyng ent [et outre que la] tranquillite et bone del commune people unqore par vertue del dit ordenance est nule chose encresse mesque diminuse; que en consideracio[n de lez] enconveniences avauntditz par auctorite dicest dit parliament ordeine est enacte et establie que bien luist al mastier ou maisters de le [minte pur le] cunage le roy deins cest terre pur le temps esteauntz de forger ferrer prenter cuner et facer de estre forge ferre cune et prende pur le [profite del commune] people et encresse del bone publique si bien iiij maners de argent ou moneyes cestassavere grosses demi grosses deniers demi deniers [de la mesme] manere come en chescun tiell lieu et lieux come il est ordeine de estre ferrue par le statute en cele parte fait en le parliament tard[e tenu] le lundie proschien apres le fest de Seint Kateryne la virgine le x ane del reigne du roy Edward le quatre[10] tarde roy Dengleterre [et par la mesme] auctorite que lez ditz iiij maneres dez cunez issint de estre forgez ferruez et cunez de estre forgez ferruez et cunez en et de lez fines en [et de] tiell assoie ove toutz tiels maneres dez remediez en le poys de chescun xx s. de ceo pur le master ou maisters avauntditz forgement [...] et ferrue overes ent come par lestatute acte et ordenaunce en une parliament du dit tarde roy tenuz a Divelyn le xij ane de son reigne fuit [enacte] de estre exercise pur le droiturell estandart del grosse demi grosse denier demi denier del cune adonqes ordeine et appelle le grosse demi grosse [denier] demi denier del cune de lez doubles come desouth le prente tarde envoie hors Dengleterre par le commaundement de nostre soveraine seignur le roy est [fait] exercise et ferrue pur le dit cune et money et ceo issint de estre uttere receive et courte entre sez subjectez dicest sa terre en different de lez prentez de son cune de son roialme Dengleterre cestassavere lez grossez demi grossez lez deniers lez demi deniers accordaunt al dit commaundement de avere en le une partie lez arms Dengleterre ove une

10 26 November 1470.

there is inconvenience and injury of the public good and nothing can be remedied by the order of that kind of mint which was sent from England and limited in weight to 37 shillings and 6 pence for each pound weight of the Tower of London to be so used in this land and the causes of which more fully appear by a certain ordinance lately made in the great council last held in this land before this said parliament; and how also inasmuch as for the reform thereof by virtue of the said ordinance it is established and ordained that the weight of every such pound should be struck and coined into the number of 450 pieces which are 30 pieces in each ounce and every such piece to be current and to be taken amongst the liege people for two pence, yet the said inconvenience is not fully remedied or the public good in any way increased thereby, because no manner of bullion brought to the said mint in cups, spoons and other silver worked in goldsmith's work could be received to be coined according to the said ordinance unless the bringer of such bullion was put to very great losses in waiting for it to be refined, and further that the tranquillity and good of the common people is yet by virtue of the said ordinance in no way increased but diminished; that, in consideration of the inconveniences aforesaid, it is ordained, enacted and established by authority of this said parliament that it shall be lawful for the master or masters of the mint for the king's coinage in this land for the time being to forge, strike, imprint, coin and cause to be forged, struck, coined and imprinted for the profit of the common people and the increase of the public good, four kinds of silver or coins, that is to say, groats, half groats, pence and halfpence, of the same kind as it is ordained to be struck in every such place and places by the statute made in that behalf in the parliament lately held on the Monday next after the feast of St Katherine the virgin in the tenth year of the reign of king Edward the fourth late king of England [26 November 1470][6]; and by the same authority, that the said four kinds of coins so to be forged, struck and coined are to be forged, struck and coined in and of the fineness in and of such assay with all such manner of remedies in the weight of every 20 shillings thereof for the master or masters aforesaid forging [. . .] and struck by workmen thereof as by the statute act and ordinance in a parliament of the said late king held at Dublin in the twelfth year of his reign[7] was enacted to be used for the lawful standard of the groat, half groat, penny and halfpenny of the coin then ordained and called the groat, half groat, penny and halfpenny of the coin of the doubles, as is made, used and struck for the said coin and money under the impression lately sent out of England by the mandate of our sovereign lord the king; and this shall be so uttered, received and current amongst his subjects of this his land different

6 10 Edward IV c.4. *Stat. Ire., 1–12 Edw. IV*, pp 650–6. 7 12–13 Edward IV c.59. *Stat. Ire., 12–22 Edw. IV*, pp 128–30.

croys tresfoile en chescun fine ove cest escripture Ricardus Dei gratia rex Anglie et dominus Hibernie et en le aultre partie del mesme iij corons une suiz le aultre ove une crosse tresfoile en chescun fine portaunt en le circumference del mesme le non del lieu en fourme avauntdit il serra loialment forge ferrue et cune des queux grosses en fourme come il est avauntdit especifie de estre fait et cune CC et xxv peces ove lez remediez avauntditz ferrount le livre del pois de Troy et chescun de eaux nient tonse ne clippe par mesme lauctorite de estre prise et passa entre toutz lez subjectes le roy par et en toute cest terre a et en la value de iiij d. et le demi grosse par mesme lauctorite de estre fait en semblable manere prentes come est avaunt especifie de lez ditz grosses ove mesme lescripture ou come il poet estre comprehende en le mesme par la discrecion del dit master ou masters ou gravers dez ditz coignes des queux demi grosses CCCC et l peces ferrount le livre del pois de T[roy ove] lez remediez avauntditz et chescun tiell pece de eaux nient tonse ne clippe par mesme le auctorite soit prise et passa entre toutz lez s[ubgettes] le roy par et en toute cest terre a et en la value de ij d. et le denier par mesme lauctorite de estre faite en semblable prentes del dit demi [grosse ove] mesme lescripture come en eaux poet comprehende par lez discrecions del master ou maisters et gravers avauntditz et dez queux deniers [DCCCC peces] ferrount le livre del pois de Troy ove lez remedies avauntditz et chescun de eaux nient tonse ne clippe par mesme lauctorite soit prise [et passa entre] toutz lez subjectes le roy dicest terre a et en la value de denier et le demi denier par mesme lauctorite de estre fait en semblable m[anere] de lez ditz deniers ove mesme le escripture come en eaux poet comprehende par lez discrecions de lez ditz master ou masteres et graver[s avauntditz et] dez queux demi deniers xviij^{c} peces ferrount le livre del pois de Troy ove lez remedies avauntditz et pur la tranquillite del commune people est ordeine [et enacte par mesme] lauctorite au meindre de ferrer le v parte ent et de chescun tiell livre en petites peces cestassavere demi grosses deniers et demi deniers et auxi par [mesme] lauctorite il bien luist al dit maister ou masters en la presence del countrouller ou countroullers dez mintes le roy ou le depute ou de[putees] de ascun de eaux pur le temps esteauntz de receiver lour stuff et toute loiall bullion amesne al minte en ciphes coclears et autre overe de [argent] pur la tranquillite del commune people qui serra entendue del fines du dit standard del double et ceo de forgier ferrer et cuner ou facer de estre forge fe[rrue et cune] en manere et fourme avauntditz et le amesnere et marchauntez de avere pur chescun unce de lour bullion et argent hors del minte iiij s. vj d. et le master et [masters] ij d. et le residue de chescun unce de estre reserve perceive et receive par le roy; et que par mesme le auctorite il bien luist al governour dicest terre pur le temp esteaunt desouth son teste si sovent come il requirera a directer lez gracieux briefs le roy a tielx persons ou person queux sacheount graver pounsons pur lez prentes del money avauntdit commaundauntez eaux

from the impressions of his coin of his kingdom of England that is to say, according to the said mandate, the groats, half groats, pence and halfpence are to have on one side the arms of England with a cross trefoil at each end with this inscription 'Richard by the grace of God king of England and lord of Ireland' and on the other side of the same three crowns one over the other with a cross trefoil at each end bearing in the circumference of the same the name of the place where it shall be lawfully forged, struck and coined in form aforesaid, of which groats to be made and coined in form as it is before specified, 225 pieces with the remedies aforesaid shall make the pound weight of Troy and by the same authority, each of them not shorn or clipped shall be taken and shall pass amongst all the king's subjects through and in all this land at and for the value of four pence; and the half groat by the same authority shall be made in like manner, imprinted as is before specified of the said groats with the same inscription or as far as it can be contained in the same at the discretion of the said master or masters or engravers of the said coins, of which half groats 450 pieces shall make the pound weight of Troy with the remedies aforesaid, and by the same authority, every such piece of them not shorn or clipped shall be taken and pass amongst all the king's subjects through and in all this land at and for the value of two pence; and the penny by the same authority shall be made in like impression as the said half groats with the same inscription as far as can be contained in them at the discretion of the master or masters and engravers aforesaid and of which pence 900 pieces shall make the pound weight of Troy with the remedies aforesaid, and by the same authority each of them not shorn or clipped shall be taken and pass amongst all the king's subjects of this land at and for the value of a penny; and the halfpenny by the same authority shall be made in like manner as the said pence with the same inscription as far as can be contained in them at the discretion of the said master or masters and engravers [...] of which halfpence 1800 pieces shall make the pound weight of Troy with the remedies aforesaid; and for the tranquillity of the common people it is ordained and enacted by the same authority that at least one fifth of every such pound shall be struck in small pieces, that is to say, half groats, pence and halfpence; and also by the same authority, that it shall be lawful for the said master or masters in the presence of the controller or controllers of the king's mints or of the deputy or deputies of any of them for the time being to receive their *stuff* and all lawful bullion brought to the mint in cups spoons and other wrought silver for the tranquillity of the common people which shall be thought to be of the fineness of the said standard of the double, and to forge, strike and coin or cause this to be forged, struck and coined in the manner and form aforesaid, and the bringer and merchants shall receive four shillings and six pence for each ounce of their bullion and silver from the mint and the master and masters shall receive two pence and the

ou luy de executer le commaundement le roy en ceo directe et que chescunz tiels briefs ou brief par mesme lauctorite de estre ajuge une loiall auctorite et discharge en ley pur sculpture del mesmez; et par mesme le auctorite touts et chescunz maners peces de argente et summez de money queux ount este forgez ferruez et cune et le sculpture de mesmez lez prentes par le master ou masters gravere et overers avauntditz ou ascun de eaux en ascun temps del primere jour de january darreine passe[11] tanque al jour del fesaunce dicest present acte et ordenaunce en grossez demi grosses deniers et demi deniers et en et de le finnes del standard del argent avauntdit de estre ajugez bons et sufficientez en ley et que toutz et chescun manere dez enditements en ascun des courtes le roy ou devaunt ascun de sez officeres ou ministres sibien envers ascun de lez ditz maisters ou gravers come auxi envers ascun de lez ditz overers amesnours de bullion a ascun des mintes le roy ou ascuns officeres ou officere occupiaunt en lez mesmez maneres lez utterers du dit money pur cele cause et occasion en ascun manere ewez et toutz et chescunz maneres dez briefs processes exigentes et utlagaries envers ascun manere de lez ditz persons pur cele parte faitz pronounciez ou ewez par mesme lauctorite soient ajugez voidez et de nule effecte en ley.

c.9

Item al requisicion des communes que en consideracion de lez graundez et cheargeous custagez et expensez queux le bon seignur Gerot [count] de Kildare depute lieutenaunt Dirland et peine de jour en aultre qil ad en defence dez subjectes le roy encountre sez irrois e[nemies] et rebelx ordeine enacte et establie par auctorite dicest parliament que bien luist al dit depute[12] duraunt le temps qil avoit e[we ou] issint avera la governaunce dicest terre de jour en aultre et annuelment de prender perceiver et receivere lez issuis profites et revenues d[e jour en] aultre et annuelment veignauntez del minte ou mintes le roy exercisez et de estre exercisez deins cest terre Dirland par lez ma[ins] del master ou masteres del dit minte ou mintes pur le temps esteauntz ou ascun aultre manere officere ou officeres dez m[intes] pur le temps esteauntz; et que par mesme lauctorite toutz et chescun manere acquittancez faitz et de estre faitz et deliverez par [le dit] count desouth son signet ou seall de armes a ascun del dit mestier ou masteres officere ou officeres avauntditz et pur chesc[un] severale parcell ou pleine recepte en lour et pur chescun de lour acquittall et discharge

11 1 January 1484. 12 Berry's note: *depute* interlined in roll.

residue of each ounce shall be reserved, taken and received by the king; and by the same authority, that it shall be lawful for the governor of this land for the time being, as often as it shall be necessary, to direct the king's gracious writs under his attestation to such persons or person who can engrave punches for the imprints of the money aforesaid, commanding them or him to execute the king's mandate therein directed and that by the same authority, every such writ or writs shall be adjudged a lawful authority and discharge in law for cutting the same; and by the same authority all and every kind of pieces of silver and sums of money which have been forged, struck and coined in groats, half groats, pence and halfpence and in and of the fineness of the standard of the silver aforesaid, and the engraving of the same imprints by the master or master engraver and workmen aforesaid or any of them at any time from the first day of January last past until the day of the making of this present act and ordinance shall be adjudged good and sufficient in law; and that by the same authority, all and every kind of indictments in any of the king's courts or before any of his officers or ministers for that cause and occasion, against any of the said masters or engravers and against any of the said workmen, persons bringing bullion to any of the king's mints or any officers or officer working in the same, and utterers of the said money and all and every kind of writs, processes, exigents and outlawries made, pronounced or had against any of the said persons in that behalf shall be adjudged void and of no effect in law.

c.9 [The deputy lieutenant of Ireland to receive the profits of the mint during his term of office][8]

Also, at the request of the commons, that in consideration of the great and burdensome costs and expenses and the daily labour which the good lord Gerald, earl of Kildare, deputy lieutenant of Ireland, has in defence of the king's subjects against his Irish enemies and rebels, it is ordained, enacted and established by authority of this parliament that it shall be lawful for the said deputy, during the time that he had or shall so have the government of this land, from day to day and yearly to take, perceive and receive the issues, profits and revenues daily and yearly coming from the king's mint or mints worked and to be worked in this land of Ireland by the hands of the master or masters of the said mint or mints for the time being or any other manner of officer or officers of the mints for the time being; and that by the same authority, all and every manner of acquittances made and to be made and delivered by the said earl under his signet or seal of arms to any of the said master or masters, officer or officers aforesaid, in acquittance

8 Irish Record Commission translation of this chapter printed by Aquilla Smith in *Numismatic Chronicle* (1881), pp 319–20.

dez ditz issues profites et revenues perceivez [et] receivez et de estre perceivez et receivez en fourme avauntdit del mesmez soient ajugez bones et effectualx en ley; et que par mesme le auctorite toutz tielx sez acquittauncez ent several-ment a chescun de lez ditz master ou masters officere et officeres issint faitz et deliverez et issint [de estre][13] faitz et deliverez de estre ajugez et allowez pur chescun de eaux une loiall et quite discharge del dette ent et de toutz maneres dez accomptes ent de estre ewe et auxi en chescun dez courtes le roy envers le roy sez officeres et ministrez accordaunt al purporte et tenour de toutz tielx acquittauncez ascun manere chose en ascun manere au contrarie ewe et de estre fait et ewe nient obstaunt.

C.10

Item al supplicacion des oratours nostre soveraine seignur le roy de jour en aultre Water abbe del meason del Benoit Virgine Marie juxt Divelin et le covent del mesme la meason illeosqes Dieu servauntez et la dit Virgine que come lez ditz abbe et covent sount seisiez en lour demesne come de fee dez certeins esglises et chappelx en la diocy de Mith' come en droite de lour dit meason et sount graundement chargez par la graunte de chescun subsidie fait al astate le roy nostre soveraine seignur; en consideracion ent ordeine est graunte establie et enacte par auctorite dicest parliament que lez ditz abbe et covent et lour successours pur toutz jours en pure et perpetuale almo[igne] desore enavaunt soient franqez clerez quitez et outrement dischargez de xxxiij s. et iiij d. et ent pardonez et relessez a chescun temps d[esore enavaunt] de ascun subsidie taxe tallage prest quote imposicion ou ascun aultre charge; et par le dit auctorite que sibien lez collectours come receivours pur le temps esteauntz eient duhe allowance et soient quitez et outrement dischargez sur lour accompte de lez ditz xx[xiij s. et] iiij d. et de chescun parte de eaux sibien devaunt lez barons del escheqer le roy en Irland come devaunt ascuns maneres [auditours] ou auditour par le governour dicest terre pur le temps esteaunt de estre assignez.

C.11

Item al supplicacion de Thomas Plunket chief justice del commune place le roy en Irland et Henrie Duff secondarie justice del dit pla[ce] que come aultres jus-tices avoient ewez et usez devaunt eaux par briefs du privelege ascun foitz par sufferaunce et ascun foitz par auctorit[e]; sur que ordeine est par auctorite dicest parliament que lez ditz justices poient avere occupier et enjoier toutz

13 Berrry's note: *de estre* omitted in transcript.

and discharge of every one of them, for each portion or in full receipt of the said issues, profits and revenues taken and received and to be taken and received in form aforesaid from the same, be adjudged good and effectual in law; and that by the same authority all such acquittances so made by him and delivered to each of the said master or masters, officer and officers shall be adjudged and allowed for each of them as a lawful and full discharge of the debt thereof and of all manner of accounts to be had thereof and also in each of the king's courts against the king, his officers and ministers according to the purport and tenor of all such acquittances, notwithstanding any manner of thing had and to be done and had in any way to the contrary.

c.10 [Grant to St Mary's abbey, Dublin, of exemption from payment of subsidy and other impositions in the diocese of Meath]

Also, at the prayer of Walter, abbot of the house of the Blessed Virgin Mary near Dublin and the convent of the same house there serving God and the said Virgin, who daily pray for our sovereign lord the king, that whereas the said abbot and convent are seised in their demesne as of fee of certain churches and chapels in the diocese of Meath as in right of their said house and are greatly burdened by the grant of every subsidy made to the estate of the king our sovereign lord; in consideration of which it is ordained, granted, established and enacted by authority of this parliament that the said abbot and convent and their successors for ever in pure and perpetual alms henceforth be free, clear, quit and altogether discharged of thirty three shillings and four pence and pardoned and released thereof at every time henceforth of any subsidy, tax, tallage, loan, quota, imposition or any other charge; and by the said authority that both the collectors and the receivers for the time being have due allowance and be quit and altogether discharged on their account of the said thirty three shillings and four pence and of every part thereof both before the barons of the king's exchequer in Ireland and before any manner of auditors or auditor to be assigned by the governor of this land for the time being.

c.11 [The justices of the common bench to enjoy procedural advantages by writ of privilege as their predecessors did]

Also, at the petition of Thomas Plunket, chief justice of the king's common bench in Ireland and Henry Duff, second justice of the said bench, that whereas other justices had had and used before them by writs of privilege, sometimes by sufferance and sometimes by authority; upon which it is ordained by authority of this parliament that the said justices may have, occupy and enjoy all manner of processes to be sued before them as any other justices

maneres processez de estre suez devaunt eaux come ascuns aultres justicez del dit commune place loialment ad ewe devaunt eaux suez devaunt cest temps et ceo saunz ascun empechement de ascun person ou persons queux voudrount suer devaunt eaux en temps avenaunt ascun acte ou ordenaunce encontrarie fait nient obstaunt issint que cest acte ne extende my ne soit prejudiciale al citte de Divelin ne al vile de Drogheda ne al cirograffer del commune place le roy en Irland pur le temps esteauntez ne a nully de eaux.

c.12

Item al requisicion dez communes que come Davy Ketyng et Patrik Ketyng furent ordeinez et faitz par commission generale receivour del roiall service le roy deins la liberte et counte de Weisford dez queux receptez ils ne avoient donez nule accompte unqore; sur que lez premissez considerez ordeine est enacte et establie par auctorite dicest parliament que lez ditz Davy et Patrik et chescun de eaux veignent et appiergent en lour propre persons en le chastell du roy de Divelin le lundie proschien apres le fest del Assension de Nostre Seignur Jesu Crist proschien avenaunt[14] et illeosqes a demurer en la garde del mareschall du dit chastell devaunt le chief justice del commune place le roy en[15] Irland jesqes al temps que ils et chescun de eaux facent duhe satisfaccion et accompte devaunt le dit justice de lez premissez avauntditz o[u] aultrement ils et chescun de eaux de monstrer sufficient discharge pur eaux et chescun de eaux pur le paiement del mesme; et si ils [ou] ascun de eaux ne appiergent my le jour et lieu avauntditz devaunt le dit justice et illoesqes a demurer en la garde del mareschall accorda[unt al] fourme avauntdit que adonqes ils et chescun de eaux de estre hors del proteccion du roy et que ils et chescun de eaux de forfaiter xx [li. al] tresnoble seignur Gerot counte de Kildare depute lieutenant Dirland et par mesme le auctorite le dit Gerot sez heires et sez assignez e[ient] pleine power de lever lez ditz xx li. a lour voluntees de touts lez terres biens et chateux queux ils ou ascun de eaux ad deins la terre Dirland issint que le dit Davy soit deins cest terre xv jours devaunt le dit lundie.

c.13

Item al requisicion dez communes que come de jour en aultre est moulte contreue et faulz mone et cune saunz loiall auctorite fait sibien par Germyn Lynche tarde coignour en et bien pres lez parties de Waterford come par diversez irrois kerdes en cestz partiez et aillours deins cest terre et par diversez

14 31 May 1484. 15 Berry's note: *en* repeated in roll.

of the said common bench lawfully have hitherto had sued before them without any hindrance of any person or persons who may wish to sue before them in time to come, notwithstanding any act or ordinance made to the contrary; provided that this act shall not extend or be prejudicial to the city of Dublin or to the town of Drogheda or to the chirographer of the king's common bench in Ireland for the time being or to any of them.

c.12 [Davy and Patrick Keating to surrender to Dublin castle to account for the royal service of the liberty of Wexford]

Also, at the request of the commons, that whereas Davy Ketyng and Patrick Ketyng were ordained and appointed by commission general receivers of the king's royal service in the liberty and county of Wexford, for which receipts they have not yet rendered any account; upon which, considering the premises, it is ordained, enacted and established by authority of this parliament that the said Davy and Patrick and each of them come and appear in person in the king's castle of Dublin on the Monday next after the feast of the Ascension of Our Lord Jesus Christ next coming [31 May 1484] and remain there in the custody of the marshal of the said castle before the chief justice of the king's common bench in Ireland until they and each of them make due satisfaction and account before the said justice for the premises aforesaid, or unless they and each of them show sufficient discharge for them and each of them for the payment of the same; and if they or either of them do not appear on the day and at the place aforesaid before the said justice and remain there in the custody of the marshal according to the form aforesaid, that then they and each of them shall be outside the king's protection and they and each of them shall forfeit twenty pounds to the very noble lord, Gerald, earl of Kildare, deputy lieutenant of Ireland; and by the same authority the said Gerald, his heirs and his assigns have full power to levy the said twenty pounds at their will on all the lands, goods and chattels which they have or either of them has in the land of Ireland, provided that the said Davy be in this land fifteen days before the said Monday.

c.13 [Resumption of grants of office in the mint made to Germyn Lynch and provisions for rejection of counterfeit coinage and action against counterfeiters][9]

Also, at the request of the commons, that whereas daily much counterfeit and false money and coin is made without lawful authority, both by Germyn

9 Irish Record Commission translation of this chapter printed by Aquilla Smith in *Numismatic Chronicle* (1881), p. 320.

persons de lour affinite uttere entre lez lieges du roy et subjectes en cest sa terre contrarie as leyes du roy et en decepte et tresmichevous lesion del bone publique dicest terre; sur que lez premisses considerez ordeine est enacte et establie par auctorite dicest parliament que bien luist a chescun dez subjectes le roy qui wineroupt ou trosverount tiell faulx et contreue argent ove ascun manere person ou ascun tiell de estre uttere en paiement entre ou a ascun dez subjectes ou lieges du roy de ceo rumper et ceo deliverer al possessour a derer; et que toutz et chescun manere dez lettres patentez dones grauntes et toutz et chescun manere dez actes et statutes du parliament devaunt cest temps en ascun manere faitz a et pur le dit Germyn de et pur le office del master du mintez le roy ou minte en Irland par auctorite dicest present parliament soient revoquez repellez et annullez et ajugez voidez et de nule effecte en ley; et que par mesme lauctorite que chescun manere seignur gentile homme et aultres persons queux desore enavaunt souffre ou soit trosve et loialment provez supportau[nt a] le dit Germyn ou ascun manere kerde saunz ascun loiall auctorite de ferrer et faire tiell contreue coigne et faulx argent de estre aju[ge en] ley come principale fesour ou fesours de mesme et de estre ajugez en tiell execucion come ley voet serroit execute envers eaux [et chescun] de eaux pur le mesme.

c.14

Item al requisicion des communes que come en une parliament del pluis excellent del benoit memorie Edward le quatre tard[e roy] Dengleterre tenuz a Lymerik devaunt le trespuissaunt et gracieux seignur Gerot count de Kildare adonqes depute lieutenaunt Dirland le vendredie proschien devaunt le fest de Cinerum le ane du reigne del dit tarde roy xxij[16] une acte fuit fait et endorse par quele endorsement le dit acte serroit avere lee al proschien adjournement del dit parliament et pur ceo que le dit tarde roy decessa en le mesne temps le dit acte ne fuit my lee accordaunt al dit endorsement; sur que lez premissez considerez ordeine est graunte establie et enacte par auctorite dicest parliament que le dit acte soit lee en cest dit parliament et ceo issint lee le avauntdit acte de estre de si graunde force et effecte et si beneficiall en ley sicome il avoit este lee al avauntdit adjournement accordaunt al dit endorsement le non lee del dit acte al dit adjournement nient obstaunt; purvieu toutz foitz que le acte suisdit ne nule article en le continue ne extendent my ne soient prejudicialx a sire

16 7 February 1483.

Lynche, late coiner in and very near the parts of Waterford, and by various Irish *kerdes* in those parts and elsewhere in this land, and uttered by persons of their kinship amongst the king's lieges and subjects in this his land contrary to the king's laws and in deception of and very mischievous injury to the public good of this land; upon which, considering the premises, it is ordained, enacted and established by authority of this parliament that it shall be lawful for every one of the king's subjects who sees or finds such false and counterfeit money with any manner of person, or any such being uttered in payment amongst or to any of the king's subjects or lieges, to break it and deliver it back to the possessor, and that all and every manner of letters patent, gifts, grants and all and every manner of acts and statutes of parliament heretofore in any manner made to and for the said Germyn of and concerning the office of master of the king's mints or mint in Ireland, by authority of this present parliament, be revoked, repealed and annulled and adjudged void and of no effect in law; and by the same authority, that every manner of lord, gentleman and other persons who shall henceforth allow the said Germyn or any manner of *kerde* to strike and make such counterfeit coin and false money without any lawful authority, or shall be found and lawfully proved to be supporting them, shall be adjudged in law as the principal doer or doers of the same and shall be adjudged in such execution as the law wills should be executed against them and every one of them for the same.

c. 14 [Confirmation of an act endorsed to be read after the adjournment of the parliament at Limerick and not read because of the death of Edward IV]

Also, at the request of the commons, that whereas in a parliament of the most excellent prince of blessed memory Edward the fourth late king of England held at Limerick before the very powerful and gracious lord, Gerald, earl of Kildare, then deputy lieutenant of Ireland, on the Friday before Ash Wednesday in the twenty second year of the reign of the said late king [7 February 1483], an act was made and endorsed by which endorsement the said act should have been read at the next adjournment of the said parliament, and because the said late king died in the meantime the said act was not read according to the said endorsement; upon which, considering the premises, it is ordained, granted, established and enacted by authority of this parliament that the said act be read in this said parliament and having been read, the aforesaid act shall be of as great force and effect and as beneficial in law as if it had been read at the aforesaid adjournment according to the said endorsement, notwithstanding the non-reading of the said act at the said adjournment; provided always that the above-mentioned act or any article contained in it do not extend

Rouland Eustace chivaler seignur de Portlester ne a ascun de sez heires en nule manere.

c.15

Item al supplicacion de Elizabeth qui fuit la famme de Johan Darcy esquier que come la dit Elizabeth est seisie de vij^{xx} vj acres de arrable terre en le Martre et de iiij li. et de xxj d. de chief rente en Alleyneston' et Fennokeston' ove lappurtenauncez come en le non del jounctour et del tierce parte dez maneres de Platyne Dunmowe et le Martre en le counte de Mithe en son demesne come de franqe tenement come en certeinez faits del dit jounctour et assignementes del dit tierce parte de lez ditz maneres faitz al dit Elizabeth par William Darcy fitz et heire al dit Johan William Hore chapleyn et Robert Warre chapleyn sicome par lez ditz faits pluis pleinement appiert; en consideracion dez premisses ordeine est enacte et establie par auctorite dicest parliament que le dit Elizabeth eit et en[joie] son dit jounctour et tierce parte come il est devaunt reherse pur terme de sa vie ascun defaulte feoffament alienacion [ou] recovere avauntdit ou ascun aultre chose par quele le dit jounctour ou tierce parte ou ascun de eaux ou ascun par[cel de] ascun de eaux serroit voide faitz ewez au contrarie devaunt cest temps a ascun aultre person ou persons ou par ascun au[ltre person] ou persons nient obstauntz issint que cest acte ne extende my ne soit prejudiciale al dit William Darcy fitz et heire [al dit] Johan Darcy ne a William Wellesley ne as heires de William Hill ne a nule de eaux en nule manere en ou [de] les deux parties de lez ditz maneres.

c.16

Item al supplicacion de Johan Pippard que come Patrik Feld porta et sua un bill de dette de ij marces envers le dit Johan Pippard devaunt le roy en sa chief place processe sur ceo continue jesqes le dit Patrik Felde avoit jugement de recoverer dez ditz ij marces ove sez dasmages sur quele le dit Johan ad sue une brief de errour retournable et retourne en cest dit parliament et sur le mesme ad assigne sez errours come appiert de recorde en la garde del clerke du parlment et pur ceo que nule scire facias ne poet my aultrement agarde a la commune ley mes al proschien parliament le quele est longe et en nule certeine ordeine est et establie par auctorite dicest parliament que le dit Patrik Felde vient et respoigne as ditz errours le primere jour del proschien prorogacion ou adjournement dicest dit parliament apres proclamacion fait et sil face defaulte et ne respoigne my que adonqes par la dit auctorite le tresnoble seignur Gerot count de Kildare depute lieutenaunt Dirland ove lez seignuries du parliament

or be prejudicial to Sir Roland Eustace, knight, lord of Portlester, or to any of his heirs in any manner.

c.15 [Confirmation of the jointure of Elizabeth, widow of John Darcy of Platin]

Also, at the petition of Elizabeth who was the wife of John Darcy esquire, that whereas the said Elizabeth is seised of one hundred and forty six acres of arable land in the Martry and of four pounds and twenty one pence of chief rent in Allenstown and Phoenixtown with the appurtenances as her jointure and of the third part of the manors of Platin, Dunmoe and the Martry in the county of Meath in her demesne as of freehold, according to certain deeds of the said jointure and assignment of the said third part of the said manors made to the said Elizabeth by William Darcy, son and heir to the said John, William Hore, chaplain, and Robert Warre, chaplain, as more fully appears by the said deed; in consideration of the premises, it is ordained, enacted and established by authority of this parliament that the said Elizabeth have and enjoy her said jointure and third part, as it is before rehearsed, for term of her life, notwithstanding any default, feoffment, alienation or recovery aforesaid or any other thing whereby the said jointure or third part or either of them or any part of either of them should be void, made or had to the contrary before now to any other person or persons or by any other person or persons; provided that this act do not extend or be prejudicial to the said William Darcy, son and heir to the said John Darcy, or to William Wellesley or to the heirs of William Hill or to any of them in any manner.

c.16 [Patrick Feld to answer to a writ of error against a judgment for debt in the king's bench]

Also, at the petition of John Pippard, that whereas Patrick Feld brought and sued a bill of debt of two marks against the said John Pippard before the king in the king's bench, process thereupon continued until the said Patrick Feld had judgment to recover the said two marks with his damages, whereupon the said John sued a writ of error returnable and returned into this said parliament and upon the same has assigned his errors as appears of record in the custody of the clerk of parliament; and because no *scire facias* can be awarded at the common law except at the next parliament which is distant and uncertain, it is ordained and established by authority of this parliament that the said Patrick Feld come and answer to the said errors on the first day of the next prorogation or adjournment of this said parliament after proclamation has been made, and if he make default and do not answer that then, by the said authority the

poient loialment proceder al examinacion de lez ditz errours et que par mesme lauctorite toute manere execucion ou execucions de cesser jesqes al temps lez ditz errours soient discussez et ajugez.

c.17

Item al supplicacion de Rogier Walcott marchaunt que come James Ketyng priour del hospitale de Seint [Johan de] Jerusalem en I[rland] et lez freres del mesme le order et hospitale par lour faite endente portaunt date del xviij jour de marche le primer an del [reigne nostre seignur le] roy Richard le tierce[17] et seale ove lour commune seall sibien de lour une assent et consent come al peticion assent et consent of[...] Lomeley une de lez ditz freres et commaundour del commaundrie de Kilsaran' en le counte de Iryell avoient donez graunt[ez et par lour] faite endente avoient confermez al dit Rogier une annuell rente ou annuite de xl marces de bone et loiall argent de I[rland] a avere perceivere et levere le dit annuell rente ou annuite de xl marces al avauntdit Rogier sez heires executours ou assignes de et en le seignurie terres et tenementez del commaundre ou seignurie de Kilsaran' avauntdit ove toutz lour appurtenaunce a deux termes par le ane cestassavere al festes de Toutz Seintes et de lez apostles Philipp et Jacob par owels parcions al [temps que le] dit Rogier sez heires executours ou assignes par icele soient loialment satisfiez paiez et contentez de CCCxxv marces iiij s. viij d. de bone et loiall argent de Irland[18] sicome pluis pleinement en le dit fait il est especifie et contenue; sur que lez premisses considerez ordeine est enacte et establie par auctorite dicest parliament que le dit fait endente done et graunte du dit annuele rente ou annuite de xl marces soient ratifiez approvez confermez donez et grauntez et ajugez bonez et effectuals en ley al dit Rogier et par mesme lauctorite a aver tener et enjoier le dit annuele rente ou annuite de xl marces et toutz et chescun manere done graunte et chose especifie en le dit fait endente al dit Rogier sez heires executours et assignes en chescun point accordaunt al purporte tenour et sentence del dit fait endente; et que toutz et chescun aultre manere choses ewe fait et de estre ewe et fait al contrarie del dit fait endente ou a cest present acte et ordenaunce par auctorite dicest [present] parliament soient restreignez et ajugez nient de estre de effecte en ley de leser ou prejudiser le dit Rogier sez heires executours [ou] assignes en et pur lez premisses ne de adnuller resumer ou en ascun manere de faire voide le dit fait endente ou le done et graunte del dit annuite ne auxi cest presente acte et ordenaunce.

17 18 March 1484. *Reigne* omitted in transcript. 18 Berry's note: *de Irland* repeated in roll.

very noble lord, Gerald, earl of Kildare, deputy lieutenant of Ireland with the lords of parliament may lawfully proceed to the examination of the said errors, and that by the same authority all manner of execution or executions shall cease until the time the said errors shall be discussed and adjudged.

c.17 [Confirmation of an annuity from the commandery of Kilsaran to Roger Walcott, merchant, in discharge of a debt]

Also, at the petition of Roger Walcott, merchant, that whereas James Ketyng, prior of the Hospital of Saint John of Jerusalem in Ireland and the brothers of the same order and Hospital by their deed indented bearing date the eighteenth day of March in the first year of the reign of our lord the king Richard the third [1484] and sealed with their common seal, by their unanimous assent and consent and at the petition, assent and consent of [Marmaduke] Lomeley, one of the said brothers and commander of the commandery of Kilsaran in the county of Uriel, had given, granted and by their deed indented had confirmed to the said Roger a yearly rent or annuity of forty marks of good and lawful money of Ireland to have, take and levy the said yearly rent or annuity of forty marks to the aforesaid Roger, his heirs, executors or assigns of and in the lordship, lands and tenements of the commandery or lordship of Kilsaran aforesaid with all their appurtenances at two terms each year, that is to say, at the feasts of All Saints and of the apostles Philip and James [1 November and 1 May], by equal portions until such time as the said Roger, his heirs, executors or assigns are fully satisfied, paid and contented of 325 marks four shillings and eight pence of good and lawful money of Ireland, as is more fully specified and contained in the said deed; upon which, considering the premises, it is ordained, enacted and established by authority of this parliament that the said deed indented, gift and grant of the said yearly rent or annuity of forty marks be ratified, approved, confirmed, given and granted and adjudged good and effectual in law to the said Roger and by the same authority to have, hold and enjoy the said annual rent or annuity of forty marks and all and every manner of gift, grant and thing specified in the said deed indented to the said Roger, his heirs, executors and assigns in every point according to the purport, tenor and intent of the said deed indented, and that all and every other manner of thing had and done and to be had and done to the contrary of the said deed indented or to this present act and ordinance by authority of this present parliament be revoked and adjudged to be of no effect in law to injure or prejudice the said Roger his heirs executors or assigns in and for the premises nor to annul, resume or in any manner make void the said deed indented or the gift and grant of the said annuity or also this present act and ordinance.

c.18

Item al supplicacion de Thomas fitz Gerot chivaler chaunceller Dirland entende de lever une chastell en la vi[le de Laghkagh'] deins le counte de Kildare que est en lez frontures del marche et si le dit chastell fuit edifie il voilet estre graund sui[rte] a toutz englois enhabitauntez del dit counte; sur que lez premissez considerez ordeine est et graunte par auctorite dicest parliam[ent que le] dit Thomas eit x li. de toutz lez communes du dit counte de lever le dit chastell et que lez sessours et collectours del subsidie darreine graunte en le dit counte facent assesser et lever lez ditz x li. et lez paier al dit Thomas; et auxi par mesme lauctorite que la vile de Laghkagh' soit franque de toute manere coigne et livere et toutz aultres subsidiez taxes et tallages durauntez vj anes; et que le viscount del dit counte eit pleine powere pur distreignere et compeller lez ditz sessours et collectours de assesser et faire leve de lez ditz x li. et faire paiement ent al dit Thomas; et que par mesme lauctorite chescun husband eiaunt une charue en le dit counte del Naas en le une parte de Anilyf et del Clane en le aultre parte face traher une charete dez peres al dit vile pur le habitacion[19] del dit chastell; et que le dit viscount compella et distreigna eaux issint affaire queux disount ou fount le contrarie deins le dit counte parissint que cest acte ne soit my prejudiciall a sire Rouland fitz Eustace ne a nule de sez tenauntez.

c.19

Item al supplicacion de Thomas Leynagh' priour del meason de Seint Dominic de Trym et le covent del mesme que come ils furent seisiez de iij^{xx} acres et x de arrable terre et pree ove lour appurtenauncez adjunauntz a lour dit meason en Trym avauntdit par le don et graunte de Richard tarde duc Deveryk a aver et tenire mesmez lez iij^{xx} acres et x et pree al dit meason et covent et lours successours en perpetuale almoigne et mesme la terre conferme al ditz meason et covent et lour successours sibien par le tresnoble prince Edwarde le iiij^{te} tarde roy Dengleterre come par Gerot count de Kildare depute lieutenaunt Dirland et Thomas fitz Morice son pier tarde [count de] Kildare quele alme Dieu reste en semble fourme as ditz meason et covent confermez cests nient obstauntz une frere Johan [...] priour del dit meason eiaunt nule covent ne conventualx freres en mesme la meason mes soulment luy mesme sole [eyaunt le] garde de touts maneres choses illeosqes et en especiale le commune seall del dit meason quele frere Johan priour forgea diversez faitz et eaux [enscella] ove le dit commune seall a diversez persons pur terme des anes seduciously a son singuler

19 Possibly an error for *habilacion*.

c.18 [Grant of £10 and cartage on the county of Kildare in aid of the building of a castle at Lackagh by Sir Thomas fitz Gerald]

Also, at the petition of Thomas fitz Gerald, knight, chancellor of Ireland, who intends to erect a castle in the town of Lackagh in the county of Kildare which is in the frontiers of the march, and if the said castle were built it would be a great security to all the English inhabitants of the said county; upon which, considering the premises, it is ordained and granted by authority of this parliament that the said Thomas have ten pounds from all the commons of the said county to erect the said castle and that the assessors and collectors of the subsidy last granted in the said county cause the said ten pounds to be assessed and levied and pay them to the said Thomas; and also by the same authority that the town of Lackagh be free of all manner of coign and livery and all other subsidies, taxes and tallages for six years; and that the sheriff of the said county have full power to distrain and compel the said assessors and collectors to assess and levy the said ten pounds and to pay them to the said Thomas; and by the same authority that every husbandman having a ploughland in the said county from Naas on the one side of the Liffey and from Clane on the other side cause a cartload of stones to be carried to the said town for the habitation[10] of the said castle, and that the said sheriff shall compel and distrain those who speak or act to the contrary in the said county to do so; provided that this act shall not be prejudicial to Sir Roland fitz Eustace or to any of his tenants.

c.19 [Annulment of grants of lands of the Dominican priory at Trim, made without the consent of the convent]

Also, at the petition of Thomas Leynagh, prior of the house of St Dominic of Trim and the convent of the same, that whereas they were seised of seventy acres of arable land and meadow with their appurtenances adjoining their said house in Trim aforesaid by the gift and grant of Richard, late duke of York, to have and to hold the same seventy acres of arable land and meadow to the said house and convent and their successors in perpetual alms, and the same land was confirmed to the said house and convent and their successors both by the most noble prince Edward the fourth late king of England and by Gerald, earl of Kildare, deputy lieutenant of Ireland and Thomas fitz Maurice, his father, late earl of Kildare, whose soul God rest, in the same form confirmed to the said house and convent, nevertheless, one brother John [...] prior of the said house, having no convent or conventual brothers in the same house but only himself alone, having the custody of all manner of things there and especially the common seal of the said house, which brother John the prior deceitfully

10 Or 'building', if the correct reading is *habilacion*.

availe laou le dit priour ne puisoit my par nule manere ley seler nule manere fait ne faites desouth le covent seall saunz assent et consent de son covent al graunde empoveri[she]ment decaie et desolacion de divine service en la dit meason saunz qil soit le pluis hastiefment remedie; sur que les premisses gracieuxment considerez enacte est ordeine et establie par auctorite dicest parliament pur ceo que lentente del donour fuit de auger [le] divine service en la dit meason en donacion de lez ditz terres et ceo et le erroniose fait del dit frere Johan priour a diminuser le dit divine service illeosqez que lez ditz frere Thomas priour et covent et lour successours poient loialment reenterer en toutz lez ditz terres et eaux a avere peisiblement saunz enterrupcion grevaunce empediment ou molestaunce de ascun person ou persons; et par mesme lauctorite si ascun person ou persons enterruptent grevent ou denient le dit priour et covent ou lour successours de lour dit reentre en lour ditz terres chescun de eaux de perdire x li. moite ent au roy et le aultre moite al dit meason et covent et lour successours et par mesme lauctorite lez ditz faitz enseallez sur la dite terre par le dit frere Johan priour de estre ajugez decrees et demez voidez et de nule effecte en ley; purvieu toutz foitz que cest acte ne extende my ne soit prejudiciale a Johan [...] de Trym marchaunt en ascun manere.

c.20

Item al supplicacion de Thomas Douedall de Divelin gentilman que come le dit Thomas est entitele de aver et receiver apres la morte de Johan Hall x marces annuelment a luy et a sez heires de son corps veignauntez del fee ferme del citte de Divelin par lez maines del maire et bailliefes de dit citte pur le temps esteauntz annuelment de estre paiez al deux festes del ane par owelx porcions come par la graunte ent fait al dit Thomas sibien par parliament come aultrement pluis largement appiert; sur que lez premisses considerez ordeine est et establie par auctorite dicest parliament que le dit Thomas et sez heires suisditz poient proferer et deliverer une generall acquittaunce al meire et bailliefes del dit citte pur le temps esteauntz annuelement pur le paiement de lez ditz x marcez a lez festes avauntditz et ils par reison del mesme de estre chargez al dit Thomas et sez heires desuis rehersez annuelment de lez ditz x marcez sur le profirre del dit acquittaunce annuelment de estre delivere par le dit Thomas et sez heires suisditz as ditz maire et bailliefes pur le tem[ps] esteauntz saunz ascun liberate de estre delivere par le dit Thomas as ditz maier et bailliefes pur le mesme; et que par la dit auctorite orde[ine est] et ajuge que la dit acquittaunce soit sufficient discharge pur lez maire et bailliefes del dit citte pur le temps esteauntez annuelment [sur] lour accompte de lez ditz x marces parcell

and to his own profit forged various deeds and sealed them with the said common seal to various persons for term of years, whereas the said prior could not, by any manner of law, seal any manner of deed or deeds under the convent seal without the assent and consent of his convent, to the great impoverishment, decay and ruin of divine service in the said house unless it be most speedily remedied; upon which, the premises graciously considered, it is enacted, ordained and established by authority of this parliament, because the intent of the donor was to increase divine service in the said house by the gift of the said lands, and this and the false deed of the said brother John the prior has diminished the said divine service there, that the said brother Thomas the prior and the convent and their successors may lawfully re-enter into all the said lands and have them peaceably without interruption, grievance, impediment or molestation by any person or persons; and by the same authority, if any person or persons interrupt, vex or deny the said prior and convent or their successors in their said re-entry into their said lands, each of them shall lose ten pounds, half to the king and the other half to the said house and convent and their successors; and by the same authority, the said deeds concerning the said land sealed by the said brother John the prior shall be adjudged, decreed and deemed void and of no effect in law; provided always that this act do not extend or be prejudicial to John [. . .] of Trim, merchant, in any manner.

c.20 [Acquittance by Thomas Dowdall for £10 received yearly from the fee farm of the city of Dublin to be sufficient discharge for the mayor and bailiffs at the exchequer]

Also, at the petition of Thomas Douedall of Dublin, *gentilman*, that whereas the said Thomas is entitled to have and receive after the death of John Hall, ten marks yearly, to him and to his heirs issuing from his body, out of the fee-farm of the city of Dublin by the hands of the mayor and bailiffs of the said city for the time being, to be paid yearly at two feasts of the year by equal portions, as more fully appears by the grant thereof made to the said Thomas both by parliament and otherwise; upon which, considering the premises, it is ordained and established by authority of this parliament that the said Thomas and his heirs aforesaid may proffer and deliver a general acquittance to the mayor and bailiffs of the said city for the time being yearly for the payment of the said ten marks at the feasts aforesaid, and they by reason of the same shall be charged to the said Thomas and his heirs before rehearsed yearly with the said 10 marks upon the proffer of the said acquittance yearly to be delivered by the said Thomas and his heirs above mentioned to the said mayor and bailiffs for the time being, without any writ of *liberate* to be delivered by the said Thomas to the said mayor and bailiffs for the same; and that by the said authority it is

del dit fee ferme devaunt lez barons del eschequier le roy Dirland pur le temps esteauntz come la graunte dez mesmez fait al dit Thomas fuit reherse paroll par paroll en la dit acquittaunce; et que par la dit auctorite ordeine est et enacte que lez barons del dit eschequirr pur le temps esteauntz allowent et dischargent lez maire et bailliefes del dit citte pur le temps esteauntz annuelment sur lour accompte de les ditz x marces come parcell del dit fee ferme sur la deliveraunce del dit acquittaunce a eaux annuelment de estre delivere par lez ditz maire et bailliefes pur le temps esteauntz pur lez ditz x marces de les termes desuis rehersez saunz ascun allocate de estre delivere par le dit Thomas et sez heires suisditz as ditz barons pur le temps esteauntz pur le allowaunce del mesme et que cest acte preigne effecte pur le paiement sibien del terme de Seint Michell dareine passe come pur toutz aultres termes en temps avenauntz; et que par mesme lauctorite que cest acte et ordenaunce ne extende my ne soit prejudicial a lez maire et bailliefes del citte de Divelyn pur le temps esteauntz ne a nule de lour successours en temps avenire ne a nule aultre person ne persons queux ount ascun chose a lour use ne a Cristofre Faunte chapleyne.

c.21

Item al supplicacion de Thomas Douedall de Divelin gentilman que come James Ketyng priour del meason del hospitale de Seint J[ohn] de Jerusalem en Irland et lez confreres del mesme par lour fait endente et desouth lour commune seall ensealle portaunt date le vij jour de feverell le prim[er] ane del reigne du roy Richard le tierce[20] par lour entier et pleine assente et consente ount donez et grauntez misez et lessez a ferme al dit Thomas toutz maneres dismes dez garbes et fene al esglis de Clontarf en ascun manere parteignauntez a avere et a tenire toutz lez ditz dismes al dit Thomas sez heires et assignes pur le terme de xxxvj anes adonqes proschiens ensuauntez le date suisdit sicome par le dit fait pluis pleinement appiert; sur que lez premisses considerez ordeine est enacte et establie par auctorite dicest parliament que la dit graunte fait al dit Thomas par les ditz priour conffreres et toute et chescun chose en le mesme contenue et chescun aultre graunte et lesse par lez ditz priour et confreres al dit Thomas forsprisez tielx grauntez queux furent faitz a Robert Douedall chivaler et al dit Thomas joinctement soient auctorisez provez confermez et ajugez bones et effectualx en ley accordaunt al tenour purporte et effecte del mesmez en toutz pointes; et que par mesme auctorite il soit decree ajuge determine et ordeine que le dit Thomas sez heires et assignes eient

20 7 February 1484.

ordained and adjudged that the said acquittance shall be a sufficient discharge for the mayor and bailiffs of the said city for the time being yearly on their account of the said ten marks, part of the said fee-farm, before the barons of the king's exchequer of Ireland for the time being, as if the grant of the same made to the said Thomas was rehearsed word by word in the said acquittance; and that by the said authority it is ordained and enacted that the barons of the said exchequer for the time being allow and discharge the said ten marks to the mayor and bailiffs of the said city for the time being yearly on their account, as part of the said fee-farm on the delivery of the said acquittance to them yearly to be delivered by the said mayor and bailiffs for the time being for the said ten marks of the terms above rehearsed, without any writ of *allocate* to be delivered by the said Thomas and his heirs above mentioned to the said barons for the time being for the allowance of the same, and that this act take effect for the payment of Michaelmas term last past and for all other terms in time to come; and that by the same authority that this act and ordinance shall not extend or be prejudicial to the mayor and bailiffs of the city of Dublin for the time being or to any of their successors in time to come, or to any other person or persons who have anything to their use, or to Christopher Faunte, chaplain.

c.21 [Confirmation of grants made by the prior of the Hospital to Sir Robert and Thomas Dowdall]

Also, at the petition of Thomas Douedall of Dublin, *gentilman*, that whereas James Ketyng, prior of the house of the Hospital of St John of Jerusalem in Ireland and the brothers of the same, by their deed indented and sealed under their common seal bearing date the seventh day of February in the first year of the reign of king Richard the third [1484] by their complete and full assent and consent have given and granted, set and let to farm to the said Thomas all manner of tithes of sheaves of corn and hay in any manner belonging to the church of Clontarf, to have and to hold all the said tithes to the said Thomas, his heirs and assigns for the term of thirty six years then next following the date above mentioned, as more fully appears by the said deed; upon which, considering the premises, it is ordained, enacted and established by authority of this parliament that the said grant made to the said Thomas by the said prior and brothers and all and everything contained in the same and every other grant and lease to the said Thomas by the said prior and brothers except such grants as were made jointly to Robert Douedall, knight and the said Thomas, be authorised, approved, confirmed and adjudged good and effectual in law according to the tenor, purport and effect of the same in all points; and by the same authority that it be decreed, adjudged, determined and ordained that the said Thomas, his heirs and assigns have, receive and enjoy all the said tithes

receivent et enjoient touts lez ditz dismez annuelment duraunt le dit terme accordaunt al dit graunte et lesse a luy faitz; et que par la dit auctorite est ordeine ajuge et decree que si ascun acte en parliament ou graund counseill soit fait en temps avenaunt en prejudice revokaunt ou adnullaunt del dit graunte lesse ou grauntez en defeasaunce ou avoidance le dit Thomas ou sez assignez de lez premissez ou ascun matier title ou cause soit allegge envers le dit Thomas ou sez assignez en defetaunt lez graunte lesse ou grauntes faitz a luy sur lez premisses par lez ditz priour et confreres ou lour successours que ascun tiell acte ou statute matier ou cause issint de estre fait ou allegge envers le dit Thomas ou sez assignez et en prejudice du dit Thomas ou sez assignez sur lez premisses soient voides et de nule effecte ne force en ley saunz que le dit Thomas ou sez assignez voudrount assenter al mesme; purvieu toutz foitz que le dit Thomas et sez assignes facent duhe paiement annuelment pur lez ditz dismes accordaunt al dit fait en toutz pointz.

c.22

Item al supplicacion de Petir Lynche de Galway marchaunt que come diverses variaunces et debates furent ewez et movez parentre le dit Petir et William Deyne del mesme marchaunt de une mese et une siller ove lez appurtenauntz en la dit vile lez queux mese et siller ove lez appurtenauntz le dit William mit en plegge ove le dit Petir pur une laste et demi des quires et xiiij marcez vj s. viij d. de argente sur queux variaunces et debates les parties avauntditz misterount eaux en agarde et arbitrement de une Martyne Lynche soveraine del dit vile et une Johan Blake del mesme ove aultres diverses persons lez queux arbitours sur duhe examinacion ewe en lez premisses par le agrement dez parties avauntditz ount ajugez decreez et agardez que le dit Petir paiereit al dit William iij hoggesheddes del vine de Spaigne et xx li. de argente a une Margarete Lynche pur son mariage sur et suis la summe suisdit et que le dit Petir averoit lez ditz mese et siller ove lez appurtenauntz a luy et a sez heires et assignes pur toutz jours sur quele agarde et jugement lez ditz arbitours misterount le dit Petir en possession dez ditz mese et siller ove lez appurtenauntz et auxi le dit Petir ad paie al dit Margarete lez ditz xx li. et issint le dit Petir ad este preste a toutz foitz de paier al dit William les ditz iij hoggeshedes de vine de Spaigne accordaunt al dit garde et jugement auxi lez ditz arbitours ount agardez que le dit William relessereit al dit Petir toute le droite et title queux il claima ou pretenda de aver al ditz mese et siller ove lappurtenauntz et ceo issint affaire refusa et unqore refuse al final anientesment du dit Petir saunz ceo qil soit gracieuxment remedie en cele partie; sur que lez premisses considerez ordeine est enacte et establie par auctorite dicest parliament que le dit Petir Lynche poient enterer aver occupier et enjoier lez ditz mese et siller ove lappurtenaunz a luy

yearly during the said term according to the said grant and lease made to him; and that by the said authority it is ordained, adjudged and decreed that if any act be made in parliament or great council in time to come in prejudice, revoking or annulling the said grant lease or grants in defeasance or avoidance of the said Thomas or his assigns of the premises, or any matter, title or cause be alleged against the said Thomas or his assigns to defeat the grant, lease or grants made to him concerning the premises by the said prior and brothers or their successors, that any such act or statute, matter or cause so to be made or alleged against the said Thomas or his assigns and in prejudice of the said Thomas or his assigns concerning the premises, be void and of no effect or force in law unless the said Thomas or his assigns assent to the same; provided always that the said Thomas and his assigns make due payment yearly for the said tithes according to the said deed in all points.

c.22 [Licence for Peter Lynch of Galway to enter a messuage and cellar there in accordance with an award made by the sovereign of Galway and John Blake in a dispute between Lynch and William Deyne]

Also, at the petition of Peter Lynche of Galway, merchant, that whereas various disputes and debates took place between the said Peter and William Deyne of the same, merchant, concerning a messuage and a cellar with the appurtenances in the said town, which messuage and cellar with the appurtenances the said William put in pledge with the said Peter for a last and a half of hides and fourteen marks, six shillings and eight pence of money, upon which disputes and debates the aforesaid parties put themselves to the award and arbitration of one Martin Lynche, sovereign of the said town, and one John Blake of the same, with various other persons, which arbitrators, after due examination was made in the premises, by the agreement of the parties aforesaid have adjudged, decreed and awarded that the said Peter should pay three hogsheads of Spanish wine to the said William and twenty pounds of money to one Margaret Lynche for her marriage, over and above the sum aforesaid, and that the said Peter should have the said messuage and cellar with the appurtenances to him and to his heirs and assigns for ever; upon which award and judgment the said arbitrators put the said Peter in possession of the said messuage and cellar with the appurtenances, and the said Peter has paid the said twenty pounds to the said Margaret and the said Peter has been ready at all times to pay the said three hogsheads of Spanish wine to the said William according to the said award and judgment; likewise the said arbitrators have awarded that the said William should release to the said Peter all the right and title which he claimed or pretended to have to the said messuage and cellar with the appurtenances and he

et a sez heires et sez assignez pur toutz jours et de receiver lez issues et profites de lez mesmes accordaunt al agarde et jugement avauntditz et si le dit Petir sez heires ou sez assignes soient grevez vexez ou distourbez de lour entre en lez ditz mese et siller ove lappurtenauntz que adonqes il ou ils ou ascun de eaux qissint offender ou distourbe si sovent foitz qils ou ascun de eaux issint face de forfaiter xl li. al dit Petir sez heires ou a sez assignez; et qil ou ils ou ascun de eaux poet avere un accion de dette devaunt le soveraine du dit vile de Galway pur lez ditz xl li. et par mesme lauctorite le dit soveraine eit pleine powere et auctorite a oier et determinere la dit accion et de agarder toute processe solonqe son discrecion et de rendire jugement et de agarder execucion sur le mesme.

c.23

Item al requisicion les communes que come James Collynge clerke ad contrarie le graund[21] seall de nostre soveraine seignur le roy de sa terre Dirland et par le mesme ad done lez lettres patentes le roy du pardon desouth le dit contreue seall a une Geffrey Artour par le non del mesme Geffrey Artur' thresourer del cathedrale esglis de Lymerik et a touts maneres delegates subdelegates maintenours counseillours autours notteries et a toutz sez adherentes de touts maneres provisions et execucions del mesme sicome par les dits lettres patentes pluis largement appiert; sur que lez premisses considerez ordeine est enacte et establie par auctorite dicest parliament que les ditz lettres patentes et chescun chose en eaux contenuez soient ajugez voidez et de nule effecte en ley; et par mesme le auctorite le dit James veient et appierge en sa propre person devaunt le chief justice del commune place le roy en Irland deins le chastell de Divelin le lundie proschien apres le fest del nativite de Seint Johan le Baptist proschien avenaunt[22] illeosqes a demurer en le garde del mareschall del mesme saunz baille ou mainprice jesqes al temps que les premisses soient duhement examinez et ajugez solonque ley et conscience et si le dit James ne vient et appierge en le garde du dit mareschall accordaunt al fourme avauntdit que adonqes le dit James soit forjuge hors de touts courtes que le roy ad en Irlande.

21 Berry's note: *graund* interlined in roll. 22 28 June 1484.

refused to do so and still refuses, to the final ruin of the said Peter unless he be graciously redressed in that behalf; upon which, considering the premises, it is ordained, enacted and established by authority of this parliament that the said Peter Lynche may enter, have, occupy and enjoy the said messuage and cellar with the appurtenances to him and to his heirs and his assigns for ever and receive the issues and profits of the same according to the award and judgment aforesaid; and if the said Peter, his heirs or his assigns be grieved, vexed or disturbed of their entry into the said messuage and cellar with the appurtenances, that then he or they or anyone who so offends or disturbs them, as often as they or any of them do so, shall forfeit forty pounds to the said Peter, his heirs or his assigns; and that he or they or any of them may have an action of debt before the sovereign of the said town of Galway for the said forty pounds; and by the same authority, the said sovereign shall have full power and authority to hear and determine the said action and to award all process according to his discretion and to give judgment and to award execution upon the same.

c.23 [James Collynge to appear to answer charges of forging the great seal of Ireland and issuing letters patent of pardon to Geoffrey Artour, treasurer of Limerick cathedral][11]

Also, at the request of the commons, that whereas James Collynge, clerk, has counterfeited the great seal of our sovereign lord the king of his land of Ireland and by the same has given the king's letters patent of pardon under the said counterfeit seal to one Geoffrey Artour by the name of the same Geoffrey Artur, treasurer of the cathedral church of Limerick, and to all manners of delegates, sub-delegates, maintainers, counsellors, agents, notaries and to all his adherents of all manners of provisions and executions of the same as by the said letters patent more largely appears; upon which, considering the premises, it is ordained, enacted and established by authority of this parliament that the said letters patent and everything contained in them be adjudged void and of no effect in law; and by the same authority that the said James come and appear in person before the chief justice of the king's common bench in Ireland in the castle of Dublin on the Monday after the feast of the Nativity of St John the Baptist next coming [28 June 1484] to remain there in the custody of the marshal of the same without bail or mainprise until the premises be duly examined and adjudged according to law and conscience; and if the said James do not come and appear in the custody of the said marshal according to the form aforesaid that then the said James shall be forejudged out of all the courts which the king has in Ireland.

11 Irish Record Commission translation of the first part of this chapter (as far as 'Limerick') printed by Aquilla Smith in *Numismatic Chronicle* (1881), p. 320.

c.24

Item al supplicacion de James Rice meire del cite de Watirford Patrik Mulgane et Philipp Bryane baillives del mesme que come lez ditz meire et baillives longe temps devaunt qils furent en office esliez firent promisse de allere en pilgrimage a Seint James du Galice en Spaigne; sur que lez premisses considerez ordeine est et establie par auctorite dicest parliament que lez ditz James Patrik et Philipp et chescun de eaux poient aller le dit pilgrimage de Seint James de Galice en Spaigne saunz ascun empechement dommache ou lesion del roy nostre soveraine seignur ou de son lieutenaunt ou depute justice ou justices ou de ascune aultres officeres ou ministres du roy nostre dit soveraine seignur esteauntz deins sa terre Dirland; purvieu que lez ditz James Patrik et Philipp et chescun de eaux firent tiell person et persons lour deputees de occupier lour ditz offices en lour absence queux serrount admittez par le advis del counseill et jurrees del mesme la cite.

c.25

Item al supplicacion de Morice Bron' citezeine del citte de Watirford que come le dit Morice est seisie en son demesne come de fee de diversez terres et tenementez deins le counte de Watirford cestassavere Rathmolane Cnokkanpadyne et Ballyloghbeg ove toutz lour appurtenaunz del done et feoffament dune Nicholas Bron' pier le dit Morice et auxi de Corballymore Ballymaquyll et Corballybege ove toutz lour appurtenauntz del done et feoffament de une William le fitz de Millone Bron' sicome pluis pleinement appiert par une inspeximus fait sur mesme le feoffament et sealle desouth le office du mairalte del dit cite et monstre en cest dit parliament dez queux terres et tenementez ove toutz lour appurtenauntz mesme le [dit][23] Morice ad este et est peisiblement seisie toutz foitz apres lez ditz feoffaments faitz a luy; et pur ceo que le dit counte de Watirford nest pas tout subduhe desouth les leyes du roy ne que les gentz del mesme le counte ne sount pas oubedientz au roy ne a sez leyes le dit Morice pur paour qil eit que ascune persons del mesme le counte voillent enterer sur luy encountre ley[24] en les ditz terrez et tenementes ou en parcell de eaux; sur que les premisses considerez ordeine est et establie par auctorite dicest parliament que le dit Morice et sez heires poient aver occupier et enjoier lez ditz terres et tenementez ove lour appurtenauntz et chescun de mesmes accordaunt as ditz feoffamentes et son possession sur les mesmes; et qil ne bien luist a nule persone ne persons de enterer sur luy ne sez heires en lez ditz terres et tenementez ne en nule parcell de eaux qil ou ils qissint fount paient al dit Morice ou sez heires sur quele ils enterount x li. si sovent foitz come ils ou

23 *dit* omitted in transcript. 24 Berry's note: *luy* in roll.

c.24 [Licence to the mayor and bailiffs of Waterford to go on pilgrimage to Santiago de Compostela]

Also, at the prayer of James Rice, mayor of the city of Waterford, and Patrick Mulgane and Philip Bryane, bailiffs of the same, that whereas the said mayor and bailiffs, long before they were elected to office, made a promise to go on pilgrimage to St James of Galicia in Spain; upon which, considering the premises, it is ordained and established by authority of this parliament that the said James, Patrick and Philip and each of them may go on the said pilgrimage of St James of Galicia in Spain without any hindrance, damage or hurt by the king our sovereign lord or by any other officers or ministers of our said sovereign lord the king being in his land of Ireland; provided that the said James, Patrick and Philip and each of them appoint such person and persons as their deputies to occupy their said offices in their absence as shall be admitted by the advice of the council and jurats of the same city.

c.25 [Confirmation to Maurice Broun, citizen of Waterford, of lands in co. Waterford]

Also, at the petition of Maurice Broun, citizen of the city of Waterford, that whereas the said Maurice is seised in his demesne as of fee of various lands and tenements in the county of Waterford, that is to say, Rathmoylan, Knockanpaddin and Ballyloughbeg with all their appurtenances, of the gift and feoffment of one Nicholas Broun, father of the said Maurice, and also of Corballymore, Ballynakill and Corballybeg with all their appurtenances, of the gift and feoffment of one William, the son of Milo Broun, as more fully appears by an *inspeximus* made of the same feoffment and sealed under the office of the mayoralty of the said city and shown in this said parliament, of which lands and tenements with all their appurtenances the same Maurice has been and is peaceably seised at all times after the said feoffments were made to him; and because the said county of Waterford is not fully subdued to the king's laws nor are the people of the same county obedient to the king or to his laws, the said Maurice is afraid that certain persons of the same county will enter upon him contrary to law in the said lands and tenements or in part of them; it is ordained and established by authority of this parliament that the said Maurice and his heirs may have, occupy and enjoy the said lands and tenements with their appurtenances and all of the same according to the said feoffments and his possession of the same and that it shall not be lawful for any person or persons to enter upon him or his heirs in the said lands and tenements or in any part of them; that he or they who do so shall pay to the said Maurice or his heirs upon whom they enter ten pounds as often as they or any of them do so; and that it shall be lawful for the said Maurice or his heirs upon

ascun de eaux issint fount et que bien luist al dit Morice ou sez heires sur quele ils enterount de aver accion de dette pur mesmez lez x li. issint forfaitez sibien deins fraunchesies come dehors et especialment devaunt lez maier et bailliefs del citte de Watirford; et que lez ditz maier et bailliefs par mesme lauctorite eient pleine power et jurisdiccion de estre juges en mesme la accion de dette et de ajuger et determinere et de agarder execucion en le mesme accion solonque lour discrecion; purvieu que chescun homme poet aver son accion envers le dit Morice et sez heires pur mesmez lez terres et tenementez et pur chescun parcell de eaux accordaunt al course de commune ley.

c.26

Item al supplicacion del soveraine [portrieffes][25] burgeises et communes del vile de Rosse que come lez ditz soveraine portrieffes burgeisez et communes sount lez foilx et humble subgittes le roy nostre soveraine seignur demurauntez et gardauntez la dit vile nient soulment a lour importablez charges et costes mes auxi de jour en aultre al extreme jeopartie de lour corpses et vies unqore si bien lez englois rebelles come irrois enemyes espoillount rubbent et depredount plusours foitz lez ditz soveraine portrieffes burgeises et communes de lour chivalx et vaches et aultres catelles labourauntez et pasturauntez hors dez mures del dit vile saunz restitucion aderer de mesmes lez biens ou satisfaccion pur eaux par lez queux lez ditz soveraine portrieffes burgeises et communes sount issint empoverisshez qils saunz gracieux aide et supportacion [. . .][26]; sur que lez premisses considerez ordeine est graunte establie et enacte par auctorite dicest parliament que bien luist al dit soveraine portrieffes burgeises et communes du dit vile pur le temps esteauntz ove toute le aide et succour qils sacheount ou sacherount faire de ensecuter chivacher aller et enterer a chescun tiell temps qils penserount pluis congrue et pur eaux expedient sibien sur tielx rebelx et ennemiez queux preigneunt rubbount et depredount lour ditz biens come lours aidours maintenours supportouts abettatours adherentez auctours fautours counseillours et receivours et sur la pais en quele ils sount succourez et favourez ou veignount ou allount entre eaux de faire ascuns tielx lesions et de prendre de eaux si moultez biens queux extendount al value dez biens prisez de lez ditz soveraine portrieffes burgeises et communes et lour successours pur le temps esteaunt est ceo saunz ascun empechement ou empediment molestaunce ou grevaunce de nostre soveraine seignur le roy sez heires officeres ou ministres et ascune aultres persons queuxconqez en temps avenire; et par la dit auctorite que queconque englois homme enterrupta ensurrexa

25 Berry's note: *burgeises* repeated in roll, presumably in error for *portrieffes*. 26 Berry's note: erasure in roll.

whom they enter to have an action of debt for the same ten pounds so forfeited both within and outside franchises and especially before the mayor and bailiffs of the city of Waterford; and that the said mayor and bailiffs by the same authority shall have full power and jurisdiction to be judges in the same action of debt and to adjudge and determine and to award execution in the same action according to their discretion; provided that every man may have his action against the said Maurice and his heirs for the same lands and tenements and for every part of them according to the course of the common law.

c.26 [Licence to the inhabitants of New Ross to pursue English rebels and Irish enemies and to seize goods to the value of their losses; alienated tenements to be forfeited to the use of the town; no person of Irish habit or condition to live there except by licence; no inhabitant of the town to be indicted for the murder of persons contravening the act, or to be compelled to pay a *saute*]

Also, at the petition of the sovereign, portreeves, burgesses and commons of the town of New Ross, that whereas the said sovereign, portreeves, burgesses and commons are the faithful and humble subjects of our sovereign lord the king dwelling in and guarding the said town, not only at their insupportable charges and costs but also from day to day at the extreme peril of their bodies and lives, yet both English rebels and Irish enemies often despoil, rob and plunder the said sovereign, portreeves, burgesses and commons of their horses and cattle and other chattels working and pasturing outside the walls of the said town without making restitution of the same goods or satisfaction for them, whereby the said sovereign, portreeves, burgesses and commons are so impoverished that without gracious aid and support they [...]; upon which, considering the premises, it is ordained, granted, established and enacted by authority of this parliament that it shall be lawful for the said sovereign, portreeves, burgesses and commons of the said town for the time being with all the aid and succour which they can or will be able to give, to follow, ride, go and enter at every such time as they shall think most fitting and expedient for them, both against such rebels and enemies as take rob and plunder their said goods and against their aiders, maintainers, supporters, abettors, adherents, agents, factors, counsellors and receivers and against the country in which they are succoured and favoured or come or go amongst them to commit any such injuries, and to take from them as much goods as reach the value of the goods taken from the said sovereign, portreeves, burgesses and commons and their successors for the time being, and this without any hindrance or impediment, molestation or grievance by our sovereign lord the king, his heirs, officers or

attempta ou dona empediment a lez ditz soveraine portrieffes burgeises et communes ou lour successours en execucion dez premissez ou de ascun de eaux que si sovent come il issint fait il courge en la peine de xx li. as ditz soveraine portrieffes bourgeoises et communes et lour successours; et par mesme lauctorite il bien luist as ditz soveraine portriefs burgeises et communes de prender lour accion ou accions en quelconque courte eaux moulx plerra pur lez ditz x li. et de recover double dasmagez; et que chescun officere devaunt quele ascun dez ditz accions serrount commensez eit pleine power et auctorite a determinere la dit accion ou accions et de agarder dasmagez et execucion et que nule proteccion tuicion lettrez patentes prive seall signet excommengement nen nule aultre dilatorie matier quelconque soient allowez admittez ne acceptez en ascun des ditz accions ne mesme la accion ou accions par iceaux soient delaiez; et pur ceo que certeinez persons eiantz franqez tenementes deinz la dit vile vendount lour ditz franqez tenementes as aultres forreins persons de irrois nacion ou irrois condicion par quele lez ditz franqes tenementes sount ruinez et gastez en graunde lesion et derogacion du dit vile; sur que ordeine est enacte et establie par auctorite dicest dit parliament que quelconque person eiaunt ascun franqe tenemente ou burgage deins la dit vile ou fraunchesie del mesme ceo venda ou le vend a ferme ou le mitta en murgage a ascun foreine person saunz ascun licence et assente del soveraine et portrieffes du dit vile pur le temps esteauntz et de lour counseill et cele licence de rester de recorde en le registre du dit vile que adonqes le dit franque tenement issint vende lesse ou mise a murgage soit forfaite as ditz soveraine portrieffes burgeises et communes et a lour successours et bien luist a eaux de enterer en le mesme et le aver teignire et reteignire al use et profite du dit vile franqement quitement et peisiblement saunz ascun suitte empechement ou vexacion et que la person quele voet faire vendicion lesser ou mittier en murgage contrarie a cest acte le dit franque tenemente ou burgage soit forfaite as ditz soveraine portrieffes burgeises et communes et lour successours xx li. et bien luist a eaux de prendre lour accion del temps en temps pur lez ditz xx li. come desuis; et outre ceo par la dit auctorite que nule manere homme de irrois habite ou irrois condicion ne soit my receive ne admitte a demurrer ou de faire residence deins la dit vile desore enavaunt saunz qil soit par licence du dit soveraine et portrieffes pur le temps esteauntz et que son non et le jour de son admission soit escrie remainaunt de recorde en le registre du dit vile; et quelconque homme de irrois habite ou condicion demura ou face residence deins la dit vile aultrement come ils est avauntdit qil forfaita xx li. as ditz soveraine portrieffes burgeises et communes et a lour successours ou si moulte bone de luy que poet estre trosve deins la dit vile et unqore nient meins de destre expelle hors du dit vile pur toutz jours; et sil avient ascun dez ditz rebelx ennemyes de estre tue fesaunt contrarie al tenour dicest presente acte ou a ascun parte ent que nule de lez ditz soveraine

ministers and any other persons whomsoever in time to come; and by the said authority, that whatever Englishman shall interrupt, resist, attack or cause impediment to the said sovereign, portreeves, burgesses and commons or their successors in the execution of the premises or of any of them that as often as he does so he shall incur the penalty of twenty pounds to the said sovereign, portreeves, burgesses and commons and their successors; and by the same authority it shall be lawful for the said sovereign, portreeves, burgesses and commons to bring their action or actions for the said ten pounds in whatever court shall best please them and to recover double damages, and that every officer before whom any of the said actions shall be commenced shall have full power and authority to determine the said action or actions and to award damages and execution, and that no protection, safeguard, letters patent, privy seal, signet, excommunication or any other dilatory matter whatsoever shall be allowed, admitted or accepted in any of the said actions, nor shall the same action or actions be thereby delayed; and because certain persons having freeholds in the said town sell their said freeholds to other outside persons of the Irish nation or Irish condition, whereby the said freeholds are ruined and wasted to the great injury and loss of the said town; upon which it is ordained, enacted and established by authority of this said parliament that whatsoever person having any freehold or burgage in the said town or franchise of the same shall sell this or set it to farm or shall put it in mortgage to any outside person without any licence and assent of the sovereign and portreeves of the said town for the time being and of their council, and that licence to remain of record in the register of the said town, that then the said freehold so sold, leased or put in mortgage shall be forfeited to the said sovereign, portreeves, burgesses and commons and to their successors and it shall be lawful for them to enter into the same and to have, hold and retain it to the use and profit of the said town freely, quit and peaceably without any suit, hindrance or vexation and that the person who sells, leases or puts the said freehold or burgage in mortgage contrary to this act shall forfeit twenty pounds to the said sovereign, portreeves, burgesses and commons and their successors and it shall be lawful for them to bring their action from time to time for the said twenty pounds as above; and moreover, by the said authority, that no manner of man of Irish habit or Irish condition be received or admitted to dwell or make his residence in the said town henceforth unless it be by licence of the said sovereign and portreeves for the time being and that his name and the day of his admission be written down and remain of record in the register of the said town; and whatsoever man of Irish habit or condition shall dwell or make his residence in the said town otherwise than is aforesaid shall forfeit twenty pounds to the said sovereign, portreeves, burgesses and commons and to their successors or so much of his goods as can be found in the said town, and yet nevertheless he shall be

portrieffes burgeises et communes ne de lour successours ne de lour aidours ne supportours soit endite moleste greve ne empeche pur icele ne compelle de paier ascun eschape ou saute pur le mesme mesque ent a toutz foitz clerez quitez et outrement dischargez; et que cest acte ne extende my ne soit prejudiciale a nule person ne persons del esglis ne a lour tenauntes ne servauntez ne a nule aultre mesque a eaux queux fount le lesion et a eaux queux maintenout eaux et supportount eaux voluntariment et ceo de estre prove loialment devaunt une competent juge.

c.27

Item al supplicacion des communes que come Katerine Aleyn famme a Thomas Cusake de Monkynton' en le counte de Mith' et Margarete Moyr sa famme a Nicholas Plunket de Clone gentilman furent en la peix de Dieu et le roy le vendredie proschien apres le feste del Annunciacion de Nostre Dame lane du reigne nostre seignur le roy qorest le primere[27] veignauntez del esglis del dit Monkynton' del masse illeosqes viegnoit une James Bath' tarde de Slane gentilman aultrement appelle James Bath' fitz a Sir Thomas Bath' chivaler tarde seignur et baron de Loueth ove diverses dez Halpennyes et aultres dez irrois ennemyez et englois rebelx et illeosqes maliciousment disposez lez ditz Katerine et Margarete pristerount et eaux vinxerount bastisterount et naufrount et eaux de lour vestures bursez et argent robba et espoila en le pluis lamentable manere et par vicious exemple de toutz aultres saunz due remedie soit ewe en cele parte; sur que les premissez considerez ordeine est enacte et establie par auctorite dicest parliament que le dit James vient et appierge en sa propre person deins le chastell du roy de Divelin et rende eins son corps en le garde de constable del mesme ou son depute ou deputees le lundie proschien apres le fest de Seint Ambrose le evesque proschien avenaunt[28] et illeosqez a demurer en le chastell et garde del constable avauntdit saunz baille ou mainprice tanque al temps qil soit delivere par le treshonourable seignur Gerount count de Kildare depute lieutenaunt Dirland et le conseill du roy del mesme la terre; et si le dit James ne appierge my al dit jour et a demurer en garde come il est desuisdit et jesqes il soit delivere come[29] il est avauntdit que adonqes par la dit auctorite il soit ajuge felon atteinte et forfaita touts lez biens et terres queux il ad ou ascun aultre person ou persons a son use et quelconque person apres le dit lundie luy receiva maintena ou supporta eaux luy conisauntz de estre atteinte que ils et chescun de eaux forfaitent lour biens et terres en sem-

27 26 March 1484. 28 5 April 1484 or 11 April 1485. 29 Berry's note: *come* repeated in roll.

expelled from the said town for ever; and if it happens that any of the said rebels or enemies are slain when acting contrary to the tenor of this present act or any part thereof, that none of the said sovereign, portreeves, burgesses and commons nor of their successors nor of their aiders or supporters shall be indicted, molested, grieved or impeached for the same, nor compelled to pay any escape money or *saute* for the same but shall be always clear, quit and fully discharged thereof; and that this act shall not extend or be prejudicial to any person or persons of the church or to their tenants or servants, or to any other save those who cause injury and to those who maintain and support them voluntarily and where this is lawfully proved before a competent judge.

c.27 [James Bath to surrender in Dublin castle to answer for various offences committed by him in Co. Meath]

Also, at the prayer of the commons, that whereas Katherine Aleyn, wife to Thomas Cusake of Monktown in the county of Meath, and Margaret Moyr, wife to Nicholas Plunket of Clonee, *gentilman*, were in the peace of God and the king on the Friday next after the feast of the Annunciation of Our Lady in the first year of the reign of our lord the king that now is [28 March 1484], coming from the church of the said Monktown from Mass there, one James Bath late of Slane, *gentilman*, otherwise called James Bath son to Sir Thomas Bath, knight, late lord and baron of Louth came with various men of the Halpennyes and others of the Irish enemies and English rebels and there, being maliciously disposed, took the said Katherine and Margaret and bound them, beat them and wounded them and robbed and despoiled them of their garments, purses and money in the most piteous manner and as a vicious example to all others unless due redress be had in that behalf; upon which, considering the premises, it is ordained, enacted and established by authority of this parliament that the said James come and appear in person in the king's castle of Dublin and surrender his body into the custody of the constable of the same or his deputy or deputies on the Monday after the feast of St Ambrose the bishop next coming [5 April 1484 or 11 April 1485][12] and remain in the castle and custody of the constable aforesaid without bail or mainprise until he is delivered by the very honourable lord, Gerald, earl of Kildare, deputy lieutenant of Ireland and the king's council of the same land; and if the said James does not appear on the said day and remain in custody as is above said until he is delivered as is aforesaid, that then by the said authority he shall be adjudged an attainted felon and shall forfeit all the goods and lands which he has or any

12 The date depends on whether the act was passed in the first or second session of this parliament. For a discussion of the evidence, see above p. xxxi.

blable manere et des estre felons atteintes et que nule pardon soit available al dit James sinon qil soit graunte par auctorite du parliament ou graunde counseille et par lassent de lez ditz Thomas Cusake Katerine et Margarete parissint que cest acte comprehende verite.

other person or persons have to his use; and whatsoever person, after the said Monday, shall receive, maintain or support him knowing him to be attainted, that they and every of them shall forfeit their goods and lands in like manner and be attainted felons and that no pardon be effective to the said James unless it be granted by authority of parliament or great council and with the assent of the said Thomas Cusake, Katherine and Margaret, provided that this act contains the truth.

2–3 Richard III

[1]Statuta ordinaciones et actus in quodam parliamento domini regis apud Dubliniam die veneris proximo post festum Sancti Patricii episcopi anno regni regis Ricardi tercii secundo[2] coram Geraldo comite Kildarie tunc deputato Johannis adtunc comitis Lyncolnie et locumtenentis ipsius nuper regis terre sue Hibernie tento edita in hunc modum:

c.1
En primes ordeine est que Seint Esglis soit franqe et eit et enjoie toutz sez franchesies et libertees saunz ascun emblemeschement sicome il ad este use devaunt cestz hoeurs.

c.2
Item ordeine est et assentue que la terre Dirland eit et enjoie toutz sez libertees et privileges sicome il ad este use devaunt cestz hoeurs.

c.3
Item ordeine est et establie que lez cittees de Divelin et Watirford et la vile de Drogheda et toutz lez aultres cittees et bons viles dedeins la dit terre Dirland eient et enjoient toutz lour franchesies et libertees privilegez bones usuages et custumes sicome ils ount owez et usez devaunt cest hoeurs.

c.4
Item al requisicion des communes que come le tresnoble seignur Gerot count de Kildare depute lieutenaunt Dirland est de jour en aultre en sa propre person attendaunt lez guerres le roy en lez marches dicest terre subduaunt sez irrois ennemiez pur le encresse del bone publique dez subgittes le roy en la mesme par le quele il ne poet my estre duhement present en parliament pur la continuaunce prorogacion ou adjournement del mesme; sur que lez premisses considerez ordeine est enacte et establie par auctorite dicest parliament que si sovent foitz il fortuner le dit depute lieutenaunt de estre absent duraunt cest dit parliament devaunt luy tenuz et de estre tenuz que bien luist al dit count si sovent come il requirer solonque son pleasure a directer son escriptour desouth

1 Differences between the Irish Record Commission (IRC) transcript and Berry's version are noted where they occur. See above pp xxvii–xxviii for details of the manuscripts used. 2 18 March 1485.

Statutes, ordinances and acts in a parliament of the lord the king held at Dublin on the Friday next after the feast of St Patrick the bishop in the second year of the reign of king Richard the third [18 March 1485] before Gerald, earl of Kildare, then deputy of John, then earl of Lincoln and lieutenant of the same late king of his land of Ireland, published in this form:

c.1 [Confirmation of the liberties of the church]

First, it is ordained that Holy Church be free and have and enjoy all her franchises and liberties without any infringement as has been customary before now.

c.2 [Confirmation of the liberties and privileges of the land of Ireland]

Also, it is ordained and assented that the land of Ireland have and enjoy all its liberties and privileges as has been customary before now.

c.3 [Confirmation of the liberties and franchises of cities and towns]

Also, it is ordained and established that the cities of Dublin and Waterford and the town of Drogheda and all the other cities and good towns within the said land of Ireland have and enjoy all their franchises and liberties, privileges, good usages and customs as they have had and used before now.

c.4 [Licence for the deputy lieutenant to continue, prorogue or adjourn parliament during his absence by deputy appointed under his privy seal]

Also, at the request of the commons, that whereas the very noble lord, Gerald, earl of Kildare, deputy lieutenant of Ireland is daily in his own person attending the king's wars in the marches of this land, subduing his Irish enemies for the increase of the public good of the king's subjects in the same, whereby he cannot be duly present in parliament for the continuance, prorogation or adjournment of the same; whereupon, considering the premises, it is ordained enacted and established by authority of this parliament that as often as it shall happen that the said deputy lieutenant is absent during this said parliament held and to be held before him, that it shall be lawful for the said earl, as often as it is necessary, according to his pleasure, to direct his writing under his privy seal to the chancellor or treasurer or to any other of the king's councillors in the same, commanding any such of them to whom any such privy seal shall be

son private seall al chaunceller ou thresourer ou a ascun aultre dez counseillours le roy en la mesme commaundaunt ascun tiell de eaux a quele ascun tiell privat seall sera directe de continuer proroger ou adjourner cest dit parliament tenuz et de estre tenuz solonque la pleasire del dit count et par mesme lauctorite il de eaux a que ascun tiell privat seall sera directe eit et soit adjuge en pleine power de continuer proroger ou adjourner cest dit parliament tenuz et de estre tenuz accordaunt al tenour del dit privat seall issint a luy directe et que toute et chescun tiell continuance prorogacion et adjournement soit ajuge si bone et si effectuall en ley sicome il fuit continue proroge ou adjourne par le dit count en sa propre person parissint que la dit continuance prorogacion et adjournement et chescun de eaux soient faitz a une competent et suffisaunt lieu deinz ascun de cestz iiij countees cest assavere lez countees de Divelin Mith Loueth et Kildare.

c.5

Item al supplicacion de Johan abbe del meason de Seint Thomas le martir juxt Divelin le oratour nostre soveraine seignur le roy de jour en aultre que come le dit abbe entende par la grace de Dieu de aller en pilgrimage en le noble roialme Dengleterre et illeosqez de visiter le dit benoit martir Seint Thomas a Cauntreburie et issint ove toute celerite enapres ove la pleasir de Dieu de resorter en la dit terre; en consideracion ent enacte est ordeine et establie par auctorite dicest parliament que le dit abbe eit licence del jour de son passage hors dicest dit terre qil poet luy absentier hors del dit terre duraunt le terme del moite de une ane adonqez proschein ensuaunt et qil en le meane temps toutz maneres dismes oblacions obvencions emoluments annuitees rentes issuez profites et toutz aultres casualtees de sez possessions sibien espiritualtees come temporaltees en ascun manere provenauntez ou cressauntez et al dit abbe parteignauntez par luy mesme sez proctours attourneez et servauntes poet receiver perceivere et eaux a disposer al pleasire et volunte du dit abbe franqement et saunz ascun empechement ou empediment molestaunce ou grevaunce de nostre soveraine seignur le roy sez heires ou successours officeres ou ministres queuxconqes en temps avenire ascuns estatutes actes ordenaunces provisions ou restriccions faitz encountre absentiers eiauntez terres tenementes ou ascunz aultres possessions deins la dit terre et sur iceaux nient residentez ne gentz defensibles en lour lieux nient trosvauntez nient obstauntez.

directed to continue, prorogue or adjourn this said parliament held and to be held, according to the pleasure of the said earl; and by the same authority the person to whom any such privy seal shall be directed shall have and be adjudged to have full power to continue, prorogue or adjourn this said parliament held and to be held according to the tenor of the said privy seal so directed to him; and that all and every such continuance, prorogation and adjournment shall be adjudged as good and as effectual in law as if it was continued, prorogued or adjourned by the said earl in his own person; provided that the said continuance, prorogation and adjournment and every one of them be made to a fit and suitable place in any of these four counties, that is to say, the counties of Dublin, Meath, Louth and Kildare.

c.5 [Licence for the abbot of St Thomas the martyr near Dublin to go on pilgrimage to Canterbury notwithstanding the statute of absentees]

Also, at the petition of John, abbot of the house of St Thomas the martyr near Dublin, who prays daily for our sovereign lord the king, that whereas the said abbot intends by the grace of God to go on pilgrimage into the noble realm of England and there to visit the said blessed martyr St Thomas at Canterbury and afterwards, if it pleases God, to return with all speed to the said land; in consideration of which it is enacted, ordained and established by authority of this parliament that the said abbot shall have licence, from the day of his passage out of this said land, to absent himself out of the said land during the term of the half year then next ensuing, and that in the meantime he may receive and perceive, in person and by his proctors, attorneys and servants, all manner of tithes, oblations, obventions, emoluments, annuities, rents, issues, profits and all other casualties of his possessions, both spiritualities and temporalities, in any manner arising or accruing and pertaining to the said abbot, and dispose of them at the pleasure and will of the said abbot freely and without any hindrance or impediment, molestation or grievance by our sovereign lord the king, his heirs or successors, officers or ministers whomsoever in time to come, notwithstanding any statutes, acts, ordinances, provisions or restrictions made against absentees having lands, tenements or any other possessions in the said land and not residing on them nor finding people able to defend them in their places.

c.6

Item al requisicion des communes que come le counte de Loueth et diverses parties de Mith sount de jour en aultre gastez et destruez par diversez gentilx homes rioteusment disposez demurauntez deins mesmez lez counte et parties; sur que lez premissez considerez ordeine est et establie par auctorite dicest parliament que Larence Dowedall de Glaspistell, Nicholas Taaff de Ballybragan, Robert Taaf de Marchalrathe, Thomas Taaff de Tillaghkewe, James Taaff, George Taaff, Roger Gernon de Gernoneston, Henrie Gernon del mesme, Johan Gernon de Killincowle, Thomas Gernon del mesme, Johan Verdon de Clonmore, Thomas Verdon bastard del mesme, George Bellewe, George Taaff, Patrik Taaff fitz a Thomas Taaff de Tilloghkele, Hopkyn Dowedall de Kilpatrik, Water Dowedall fitz al avauntdit Laurence Dowedall, Thomas Dowedall de Glaspistell, Edward Dowedall, Laurence Haddesors de Keppoke, Johan Verdon fitz a Cristofre Verdon, Cristofre Drake de Gernoneston en le counte de Mith, Nicholas Drake, Richard Drake fitz al dit Cristofre, George Clynton de Drumcasshell et Johan Clynton son fitz, Piers Nugent de Clonaghery et William Sprynger qils et chescun de eaux rendent lour et son corps en le chastell le roy de Trym al xvme de Pasque proschien avenaunt[3] et illeosqes a demurer saunz baille ou mainprise a respoundre a toutz compleintes et defaultes queux serrount alleggez envers eaux ou ascun de eaux jesqez a tiell temps qils et chescun de eaux sount deliverez par le treshonourable seignur Gerot count de Kildare depute lieutenaunt Dirland et tielx del counseill le roy queux le dit depute appeller a luy; et sils et chescun de eaux ne rendent my lour corps en le dit chastell al dit xvme come il est desuis reherse que adonqez ils et chescun de eaux soient ajugez par mesme lauctorite felons atteintez et forfaitent toutz lour bons et chateux terres et tenementes queux ils ount ou ascun aultre a lour use; et que nule pardon sera a eaux ne a nule de eaux available sinon qil soit graunte par auctorite du parliament; purvieu que cest acte ne extende my ne soit prejudiciale a ascun de lez fammez de ascun de lez persons avauntditz en ou de lour jounctour ou dowery ou jounctour ou dowery de ascun de eaux en temps avenire.

Statuta ordinaciones et actus in parliamento predicto apud Trym die lune proximo post festum Corporis Christi tunc proxime sequens[4] coram prefato deputato similiter tento necnon per ipsum deputatum ad idem locum adjornato ibidem ad predictum diem lune tenendo edita in hec verba:

3 17 April 1485. 4 6 June 1485.

c.6 [Certain gentlemen of cos. Louth and Meath to surrender to Trim castle to answer charges to be determined by the deputy and council]

Also, at the request of the commons, that whereas the county of Louth and various parts of Meath are daily wasted and destroyed by various riotously disposed gentlemen living in the same county and parts; whereupon, considering the premises, it is ordained and established by authority of this parliament that Laurence Dowedall of Glaspistol, Nicholas Taaff of Braganstown, Robert Taaff of Marshallrath, Thomas Taaff of Tullakeel, James Taaff, George Taaff, Roger Gernon of Gernonstown, Henry Gernon of the same, John Gernon of Killincoole, Thomas Gernon of the same, John Verdon of Clonmore, Thomas Verdon bastard of the same, George Bellewe, George Taaff, Patrick Taaff son of Thomas Taaff of Tullakeel, Hopkyn Dowedall of Kilpatrick, Walter Dowedall, son of the aforesaid Laurence Dowedall, Thomas Dowedall of Glaspistol, Edward Dowedall, Laurence Haddesors of Cappoge, John Verdon son of Christopher Verdon, Christopher Drake of Gernonstown in the county of Meath, Nicholas Drake, Richard Drake son of the said Christopher, George Clynton of Drumcashel and John Clynton his son, Piers Nugent of Clonaghery[1] and William Sprynger, all and every one of them, surrender their bodies in the king's castle of Trim on the quindene of Easter next coming [17 April 1485] and remain there without bail or mainprise to answer to all complaints and defaults which shall be alleged against them or any of them, until such time as they and every one of them are delivered by the very honourable lord, Gerald, earl of Kildare, deputy lieutenant of Ireland, and such of the king's council as the said deputy will call to him; and if they and every of them do not surrender their bodies into the said castle at the said quindene as it is stated above, that then they and every one of them shall be adjudged by the same authority attainted felons and shall forfeit all their goods and chattels, lands and tenements which they have or any other person has to their use; and that no pardon shall be available to them or to any of them unless it be granted by authority of parliament; provided that this act shall not extend or be prejudicial to any of the wives of any of the persons aforesaid in or of their jointure or dower or the jointure or dower of any of them in time to come.

Statutes, ordinances and acts in the aforesaid parliament similarly held at Trim on Monday next after the feast of Corpus Christi then next following [6 June 1485] before the aforesaid deputy and adjourned by the same deputy to the same place to be held there on the aforesaid Monday, published in these words:

1 ? Clonnageeragh, co. Westmeath

c.7

Item al supplicacion de Gerot count de Kildare et Alice sa famme Thomas fitz Gerot chivaler chaunceller Dirland Rouland fitz Eustace chivaler seignur de Portlester thresourer Dirland Philipp Bermyngeham chief justice del chief place nostre soveraine seignur le roy de sa terre Dirland Richard Bellewe esquier William Heneman vicary de Dundalke et William Brystowe del mesme ordeine est et graunte par auctorite dicest parliament que lez lettres patentes le roy soient faitz a eaux en la fourme qui ensuit:

> Ricardus Dei gratia rex Anglie et Francie et dominus Hibernie omnibus ad quos presentes littere pervenerint salutem. Sciatis quod cum predilectus consanguineus noster Geraldus comes Kildarie et Alicia uxor eius Thomas fitz Gerot miles cancellarius noster terre nostre Hibernie Rolandus fitz Eustace miles dominus de Portlester thesaurarius noster terre nostre Hibernie Philippus Bermyngeham capitalis justiciarius noster ad placita coram nobis in terra nostra Hibernie tenenda Ricardus Bellewe armiger Willelmus Heneman vicarius de Dundalke et Willelmus Brystowe de eadem fervore devocionis succensi quandam cantariam perpetuam trium capellanorum in honore Dei Beate Marie Virginis Sancti Nicholai et Sancti Ricardi de Dundalke ad divina celebranda in ecclesia Sancti Nicholai de Dundalke predicti pro statu nostro ac pro animabus dictorum fundatorum parentum et amicorum suorum necnon pro animabus omnium fidelium defunctorum et precipue pro anima Cristofori Douedall nuper de Dundalke defuncti de novo inire et fundare proponunt unde nobis supplicarunt ut sibi ad hoc quantum in nobis est licenciam nostram regiam in ea parte concedere graciose dignaremur nos pium et salubre propositum ipsorum comitis Alicie Thome Rolandi Philippi Ricardi Willelmi et Willelmi commendantes cupientesque divinum servicium nostris temporibus adaugeri ac volentes ea consideracione ad eorum supplicatum favorabilius condecendere ut tam perfecte caritatis participes effici valeamus de gracia nostra speciali de assensu predilecti consanguinei nostri Geraldi comitis Kildarie deputati precarissimi nepotis nostri Johannis comitis Lyncolnie locum nostrum tenentis terre nostre Hibernie ac dominorum spiritualium et temporalium procuratorum et communitatis terre nostre Hibernie in parliamento nostro apud Dubliniam die veneris proximo post festum Sancti Patricii episcopi ultimo preteritum[5] coram prefato deputato tento et abinde ad villam de Trym adjornato usque diem lune proximum post festum Corporis Christi tunc proxime sequens[6] conces-

5 18 March 1485. 6 6 June 1485.

c.7 [Licence for the earl of Kildare and others to found a chantry in the church of St Nicholas, Dundalk]

Also, at the petition of Gerald, earl of Kildare, and Alice his wife, Thomas fitz Gerald, knight, chancellor of Ireland, Roland fitz Eustace knight, lord of Portlester, treasurer of Ireland, Philip Bermyngeham, chief justice of the king's bench in his land of Ireland, Richard Bellewe esquire, William Heneman, vicar of Dundalk, and William Brystowe of the same, it is ordained and granted by the authority of this parliament that the king's letters patent be made to them in the form which follows:

> Richard, by the grace of God king of England and France and lord of Ireland, to all to whom the present letters shall come, greeting. Know that whereas our dearly beloved cousin, Gerald, earl of Kildare, and Alice his wife, Thomas fitz Gerald, knight, our chancellor of our land of Ireland, Roland fitz Eustace, knight, lord of Portlester, our treasurer of our land of Ireland, Philip Bermyngeham, our chief justice for pleas to be held before us in our land of Ireland, Richard Bellewe, esquire, William Heneman, vicar of Dundalk, and William Brystowe of the same, inflamed with the fervour of devotion propose to begin anew and found a certain perpetual chantry of three chaplains in honour of God, the Blessed Virgin Mary, St Nicholas and St Richard of Dundalk, to celebrate divine service in the church of St Nicholas of Dundalk aforesaid, for our estate and for the souls of the said founders, their parents and friends and also for the souls of all the faithful departed and especially for the soul of Christopher Douedall, late of Dundalk, deceased, wherefore they have petitioned us that we should graciously deign to grant them, so far as in us lies, our royal licence in this behalf, we, commending the pious and salutary purpose of the same earl, Alice, Thomas, Roland, Philip, Richard, William and William, and desiring that divine service should be increased in our times and willing for that consideration to condescend the more favourably to their petition, so that we may be made as far as possible participators in the charity of our special grace, with the assent of our dearly beloved cousin, Gerald, earl of Kildare, the deputy of our dearest nephew, John, earl of Lincoln, our lieutenant of our land of Ireland, and of the lords spiritual and temporal, the proctors and commons of our land of Ireland in our parliament held at Dublin before the aforesaid deputy on the Friday next after the feast of St Patrick the bishop last past [18 March 1485] and from thence adjourned to the town of Trim to the Monday next after the feast of Corpus Christi then next following [6 June 1485] have granted and given licence by the authority of our parliament aforesaid to the afore-

simus et licenciam dedimus auctoritate[7] parliamenti nostri predicti prefatis comiti Alicie Thome Rolando Philippo Ricardo Willelmo et Willelmo quod ipsi et eorum quilibet huiusmodi cantariam de novo inire fundare facere constituere et construere possint et possit imperpetuum; quodque iidem comes Alicia Thomas Rolandus Philippus Ricardus Willelmus et Willelmus et quilibet eorum dare et concedere valeant et valeat prefatis capellanis in forma predicta in dicta cantaria fundatis vigore et auctoritate presencium terras tenementa redditus et servicia cum pertinenciis usque ad valorem triginti librarum per annum ultra onera et reprisas inde licet de nobis teneant in capite sive de aliis absque aliquo brevi nostro ad quod dampnum habenda et tenenda prefatis capellanis in cantaria predicta fundatis et successoribus suis capellanis in cantaria huiusmodi fundatis successive imperpetuum sine aliqua alia licencia nostra heredum vel successorum nostrorum inde optinenda sive prosequenda; et ulterius de gratia nostra uberiori ac ex assensu et auctoritate predictis concessimus et licenciam dedimus quod prefati capellani in dicta cantaria sic fundati et successores sui possint perquirere et adquirere ac recipere terras tenementa redditus et servicia cum suis pertinenciis ad valorem decem librarum per annum ultra onera et reprisas inde licet de nobis sive de aliis teneantur habenda et tenenda sibi et successoribus suis imperpetuum absque aliquo brevi nostro ad quod dampnum in hac parte perquirendo sive optenendo statuto de terris et tenementis ad manum mortuam non ponendis edito seu quocumque alio statuto actu ordinacione prosecucione re vel materia inde in contrarium similiter edito proviso ordinato aut habito in aliquo non obstante; et insuper de gratia nostra habundanti ac de assensu et auctoritate predictis concessimus et quantum in nobis est licenciam pro nobis heredibus et successoribus nostris dedimus specialem quod predicti capellani in dicta cantaria fundati et successores sui omnia predicta terras tenementa redditus et servicia cum suis pertinenciis sic data et concessa ante hec tempora sive imposterum danda et concedenda recipere habere occupare et eis gaudere possint et quilibet eorum possit sibi et successoribus suis imperpetuum absque alia licencia a nobis heredibus vel successoribus nostris inde perquirenda sive optinenda; ulteriusque de uberioris gratie amplitudine ac ex assensu et auctoritate predictis concessimus priori de Dundalke ac vicario ecclesie Sancti Nicholai de Dundalke necnon ballivis ville de Dundalke pro tempore existentibus et successoribus suis imperpetuum quod ipsi successive huiusmodi capellanos in dicta cantaria fundatos et quemlibet eorum

7 Berry's note: *auctoritati* in roll.

said earl, Alice, Thomas, Roland, Philip, Richard, William and William that they and every one of them may begin anew, found, make, constitute and erect for ever such chantry and that the same earl, Alice, Thomas, Roland, Philip, Richard, William and William and every one of them may give and grant to the aforesaid chaplains in the form aforesaid in the said chantry founded by force and authority of these present letters, lands, tenements, rents and services with the appurtenances up to the value of thirty pounds yearly beyond the charges and reprises thereof, whether they hold of us in chief or of others, without any writ of *ad quod dampnum*, to have and to hold to the aforesaid chaplains established in the aforesaid chantry and their successors, chaplains established in such chantry successively for ever, without obtaining or suing any other licence from us, our heirs or successors; and further, of our more abundant grace and with the assent and authority aforesaid, we have granted and given licence that the aforesaid chaplains so established in the said chantry and their successors may purchase and acquire and receive lands, tenements, rents and services with their appurtenances to the value of ten pounds yearly beyond the charges and reprises thereof, whether they be held of us or of others, to have and to hold to them and their successors for ever, without purchasing or obtaining any writ of *ad quod dampnum* in this behalf, notwithstanding the statute published against putting lands and tenements in mortmain or whatsoever other statute, act, ordinance, suit, thing or matter to the contrary thereof similarly published, provided, ordained or had in any wise; and further, of our abundant grace and with the assent and authority aforesaid, we have granted and so far as in us lies have given special licence for us, our heirs and successors that the aforesaid chaplains established in the said chantry and their successors and every one of them may receive, have, occupy and enjoy all the aforesaid lands, tenements, rents and service, with their appurtenances, so given and granted before now or to be given and granted in the future to them and their successors for ever, without purchasing or obtaining any other licence from us, our heirs or successors; and further, of the amplitude of our more abundant grace and by the assent and authority aforesaid, we have granted to the prior of Dundalk and the vicar of the church of St Nicholas of Dundalk and also to the bailiffs of the town of Dundalk for the time being and their successors for ever, that they successively, for defects, culpable causes, bad rule, negligence, ignorance, excesses, death, resignation, translation, surrender or for example, on account of deficiency of knowledge or other reasonable cause, as often as it shall be necessary, may discharge, depose and remove from such service such

propter defectus causas culpabiles malam gubernacionem necligenciam ignoranciam excessus decessum resignacionem translacionem sursum reddicionem vel utputa non propter defectum sciencie seu aliam causam racionabilem tociens quociens necesse fuerit ab huiusmodi servicio exonerare deponere et amovere aliumque capellanum seu alios capellanos idoneum vel idoneos vice et loco ipsius vel ipsorum exoneratorum depositorum et ammotorum facere ordinare et constituere possint de tempore in tempus nolentes quod predicti comes, Alicia Thomas Rolandus Philippus Ricardus Willelmus Willelmus prior vicarius et ballivi seu eorum aliquis heredes aut successores sui aut heredes vel successores alicuius eorum racione premissorum per nos heredes vel successores justiciarios locumtenentes deputatos gubernatores escaetores vicecomites ballivos seu ministros nostros heredum vel successorum nostrorum occasionentur molestentur in aliquo seu graventur proviso quod non extendat nec sit prejudicialis Ricardo Bellewe de la Roche armigero nec alicui heredum suorum quoquo modo imperpetuum salvis semper capitalibus dominis feodi illius serviciis inde debitis et de jure consuetis. In cuius etc. Teste etc.

et ceo saunz ascun fine de estre fait et pur une soule fee de xx s. de estre paiez en le hanaper le roy de sa chauncerie Dirland pur le fee du graund seall illeosqes.

c.8[8]

Item al requisicion dez communes que le statute de Henry fitz Emprice ordeine pur la eleccion del governour de estre ewe en cest terre en ascun temps quaunt il fortuner de estre voide de ascun loiall governour par auctorite dicest parliament soit conferme ratifie et ajuge bone et effectuale en ley; et quaunt il fortuner cest terre Dirland en ascun temps avenaunt en ascun manere de estre voide de ascun tiell manere governour que adonqes si sovent come il fortuner issint de estre voide par auctorite dicest parliament Thomas fitz Gerrald chaunceller Dirland sire Rouland fitz Eustace tresorer Dirland Philipp Bermyngham chief justice del chief place le roy en Irland Olivere Eustace chief baron del escheqer le roy en Irland ou son depute pur le temps esteaunt Thomas Dowedall clerke et gardeine dez roulles et recordes le roy en sa chauncerie en Irland Johan Estrete serjeaunt le roy a sez leyes en Irland et chescun de eaux severalment par auctorite dicest dit parliament soient ajugez pleinement en chescun de lour dit severale office severalment a aver et tenire

8 This chapter is printed in Richardson & Sayles, *Ir, parl. in middle ages*, pp 330–1.

> chaplains established in the said chantry and every one of them, and make, ordain and appoint another fit chaplain or other fit chaplains in the stead and place of him or them discharged, deposed and removed from time to time, not willing that the aforesaid earl, Alice, Thomas, Roland, Philip, Richard, William, William, prior, vicar and bailiffs or any of them, their heirs or successors or the heirs or successors of any of them by reason of the premises be harassed, molested or grieved in any respect by us, our heirs or successors, or the justices, lieutenants, deputies, governors, escheators, sheriffs, bailiffs or ministers of us, our heirs or successors; provided that it shall not extend or be prejudicial to Richard Bellewe of the Roche, esquire, or to any of his heirs in any way, for ever; saving always to the chief lords of that fee the services thereout due and of right accustomed; in witness whereof etc. Witness etc.[2]

and this without any fine to be made and for a single fee of twenty shillings to be paid in the king's hanaper of his chancery of Ireland for the fee of the great seal there.

c.8 [Confirmation of the statute of Henry fitz Empress]
Also, at the request of the commons, that the statute of Henry fitzEmpress ordained for the election of a governor to be made in this land at any time when it shall happen to be without any lawful governor be confirmed, ratified and adjudged good and effectual in law by authority of this parliament; and when it shall happen that this land of Ireland at any time in the future in any manner shall be without any such manner of governor, that then, as often as the office shall happen so to be vacant, by authority of this parliament, Thomas fitz Gerald, chancellor of Ireland, Sir Roland fitz Eustace, treasurer of Ireland, Philip Bermyngham, chief justice of the king's bench in Ireland, Thomas Plunket, chief justice of the king's common bench in Ireland, Oliver fitz Eustace, chief baron of the king's exchequer in Ireland or his deputy for the time being, Thomas Dowedall, clerk and keeper of the king's rolls and records in his chancery in Ireland, John Estrete, the king's serjeant at laws in Ireland and every one of them separately by authority of the said parliament, shall be

2 No patent rolls for the reign of Richard III are calendared in *Rot. pat. Hib.*

chescun de eaux severalment son office pur terme de sa vies ascun maner matier cause ou chose ewe et de estre ewe au contrarie nient obstaunt; et que par mesme lauctorite il bien luist sibien a eaux ou la greindre parte de eaux come a toutz aultres maners persons ou la greindre parte de eaux queux issint severalment averount et teignerount ascun de lez ditz offices par reison del morte de ascun officer de lez ditz offices par done desouth le testmoignaunce de Gerrald count de Kildare en ascun manere come governour dicest terre accordaunt al tenour usage et execucion del dit estatute de Henry fitz Emprice ove lassent dez noblez dicest terre accordaunt come il est especifie en mesme lestatute sur chescun tiell avoidaunce de estre ewe de eslier une noble seignur de estre governour et eit la governance come justice Dirland ceo de aver et enjoier accordaunt al auncient usage use et execute devaunt cest temps; et que par mesme lauctorite il bien luist a chescun tiell governour issint eslie a tenire parliaments et graundez counseils et de faire que lez leyes dicest terre pur le bone publique del mesme duhement soient excercisez en la mesme et executez en toute manere come par ascun manere governour del mesme il ad este fait done et excercise et ceo de estre ajugez si bien et effectuale en ley come ascun tiell qui ad este par ascun manere governour dicest terre en ascun temps passe par issint que la dit eleccion soit fait chescun foitz par lez seignurs espirituelx et temporalx et lez noblez del dit terre et par issint auxi que nule parliament soit comense forsque une foitz par ane.

c.9

Item al requisicion des communes que come le tres reverend pier en Dieu Johan erchevesque tarde de Develyn de son tres entier et favourable amour que ad al natiefs englois subgittez le roy en cest sa terre resigna sez dignite et erchevesqery avauntditz al entente que le tresreverend pier en Dieu Water fitz Symond ore esteaunt erchevesque de Develyn natief et nee en cest terre pur luy mesme et aultres en semblable manere natief apres luy enjoierount lour promocions et consecracions del dignite et erchevesqery avauntditz lez queux par long temps passe en la person de ascun tiell manere natief person ne ad my este viewe enjoie ne possede; que en consideracion sibien ent que come le dit tresreverend pier en Dieu Johan erchevesque tarde de Develyn parmy toute la province de Develyn fuit metropolitane et pier desouth Dieu pur le quele il ne doit estre viewe mesque qil avera une continuell substaunce pur sa sustentacion ordeine este enacte et establie par auctorite dicest parliament que le dit Johan erchevesque tarde de Develyn soit ajuge personate en lez leyes du roy en cest sa terre de empledere et desore enavaunt de estre empledde en chescun dez courtes le roy et aillours en la mesme et auxi ajuge personate de enjoier le benefice franqe done avauntage et privilege dez leyes du roy en chescun

adjudged fully in every of their said separate offices separately to have and to hold each of them separately his office for term of his life, notwithstanding any manner of matter, cause or thing had and to be had to the contrary; and that by the same authority it shall be lawful as well for them or the greater part of them, as for all other manners of persons or the greater part of them, who shall so separately have and hold any of the said offices by reason of the death of any officer of the said offices by gift under the testimony of Gerald, earl of Kildare in any manner as governor of this land, according to the tenor, usage and execution of the said statute of Henry fitz Empress, with the assent of the nobles of this land according as it is specified in the same statute, upon every such vacancy to be had, to elect a noble lord to be governor and have the government as justiciar of Ireland, to have and enjoy this according to the ancient usage used and executed before now; and by the same authority that it shall be lawful for every such governor so elected to hold parliaments and great councils and to see that the laws of this land for the public good of the same be duly carried out in the same and executed in every way as it has been done, given and carried out by any manner of governor of the same, and this shall be adjudged as good and effectual in law as any such which has been by any manner of governor of this land at any time past; provided that the said election be made every time by the lords spiritual and temporal and the nobles of the said land and provided also that no parliament be commenced except once a year.

c.9 [Grant of an annuity of £100 out of the archbishopric of Dublin to John, former archbishop]

Also, at the request of the commons, that whereas the very reverend father in God John, late archbishop of Dublin[3], out of the most entire and favourable love which he has for the king's native English subjects in this his land, resigned his dignity and archbishopric aforesaid to the intent that the very reverend father in God Walter fitz Symond, now being archbishop of Dublin, a native and born in this land, for himself and others in like manner natives after him, shall enjoy their promotions and consecrations to the dignity and archbishopric aforesaid which for a long time past has not been seen, enjoyed or possessed in the person of any such manner of native person; that in consideration both of this and of the fact that the said very reverend father in God, John, late archbishop of Dublin, was metropolitan and father under God throughout the whole province of Dublin, wherefore it ought not to be seen but that he shall have continuing provision for his sustenance, it is ordained, enacted and established by authority of this parliament that the said John, late

3 John Walton OSA, resigned 14 June 1484.

manere si franqement et si liberalment come ascun aultre manere person dez subgittes le roy par son duhete de sa ligeaunce est enheritable a aver enjoier et user[9] lez mesmez; et que par mesme lauctorite pur la sustentacion avauntdit de estre ewe quaunt le dit erchevesqery en ascun manere desore enavaunt sera proschien voide par morte ou resignacion del dit Water erchevesque que adonqes toute le seignurie et manere de Swerdes en le counte de Develyn par mesme lauctorite soit ajuge en la possession del dit Johan erchevesque tarde de Develyn; et que bien luist a luy de enterer et aver et teignire adonqez toute le dit seignurie et manere de Swerdes et lez annuelx issues et profites ent ove toutz et chescun del appurtenaunce al avauntdit Johan erchevesque tarde de Develyn et a sez assignes pur terme de sa vie quitement saunz de estre charge ove ascun manere accion demaunde et empechement de gaste de ascun manere person et saunz liverey de estre sue ou ewe de nostre soveraine seignur le roy ou sez heires; purvieu que le dit erchevesque tarde de Develyn apres la morte del dit Water ore erchevesque de Develyn et en le temps de son successour eit C li. annuelment del dit manere enterment outre toutz lez chargez et purvieu auxi que cest acte ne extende my ne soit prejudiciale a nully qui ad ascun graunte desouth lez iij sealx.

C.10

Item al supplicacion de Watier erchevesque de Divelin primate Dirland que pur ceo que diverse benefices de sez diocez sount scituatez enter lez irrois ennemyes le roy dez queux lez advocions a luy apparteignount par reison de son erchevesqery et a sez predecessours ount parteignez devaunt le temps que nule memorie est et en lez ditz benefices poet nule englois home suirment enhabite ne a eaux peisiblement ne surement passer ne venire et diversez dez englois clerkes queux sount hablez de aver cure dez almes sount enexpertez del irroys langage et tielx queux del mesme ount experiment ascuns disdaignount de enhabiter entre lez irroys people et aultres ne osont my pur que divine service est diminuse et cure dez almes piteuxment neclecte; sur que lez premisses considerez ordeine est establie et enacte par auctorite dicest parliament que bien luist al dit erchevesque pur la space de ij anes proschiens ensuantez a toutz foitz tielx benefices de collater et de doner as irroys clerkes de irroys nacion et langage saunz ascun empechement vexacion ou grevaunce de nostre soveraine

9 Berry's note: *usa* in roll.

archbishop of Dublin, be adjudged personate in the king's laws in this his land to implead and henceforth to be impleaded in all the king's courts and elsewhere in the same, and also adjudged personate to enjoy the benefit, freedom, gift, advantage and privilege of the king's laws in every respect as freely and as liberally as any other manner of person of the king's subjects is entitled by his duty of allegiance to have enjoy and use the same; and that by the same authority, in order that his aforesaid sustenance be had when the said archbishopric in future shall in any manner next be vacant by the death or resignation of the said Walter the archbishop, that then the whole lordship and manor of Swords in the county of Dublin, by the same authority be adjudged in the possession of the said John, late archbishop of Dublin; and that it shall be lawful for him then to enter and have and hold all the said lordship and manor of Swords and the yearly issues and profits thereof with all and every one of the appurtenances to the aforesaid John, late archbishop of Dublin, and to his assigns for term of his life freely without being burdened with any manner of action, demand and impeachment of waste of any manner of person and without livery to be sued or had of our sovereign lord the king or his heirs; provided that the said late archbishop of Dublin, after the death of the said Walter now archbishop of Dublin, and in the time of his successor shall have one hundred pounds yearly out of the said manor entirely beyond all the charges; and provided also that this act shall not extend not be prejudicial to anyone who has any grant under the three seals.

c.10 [Licence for two years for the archbishop of Dublin to provide Irish clergy to benefices in his gift]

Also, at the petition of Walter, archbishop of Dublin, primate of Ireland, that whereas various benefices of his dioceses are situated amongst the king's Irish enemies, the advowsons of which belong to him by reason of his archbishopric and have belonged to his predecessors from beyond the time of memory, and no Englishman can safely occupy the said benefices nor go to them nor come from them peaceably and safely, and various English clerks who are fit to have the cure of souls are inexpert in the Irish language, and of those who are practised in the same, some disdain to live among the Irish people and others dare not, whereby divine service is diminished and the cure of souls sadly neglected; whereupon, considering the premises, it is ordained, established and enacted by authority of this parliament that it shall be lawful for the said archbishop for the space of the two years next ensuing at all times to collate and give such benefices to Irish clerks of the Irish nation and language without any hindrance, vexation or grievance by our sovereign lord the king, his heirs, officers or ministers in any manner, notwithstanding any act or ordinance

seignur le roy sez heires officeres ou ministres en ascun manere ascun acte ou ordenaunce devaunt cest temps fait nient obstaunt et que lez avauntditz beneficeres soient jurrez de estre foialx a nostre soveraine seignur le roy et sez subgittes son depute ou justice dicest terre.

c.11

Item al supplicacion de Simon Byrford fitz et heire a Esmond Byrford de Kilrowe que come le dit Esmond fuit seisie del manere de Kilrowe avauntdit ove lez appurtenauntz en son demesne come de fee taille et ceo teignoit[10] del manere de Rathtouth en socage et nient par roiall service et issint murist seisie apres que morte le dit manere de Kilrowe ove lez appurtenauncz descenda al dit Simon come fitz et heire al dit Esmond et cestz nient obstauntz le dit Simon est interrupte de prendre lez profites del dit manere de Kilrowe par Thomas Plunket chief justice del commune place le roy en Irland par une colour que le dit manere de Kilrowe serroit tenuz del manere de Rathtouth par roiall service lou en veraite il nest pas tenuz del dit manere par roiall service mesque en socage sicome pluis pleinement appiert en le ruge livre de Trym; sur que lez premisses considerez ordeine est enacte et establie par auctorite dicest parliament que bien luist al dit Simon de enjoier son possession en le dit manere de Kilrowe ove lez appurtenauncz et ceo de lesser a son pleasire et de prendre lez profites del mesme saunz ascun enterrupcion del dit Thomas ou ascun aultre person ou persons; et que par mesme lauctorite le dit Simon soit ajuge a tegnire le dit manere de Kilrowe ove lez appurtenauntez del dit manere de Rathtouth par sogage et nient par roiall service.

c.12

Item al supplicacion de Rouland Eustace chivaler seignur de Portlester thesorer Dirland que laou Halloueston' en le paroche de Ardbrekan est moite de une charue de terre et Bayardeston' juxt le mesme en quele est si moulte terre come en Halloueston' est mesque une quarter de une charue de terre et en Aronane par mesme nest pas forsque xj acres lez queux sount ore gastez; et pur cause que la dit Halloueston' est assesse pur le subsidie moite de une charue de terre la quele serroit forsque une quarter de une charue de terre sil fuit assesse come la dit Bayardeston' et aultres viles bien pres sount et sils ne sount pas remediez et meindre assessez ils voudrount estre toute outrement gastez; sur que les premisses considerez ordeine est par auctorite dicest parliament que la dit

10 IRC *teignoit*; Berry *tegnent*.

heretofore made; and that the aforesaid benefice holders shall be sworn to be faithful to our sovereign lord the king and his subjects, his deputy or justiciar of this land.

c.11 [Confirmation to Simon Byrford of quiet possession of the manor of Kilrue, held of the manor of Ratoath in common socage]

Also, at the petition of Simon Byrford, son and heir to Esmond Byrford of Kilrue, that whereas the said Esmond was seised of the manor of Kilrue aforesaid with the appurtenances in his demesne as of fee tail and held it of the manor of Ratoath in socage and not by royal service and so died seised, after whose death the said manor of Kilrowe with the appurtenances descended to the said Simon as son and heir of the said Esmond, notwithstanding this the said Simon is stopped from taking the profits of the said manor of Kilrowe by Thomas Plunket, chief justice of the king's common bench in Ireland by the pretext that the said manor of Kilrue should be held of the manor of Ratoath by royal service, whereas in truth it is not held of the said manor by royal service but in socage as more fully appears in the red book of Trim; whereupon, considering the premises, it is ordained, enacted and established by authority of this parliament that it shall be lawful for the said Simon to enjoy his possession of the said manor of Kilrue with the appurtenances and to let it at his pleasure and to take the profits of the same without any interruption by the said Thomas or any other person or persons; and by the same authority that the said Simon be adjudged to hold the said manor of Kilrue with the appurtenances of the said manor of Ratoath by socage and not by royal service.

c.12 [Reduction in the valuation for subsidy of Sir Roland fitz Eustace's lands in Hanlonstown and Aronane]

Also, at the petition of Roland Eustace, knight, lord of Portlester, treasurer of Ireland, that whereas Hanlonstown in the parish of Ardbraccan is half of a ploughland and Boyerstown near the same, in which is as much land as in Hanlonstown, is but a quarter of a ploughland, and in Aronane by the same, there is only eleven acres, which are now waste, and because the said Hanlonstown is assessed for the subsidy at half a ploughland, which would be only a quarter of a ploughland if it was assessed as the said Boyerstown and other vills very near it are and if they are not remedied and assessed at less they will be all utterly waste; whereupon considering the premises, it is ordained by authority of this parliament that the said Hanlonstown and Aronane shall be

Halloueston' et Aronane ne soient my forsque une quarter de une charue de terre desore en avaunt pur toutz jours et de estre issint assessez en toutz subsidies et tallages.

c.13

Item al supplicacion de Alexander Plunket chivaler que come le dit sire Alexander fuit charge quaunt il fuit viscount del counte de Mithe de lever lez gages del Oconghore le temps de son office come il fuit del auncient temps use en le dit counte lez ditz gagez de estre paiez; sur que les premissez considerez ordeine est par auctorite dicest parliament que bien luist al dit sire Alexander pur distreiner pur la parcell de lez ditz gages esteaunt aderere duraunt le temps que le dit sire Alexander fuit viscount lez distressez rehersez de estre faitz en tielx baronies come ils doient estre faitz et si ascun homme resiste encountre le dit sire Alexander il bien luist a luy pur luy defender envers lez resisteres et outre ceo lez resisteres de paier luy pur tielx lesions queux il preigne pur la fesaunce de cele distresse.

c.14

Item al requisicion des communes que en consideracion que diversez dez irrois ennemyez le roy sount confederez[11] ensemblement de faire guerre sur lez foialx lieges et subgittes le roy quele est semble de estre le extreme anientesment de eaux si lez ditz irrois enemies ne soient my resistez et auxi que pur le adsistence dez mesmez nule dez subgittes le roy ore esteauntz residentes deins la citte de Divelin et aultres porte viles de les iiij countees cest assavere Divelin Mithe Kildare et Uriell et de diversez aultres lieux de lez mesmz sount enfectez ove cest perillose plage de pestelence reignaunt entre eaux ne poient my estre appellez de estre en la company del tresbone et noble seignur Gerot count de Kildare depute lieutenaunt Dirland en defense del mesmez pur le eminent perill del dit plage; ordeine est enacte et establie par auctorite dicest parliament que bien luist al dit count de aver faire leve et perceiver de lez enhabitauntez de les ditz iiij countees C li. cest assavere lxx marcez sur lez charues de terre rentes et possessions de lez seignurs espiritualx et temporelx chivalers esquiers gentilx et franqes tenauntez del dit counte de Mithe sibien del counte come del croce et clergie del mesme exemptez et nient exemptez et xl marcez sur lez charues de terre rentes et possessions de lez seignurs espiritualx et temporalx chivalers esquiers gentilx et franqes tenauntes del dit counte de Divelin sibien

11 IRC *confederez*; Berry *considerez*.

no more than a quarter of a ploughland henceforth for ever and be so assessed in all subsidies and tallages.

c.13 [Licence for Sir Alexander Plunket, former sheriff of Meath, to levy the balance of O'Connor's wages]

Also, at the petition of Alexander Plunket, knight, that whereas the said Sir Alexander was charged when he was sheriff of the county of Meath to levy the wages of O Conghore during the time of his office, as it was customary in the said county in ancient times for the said wages to be paid; whereupon, considering the premises, it is ordained by authority of this parliament that it shall be lawful for the said Sir Alexander to distrain for the portion of the said wages which were in arrear during the time that the said Sir Alexander was sheriff, the aforesaid distresses to be made in such baronies as they ought to be made in, and if any man resist the said Sir Alexander, it shall be lawful for him to defend himself against the resisters and moreover the resisters shall pay him for such injuries as he may receive in the making of such distress.

c.14 [Grant to the deputy of £100 subsidy from Cos. Dublin, Meath, Kildare and Louth for defence during the present time of plague]

Also, at the request of the commons, that in consideration of the fact that various of the king's Irish enemies are confederated together to make war on the king's faithful liegemen and subjects, which is likely to be their total destruction if the said Irish enemies are not resisted, and also that for the assistance of the same, none of the king's subjects now being resident in the city of Dublin and other walled towns of the four counties, that is to say, Dublin, Meath, Kildare and Louth and of various other places of the same which are infected with this dangerous plague of pestilence prevailing amongst them, can be summoned to be in the company of the very good and noble lord Gerald earl of Kildare, deputy lieutenant of Ireland, in defence of the same due to the great danger of the said plague; it is ordained, enacted and established by authority of this parliament that it shall be lawful for the said earl to have, levy and receive from the inhabitants of the said four counties one hundred pounds, that is to say, seventy marks on the ploughlands, rents and possessions of the lords spiritual and temporal, knights, esquires, gentlemen and freeholders of the said county of Meath, both of the county and of the cross and clergy of the same, exempt and not exempt, and forty marks on the ploughlands, rents and possessions of the lords spiritual and temporal, knights, esquires, gentlemen and freeholders of the said county of Dublin, both of the same county and of

del mesme le counte come del croce et clergie deane et chapitrees exemptez et nient exemptez et xx marces sur lez charues de terre rentes et possessions de lez seignurs espiritualx et temporalx chivalers esquiers gentilx et franqes tenauntez del dit counte de Kildare et que si bien de mesme counte come del croce et clergie del mesme exemptez et nient exemptez et xx marces sur lez charues de terre rentes et possessions de lez seignurs espiritualx et temporalx chivalers esquiers gentilx et franqes tenauntez del dit counte de Uriell et que sibien mesme le counte come croce et clergie del mesme exemptez et nient exemptez et lez ditz C li. en fourme avantdit de estre ratez et levez par sessours et collectours de estre nosmez en chescun counte sibien pur le laife come pur le clergie et croce solonque la manere et fourme come il ad este fait et use del commune subsidy devaunt cest temps graunte et que par la dite auctorite que chescun de lez ditz seignurs espiritualx et temporalx chivalers esquiers gentilx et franqez tenauntez face allower a chescun de lour tenauntez si moulte del dit summe que chescun de eaux paie en discharge de chescun de lour ditz seignurs espiritualx et temporalx chivaleres esquiers gentilx et franqes tenauntez al proschien terme en paiement de lour rente sur peine de forfaitoure de x li. al dit depute de estre levez de chescun de lez ditz seignurs espiritualx et temporalx chivalers esquiers gentilx et franqez tenauntes queux ne allowent my a lour tenauntes come il est avauntdit; purvieu toutz foitz que les persons nosmez par les seignurs espiritualx et temporalx de estre sessours sibien pur lez deanes chapitelx clergies et croces de chescun de lez ditz countees come pur mesmez lez countees soient sessours accordaunt et forsprise que nule peine sera done par force dicest acte envers le prioure de Kilmaynan'.

c.15

Item al requisicion des communes que come le tresnoble et tresbone seignur Gerot count de Kildare depute lieutenaunt Dirland est edifiaunt une chastell en Testeldermote quele chastell edifie et perfourme voudra este la vray readepcion de toutz lez terrez gastez del counte de Cathirlagh de estre enhabitez ove lez subgittes le roy; que en consideracion ent ordeine este enacte et establie par auctorite dicest parliament que lez baronies de Balrothery Castelknok et Cowlok et la croce del aultre parte del ewe en Fyngall en le counte de Divelin soient charges en xij charetes de amesner culme de Divelin al dit chastell a Testeldermot et lez charettes de estre cessez et chargez de venire hors de celes parties par la discrecion de Philipp Bermyngham chief justice del chief place le roy en Irland et Thomas Douedall clerk et gardeine des roulles le roy de sa chauncerie en Irland et sur ceo de aver le garnisement de viij jours par le viscount del mesme le counte et auxi outre ceo v charetes issint hors del baronie de Dunboyng et vij charetes issint hors del baronie de Rathtouth de carier

the cross and clergy, dean and chapters, exempt and not exempt, and twenty marks on the ploughlands, rents and possessions of the lords spiritual and temporal, knights, esquires, gentlemen and freeholders of the said county of Kildare and that both of the same county and of the cross and clergy of the same, exempt and not exempt, and twenty marks on the ploughlands, rents and possessions of the lords spiritual and temporal, knights, esquires, gentlemen and freeholders of the said county of Louth and that both of the same county and the cross and clergy of the same, exempt and not exempt, and the said one hundred pounds in form aforesaid to be rated and levied by assessors and collectors to be named in every county both for the lay fee and for the clergy and cross according to the manner and form as has been done and practised with regard to the common subsidy granted before now; and that by the said authority that each of the said lords spiritual and temporal, knights, esquires, gentlemen and freeholders make allowance to each of their tenants of so much of the said sum as each of them pays in discharge of each of their said lords spiritual and temporal, knights, esquires, gentlemen and freeholders at the next term in payment of their rent on pain of forfeiture of ten pounds to the said deputy to be levied of each of the said lords spiritual and temporal, knights, esquires, gentlemen and freeholders who do not make allowance to their tenants as is aforesaid; provided always that the persons named by the lords spiritual and temporal to be assessors, both for the deans, chapters, clergy and crosses of each of the said counties, and for the same counties, shall be assessors accordingly, and that no penalty shall be given by force of this act against the prior of Kilmainham.

c.15 [Assessment of labourers and carts to build the earl of Kildare's castle at Castledermot for the recovery of lands in co. Carlow]

Also, at the request of the commons that whereas the very noble and very good lord, Gerald, earl of Kildare, deputy lieutenant of Ireland, is building a castle at Castledermot, which castle when built and completed may be the true means of recovering all the waste lands of the county of Carlow to be populated by the king's subjects; that in consideration thereof it is ordained, enacted and established by authority of this parliament that the baronies of Balrothery, Castleknock and Coolock and the cross of the other side of the water in Fingal in the county of Dublin be charged with twelve carts to bring culm from Dublin to the said castle at Castledermot and the carts to be assessed and charged to come from those parts at the discretion of Philip Bermyngham, chief justice of the king's bench in Ireland and Thomas Douedall, clerk and keeper of the king's rolls of his chancery in Ireland, and to have eight days warning of this by the sheriff of the same county and also in addition to this,

culme en fourme avauntdit et lez ditz v charetes queux issint viendrount hors del baronie de Dunboyng de estre cessez et charges par la discrecion de Richard Feypowe gentilman Nicholas Husse gentilman et le portrief de Dunboyng et lez ditz vij charetes queux issint viendrount hors del dit baronie de Rathtouth de estre cessez et charges par la discrecion de Richard Sedygrave gentilman et Johan Ley gentilman et sur ceo de aver le garnisement de viij jours par le viscount del mesme le counte et pur chescun charete de ceaux ditz charetes queux en fourme avauntdit serrount issint assessez que face defaulte cele persone ou persons sur quele il est issint assesse et face defaulte de forfaiter et perdire al dit depute xl s. de estre levez de lour terres et tenementez bones et chateux al volunte du dit depute et que par mesme le auctorite chescun person ou persons eiaunt une entier charue deins la baronie de Newcastell et la croce del mesme envoia une hable homme a Testeldermot illeosqes de estre continuelment laboraunt sur lour propre custages iij jours apres le garnisement de viij jours done a luy par le viscount de counte de Divelin ou le sejeaunt del dit baronie et que chescun de les viscountes sibien del counte de Divelin come Mith ou chescun de lour deputees soient a Testeldermot de faire lour retournez de les nons de lez ditz persons queux par eaux ou ascun dez serjeauntes issint sount garnisez et summonez et ceo sur la peine de chescun person qui face defaulte de forfaiter et perdire al dit depute vj s. viij d. de estre levez de lour biens et chateux al volunte del dit depute et si ascun de lez ditz viscountes en icele face defaulte de forfaiter al dit depute x li. et le dit serjeaunt en semble manere de forfaiter xx s. si sovent foitz come ascun de eaux en ascun manere avauntdit offende.

c.16

Item al requisicion des communes del counte de Loueth aultrement appelle Uriele que come Nicholas Taaff de Ballybragan' esquier et Robert Taaff de Marchalrath gentilman ore tarde ount gages et reteignez certeines irrois kernes deins le dit counte promittauntz a eaux duhe paiement pur lour service al fine del terme parentre eaux aggree les queux kernes apres lour dit service fait et terme finie desirauntez lez ditz Nicholas et Robert de paier eaux pur lour ditz service lez queux Nicholas et Robert ne ount my eaux paiez pur que lez ditz kernes a et juxt le Lorgen' en le lundie jour del marchee a Dundalke pristerount William Webley de Kilcloghir Thomas Fisher de Terfeghen' et William Bron' del Newton' de Dromysken et aultres diversez dez foialx subgittes le roy enhabitauntez deins le dit counte hommes et tenauntez de erchevesque de Ardmagh' primat Dirland le abbe de Mellifonte et sire Rouland Eustace seignur de Portlester prisoneres et eaux pristerount al pais de Hanweyn et eaux

five carts similarly from the barony of Dunboyne and seven carts so from the barony of Ratoath to carry culm in form aforesaid, and the said five carts which shall so come from the barony of Dunboyne to be assessed and charged at the discretion of Richard Feypowe, *gentilman*, Nicholas Husse, *gentilman*, and the portreeve of Dunboyne, and the said seven carts which shall come from the said barony of Ratoath to be assessed and charged at the discretion of Richard Sedygrave, *gentilman*, and John Ley, *gentilman*, and to have eight days warning of this by the sheriff of the same county; and for each cart of those said carts assessed in the form aforesaid which make default, the person or persons upon whom it is so assessed and who makes default shall forfeit and lose to the said deputy forty shillings to be levied from their lands and tenements, goods and chattels at the will of the said deputy; and by the same authority that every person or person having an entire ploughland in the barony of Newcastle and the cross of the same shall send an able man to Castledermot there to labour continuously at their own costs for three days after the warning of eight days given to him by the sheriff of the county of Dublin or the serjeant of the said barony; and that each of the sheriffs, as well of the county of Dublin as Meath or each of their deputies shall be at Castledermot to make their returns of the names of the said persons who are so warned and summoned by them or any of the serjeants and this upon the penalty that every person who makes default shall forfeit and lose to the said deputy six shillings and eight pence to be levied from their goods and chattels at the will of the said deputy and if any of the said sheriffs make default therein he shall forfeit to the said deputy ten pounds and the said serjeant in like manner shall forfeit twenty shillings as often as any of them offend in any manner aforesaid.

c.16 [Grant of a subsidy of 43 marks from co. Louth for the relief of certain tenants held to ransom by Irish kerns]

Also, at the request of the commons of the county of Louth otherwise called Uriel, that whereas Nicholas Taaff of Braganstown, esquire, and Robert Taaff of Marshallrath, *gentilman*, now lately have hired and retained certain Irish kerns in the said county promising to them due payment for their service at the end of the term agreed on between them, which kerns, after their said service was performed and the term finished, desired the said Nicholas and Robert to pay them for their said service which Nicholas and Robert have not paid them, and because of this the said kerns at and near the Largen[4] on the Monday market day at Dundalk took prisoner William Webley of Kilclogher[5], Thomas Fisher of Termonfeckin and William Broun of the Newtown of Dromiskin and

4 ? Lurgankeel, co. Louth. 5 ? Clogher, co. Louth.

illeosqes estreitement garderount en prison jesqes al temps qils par cohersion de emprisonement de necessite covient[12] paier severalx ransons lez queux extenderount al summe de xliij marces devaunt qils puissoient estre deliverez al final anientesment de lez ditz subgittes saunz qils soient relevez a cest temps; in consideracion de lez premisses ordeine est establie et enacte par auctorite dicest parliament que incontinent[13] apres le viewe dicest acte engrosse et enacte il bien luist al dit erchevesque et primate et qil eit pleine auctorite et power de assesser le avauntdit summe sur lez enhabitauntez de chescun charue de terre sibien croce come laife deins le dit counte forsprise la baronie de Dundalke et de faire leve ent et le adeliverer a chescun de lez subgittez accordaunt al rate de chescun de lour finaunce et queconque person defors ascun collectour del dit summe qil forfaita xl s. au roy de estre levez a son volunte et qils devaunt cest temps chargez ove le exhibicion de lez ditz kernez soient dischargez a cest temps solonque la rate de lour primere charge.

Quodquidem parliamentum prorogatum fuit usque diem lune proximum post festum Sancti Petri quod dicitur ad vincula tunc proxime sequens[14] ad quem diem lune prefatus deputatus ad parliamentum predictum non venit nec aliquod statutum actus sive ordinacio edita fuerunt set quidem Thomas Douedall clericus et custos rotulorum cancellarie domini regis in Hibernia tam virtute cuiusdam actus in isto dicto parliamento editi quam pretextu cuiusdam littere prefati deputati tam eidem Thome quam aliis ad adjornandum dictum parliamentum directe idem parliamentum usque diem lune proximum post festum Sancti Luce evangeliste tunc proxime futurum[15] de supradicta villa de Trym ad civitatem Dublinie adjornavit.

Statuta ordinaciones et actus in parliamento predicto apud Dubliniam predictam die lune proximo post dictum festum Sancti Luce evangeliste anno regni regis supradicti tercio[16] coram prefato deputato similiter tento ac ibidem finito et terminato edita in forma que sequitur:

c.17[17]

Item al requisicion des communes que en consideracion des bonez et notablez services faitz a nostre soveraine seignur le roy par le trespuissaunt et gracieux

12 IRC *covient*; Berry *coment*. 13 IRC *incontinent*; Berry *entoutment*. 14 8 August 1485. 15 24 October 1485. 16 24 October 1485. 17 Extracts from this chapter are printed in Bryan, *Great earl of Kildare*, pp 83, 282–3.

various others of the king's faithful subjects dwelling in the said county, men and tenants of the archbishop of Armagh, primate of Ireland, the abbot of Mellifont and Sir Roland Eustace, lord of Portlester, and brought them to the country of Hanweyn and kept them strictly in prison there until they, by coercion of imprisonment, were compelled to pay several ransoms which amounted to the sum of forty-three marks before they could be delivered, to the final ruin of the said subjects unless they be now relieved; in consideration of the premises, it is ordained, established and enacted by authority of this parliament that immediately after the sight of this act engrossed and enacted it shall be lawful for the said archbishop and primate, and he shall have full authority and power, to assess the aforesaid sum upon the inhabitants of every ploughland, both cross and lay fee, within the said county, except the barony of Dundalk, and to cause it to be levied and to deliver it to every one of the subjects according to the rate of each one's ransom; and that whatsoever person shall withhold the said sum from any collector shall forfeit forty shillings to the king to be levied at his will and that those heretofore charged with the maintenance of the said kerns shall be now discharged according to the rate of their first charge.

Which parliament was prorogued to the Monday next after the feast of St Peter which is called ad Vincula then next following [8 August 1485], on which Monday the aforesaid deputy did not come to the aforesaid parliament nor was any statute, act or ordinance published but a certain Thomas Douedall, clerk and keeper of the rolls of the lord the king's chancery in Ireland, both by virtue of a certain act published in this said parliament, and by pretext of a certain letter of the aforesaid deputy directed both to the same Thomas and to others for the adjourning of the said parliament, adjourned the same parliament to the Monday next after the feast of St Luke the evangelist then next coming [24 October 1485] from the aforesaid town of Trim to the city of Dublin.

Statutes, ordinances and acts in the aforesaid parliament similarly held at Dublin on the aforesaid Monday next after the said feast of St Luke the evangelist in the third year of the reign of the above mentioned king [24 October 1485] before the aforesaid deputy and there finished and terminated, published in the form which follows:

c.17 [Grant to the deputy of a subsidy of one mark per ploughland from cos. Dublin, Meath, Louth and Kildare]

Also, at the request of the commons, that in consideration of the good and notable services done to our sovereign lord the king by the very powerful and gracious lord, Gerald, earl of Kildare, deputy lieutenant of Ireland, and the

seignur Gerot count de Kildare depute lieutenaunt Dirland et dez graundez et emportablez chargez et labours queux le dit depute susteigne et porte de jour en aultre resistaunt la malice des irrois ennemyes et englois rebelx ordeine est done et graunte par auctorite dicest parlement al dit depute qil eit xiij s. iiij d. de chescun charue de terre deins lez countees de Divelin Mith Loueth et Kildare et chescun counte deins la dit terre de estre assessez et levez sur et de lez enhabitauntez sibien de lez ditz charues de terre come croces et clergees de chescun de lez ditz countees exemptez et nient exemptez ascun acte ou ordenaunce au contrarie fait nient obstaunt et que par la dit auctorite sibien chivalers pur countees et proctours pur clergees deanes et chapitrees et chescun de eaux eient pleine power cest assavere lez chivalers pur countees pur lez charues de terre come lez proctours pur lour spiritualx possessions et que toutz loialx gastes et deforces soient allowez et que lez clergees et croces ne sount my forsque dowblement chargez et que par auctorite dicest parliament lez chivalers pur countees et proctours pur clergees et chapitrees mittent eins al clerke du roulles ou al clerke del parlement suffissauntez collectours nosmez pur la leve del dit subsidy parentre cy et dimenche proschien avenire[18] et si ils ou ascun de eaux departent et ne mittent my eins lez nons de lez ditz collectours par le dit jour come est avauntdit que adonqez il ou ils qissint departount chescun de eaux de[19] forfaitent et perdent xx li. al dit depute de estre levez de lour biens et chateux terres et tenementes al volunte du dit depute; purvieu toutz foitz que lez clergees de Ardmagh' Divelin Mithe et Kildare eient ij semayns apres le dit dimanche del space de eslier lour collectours.

c.18

Item al requisicion des communes que come Cahir O Conghir capiteigne de sa nacion ad fait bone et foiale service a nostre soveraine seignur le roy en sez guerres deins cest sa terre Dirland en la companie del trespuissaunt seignur Gerot count de Kildare depute lieutenaunt Dirland et est arere de sez gages pur le ane darreine passe ordeine est et graunte par auctorite dicest parliament que le dit O Conghir eit xl d. de chescun charue de terre deins le counte de Mithe de estre levez par lez collectours del graunde subsidie graunte al dit depute a cest temps et que toutz loialx gastez et deforces soient allowez.

18 29 October 1485. 19 Berry's note: thus in roll.

great and unbearable charges and labours which the said deputy sustains and bears from day to day resisting the malice of the Irish enemies and English rebels, it is ordained, given and granted to the said deputy by authority of this parliament that he have thirteen shillings and four pence from every ploughland in the counties of Dublin, Meath, Louth and Kildare and every county in the said land, to be assessed and levied upon and from the inhabitants both of the said ploughlands and of the crosses and clergy of every one of the said counties, exempt and not exempt, notwithstanding any act or ordinance made to the contrary; and that by the said authority, both knights for counties and proctors for clergy, deans and chapters and every one of them have full power, that is to say, the knights for counties for the ploughlands and the proctors for their spiritual possessions and that all lawful wastes and withholdings shall be allowed and that the clergy and crosses shall be charged no more than double; and by authority of this parliament that the knights for counties and proctors for clergy and chapters send in to the clerk of the rolls or to the clerk of parliament, between this and Sunday next coming [29 October 1485], the names of sufficient collectors for the levy of the said subsidy; and if they or any of them depart and do not send in the names of the said collectors by the said day as is aforesaid that then he or they who so depart shall each of them forfeit and lose twenty pounds to the said deputy to be levied from their goods and chattels, lands and tenements, at the will of the said deputy; provided always that the clergy of Armagh, Dublin, Meath and Kildare have two weeks after the said Sunday as time to choose their collectors.

c.18 [Grant to Cahir O'Connor of his wages of 3s. 4d. per ploughland in Co. Meath][6]

Also, at the request of the commons, that whereas Cahir O Conghir, captain of his nation, has done good and faithful service to our sovereign lord the king in his wars in this his land of Ireland in the company of the very powerful lord, Gerald, earl of Kildare, deputy lieutenant of Ireland, and is in arrear of his wages for the year last past, it is ordained and granted by authority of this parliament that the said O Conghir have forty pence from every ploughland in the county of Meath, to be levied by the collectors of the great subsidy now granted to the said deputy, and that all lawful wastes and withholdings be allowed.

6 A translation of this chapter is printed in Bryan, *Great earl of Kildare*, pp 82–3.

[Letter of the deputy lieutenant for the adjournment of parliament][20]
Gerot erle of Kildare depute lieutenaunt of Irland to oure right trusty and welbiloved Thomas fitz Gerot knight chaunceller of Irland Rouland fitz Eustace knight lord of Portlester and thresourer of Irland Thomas Douedall maister and kepier of the kinges recordes and roulles in his chauncery in Irland and to John Estrete serjeaunt at the kinges lawes in Irland and to every of you greting. And whereas by a certeine acte and ordenaunce bi auctorite of parliament holden before us at Divelin the Friday next after the fest of Seint Patrik the bishop last past[21] and from thens adjournet and holden at Trym the Moneday next after the fest of Corporis Christi than next ensuyng[22] and so proroget till the Moneday next after the fest of Seint Petre the advincle next commyng[23] ther than to be hold it is ordeinet to be lefull to us as efte as it shall require after oure pleasire for certeins consideracions of oure absence specified in the same acte and ordenaunce to direct oure privat seall to the chaunceller thresourer or to any othir of the kinges counseill in this land commaunding any suche of theym to whom any suche privat seall be directed to contynue proroge or adjourne this present parliament holden and to be holden after oure pleasire as more pleinly it is conteignet and specified in the same acte and ordenaunce.[24] We therfor in consideracion of the premissez for as muche as we may not be at Trym in oure propre person the said Moneday for certeine causes ordeigne and commaunde you iiij iij ij or one of you to be at Trym the said Moneday and ther than in oure absence bi vertue of the said acte and ordenaunce and bi auctorite of oure privat seall to adjourne this present parliament to be holden before us at Divelin the Moneday next after the fest of Seint Luke the evangelist next cum.[25] Yoven under oure privat seall a Testildermot the xxj day of Juyll[26].

20 Printed in Bryan, *Great earl of Kildare*, p. 87. **21** 18 March 1485. **22** 6 June 1485. **23** 8 August 1485. **24** Above c.4. **25** 24 October 1485. **26** 21 July 1485.

8 Henry VII

Parliamentum tentum apud Dubliniam die veneris proximo post festum nativitatis Sancti Johannis Baptiste anno regni regis Henrici septimi octavo[1] coram Waltero archiepiscopo Dublinensi deputato Jasparis ducis Bedfordie et comitis Pembrockie locumtenentis domini regis terre sue Hibernie.

c.1

Item al requisicion dez communes que lou sire Rouland Eustace chivalier seignur de Portlester tarde chaunceller et thresourer dicest terre Dirland de veray displeasir ne et malice propsense qil avoit al tresreverend pier en Dieu Waltier erchevesque du Divelyn primat Dirland ad laboure et procure divers enquestes de ses mesmez tenauntz et aultres queux noes my dire ou faire ascun chose encountre sa entent et avoit le dit tresreverend pier en Dieu endite dez divers treisons feloniez trespasez offensez et contemptz sourmisez destre faitz par le dit erchevesque encountre le roy et sez leiez et avoit divers brevez de subpena directz al dit erchevesque et luy sour mesmez grevousment amercie par colour de quele le dit sire Roland fest tenerz lez temporalteez que le dit erchevesque avoit en Irland en lez mains nostre seignur le roy et lez issuez et proffites de eulx preigne et perceyve et divers aultres biens et chateulx del mesme erchevesque nient a petit somme saunz tout reason ou bon conscience al importable lesion et hindraunce de dit erchevek et graund diminucion a son astate et dignite; lez premissez considerez ordeine est enacte et estable par auctorite dicest present parlment que touz maners inquisicions enditementes presentementes verdites amercimentes recordes forfeturs et seisiers ewez ou prisez envers le dit erchevesque par quelconque non qil soit appelle ou nuncupe en lez premissez ou ascun de eulx et estauntz de recorde en ascun courte que le roy ad deins cest terre envers le dit erchevesque en ascun maner soient annullez revokez cassez et adjugez voids et de null enfect en ley; et par mesme lauctorite ordenie est enacte et establie que severels briefs hors du chauncerie soient directz sibien as justicez du bank du roy de sa terre Dirland et al chief clerk du mesme come al clerk ou gardein dez roulles del chauncerie en Irland et as thresourer et barons et chamberli[ns] del eschequir du roy et al chief remembracer du mesme et a chescun de eulx comaundaunt eux streitment en le non du roy et sour peyne du perdaunce de lour officez de dampner annuller canceller et faire voide touz maners tiels inquisicions enditementes presentementes amercimentes recordez seisiers et forfeturs et touz empechmentz jugementes entrees et exe[cucions] par reason de lez premissez et touz et chescun aultres briefs et commissions et recordez esteauntz en ascun manere de

1 28 June 1493.

Parliament held at Dublin on the Friday after the feast of the Nativity of St John the Baptist in the eighth year of the reign of king Henry the seventh [28 June 1493] before Walter, archbishop of Dublin, deputy of Jasper, duke of Bedford and earl of Pembroke, lieutenant of the lord the king of his land of Ireland.

c.1 [Annulment of all indictments and judgements against Walter, archbishop of Dublin]

Also, at the request of the commons, that whereas Sir Roland Eustace, knight, lord of Portlester, late chancellor and treasurer of this land of Ireland, out of the real hatred and malice aforethought which he bore to the very reverend father in God Walter, archbishop of Dublin, primate of Ireland, laboured and procured various inquisitions by his own tenants and others who do not dare to do or say anything against his intentions and had indicted the said very reverend father in God of various treasons, felonies, trespasses, offences and contempts alleged to have been committed by the said archbishop against the king and his laws and had directed various writs of *sub poena* to the said archbishop and grievously amerced him upon the same, on account of which the said Sir Roland caused the temporalities which the said archbishop had in Ireland to be held in the hands of our lord the king, and takes and receives the issues and profits thereof and various other goods and chattels of the same archbishop to no small amount without any reason or good conscience to the unbearable injury and hindrance of the said archbishop and great diminution of his estate and dignity; in consideration of the premises, it is ordained, enacted and established by authority of this present parliament that all kinds of inquisitions, indictments, presentments, verdicts, amercements, records, forfeitures and seizures had or taken against the said archbishop by whatsoever name that he be called or named in the premises or any of them, and being of record in any manner against the said archbishop in any court which the king has in this land, be annulled, revoked, quashed and adjudged void and of no effect in law; and by the same authority it is ordained, enacted and established that several writs out of the chancery be directed to the justices of the king's bench of his land of Ireland and to the chief clerk of the same, and to the clerk or keeper of the rolls of the chancery in Ireland and to the treasurer and barons and chamberlains of the king's exchequer and to the chief remembrancer of the same and to each of them, strictly commanding them in the king's name and under pain of loss of their offices to nullify, annul, cancel and make void all manner of such inquisitions, indictments, presentments, amercements, records, seizures and forfeitures and all impeachments, judgments, entries and executions by reason of the premises, and all and every other writs and com-

recorde devaunt eux en lez ditz courtz ou ascun de eulx envers le dit erchevesque pour ascun dez causez avauntditz en semblable maner et par la dit auctorite ordenie est enacte et estable que lez mains du roy soient ammovez de touz lez temporalteez le dit erchevesque et chescun parcell de eulx ove lour appurtenaunces et que le dit erchevesque soit restore as ditz temporalteez et chescun parcell de eulx ove lour appurtenaunces et a toutz biens et chatels apertenauntz a luy en ascun manere en semblable manere et fourme et semblable condicion come il fuit al temps du dit seisir ou forfaitur ou ascun temps donque apres et eulx et chescun parcell de eulx a aver perceiver tener et enjoier frankement a luy et a sez assignez saunz ascun empechement vexacion ou perturbacion de nostre soverain seignur le roy sez heirs officiers ou ministrez queuxconques entemps avener ascunz enditementes presentmentes verditz inquisicions forfeiturs seisiers ou assignementes al contrary faitz ou esteauntz de record en ascun dez ditz courtes nient obstauntz; et que par la dit auctorite ordenie est et enacte que le dit erchevesque par quelconque non qil soit nosme soit pardone et relesse de touz maners treisons feloniez trespasez contemptz et offensez queuxconques faitz par luy en ascun manere devaunt cestz heurs al nostre soverain seignur le roy encountre sez leiez et statutes et de touz maners dettz accomptz fins issuez forfeturs et amerciments queuxconques par le dit erchevesque severalment ou jointement ove ascuns aultrez persons ou persone devaunt cestz heurs a nostre dit soverain seignur le roy ou a ascun de sez noblez progenitours ou predecessours roiez de Engleterre duhement devauntes spectauntz ou purtenauntes en ascun maner ascun estatut act ou ordenaunce ou provision al contrary devaunt cestz heurs fait ou ordeine nient obstaunt.

c.2

Item al requisicion dez communez que lou sount divers beneficiez entour lez irrois enemiez du roy dez queux benefices le tresreverend pier en Dieu Watere erchevesque de Divelyn primat Dirland est patron par reson de son erchevesquery entour lez queux irrois enemiez la ne voilent les englois subjectes du roy a demorere ne enhabiter par reason de quell lavaundit erchevesque ne poet collater null englois clerk a null dez ditz benefices come ils fortunerount de estre voidez; in consideracion de quell ordenie establie et enacte est par auctorite dicest present parlment que le dit Waltere erchevesque et sez successours poient loialment collater et presenter a chescun dez ditz benefices esteauntz voidez ou en temps avener serrount fortunez destre voidez a ascun person dirrois nacion saunz ascun molestacion ou grevaunce de nostre soverain seignur le roy sez heirs officiers ou ministrez ou ascun aultre person ou persons

missions and records being in any manner of record against the said archbishop before them in the said courts or any of them for any of the causes aforesaid; in like manner and by the said authority it is ordained, enacted and established that the king's hands be removed from all the temporalities of the said archbishop and every part of them with their appurtenances, and that the said archbishop be restored to the said temporalities and every part of them with their appurtenances and to all goods and chattels in any manner belonging to him in the same manner and form and the same condition as it was at the time of the said seizure or forfeiture or at any time thereafter and to have, receive, hold and enjoy freely them and every parcel thereof to him and to his assigns without any hindrance, vexation or disturbance by our sovereign lord the king, his heirs, officers or ministers whomsoever in time to come, notwithstanding any indictments, presentments, verdicts, inquisitions, forfeitures, seizures or assignments to the contrary made or being of record in any of the said courts; and that by the said authority it is ordained and enacted that the said archbishop by whatever name that he be named, be pardoned and released of all manner of treasons, felonies, trespasses, contempts and offences whatsoever done by him in any manner before now to our sovereign lord the king contrary to his laws and statutes, and of all manner of debts, accounts, fines, issues, forfeitures and amercements whatsoever duly owing by the said archbishop severally or jointly with any other persons or person heretofore, belonging or appertaining to our said sovereign lord the king or to any of his noble progenitors or predecessors kings of England, in any manner, notwithstanding any statute, act or ordinance or provision to the contrary heretofore made or ordained.

c.2 [Licence for Irishmen to be presented to benefices]
Also, at the request of the commons, that whereas there are various benefices amongst the king's Irish enemies of which benefices the very reverend father in God, Walter, archbishop of Dublin, primate of Ireland, is patron by reason of his archbishopric and the king's English subjects are not willing to remain or dwell amongst which Irish enemies there; by reason of which the aforesaid archbishop cannot collate any English clerk to any of the said benefices when they happen to be vacant; in consideration of which it is ordained, established and enacted by authority of this present parliament that the said archbishop Walter and his successors may lawfully collate and present any person of Irish nation to every of the said benefices being vacant or which in time to come shall happen to be vacant, without any molestation or grievance by our sovereign lord the king, his heirs, officers or ministers or any other person or persons,

ascun act ou ordenaunce par auctorite du parlment ou graund counseill a contrary fait nient obstaunt.

c.3

Item al supplicacion de mair bailliffes et communes del cite de Waterford que lou ils ove divers enhabitauntes du dit cite sour ascuns faux feinez causez ou faulx sourmysez furent atteintz par auctorite du parlment en le temps du Gerot count de Kildare adonques esteaunt depute lieutenaunt Dirland en le reigne tresredoubte nostre soverain seignur quorest pour quelx atteindrez ils ount faitz[2] streit et due serch et ils ne poient en ascun maner destre trovez deins lez roullez ou recordez du roy en ascun de sez courtes pour que provise soit pur eulx en icell parte que par quelconque non come par non du mair bailliffes et communes ou par mair et communez ou ascun aultre manere polletique non cause ou quarell ils ou ascun de eux ou ascun dez enhabitauntz del dit cite devaunt cestz heurez furent atteintz en ascun maner a ascun temps du primere joure du moiz de novembre le primer an du reigne nostre soverain seignur le roy quorest[3] tanque al primer jour dicest present moiz[4] que toutz tiels maner atteindrez ou enditementis et toutz aultrez manerez actis ou ordenaunciz devaunt cestez heurez faitz prejudiciale as ditz maire bailliffes et communes par auctorite du cest parlement soient adnullez quassez et repellez et faitz voidez en ley a eulx et chescun de eulx ensi de estre beneficiale et al toutz maner enhabitauntis del dit citte en si ampil et large fourme come si chescun de eulx furent deinz cest act nommez et specifiez; et auxi en consideracion del nient doubte verite du perseveraunce et charge et burdon pur le mesme qils ount suffres il pleaset nostre dit soverain seignur de son tresnoble et habundaunt grace a ratifiere confirmer et approver toutz manerez lour auncient libertees privilegis custumez grauntes et usez par eulx ou lour predecessours mairez bailliffes et communez de Waterford usez enjoiez et custumez et oustre a graunter et doner a eulx ove aulterez divers maner grauntez auctoriteez liberteez et privilegis et en especiale entre aulterez auctorite et powere del deliveraunce de gaole du roy illeoques coket poundage et le annuele rent du xxx li. de le fee ferme de la dit citte al dit maire bailliffes et communes et al lour successours a toutz jours queulx grauntez furent enrollez en divers places del courtis du roy quore sount embesliez et ne purrount destre ewez; sour que lez premissez considerez[5] que accordaunt al memory et plesaunce del nostre dit soverain seignur que toutz manerez grauntez auctoriteez privilegis usez et custumez a eulx grauntez ou confirmez desoubtz le graunde seall Dengleterre ou

2 *fuitz* in transcript. 3 1 November 1485. 4 1 June 1493. 5 It appears that the words of enactment have been omitted here.

notwithstanding any act or ordinance to the contrary made by authority of parliament or great council.

c.3 [Indictments against the mayor, bailiffs and commons of Waterford city to be void]

Also, at the prayer of the mayor, bailiffs and commons of the city of Waterford, that whereas they with various inhabitants of the said city were attainted upon certain false pretended causes or false surmises by authority of parliament in the time of Gerald, earl of Kildare, then being deputy lieutenant of Ireland in the reign of our very redoubted sovereign lord that now is, for which attainders they have made strict and due search and they cannot in any way be found in the king's rolls or record in any of his courts; wherefore let it be provided for them in that behalf that by whatever name, either by name of the mayor, bailiffs and commons or by mayor and commons or any other manner of politic name, and for whatever cause or quarrel they or any of them or any of the inhabitants of the said city were heretofore attainted in any manner at any time from the first day of the month of November in the first year of the reign of our sovereign lord the king that now is [1 November 1485] until the first day of this present month [1 June 1493], that all such manner of attainders or indictments and all other manner of acts or ordinances heretofore made prejudicial to the said mayor, bailiffs and commons by authority of this parliament be annulled, quashed and repealed and made void in law, so as to be beneficial to them and every one of them and to all manner of inhabitants of the said city in as ample and large form as if every one of them were named and specified in this act; and also, in consideration of the undoubted truth of the consequence and charge and burden which they have suffered through the same, it has pleased our said sovereign lord of his very noble and abundant grace to ratify, confirm and approve all kinds of ancient liberties, privileges, customs, grants and usages used, enjoyed and accustomed by them or their predecessors, mayors, bailiffs and commons of Waterford, and further to grant and give to them, with various other kinds of grants, authorities, liberties and privileges and especially amongst other things the authority and power of delivery of the king's gaol there, cocket, poundage and the yearly rent of thirty pounds of the fee farm of the said city to the said mayor, bailiffs and commons and to their successors for ever, which grants were enrolled in various places of the king's courts and are now embezzled and cannot be had; upon which, in consideration of the premises, according to the remembrance and pleasure of our said sovereign lord, that all manner of grants, authorities, privileges, usages and customs granted or confirmed to them under the great seal of England or the great seal of Ireland by our said sovereign lord, his predecessors or progenitors

le graunde sele Dirland par nostre dit soverain seignur sez predecessours ou progenitours roiez Dengleterre soient par auctorite du cest present parlement grauntes ratifiez confirmez et approwez ove cest clause licet non fuerunt usi vel abusi ascun act ordynaunce ou graunt fait al contrary nient obstaunt.

c.4

Item al supplicacion de Morice Wise cittezein del citte de Waterford que laou il et sez auncestrez furent seisez en lour demesne come de fe taile du toutz lez terrez et tenementz en Ilany Ken' et Ballydermyd deinz le counte de Waterford jesques ore tarde temps fuit disseisie et par violente myse hors par lez rebelles du roy par le maintenaunce del graund seignurez cestassaver Richard Mc Shaun, Morice Mc Shaun, Robert Mc Shaun, Davi Mc Shaun, Thomas Mc Shaun et le possession dicele avount tenuz entaunt que le dit Morice Wyse ne poet pur doubt et le yeopardy da sa vie reentre ou regresse faire sur lez ditz terrez et ne poet estre remedie par le commen ley le roy illeoques en default du officerez et mynystres dicele jesques cel temps; en consideracion du cestez myschauncez est establie enacte et ordine que si lez ditz deforsourez ne apperent devaunt cel parlement proroge ou adjourne ou fynyshe que le dit Morice soit restore al possession du sez ditz terrez et tenementz ove lez damagez du lxxx li.; et auxi ordine est que si lez ditz persones ou ascun de eulx entra depuise sour le dit Morice en ascun du cestez ditz terrez ou tenementz qils et chescun de eulx forfet C s. en noun de peyn et pour le mesme et pour sez ditz damagis du aver accions du dett en ascun courte que le roy ad ascun act or ordynaunce fait al contrary neint obstaunt.

c.5

Item al supplicacion dez communez que lou en ascun parliament ou graund counsaill tenuz sibien deins cest terre Dirland come deins le realme Dengleterre touz manerez liberteez franchesez privelegez et customez ount [este][6] usez et grauntez a nostre mier Seint Esglise sount auctorisez approvez et confermez et auxi par auctorite de diverse parlmentes devaunt cestz heurs fuit ordeine et enacte que null manere extorcion coigne ne lyvere devoit estre prise ne usee ne en ascun manere mise sour ascun homme de Seint Esglise ne sour ascun enhabitaunt deins la glebe de Seint Esglise queux liberteez franchesez privilegz custumez et actes du parlment ensy grauntez a nostre dit mier

6 *este* omitted in transcript.

kings of England be granted, ratified, confirmed and approved by authority of this present parliament, with this clause "although they were not used or were abused", notwithstanding any act, ordinance or grant made to the contrary.

c.4 [Restoration of Maurice Wise to the lands of Islandikane and Ballydermody, Co. Waterford]

Also, at the petition of Maurice Wise, citizen of the city of Waterford, that whereas he and his ancestors were seised in their demesne as of fee tail of all the lands and tenements in Islandikane and Ballydermody in the county of Waterford until now in recent times he was disseised and expelled by violence by the king's rebels by the maintenance of the great lords, that is to say, Richard Mc Shaun, Maurice Mc Shaun, Robert Mc Shaun, Davi Mc Shaun, Thomas Mc Shaun and they had held possession thereof so that the said Maurice Wise, for doubt and peril of his life, cannot re-enter or return to the said lands, and cannot be remedied by the king's common law there in default of officers and ministers thereof up to this time; in consideration of these misfortunes, it is established, enacted and ordained that if the said deforcers do not appear before this parliament is prorogued or adjourned or finished, that the said Maurice be restored to the possession of his said lands and tenements with damages of eighty pounds; and it is also ordained that if the said persons or any of them afterwards shall enter upon the said Maurice in any of these said lands or tenements that they and every one of them shall forfeit one hundred shillings by way of penalty and that he shall have actions of debt for the same and for his said damages in any court which the king has, notwithstanding any act or ordinance made to the contrary.

c.5 [Confirmation of the liberties of the church]

Also, at the petition of the commons, that whereas in every parliament or great council held both in this land of Ireland and in the kingdom of England, all kinds of liberties, franchises, privileges and customs which have been used and granted to our mother Holy Church are authorised, approved and confirmed, and also by authority of various parliaments before now it was ordained and enacted that no manner of extortion, coign or livery should be taken or used or in any manner imposed upon any man of Holy Church nor upon any dweller in the glebe of Holy Church, which liberties, franchises, privileges, customs and acts of parliament so granted to our said mother Holy Church for the most part are broken and lost and despised by every temporal person at war within this land, not sparing or showing reverence to the altar where Our Blessed

Seint Esglise pour le greindre parte sount rumpuz et perduz et despisez ove chescun temporell persone usaunt la guerre deins cest terre nient parcauntz ne reverencez fesauntz ne aultere lou nostre benoit saviour Jesu Crist en fourme du payne est consecrate et agarder destre ministre en sacrament a chescun veray christien homme pour relief de sa alme il gisaunt en sez darreins jours nient puys que estoit une cotage dez porkes ou stye oultre abhominable a chescun veray christien homme de veer ou oier a graund displesir de Dieu et touz seintes queux par tout semblable presumpcion de graund miserie et plage queux cestz certains anez ount sour lez ditz communez en amendaunce de quell inhumane et dampnable extorsion ordeine est enacte et establie par auctorite dicest present parlment que nostre dit mier Seint Esglise et touz prelatz et spirituelx hommez et femmez de Seint Esglise et la glebe du mesme deins cest terre Dirland eient exercisent et enjoient touz maners liberteez franchisez privelegz a eulx et chescun de eulx du veile temps grauntz usez ou ewez et que par la dit auctorite touz maners estatutz actz du parlment provisions ou ordenauncez faitz ordeinez ou grauntez a nostre dit mier Seint Esglise ou ascun erchevesque evesque suffragan prelate clerk ou espirituell ministre del esglise auxibien deins le realme Dengleterre ou deinz cest terre Dirland par nostre soverain seignur le roy quorest ou ascun de sez noblez progenitours ou predecessours roiez Dengleterre par sez lettrez patentz ou lez lettrez patentz dascun de eulx a ascun temps ou par auctorite du parlment ou graund counsaill ou aultrement en ascun manere devaunt cest temps done ou graunte enacte approve ou conferme par auctorite dicest present parlement soit auctorise approve conferme et adjuge bon et effectual en ley pour lez ditz prelatz et persons du Seint Esglise et chescun de eulx ascun usage ou nient loiall mesprision ou ascun estatut act ou ordenaunce al contrary devaunt cestz heurs ewe use ou fait nient obstaunt et queuxconqzs persons ou person en apres entrude attempte ou fait ascun chose a contrary dez ditz liberteez franchesiez ou grauntz ou ascun de eulx ou encontre ascun spirituell persons ou person par auctorite dicest present parliment est deme et ajuge felon atteinte.

c.6[7]

Item al supplicacion du dean et chapeter du cathedrall esglise de Seint Patrik de Dyvelin entaunt que lez ditz esglise et college est du fundacion nostre soverain seignur le roy et le dit esglise et close en scite de terre stest en basse valey nient obstaunt par sage consideracion et dilligent provision lez ditz dean et chapeter eiauntz paour du violences dez ewez alivious dez flotz a sez graundez chargez et costagz pour le saufgard dez ditz esglise et close ount faitz

7 Printed in *Statutes at large.*

Saviour Jesus Christ is consecrated in the form of bread and kept to be administered in the sacrament to every true Christian man for relief of his soul, he lying in his last days, any more than if it were a house for pigs or sty, altogether abominable to every true Christian man to see or hear, to the great displeasure of God and all the saints, which through all such presumption have brought great misery and pestilence upon the said commons for some years; in amendment of which inhuman and damnable extortion it is ordained, enacted and established by authority of this present parliament that our said mother Holy Church and all the prelates and spiritual men and women of Holy Church and the glebe of the same in this land of Ireland have, exercise and enjoy all manner of liberties, franchises, privileges to them and every one of them in ancient times granted, used or had; and that by the said authority all manner of statutes, acts of parliament, provisions or ordinances made, ordained or granted to our said mother Holy Church or any archbishop, bishop, suffragan, prelate, clerk or spiritual minister of the church both in the kingdom of England and in this land of Ireland by our sovereign lord the king that now is or any of his noble progenitors or predecessors kings of England by his letters patent or the letters patent of any of them at any time, or by authority of parliament or great council or otherwise in any manner heretofore given or granted, enacted, approved or confirmed, by authority of this present parliament be authorised, approved, confirmed and adjudged good and effectual in law for the said prelates and persons of Holy Church and every one of them, notwithstanding any usage or unlawful misprision or any statute, act or ordinance to the contrary had, used or made heretofore; and whatsoever persons or person hereafter intrudes, attempts or does anything contrary to the said liberties, franchises or grants or any of them or against any spiritual persons or person by authority of this present parliament is deemed and adjudged an attainted felon.

c.6 [Dwellers on the Poddle river in Dublin to clean their tenements to prevent flooding]

Also, at the petition of the dean and chapter of the cathedral church of St Patrick of Dublin, because the said church and college is of the foundation of our sovereign lord the king and the site of land of the said church and close stands in a low valley, notwithstanding this, by wise consideration and diligent foresight, the said dean and chapter through fear of the violence of the alluvious waters of the floods, at their great charges and costs, for the safeguard of the said church and close have made various outlets and sewers for the free

diverse issuez et gowtez pour frank avoidaunce de touz tielx sodein flotes aunxi il fuit de viell temps et maintenaunt sount ij ryvers ou passages dez ewez un sour chescun partie de le strete du Seint Patrik appelle le Podell par que touz tielx ewez avoient loiall course et large passage saunz ascun empediment jesques ore tarde que lez ditz ryvers et Podels sount garriz et estoupez par enhabitauntz dez measons sour lez ditz Podels sibien enhabitauntz sour lez ditz podels en estopaill ou rettaill du stopaunce de lour measons come fune dez bestez come par ciroters et fruniters fesauntz fossez ou dampinges de ewe lour pelux en taunt qils ount estoupez ambedeux partez du Podell que le ewe ne purroit aver son loiall et frank course et passage entaunt que deins poy dez ans et tarde jours lez ditz esglise et college ount estez sourfluez ove graundez superfluiteez et habundaunce dez ewez al graund lesion et damages du ditz dean et chapeter et college; lez premissez considerez enacte est establie et ajuge par auctorite dicest present parlment que chescun homme qui demore ou enhabite ou eit meson ou shop' sour le dit Podell sour chescun parte dicell fait purger ou munder le dit rowm' et precinct du son tenement ou enhabitaunce al dit chanell sicome fuit de viell temps deins ij moisez apres cest present act passe sour pein de xx s. destre leve par le proktour del esglis de Seint Patrik avauntdit pour le temps esteaunt saunz ascun aultre auctorite ou impediment; et desor enavaunt sour la dit peyn en semblable manere destre leve que null homme ne fame par null mesnez estoupa ne distourba le cours et frank passage dez ditz ewez.

c.7

Item ad supplicacionem Walteri abbatis domus beate Marie virginis juxta Dubliniam et conventus eiusdem quod ubi tenentes sui parochie de Ballibaghill' nunquam fuerunt onerati nisi cum una biga ad hostilia viagia egressus vel itinera et iam istis duobus vel tribus annis fuerunt onerati cum duobus bigis in contrarium bonorum antiquorum usuum et consuetudinum premissis consideratis inactitatur et stabilitur auctoritate presentis parliamenti quod dicta parochia de Balybaghill' non sit onerata decetero nisi cum una biga et quod illa biga serviet predictis abbati et conventui et familiaribus suis proficiscentibus ad aliqua hostilia viagia egressus vel itinera in futurum; et si aliqua persona vel persone perturbent vel vexent dictos tenentes vel eorum aliquem in contrarium presentis actus quod tociens ipsi vel eorum aliquis taliter facient[8] forisfaciant decem libras medietate domino regi aliaque medietate dictis abbati et conventui reservata; et quod ipsi abbas et conventus habeant suam accionem debiti super dicta forisfactura in qualibet curia regia.

8 *facienda* in transcript.

draining of all such sudden floods, also there was in times past and now there are two rivers or passages of waters, one on each side of St Patrick's Street, called the Poddle, through which all such waters had lawful course and wide passage without any impediment until now recently the said rivers and Poddles are choked and stopped by the inhabitants of the houses on the said Poddles, both by those dwelling on the said Poddles stopping or casting stoppance, such as dung of beasts, out of their houses, and by glovers and tanners making ditches or dams to water their skins, inasmuch as they have stopped both parts of the Poddle so that the water cannot have its lawful and free course and passage and as a result for a few years past and recently the said church and college have been overflowed with great superfluities and abundance of waters to the great injury and damages of the said dean and chapter and college; in consideration of the premises, it is enacted, established and adjudged by authority of this present parliament that every man who dwells or inhabits or has a house or shop on either side of the said Poddle shall clear or cleanse the said space and precinct of his tenement or habitation to the said channel, as it was in times past, within two months after the passing of this present act, under pain of twenty shillings to be levied by the proctor of the church of Saint Patrick aforesaid, for the time being, without any other authority or impediment; and that henceforth no man or woman shall stop or disturb the course and free passage of the said waters by any means under the said pain, to be levied in like manner.

c.7 [Parish of Ballyboghil, co. Dublin, to supply only one horse cart when necessary for expeditions of war]

Also, at the petition of Walter, abbot of the house of the Blessed Virgin Mary near Dublin and the convent of the same, that whereas their tenants of the parish of Ballyboghil were never charged with more than one cart for warlike expeditions, sallies or journeys, and now for the past two or three years they have been charged with two carts contrary to the ancient good usages and customs; in consideration of the premises, it is enacted and established by authority of the present parliament that the said parish of Ballyboghil be charged henceforth only with one cart and that cart shall serve the aforesaid abbot and convent and their servants when going upon any warlike expeditions, sallies or journeys in future; and if any person or persons disturb or vex the said tenants or any of them contrary to the present act, that as often as they or any of them do so, they shall forfeit ten pounds, half reserved to the lord the king and the other half to the said abbot and convent, and that the said abbot and convent shall have their action of debt upon the said forfeiture in any of the king's courts.

c.8

Item ad supplicacionem Walteri abbatis domus beate Marie virginis juxta Dubliniam consideracione veri et fidelis obsequii quod idem abbas summo domino nostro regi qui nunc est impendit ordinatur inactitatur et stabilitur auctoritate presentis parliamenti quod dictus abbas perdonetur relaxetur et quiete exoneretur de omnibus et singulis prodicionibus feloniis murdris mesprisionibus contemptibus ac de omnibus aliis offensis per ipsum abbatem perpetratis et commissis ante hec tempora et eadem auctoritate idem actus sit ita beneficialis[9] eidem abbati consimili forma sicut ipse esset perdonatus sub magno sigillo regis Anglie; ac eadem auctoritate omnia et singula presentamenta indictamenta impeticiones inquisiciones utlagarie attincte seisine littere patentes donaciones vel concessiones inde facta vel aliquis processus habitus vel pendens racione premissorum vel alicuius eorum versus dictum abbatem revocetur repellatur et adjudicetur vacuum et de nullo effectu in lege; et eadem auctoritate omnia benivolencie adjutoria taxaciones vel alique alie imposiciones habite vel concesse de quibus dictus abbas dedit suum assensum vel concensum quod ipse inde perdonetur relaxetur et quiete inde exoneretur aliquo actu statuto materia vel causa in contrarium premissorum seu alicuius eorundem non obstante.

c.9

Item al supplicacion de Richard Tirrell gentilman que lou come il est seisie de certains mesez et iij^{xx} acrez de terre arable ove lez appurtenaunt[es][10] en Balydowd' del parish de Eskirre en le counte de Dyvelyn en son demesne come de fee queux terrez sount tenuz de nostre soverain seignur le roy come de son manoir de Eskirre avauntdit par service et fealte de xliij s. et iiij d. de annuel rent le quell terre maintenaunt gist gaste et dekaie par reason du guerre et extorcion de coigne et lyvere que ad longement continue en le mesme ensy que le dit Richard est semblable de estre disherite del proffite du dit terre sinon qil soit remedie; lez premissez considerez et le beucoup et plusours bonz servicez queux le dit Richard ad fait a nostre dit soverain seignur en sez guerrez come aultrement et ensy entend de continuer et que le dit annuell rent est sy graund et lez ditz chargez du coigne et lyvere considerez ensemblement al entent que lez ditz mesez et terrez purroient estre reedifiez et tillez enacte est et establie par auctorite dicest present parlement que lez ditz mesez et lx acrez du terre soient dischargez del dit annuell rent duraunt le space de lx ans prochiens apres cest present act; et que le dit Richard et sez heirs purroient loialment faire rescous as fermours ou receyvours du dit terre pour le temps esteauntz dascun

9 *beneficial* in transcript. 10 Transcript torn.

c.8 [Pardon to the abbot of St Mary's, Dublin, of all treasons and other offences]

Also, at the petition of Walter, abbot of the house of the Blessed Virgin Mary near Dublin, in consideration of the true and faithful service which the same abbot has rendered to his highness our lord the king that now is, it is ordained, enacted and established by authority of the present parliament that the said abbot be pardoned, released and fully exonerated of all and singular treasons, felonies, murders, misprisions, contempts and of all other offences before now perpetrated and committed by the same abbot; and by the same authority, that the same act be as beneficial to the same abbot in like form as if he had been pardoned under the king's great seal of England; and by the same authority that all and singular presentments, indictments, impeachments, inquisitions, outlawries, attainders, seisins, letters patent, gifts or grants thereupon made or any process had or pending by reason of the premises or any of them against the said abbot be revoked, repealed and adjudged void and of no effect in law; and by the same authority, that he be pardoned, released and fully exonerated of all benevolences, aids, taxes or any other impositions had or granted concerning which the said abbot gave his assent or consent, notwithstanding any act, statute, matter or cause to the contrary of the premises or of any of them.

c.9 [Ballydowd in the parish of Esker, co. Dublin, to be discharged from payment of rent]

Also, at the petition of Richard Tirrell, *gentilman*, that whereas he is seised in his demesne as of fee of certain messuages and sixty acres of arable land with the appurtenances in Ballydowd in the parish of Esker in the county of Dublin, which lands are held of our sovereign lord the king as of his manor of Esker aforesaid, by service and fealty of forty-three shillings and four pence of yearly rent, which land now lies waste and decayed by reason of war and extortion of coign and livery which has long continued in the same, so that the said Richard is likely to be disinherited of the profit of the said land unless he be redressed; in consideration of the premises and the great and many good services which the said Richard has done to our said sovereign lord in his wars and otherwise and so intends to continue and in consideration likewise of the fact that the said yearly rent is so great and the said charges of coign and livery, to the intent that the said messuages and lands may be rebuilt and tilled, it is enacted and established by authority of this present parliament that the said messuages and sixty acres of land be discharged of the said yearly rent for sixty years after this present act, and that the said Richard and his heirs may lawfully make rescue from the farmers or receivers of the said land for the time being of any distress to be taken for the said yearly rent without any hindrance thereof to be had against

distresse apprendiers pour le dit annuell rent saunz ascun empechement ent destre ewe envers le dit Richard et sez heirs durauntz lez ditz lx ans par nostre dit soverain seignur le roy sez heirs officers ou ministrez queuxconques.

C.10

Item al requisicion dez seignurez spirituals et temporals et communez del counte de Kilkeny et Waterford que lou ils de jour en aultre sount robbez et expellez de lour biens et terrez [par][11] riotment disposez personez par le colour du droit feyne ou surmyse pur lez queulx lesions ils ne purrount faire nule maner sute ou labours a tout temps as officerez du roy en cestez partiez pur paoure et daunger et perile du chymyn et en maner saunz remedy a sibien labrigement dez revenuz issuez et profitez du roy come a lour oultre myschaunce et disheeritaunce; lez premissez considerez a purveuer establyer et enacte que tresdiscrete sage[12] person del counseill du roy soit ordinie et fait commissioner et justice del dit counte la a mynystrer et determyner lez leyez du roy en chescun causez entre eulx a tout temps du necessite pur que ils conust treshable expedient et necessare pur la honoure du roy et lour commen profite Johan Wyse chief baron del eschekere du roy quele Johan ils priount destre admyse ordine et depute justice du mesme par auctorite du cest present parlement duraunt sa vie accordaunt a un patent sour icele destre fete en si ample et large fourme come il purroit estre le quele Johan en consideracion de premissez par auctorite de cest parlement est admyse et depute.

C.11

Item al requisicion dez communes que toutz et chescun maner graunt ou grauntis du rent charges annuytees pensions lesez pur terme du vie ou anez grauntes du officez du constabulry seneschalry viscount ou dascun aultre maner officez ewez ou grauntez en ascun maner a ascun person ou persones par le tresnoble seignur du benoit memory Jamys jaditz count de Ormond et Johan son fitz jaditz count de Ormond et chescun de eulx par auctorite du cest present parlement soient resumez revokez repellez et adjugez voyed et de nule effect en ley en semble maner sicome jammez ascun tiel graunte ou grauntes et toutz aulterez premissez et chescun de eulx ewe fait ou graunte ascun act statute mater cause ou restreint al contrary fait ou ordeine nient obstaunt purvieu toutz foitz que cest act de resumpcion nextend my ne en ascun maner

11 *et* in transcript. 12 Berry's note: *sage* repeated in roll.

the said Richard and his heirs during the said sixty years by our said sovereign lord the king, his heirs, officers or ministers whomsoever.

c.10 [John Wyse, chief baron of the exchequer, to be appointed special justice in cos. Kilkenny and Waterford]

Also, at the request of the lords spiritual and temporal and commons of the county of Kilkenny and Waterford, that whereas they are from day to day robbed and expelled from their goods and lands by riotously disposed persons by reason of feigned or pretended right, for which injuries they cannot make any manner of suit or labours at any time to the king's officers in those parts, through fear and the danger and peril of the road, and are in a manner without redress both to the diminution of the king's revenues, issues and profits and to their utter misfortune and disinheritance; in consideration of the premises, to provide, establish and enact that a very discreet wise person of the king's council be appointed and made commissioner and justice of the said county, to administer and determine the king's laws there in all causes between them at all times of necessity, for which they know John Wyse, chief baron of the king's exchequer, to be very skilful, expedient and necessary for the king's honour and their common profit, and they pray that John may be admitted, appointed and deputed justice of the same by authority of this present parliament during his life, according to a patent thereupon to be made in as ample and large form as may be, which John, in consideration of the premises, by authority of this parliament is admitted and deputed.

c.11 [Resumption of grants made by James, earl of Ormond, and John, earl of Ormond]

Also, at the request of the commons, that all and every manner of grant or grants of rent-charges, annuities, pensions, leases for term of life or years, grants of the offices of constable, seneschal, sheriff or of any other manner of offices had or granted in any manner to any person or persons by the very noble lord of blessed memory, James, late earl of Ormond, and John his son, late earl of Ormond, and each of them, by authority of this present parliament be resumed, revoked, repealed and adjudged void and of no effect in law in like manner as if any such grant or grants and all other premises and every one of them had never been had, made or granted, notwithstanding any act, statute, matter, cause or restraint made or ordained to the contrary; provided always that this act of resumption do not extend or be in any way prejudicial to any

soit prejudiciale a ascun graunt ou don fait ou graunt a Nicholas Tournoure gentilman en et de le office du chief justice de liberte de Typerary.

c.12

Item al supplicacion du Edward Bermyngham gentilman que lou le dit Edward et sez auncestrez furent seisez du le office du chief serjaunt du le counte du Mithe hors du temps du memory ceste nient obstaunt le dit Edward et sez auncestrez furent par divers temps vexez et troublez en le dit office contrarie al droit et conscience; lez premissez considerez est ordeine enacte et establie par auctorite du cest parlement que le dit Edward avera occupiera et enjoiera le office du chef serjaunty du le counte du Mithe a luy et sez heirs a toutz jours ascun act ordenaunce ou graunt faitz a contrarie a ascun aultre person ou persons nient obstauntz et que le dit Edward et sez heirs et le dit office soient quietez et clarement dischargez de toutz maner seisiez forfetz et toutz sommes du mone que sount encurrez ou passez sur le dit office en ascun courte que le roy eit.

c.13

Item al requisicion dez communez ordeine est enacte et establie par auctorite du cest present parlement qil soit loiall a tresreverend pier en Dieu Water archevesque du Dyvelin depute lieutenaunt Dirland de provyser toutz et chescun maner person et persons pur ascun manere graunt ou grauntz actz du parlement faitz par nostre soverain seignur le roy qui ore est ou ascun de sez noble progenitours ou predecessours si bene desoubz le graund sele de Engleterre come desoubz le graund sele Dirland ou par auctorite du parlement graund conseill ou aultrement a toutz foitz a son plesire jeques cest present parlement serra dissolue; et que nule act[13] fait en cest present parlement soit prejudiciall as tils persons ou person pur queux le dit tresreverend piere en Dieu depute lieutenaunt provysera jesques cest present parlement serra dissolver.

13 *aut* in transcript.

grant or gift made or granted to Nicholas Tornoure, *gentilman*, in and of the office of chief justice of the liberty of Tipperary.

c.12 [Edward Bermingham and his heirs to have the office of chief serjeant of co. Meath]

Also, at the petition of Edward Bermyngham, *gentilman*, that whereas the said Edward and his ancestors were, since beyond the time of memory, seised of the office of chief serjeant of the county of Meath, notwithstanding this, the said Edward and his ancestors were at various times vexed and troubled in the said office contrary to right and conscience; in consideration of the premises, it is ordained, enacted and established by authority of this parliament that the said Edward shall have, occupy and enjoy the office of the chief serjeanty of the county of Meath to him and his heirs for ever, notwithstanding any act, ordinance or grant to the contrary made to any other person or persons; and that the said Edward and his heirs and the said office be quit and clearly discharged of all manner of seizures, forfeitures and all sums of money which are incurred or passed upon the said office in any of the king's courts.

c.13 [Deputy lieutenant empowered to make provisos until the dissolution of the present parliament]

Also, at the request of the commons, it is ordained, enacted and established by authority of this present parliament that it be lawful for the very reverend father in God, Walter, archbishop of Dublin, deputy lieutenant of Ireland, to provide[1] all and every manner of person and persons for any manner of grant or grants or acts of parliament made by our sovereign lord the king that now is or any of his noble progenitors or predecessors, both under the great seal of England and under the great seal of Ireland or by authority of parliament, great council or otherwise, at all times at his pleasure until this present parliament shall be dissolved, and that no act made in this present parliament be prejudicial to such persons or person for whom the said very reverend father in God, the deputy lieutenant, shall provide until this present parliament shall be dissolved.

1 i.e. to make provisos in favour of.

c.14

Item al supplicacion de Clement Fitzlenes de Divelyn gentilman que laou un frere James Ketyng priour de hospitall du Seint Johan Jerusalem en Irland et lez confreers dicel lieu par lour fait desouth loure commen seall portaunt date le tierce jour de jully lan du Nostre Seignur Jesu Crist MCCCClxxvij[14] donerount et graunterount a lavaundit Clement un annuell rent de xx marces destre leyverez et parceyverez annuelment de toutz lez terres et tenementz in Clonetarffe deins le countie de Divelyn as deux termes del an cestassavoir as festes du Seint Michell et Pasch' par ewels porcions a aver et teigner le dit annuel rent al avauntdit Clement tanque il ad resceive de lez ditz terrez et tenementz lez ditz xx marcez laou lavauntdit priour longtemps devaunt le dit graunt fait al dit Clement dimist et grauntest lez ditz terrez a ferme pur certaine ans a un William Porter et Johan Bekete rendantz annuelment al dit priour et cez successours xviij li. as deux termes de lan cestassavoir ix li. al fest de Seint Michell larchangell et ix li. al fest de Pac' de quell terme ils ount treis ans aveners et pluis issint que vostre suppliaunt ne poet my distreigner durant le dit terme laou le dit priour promytta que le dit Clement receiveroit le prochien terme puis le dit graunt; lez premissez considerez soit il ordeigne enacte et establie par lauctorite de cest present parliament que le dit William Porter et Johan Beket face paiement et contenter le dit Clement ix li. al fest de Pac' prochien avener parcell de lez ditz xviij li. lez queux ilz paiount annuelment al dit priour et iiij li. vj s. viij d. parcell de lez ditz ix li. al fest de Seint Michell larchangell adonqs prochein ensuauntz parcell de lez ditz ix li. lez queux serront duez al dit fest lez queux ix li. iiij li. vj s. viij d. amounta al somme de xx marces desuis reherse; et par mesme lauctorite que le paiement de lez ditz sommes a le dit Clement soit sufficiant discharge devers le dit priour et cez successours pur lez ditz William et John; et si le dit priour vexera ou troublera lez ditz William et Johan pur lez ditz sommez quil forfaita a le dit suppliaunt xx li. tantost quil issint facera; et par mesme lauctorite que le dit Clement poet loialment distreigner en toutz lez ditz terrez et tenementz puis chescun de lez avauntditz festis pour le noun paiement de lez ditz sommes et chescun parcell deux et le dit distreint a reteigner et a garder tanque qil soit contente de lez ditz sommes et chescun parcell dicell; et si le dit priour ou ascun autre person ou persone disturbe ou interupt le dit Clement a distreigner en lez ditz terrez pur lez ditz sommes ou chescun parcell dicell ou face rescuce quil ou ils queux issint facent forfaitent xl li. a lavauntdit Clement; et que le dit Clement puisseit aver accion de dette en chescun court que le roy ad par breve ou par bille pur lez ditz xl li. issint forfaitz et que null maner discharge de lez

14 3 July 1477.

c.14 [William Porter and John Beker to pay rents to Clement fitz Lenes of Dublin]

Also, at the petition of Clement fitz Lenes of Dublin, *gentilman*, that whereas one brother James Ketyng, prior of the hospital of St John of Jerusalem in Ireland and the brothers of that place, by their deed under their common seal bearing date the third day of July in the year of Our Lord Jesus Christ 1477, gave and granted to the aforesaid Clement a yearly rent of twenty marks to be levied and received yearly out of all the lands and tenements in Clontarf in the county of Dublin at two terms in the year, that is to say, at the feasts of St Michael and Easter, by equal portions, to have and to hold the said yearly rent to the aforesaid Clement until he has received the said twenty marks from the said lands and tenements; and whereas the aforesaid prior, long before the said grant was made to the said Clement, demised and granted the said lands to farm for a certain number of years to one William Porter and John Beket, paying annually to the said prior and his successors eighteen pounds at two terms of the year, that is to say, nine pounds at the feast of St Michael the archangel and nine pounds at the feast of Easter, of which term they have three years and more to come, so that your suppliant cannot distrain during the said term; and whereas the said prior promised that the said Clement would receive the next term after the said grant; in consideration of the premises, be it ordained, enacted and established by authority of this present parliament that the said William Porter and John Beket pay and satisfy the said Clement nine pounds at the feast of Easter next coming, part of the said eighteen pounds which they pay yearly to the said prior, and four pounds, six shillings and eight pence, part of the said nine pounds, at the feast of St Michael the archangel then next following, part of the said nine pounds which will be due at the said feast, which nine pounds and four pounds, six shillings and eight pence will amount to the sum of twenty marks above rehearsed; and by the same authority that the payment of the said sums to the said Clement be a sufficient discharge towards the said prior and his successors for the said William and John; and if the said prior shall vex or trouble the said William and John for the said sums, that he shall forfeit to the said petitioner twenty pounds whenever he does so; and by the same authority that the said Clement may lawfully distrain in all the said lands and tenements after each of the aforesaid feasts for the non-payment of the said sums and every part of them and retain and keep the said distress until he be satisfied of the said sums and every part of them; and if the said prior or any other person or persons disturb or interrupt the said Clement in distraining in the said lands for the said sums or every part of them or make rescue that he or they who do so shall forfeit forty pounds to the aforesaid Clement; and that the said Clement may have an action of debt for the said forty pounds so forfeited in every court which the king has, by writ or by bill, and that no manner

ditz xviij li. faitz ou donez par le dit prioure ou cez successours a lez ditz William et Johan soit available ne effectuell.

c.15

Item al supplicacion du Philipp Flatisbery gentilman fitz et heir al Cristofor Flatisbery jaditz seignur du Osberteston' en le counte de Kildare que lou un Symon Flatisbery fuit seisy en son demesne come de fee du une mese et iij caruez de terre en Osberteston' ove lour appurtenaunces une mese et iij charuez de terre en Johaneston' ove lour appurtenaunces une mese et j charue de terre en Palmereston' ove lour appurtenaunces une mese et lij acres de terre et iij li. et xiiij s. du chiefrent en Yagoston' juxt le Naas ove lour appurtenaunces le quel Symon ensy dent estent seisy dona et graunta al sire Johan Cornic' et Richard fitz Rere chapelleynes toutz lez ditz mesez terrez tenementez chiefrentes et services ove lour appurtenaunces a aver et tenir toutz lez ditz mesez terrez tenementes rentes et servicez ove lour appurtenaunces al dit Johan et Richard et lour heirez a toutz jours par vertue de quel don lez ditz Johan et Richard furent seisez en lour demesne come de fee de toutz lez ditz mesez terres tenementz rentes et servicez ove lour appurtenaunces; et lez ditz Johan et Richard ensy dent estant seisi dona et graunta touts lez ditz mesez terres tenementes rentes et servicez ove lour appurtenaunces al dit Symon a aver et tenir toutz lez ditz mesez terres tenementes rentes et services ove lour appurtenaunces al dit Symon pur terme de sa vie apres quel morte que adonqes toutz lez ditz mesez terres tenementes rentes et services ove lour appurtenaunces remanderount al Henry Flatisbery leisne fitz al dit Symon a aver et tenir toutz lez mesez terres tenementes rentes et services ove lour appurtenaunces al dit Henry et sez heires masculez du son corps veynaunt; et si avient le dit Henry a morire saunce heirez masculez du son corps veynaunte que adonques toutz lez ditz mesez terres tenementes rentes et services ove lour appurtenaunces remanderount al Robert Flatisbery son frere a aver et tenir toutz lez ditz mesez terres tenementes rentes et services ove lour appurtenaunces al dit Roberte et sez heires masculez de son corps veynaunte; et sil vient le dit Roberte morire saunce heirez masculez de son corps veynaunte que adonques toutz lez ditz mesez terres tenementes rentes et services ove lour appurtenaunces remanderount as droiturels heirs du le dit Symon a toutz jours par vertue de quele don le dit Symon fuit seisy du ditz lez mesez terres tenementes rentes et services ove lour appurtenaunces en son demesne come de frantenement le dit Henry avoit issue mascule Richard et morist vyvaunte le dit Symon et tantost apres le dit Symon morist apres quel mourt le dit Richard en toutz lez ditz mesez terres tenementes rentes et servicez ove lour appurtenaunces entra et du cele fuist seisy en son demesne come de fee taill par vertue du don avauntdit et du cele morist seisi saunce heirez masculez

of discharge of the said eighteen pounds made or given by the said prior or his successors to the said William and John shall be valid or effectual.

c.15 [John and Margaret fitz John to appear to show title to Osberstown and other lands in co. Kildare]

Also, at the petition of Philip Flatisbery, *gentilman*, son and heir of Christopher Flatisbery, formerly lord of Osberstown in the county of Kildare, that whereas one Simon Flatisbery was seised in his demesne as of fee of one messuage and three ploughlands in Osberstown with their appurtenances, one messuage and three ploughlands in Johnstown with their appurtenances, one messuage and one ploughland in Palmerstown with their appurtenances, one messuage and fifty-two acres of land and three pounds and four shillings of chief rent in Yagostown near Naas with their appurtenances; which Simon being so thereof seised gave and granted to Sir John Cornic and Richard fitz Rere, chaplains, all the said messuages, lands, tenements, chief rents and services, with their appurtenances, to have and to hold all the said messuages, lands, tenements, rents and services with their appurtenances to the said John and Richard and their heirs for ever; by virtue of which gift the said John and Richard were seised in their demesne as of fee of all the said messuages, lands, tenements, rents and services, with their appurtenances; and the said John and Richard so being seised thereof gave and granted all the said messuages, lands, tenements, rents and services with their appurtenances to the said Simon, to have and to hold all the said messuages, lands, tenements, rents and services, with their appurtenances to the said Simon for the term of his life, and after whose death all the said messuages, lands, tenements, rents and services with their appurtenances should remain to Henry Flatisbery, the eldest son of the said Simon, to have and to hold all the messuages, lands, tenements, rents and services with their appurtenances, to the said Henry and his heirs male of his body issuing; and if it should happen that the said Henry die without heir male of his body issuing, that then all the said messuages, lands, tenements, rents and services, with their appurtenances should remain to Robert Flatisbery, his brother, to have and to hold all the said messuages, lands, tenements, rents and services, with their appurtenances to the said Robert and his heirs male of his body issuing; and if it should happen that the said Robert died without heirs male of his body issuing, that then all the said messuages, lands, tenements, rents and services, with their appurtenances should remain to the right heirs of the said Simon for ever; by virtue of which gift the said Simon was seised of the said messuages, lands, tenements, rents and services, with their appurtenances, in his demesne as of freehold; the said Henry had issue male, Richard, and died in the lifetime of the said Simon and shortly afterwards the said Simon died;

du son corps aveynaunte apres quele mourt le dit Roberte en toutz lez ditz mesez terres tenementes rentes et services ove lour appurtenaunces entra et du cele fuit seisi en son demesne come de fee taile par vertue du don avauntdit et avoit issue male du son corps aveynaunte Patrik et Philipp et du cele morist seisi apres quele mourt le dit Patrik come fitz et heir al dit Roberte en toutz lez ditz mesez terres tenementes rentes et services ove lour appurtenaunces entra et du cele fuit seisi en son demesne come de fee taile par vertue du dit don et avoit issue male Jamys et du cele morist seisi apres quel mourt le dit Jamys come fitz et heir al dit Patrik en toutz lez ditz mesez terres tenementes rentes et services ove lour appurtenaunces entra et du cele fuit seisy a son demesne come de fee taile par vertue du dit don et avoit issue male Thomas et du cele morist seisi apres quel mourt le dit Thomas come fitz et heir al dit Jamys en toutz lez ditz mesez terres tenementes rentes et services ove lour appurtenaunces entra et du cele fuit seisie en son demesne come de fee tail par vertue du dit don et du cele morist seisie saunce heir male de son corps aveynaunt apres quel mourt donques le dit Cristofor Flatisbery pier al dit Philipp Flatisbery come cosyn et heir al dit Thomas cestasaver fitz al dit Philipp fitz al dit Roberte en toutz lez ditz mesez terres tenementes rentes et services ove lour appurtenaunces entra et du cele fuit peisiblement[15] seisie en son demesne come de fee taile par vertue du dit don et auxi le dit Philipp fuit seisi en son demesne come de fee du j charue de terre en le Moche Fournaght ove lour appurtenaunce et du xxxvij acrez de terre en Poncheston' juxt le Naas ove lour appurtenaunces deinz le counte de Kildare le quel Philipp ensy dent estaunt seisi dona et graunta al Richard Flatisbery vikery de Kildroght et Nicholas Alger[16] vikery de la Naas toutz lez ditz parcellez du terre ove lour appurtenaunces a aver et tenir toutz lez ditz terrez ove lour appurtenaunces al ditz Richard et Nicholas et sez heires a toutz jours par vertue de quel don lez ditz Richard et Nicholas furent seisiez en lour demesne come de fee du toutz lez ditz terrez ove lour appurtenaunces; et lez ditz Richard et Nicholas ensy dent estant seisez tantost apres le dit Nicholas morist apres quel mourt le dit Richard enfeffa en et du toutz lez ditz terrez ove lour appurtenaunces le dit Cristofor come fitz et heir al dit Philipp a aver et tenir toutz lez ditz terrez ove lour appurtenaunces al dit Cristofor sez heirs et assignes a toutz jours par vertue du quel feffament le dit Cristofor pier al dit Philipp fuit pesiblement seisy en son demesne come de fee de toutz lez ditz terrez ove lour appurtenaunces jesques un Johan fitz Johan aultrement appelle Shan Mc Shan et Margaret sa fesme viendront ove force et armez le sabbat dye prochien devaunt le feste du Corpus Christi lan du regne du roy Henry le vj xxxvij[17] en fourme du guerre ove graunde multitude du lez irroiez enemyez du roy et englissh rebellez

15 Berry's note: *peisiblement* interlined in roll. 16 Berry's note: *Alger* interlined in roll. 17 20 May 1459.

after whose death the said Richard entered into all the said messuages, lands, tenements, rents and services, with their appurtenances and was seised thereof in his demesne as of fee tail by virtue of the aforesaid gift and died seised thereof without heir male of his body issuing; after whose death the said Robert entered into all the said messuages, lands, tenements, rents and services, with their appurtenances and was seised thereof in his demesne as of fee tail by virtue of the aforesaid gift and had issue male of his body issuing, Patrick and Philip, and died seised thereof; after whose death the said Patrick, as son and heir to the said Robert, entered into all the said messuages, lands, tenements, rents and services with their appurtenances and was seised thereof in his demesne as of fee tail by virtue of the said gift and had issue male, James, and died seised thereof; after whose death the said James, as son and heir to the said Patrick, entered into all the said messuages, lands, tenements, rents and services with their appurtenances, and was seised thereof in his demesne as of fee tail by virtue of the said gift and had issue male, Thomas, and died seised thereof; after whose death the said Thomas, as son and heir to the said James, entered into all the said messuages, lands, tenements, rents and services with their appurtenances and was seised thereof in his demesne as of fee tail by virtue of the said gift and died seised thereof without heir male of his body issuing; after whose death then the said Christopher Flatisbery, father of the said Philip Flatisbery, as cousin and heir of the said Thomas, that is to say, as son of the said Philip, son of the said Robert, entered into all the said messuages, lands, tenements, rents and services with their appurtenances and was peaceably seised thereof in his demesne as of fee tail by virtue of the said gift; and also the said Philip was seised in his demesne as of fee of one ploughland in Forenaghts Great, with its appurtenances and of thirty-seven acres of land in Punchestown near Naas, with their appurtenances, in the county of Kildare, which Philip being so seised thereof gave and granted to Richard Flatisbery, vicar of Celbridge, and Nicholas Alger, vicar of Naas, all the said parcels of land with their appurtenances to have and to hold all the said lands with their appurtenances to the said Richard and Nicholas and their heirs for ever; by virtue of which gift the said Richard and Nicholas were seised in their demesne as of fee of all the said lands with their appurtenances; and the said Richard and Nicholas so being seised thereof, soon afterwards the said Nicholas died; after whose death the said Richard enfeoffed the said Christopher as son and heir of the said Philip, in and of all the said lands with their appurtenances, to have and to hold all the said lands with their appurtenances to the said Christopher, his heirs and assigns for ever; by virtue of which feoffment the said Christopher, father of the said Philip was peaceably seised in his demesne as of fee of all the said lands with their appurtenances until one John fitz John, otherwise called Shan Mc Shan, and Margaret his wife, came with force and

et par le mayntenaunce du lez Gerrotyns entra et luy disseisia come en le droit du dit Margaret sa femme et luy ousta hors de sa possession de touz lez ditz mesez terrez tenementes rentes services ove lour appurtenaunces et ensy le dit Johan fitz Johan et le dit Margaret sa femme occupierent et receverent toutz maner issuez rentes et profitez de toutz lez ditz mesez terres tenementes rentes et services ove lour appurtenaunces a cele jour jesques al cel temps et ceo saunce droit ley ou conscience eiantez null maner devidence ne title amonstrer pur eux que est al finall anientisment du dit Philipp sil ne soit remedy; lez premissez considrez ordeine est enacte et establie par auctorite du cest present parliament que le dit Johan fitz Johan et le dit Margaret sa femme devyendra et appieria en lour propre person ou personez en le xv du Seint Michell larchangell prochein avenaunte[18] ou[19] al chastell le roy du Divelyn et illoques ils adonques a rendre lour corpsez al garde du constabill du dit chastell saunz baill ou maynprice jesques le droit et title du lez premissez soient determinez par le triell et jugement du le juge ou juges de le commen place du roy en Irland; et par mesme auctorite que lez ditz juge ou juges de aver pleyn power a trier determiner et juger lez premissez et que le determinacion et jugement du ditz juge ou juge serra de sy taunte force en ley come sy fuerent determiner par le course du commen ley en ycele parte; et si le dit Johan fitz Johan et le dit Margaret sa femme ny veynaunt le dit jour al dit chastell sy come est avauntdit que adonques par le dit auctorite du cest dit parliament quils et chescun deux lour heires et assignez du chescun deux soient oulterment exclusez et deperderent lour droit title et claym du lez premissez a toutz yours queux ils avoient ou claymount al aver al toutz lez ditz mesez terres tenementes rentes et services ove lour appurtenaunces ou en aschun parcell ducele; et sur ycele soit loyalment al dit Philipp al entra a aver occupier et enjoier toutz dez ditz mesez terres tenementes rentes et services ove lour appurtenaunces acordaunte al lez premissez en toutz chosez sy come est devaunte reherse; purveue tout foitz par le mesme auctorite que lou come Mathow Bath come en le droit du Anastace sa femme soer al dit Margaret clayme title al lez premissez quils veynent et apperent le dit jour sy come est avauntdit al monstrer lour title du lez premissez et si ils ne veynent que par le mesme auctorite ils forfeta[20] lour droit du premissez forspris lez terres et tenementez du Mathow Bath acordaunt al ley.

18 13 October 1493. **19** Thus in transcript. **20** Berry's note: *forteta* in roll.

arms on the Saturday before the feast of Corpus Christi in the thirty-seventh year of the reign of king Henry the sixth [20 May 1459], in form of war, with a great multitude of the king's Irish enemies and English rebels, and by the maintenance of the Geraldines, entered and disseised him as in right of the said Margaret his wife and ousted him from his possession of all the said messuages, lands, tenements, rents and services with their appurtenances; and so the said John fitz John and the said Margaret his wife occupy and receive all manner of issues, rents and profits of all the said messuages, lands, tenements, rents and services with their appurtenances from that day to now and this without right, law or conscience, having no manner of evidence or title to show therefor, which is to the utter destruction of the said Philip unless he be redressed; in consideration of the premises, it is ordained, enacted and established by authority of this present parliament that the said John fitz John and the said Margaret his wife shall come and appear in their own person or persons on the quindene of St Michael the archangel next [13 October 1493] at the king's castle of Dublin, and there they then shall surrender their bodies to the custody of the constable of the said castle without bail or mainprise until the right and title of the premises be determined by the trial and judgment of the judge or judges of the king's common bench in Ireland; and by the same authority that the said judge or judges shall have full power to try, determine and judge the premises, and that the determination and judgment of the said judge or judges shall be of as great force in law as if they were determined by the course of the common law in that behalf; and if the said John fitz John and the said Margaret his wife do not come on the said day to the said castle as is aforesaid that then, by the said authority of this said parliament, they and each of them and the heirs and assigns of each of them, shall be totally excluded and shall lose their right, title and claim to the premises for ever, which they had or claim to have to all the said messuages, lands, tenements, rents and services with their appurtenances or in any parcel thereof; and it shall be lawful for the said Philip to enter thereon, to have, occupy and enjoy all the said messuages, lands, tenements, rents and services with their appurtenances according to the premises in all things as is before rehearsed; provided always by the same authority that whereas Matthew Bath, as in right of Anstace his wife, sister to the said Margaret, claims title to the premises, that they come and appear on the said day, as is before said, to show their title to the premises; and if they do not come, that by the same authority, they shall forfeit their right in the premises, except the lands and tenements of Matthew Bath, according to law.

c.16

Item al supplicacion de Cristofre Bernewall de Krikeston' esquier que lou il et touz sez auncestrez dehers temps du memorie ewe furent pesiblement seisiez en et de le manere de Castelknoc ove lez appurtenauncez en le counte de Dyvelin et de touz lez terrez mesez et tenementz rents et services ove lour appurtenaunces qils ount en lez vils et vill[ages] de Cabragh et Hunteston' Dunbro Killoserie et Godamendy ove lez appurtenaunces en le dit counte de Dyvelin jesques al temps qil dicell fuit expulse dehors dicell par reson de diverse nient resonable actes du parliament rem[21] encountre ley et conscience sue par sire Roland Eustace chivaler adonque thresorer Dirland encountre le dit Cristofre en un parlment tenuz a Dyvelin le vendredie prochen apres le fest del Concepcion du Nostre Dame lan del reigne du roy Edward le quart xviij[22] devaunt Gerot count de Kildare adonque depute lieutenaunt Dirland quell count ad marie la fele du dit sire Roland a ses temps as queux actes le dit Cristofre ne poet my de estre receyve a ministre ne declare son title et droit en le mesme mez de rendre son corps al chastell de Dyvelin et illesqes de remayner tanque il fuit amesne dehors du mesme chastell et myse sour un sowe devaunt le dit manere de Castellknoc par reson de cell le gard adonques esteaunt en Castelknoc avauntdit pur[23] la securite dicell remove par force dicell a departire le mesme pur le conservacion du vie du dit Cristofre et ensy par cell cruell et illoiall fesauncez et par reson daultres feines et illoials recovers et par embracementes par reson de pretense dun fyn sourmise de estre leve al dame Margaret Jenico adonques esteaunt femme du dit sire Roland que lou le dit fyn fuit et est voide et de null effect en ley; en consideracion de quell que le dit Cristofre ne savoit ne purroit aver la ley ministre a luy pur lez consideracions avauntditz mez pour power et force il du cest veile enheritaunce saunz ascun loiall ou due ordre ou recover par le course du ley du roy ordine enacte et establie par auctorite du cest present parlment que le dit act ou actes ewes ou passez pur lenterest ou profit du dit sire Roland et dame Margaret sa femme ou ascun de eux en le dit parlment ou en ascun aultre parlment encountre le dit Cristofre et auxi le pretense fyn avaunce dit soient annullez revokez et adjugez voide et de null effect en ley en semblable manere sicome jammez null tiel act ou actez furent faitz; et par le mesme auctorite qil soit loiall al dit Cristofre et sez heirs dentrer en le dit manere et en touz aultres terrez mesez et tenementes rents et servicz ove lour appurtenaunces en les viles et villages suisditz et chescun de eaux esteaunt come est devaunt reherce et eux et chescun de eux ov lour appurtenaunces a aver et enjoier accordaunt all son veile title et droit ascun estatut act ou ordenaunce al contrary fait nient obstaunt; et par la mesme auc-

21 Thus in transcript. 22 *Recte* xix (10 December 1479). 19–20 Edward IV c.8, 52. *Stat. Ire.*, 12–22 Edw. IV, pp 698–702, 786–94. 23 *par* in transcript.

c.16 [Repeal of all acts against Christopher Barnewall]

Also, at the petition of Christopher Bernewall of Crickstown, esquire, that whereas he and all his ancestors from beyond the time of memory were peaceably seised in and of the manor of Castleknock with the appurtenances in the county of Dublin and of all the lands, messuages and tenements, rents and services with their appurtenances which they have in the vills and villages of Cabragh and Huntstown, Dunbro, Killossery and Goddamendy with the appurtenances in the said county of Dublin, until the time that he was expelled by means of various unreasonable acts of parliament, a thing contrary to law and conscience, sued by Sir Roland Eustace, knight, then treasurer of Ireland against the said Christopher in a parliament held at Dublin on the Friday next after the feast of the Conception of Our Lady in the nineteenth year of the reign of king Edward the fourth [10 December 1479] before Gerald, earl of Kildare, then deputy lieutenant of Ireland which earl has married the daughter of the said Sir Roland in his time; on account of which acts the said Christopher can not be received to offer or declare his title and right in the same, but had to surrender his body to the castle of Dublin and remain there until he was brought out of the same castle and set upon a sow[2] before the said manor of Castleknock, by reason of which the guard then being in Castleknock aforesaid for the safety thereof was compelled by force thereof to depart from the same to preserve the life of the said Christopher; and so by these cruel and unlawful actions and by reason of other feigned and illegal recoveries and by embraceries by means of the pretence of a fine claimed to be levied to Dame Margaret Jenico, then being the wife of the said Sir Roland, whereas the said fine was and is void and of no effect in law; in consideration of which and because the said Christopher could not nor might have the law administered to him for the considerations aforesaid, but by strength and force was deprived of this old inheritance without any lawful or due order or recovery by the course of the king's law, it is ordained, enacted and established by authority of this present parliament that the said act or acts had or passed for the interest or profit of the said Sir Roland and Dame Margaret his wife or either of them in the said parliament or in any other parliament against the said Christopher and also the pretended fine aforesaid be annulled, revoked and adjudged void and of no effect in law, in like manner as if such act or acts were never made; and by the same authority that it be lawful for the said Christopher and his heirs to enter into the said manor and into all other lands, messuages and tenements, rents and services, with their appurtenances in the towns and villages before

2 'A moveable structure having a strong roof, used to cover men advancing to the walls of a besieged town or fortress, and to protect them while engaged in sapping and mining or other operations' (*O.E.D.*)

torite en consideracion que le dit Roland ad par le space de xiiij ans et pluis receive lez issuez et profites del dit manere et terrez tenementz rentes et servicz ove lour appurtenaunces al summe de xiiij^{c} li. par colour del avauntditz illoials actes et recoverez eiauntz nul perfite droit ne bon title a icell al oultre[24] anientesment du dit Cristofre pur que establie et enact est que soit loiall al dit Cristofre et a sez heirs ou assignes denterer en tout et chescun manere ou manerez terrez mesez et tenements que le dit sire Roland ad ou ascun aultre a son ups dicest propre enheritaunce ou que le dit sire Roland et [. . .][25] droit du dit dam Margaret duraunt son interest et lez issuez et profites dicell daver et perceyver jesques tiell temps que le dit Cristofre serra satisfie et content del dit somme de xiiij^{c} li. queux le dit sire Roland et dam Margaret ount receivez de cest dit enheritaunce purvieu touz foitz que le dit Cristofre ne recevera pluis pur lez ditz xiiij^{c} li. que ij^{c} marcz par la mesme auctorite que cest act ne soit my prejudiciall ne extend a Elizabeth Talbot en ascun manere.

c.17

Item al supplicacion de Cristofre Bernewall de Krikeston' esquier [que lou] un Thomas Plunket pursue un act du parlment envers le dit Cristofre en un parlment tenuz a Dyvelyn devaunt Gerot count de Kildare a qui le dit Cristofre nad my respounse et auxi araina un assis de novell disseisin envers le dit Cristofre de lez maners de Loghgowre Dirloghgowre et Molinam[26] deins le[27] counte de Mithe le quell assise fuit prise devaunt le lewe de solant que le dit Cristofre ne fuit jammes attache a icell a respondre ne avoit ascun conusaunz dicell a son oultre disheriteson et un de puis parelous ensample que unques fuit use que ascun homme perderoit ses terrez par tiels subtilx et faux avenez; lez premissez considerez ordeine est enacte et estable par auctorite du dit parlment que le dit act du parlment soit revok repelle reverse et adjuge void et de null effect en ley ensy que null tiel act fuit trove ascun act restreint manere ou cause al contrarie nient obstaunt; et par le mesme auctorite ordine est que al tiel temps qun breve derrour serra delivere de remover le dit recovere en assise si le dit record ne soit mys et delivere parentre ceo et le xvme de Seint Michell prochien avener[28] accordant al tenour du dit breve que adonqez le dit recorde

24 *aultre* in transcript. 25 Blank in transcript but no explanation is given. 26 *Molmain* in transcript. 27 *de* in transcript. 28 13 October 1493.

mentioned and every one of them, as is before rehearsed, and to have and enjoy them and every of them with their appurtenances according to his old title and right, notwithstanding any statute, act or ordinance made to the contrary; and by the same authority in consideration of the fact that the said Roland, for the space of fourteen years and more has received the issues and profits of the said manor and lands, tenements, rents and services, with their appurtenances, to the sum of 1400 pounds by reason of the aforesaid illegal acts and recoveries, having no perfect right or good title thereto, to the utter ruin of the said Christopher, wherefore it is established and enacted that it be lawful for the said Christopher and for his heirs or assigns to enter into all and every manor or manors, lands, messuages and tenements which the said Sir Roland has, or any other person has to his use, of his own inheritance or which the said Sir Roland and [...] right of the said Dame Margaret during his interest and to have and receive the issues and profits thereof until such time as the said Christopher shall be satisfied and contented of the said sum of 1400 pounds which the said Sir Roland and Dame Margaret have received of this said inheritance; provided always that the said Christopher shall not receive more for the said 1400 pounds than 200 marks; by the same authority that this act be not prejudicial nor extend to Elizabeth Talbot in any manner.

c.17 [Repeal of act against Christopher Barnewall]

Also, at the petition of Christopher Bernewall of Crickstown, esquire, that whereas one Thomas Plunket sued an act of parliament against the said Christopher in a parliament held at Dublin before Gerald, earl of Kildare[3], to which the said Christopher has no answer and also arraigned an assize of novel disseisin against the said Christopher of the manors of Lagore, Dirloghgowre[4] and Mullinam in the county of Meath, which assize was taken before sunrise and the said Christopher was never attached thereto to answer nor had he any knowledge thereof to his utter disinheritance, and as one of the most dangerous examples that was ever used that any man should lose his lands by such cunning and false means; in consideration of the premises, it is ordained, enacted and established by authority of the said parliament that the said act of parliament be revoked, repealed, reversed and adjudged void and of no effect in law, as if no such act was found, notwithstanding any act, restraint, manner or cause to the contrary; and by the same authority it is ordained that at such time as a writ of error shall be delivered to remove the said recovery in assizes if the said record be not sent in and delivered between now and the quindene

3 19–20 Edward IV c.59; 20 Edward IV c.12. (*Stat. Ire., 12–22 Edw. IV*, pp 826–8, 858–60).
4 Possibly Little Lagore, co. Meath.

et tout en tiell conteine soit adnule revoke reverse et adjuge voide et de null effect en ley.

c.18

Item al supplicacion de Elizabeth Bernewall widowe jaditz femme a Nicholas Hussee jaditz baron de Galtrym que lou Johan fitz et heir al dit Nicholas apres la morte du dit Nicholas endowa la dit Elizabeth ove viij marcez de loial mone et aultres diverse casualteez et custumz partenauntz al droit de sa dower queux el possessa et enjoya divers ans pesiblement tanque le temps que le dit Johan murist donques le heir du dit Johan esteaunt deins age le roy entra par le non age as tielx terrez et tenementes ove lour appurtenaunces et aultres casualtees sicome el fuit endowe en le dit seignurie de Galtrym et il est tenu et garde en lez mains du roy vj ans et pluis a son graund damage et empoverishment; lez premissez considerez et coment le roy ne null de sez officers de droit doient seisier ne garder le dit par le reson avauntdit ordein est par auctorite dicest present parlment que la dit Elizabeth entra en cest dit dower et chescun parcell dicell et lez possesser et enjoier accordaunt al droit et conscience saunz ascun empechement ou impediment du roy ou sez heirz ou ascun de sez officers ou ministrez quelconques en temps avener ascun estatut act ou ordenaunce don ou graunt del dit dower a ascun persone ou persons ent fait ou graunt devaunt cestz heurs nient obstaunt.

c.19

Item al supplicacion de Edmon Botiller baron de Donboigne que lou le dit Edmon et sez auncestrez ount este seisiez en lour demesne come de fee de lez seignuries de Molynger et la vile appelle le Irishton' juxt Molynger deins le counte du Mithe et lez issuez et proffities de eux receivez pesiblement saunz ascun contradiccion tanque le temps qun Janyn Petite par force et maintenaunce de ceux[29] qui porterount la ruyle du cest terre desouz nostre soveraine seignur le roy ove force et armez entrera et gardera ove tort lez ditz seignuries de Molynger et Irishton' ove lour appurtenaunces saunz ascun loiall title du droit et gardera lez ditz Molynger et Irishton' ove lour appurtenauncz ove tort et maintenaunce jesques a cest temps al disheriteson et finall destruccion del

29 *e eux* in transcript.

of St Michael next coming [13 October 1493], according to the tenor of the said writ, that then the said record and everything contained in it be annulled, revoked, reversed and adjudged void and of no effect in law.

c.18 [Elizabeth Barnewall, widow of Nicholas Hussey, baron of Galtrim, to have her dower]

Also, at the petition of Elizabeth Bernewall, widow, formerly wife of Nicholas Hussee, late baron of Galtrim, that whereas John, son and heir of the said Nicholas, after the death of the said Nicholas, endowed the said Elizabeth with eight marks of lawful money and various other casualties and customs appertaining to the right of her dower which she possessed and enjoyed peaceably for several years until the time that the said John died; then, because the heir of the said John was under age, the king, on account of the minority of the heir, entered upon such lands and tenements with their appurtenances and other casualties as she was endowed with in the said lordship of Galtrim and it has been held and kept in the king's hands for six years and more, to her great damage and impoverishment; in consideration of the premises, and of how the king or any of his officers of right ought not to seize or keep the said dower for the reason aforesaid, it is ordained by authority of this present parliament that the said Elizabeth shall enter into this said dower and every part thereof and possess and enjoy them according to right and conscience, without any hindrance or impediment by the king or his heirs or any of his officers or ministers whomsoever in time to come, notwithstanding any statute, act or ordinance, gift or grant of the said dower to any person or persons thereof made or granted heretofore.

c.19 [Simon Petit to appear to show title to Mullingar and the Irishtown there, at the request of Edmond Botiller, baron of Dunboyne]

Also, at the petition of Edmond Botiller, baron of Dunboyne, that whereas the said Edmond and his ancestors have been seised in their demesne as of fee of the lordships of Mullingar and the town called the Irishtown near Mullingar in the county of Meath and have received the issues and profits thereof peaceably without any opposition until the time that one Janyn Petit by the force and maintenance of those who bore the rule of this land under our sovereign lord the king with force and arms entered and wrongfully kept the said lordships of Mullingar and Irishtown with their appurtenances without any lawful title of right and kept the said Mullingar and Irishtown with their appurtenances, by wrong and maintenance to this time, to the disinheritance and utter ruin of the

dit Edmon sil ne soit remedie et dent provise; et en taunt que le dit Edmon est remote del commune ley et aunxi il stest en daunger dez ditz seignuries ensy qil nosa my dapparer de pursuer al commune ley le droit du mesme pur cause du favour dez ditz seignuries ewe al dit Janyn Petite lez premises considerez ordeine est enacte et establie par auctorite dicest present parlment que Symon Petit cousin et heire al dit Janyn Petit qui tortousement reteine lez ditz seignuries et villages ove lez appurtenaunces veigne et rende son propre person all chastell de Dyvelyn le lundye prochein devaunt le fest du Seint James lapostle prochein avener[30] illesques a demorer en le garde du counstable la saunz baill ou mainprice jesques al temps qil mostra son title et droit devaunt tielx juges come le tresreverend pier en Dieu Watere erchevesque de Dyvelyn et sire James Dormond governour et tresourer voillent assigner a determiner le droit et title du dit Edmon et le droit du dit Symon dez ditz seignuries de Molynger et Irishton' ove lez appurtenaunces; et si le dit Symon ne veigne pas et appierge lez jour et lieu avaunt rehercez que adonque le dit Symon perdera touz sez droit et title as ditz seignuries de Molynger et Irishton' ove lez appurtenaunces et par mesme auctorite qil soit loiall al dit Edmon dentrer en lez ditz seignuries de Molynger et Irishton' ove lez appurtenaunce et que lez ditz juges issint assignez par mesmes ambedeux seignurs eient auctorite a determiner le droit dez ditz ambedeux parties aunxi bien come il ad este commense par le course du commune ley et le jugement ensy rendue par eux de estre de sy graund force et effect come il ad este commense par due processe de commune ley devaunt lez juges en Irland.

c.20

Item al requisicion dez communes en consideracion du le penury et poverte en queux ils sount et par graund roberiez oppressions injuriez extorsionez coignez et liverers dez englez rebellez come par continuel guerre du iroish enymyez ensi que le ditz communez ne poient a departier ove lour bienez si large come lour duete ou volunte requirunt pur le defens et relief du mesme terre Dirland; ordeine est et enacte par auctorite du cest present parlement que soient resumez prisez et seisiez en lez mainez nostre soverain seignur le roy a prymer ane du reyng du roy Henry le vj darreyn passe[31] toutz manerez chatels seignuriez manerez vilez villagz terrez tenementz rentz servicez custumez revenuez annueteez rentchargez servicez reversionez feez fefermez de queux nostre dit soverain seignur le roy est ou fuist entitle par le droit du son coron ou de son enheritaunce gardz mariagez et forfetourez du mariagez licencez du

30 29 July 1493. 31 1 September 1422.

said Edmond if he be not redressed and provided therein; and inasmuch as the said Edmond is remote from the common law and also he stands in danger of the said lords so that he dares not appear to sue the right of the same at the common law by reason of the favour of the said lords had to the said Janyn Petit; in consideration of the premises, it is ordained, enacted and established by authority of this present parliament that Simon Petit, cousin and heir to the said Janyn Petit, who wrongfully retains the said lordships and villages, with the appurtenances, come and surrender himself in person at the castle of Dublin on the Monday next before the feast of St James the apostle next coming [29 July 1493], to remain there in the custody of the constable there, without bail or mainprise, until such time as he shall show his title and right before such judges as the very reverend father in God, Walter, archbishop of Dublin and Sir James of Ormond, governor and treasurer, will assign to determine the right and title of the said lordships of Mullingar and Irishtown with the appurtenances; and if the said Simon do not come and appear at the day and place before rehearsed, that then the said Simon shall lose all his right and title to the said lordships of Mullingar and Irishtown, with the appurtenances; and by the same authority that it shall be lawful for the said Edmond to enter into the said lordships of Mullingar and Irishtown with the appurtenances; and that the said judges so assigned by the same two lords have authority to determine the right of the said two parties as well as if it had been commenced by the course of the common law, and the judgment so given by them shall be of as great force and effect as if it had been commenced by due process of common law before the judges in Ireland.

c.20 [Act of resumption]

Also, at the request of the commons, in consideration of the penury and poverty in which they are, both through great robberies, oppressions, injuries, extortions, coigns and liveries of the English rebels and by continual war of the Irish enemies, so that the said commons cannot part with their goods as amply as their duty or will require for the defence and relief of the same land of Ireland, it is ordained and enacted by authority of this present parliament that there be resumed, taken and seized into the hands of our sovereign lord the king from the first year of the reign of king Henry the sixth last past [1 September 1422], all manner of castles, lordships, manors, towns, villages, lands, tenements, rents, services, customs, revenues, annuities, rent-charges, services, reversions, fees and fee-farms to which our said sovereign lord the king is or was entitled in right of his crown or of his inheritance, wardships, marriages and forfeitures of marriages, licences of absence, offices, fees, wages, rewards, with their appurtenances, and every one of them whatsoever, that

absentez officez feez gagez regardez ove lour appurtenauncez et chescun du eux quelconques ils ount deinz le dit terre sibien par nostre soverain seignur le roy qui or est que par ascun du sez predecessours ou ascun de eux a ascun temps a le dit prymer ane sibien par lettrez patentz en faitez ou ascun de eux si par auctorite du parlement ou en ascun aultre manere grauntez ou faitz a ascun person ou persons du lez premissez ou ascun de eaux en fee symple fee taile terme du vie ou anez ou al volunte devaunt cest temps faitz ou grauntez; et que toutz maner grauntez donez ordenauncez confirmacions ratificacions et approbacions du mesme ou ascun manumyssions quietclaymez dischargez du rentz et du fee fermez queuxconques ils sount et de queconque chose ils ou ascun de eux sount par nostre dit soverain seignur le roy qui or est ou ses predecessours ou ascun du eaux devaunt cest temps a le dit primer ane jesque cest temps grauntz a ascun temps par auctorite de parlement ou en ascun aultre manere par auctorite du cest present parlement soit void et de nule effecte en ley; purvieu que cest act du resumpcion nextend my ne soit prejudiciall a le tresreverend pier en Dieu Water archivesque du Divelin depute lieutenaunt du cest terre Dirland ne a James Ormond chivaler pur le corps du roy governour et tresorer Dirland ne a Alexandre Plunket chivalier ne a reverend pier en Dieu Water abb del[32] abbay Nostre Dame juxt Divelin et ses successours ne a maire balivez et communes du le cite du Waterford ne a Johan Wise chief baron de leschequer du roy ne a Thomas Botiller maister du rollis ne a Edward Bermyngham chief serjaunt del counte du Mithe ne a sez heirs; et que le dit depute eit poier par auctorite du dit parlement du purvier toutz seulx que luy plerra durant le dit parlement et le prorogacion et le adjournement du mesme; et que le dit act nextend my a nostre Seint mere Seint Esglise ne as clerkis et parsons du mesme; et purvieu toutz foitz que cest act du resumpcion nextend ne soit my prejudiciall a Matheou Bath de Rathfegh gentilman du ascun act du parlement ou ordenaunce graunt ou grauntz faitz a le dit Matheou ou a son profit par nostre soverain seignur le roy qui ore est en ou ascun de ses predecessours en ascun maner foitz; purvieu a toutz foitz que cest act du resumpcion ou ascun aultre act feit ou fera en cest present parlement nextend my ne soit prejudiciall ou grefe ou damage en ascun maner foitz a le reverend pier en Dieu Octavian primat de tout Irland a ascun graunt ou grauntz act ou actz faitz a le dit primat ou ascun du sez predecessours ou a sez successours ou a eaux ou ascun de eaux sibien par nostre soverain seignur le roy qui or est desoubz son sele Dengleterre ou Dirland come par ascun de sez noblez progenitours ou predecessours en temps passe; purvieu toutz foitz que cest act du resumpcion nextend my ne en ascun maner soit prejudiciall al William English du Divelin mercer en ou de loffice de ballishup de Dalkey done ou graunt a luy par le dit

32 *abb del* repeated in transcript.

they have in the said land by our sovereign lord the king that now is or by any of his predecessors or any of them at any time from the said first year, by letters patent made by him or any of them or by authority of parliament or in any other manner granted or made to any person or persons of the premises or any of them, in fee simple, fee tail, term of life or years, or at will, and that all manner of grants, gifts, ordinances, confirmations, ratifications and approbations of the same or any manumissions, quitclaims, discharges of rents and of fee farms, whatsoever they are and of whatsoever thing they or any of them are, granted by our said sovereign lord the king that now is or his predecessors or any of them heretofore from the said first year to this time at any time by authority of parliament or in any other manner, by authority of this present parliament be void and of no effect in law; provided that this act of resumption do not extend or be prejudicial to the very reverend father in God, Walter, archbishop of Dublin, deputy lieutenant of this land of Ireland, or to James Ormond, knight for the body of the king, governor and treasurer of Ireland, or to Alexander Plunket, knight, or to the reverend father in God, Walter, abbot of the abbey of Our Lady near Dublin, and his successors, or to the mayor, bailiffs and commons of the city of Waterford, or to John Wise, chief baron of the king's exchequer, or to Thomas Botiller, master of the rolls, or to Edward Bermyngham, chief serjeant of the county of Meath, or to his heirs; and that the said deputy have power by authority of the said parliament to provide all those whom it shall please him during the said parliament and the prorogation and the adjournment of the same; and that the said act do not extend to our Holy Mother, Holy Church, or to the clerks and persons of the same; and provided always that this act of resumption do not extend or be prejudicial to Matthew Bath of Rathfeigh, *gentilman*, as regards any act of parliament or ordinance, grant or grants thereof made to the said Matthew or to his profit by our sovereign lord the king that now is or any of his predecessors at any time; provided always that this act of resumption or any other act made or to be made in this present parliament do not extend or be prejudicial to, or grieve or damage at any time the reverend father in God Octavian, primate of all Ireland, as to any grant or grants, act or acts made to the said primate or any of his predecessors or to his successors or to them or any of them by our sovereign lord the king that now is under his seal of England or Ireland, or by any of his noble progenitors or predecessors in time past; provided always that this act of resumption do not extend or in any way be prejudicial to William English of Dublin, mercer, in or of the office of bailiff of Dalkey, given or granted to him by the said John, predecessor to the said very reverend father, Walter, under the seal of the said John and the seals of the chapters for term of the life of the said William or in or of the wages, fees, profits and commodities belonging to the said office in any manner; and by the said authority that this act of resumption

Johan predecessour a le dit tresreverend pier Waltere desoubz le seall de le dit Johan et lez sealez du lez chapiterez pur terme du vie du le dit William ou en ou de lez gagez feez profitez et commoditeez appurteignauntz al dit office en ascun manere; et par le dit auctorite que cest act du resumpcion nextend ne soit prejudiciall al priour et covent del frers prechours du Drogheda ne a lour successours en nule manere; purvieu aunxi que cest act du resumpcion nextend my ne soit prejudiciall en ascune manere a lez soverain portreffes et communez du le vile du Rosse en Leynyster en ascun graunt ou grauntz faitz a eaux ou lour successours par nostre soverain seignur le roy qui or est ou ascun du sez noblez progenitours ou predecessours en temps passe; purvieu toutz foitz que cest act du resumpcion nextend my ne soit prejudiciall a maister Richard Walsh' parson du Trym en ascun foitz; et par le dit auctorite que cest act du resumpcion nextend my ne soit prejudiciall a le priour et covent del meason du lez frers prechours du Trym ne a lour successours en nule manere; purvieu que cest acte du resumpcion ne nule aultre act fait nextend my ne soit prejudiciall ne lesion a Johanet jaditz famme a Robert Douedall chevalier pur ascun graunt fait a ele et Johan Benet jaditz son baron jointement severalment par nostre soverain seignur le roy qui or est ou par ascun du sez progenitours ou predecessours; purvieu toutz foitz que cest act du resumpcion nextend ne soit prejudiciall ne lesion en ascun manere graunt ou grauntez act ou actz faitz al reverend pier en Dieu Johan evesque du Mith ou ascun de sez predecessours et a lour successours ou ascun de eaux; et par le dit auctorite que cest act du resumpcion nextend my ne soit prejudiciall al priour et covent del meason frers prechours du Divelin ne a lour successours en nule manere; purvieu toutz foitz que cest act du resumpcion ou ascun act fait nextend my ne soit prejudiciall ne lesion en ascun maner a Henry priour del meason du benoit virgin Marie du Lanthon' juxt Gloucestre en Engleterre ne a ses friers deputeez proctours en le terre Dirland a ascun graunt ou grauntz act ou actz faitz al dit priour et covent et lour successours ou a ascun de lour predecessours et a lour successours ou a eux ou a le successour ou dascun de eaux sibien par nostre soverain seignur le roy qui or est desoubz son graund seale ou sealis Dengleterre ou Dirland come par ascun de ses nobles progenitours ou predecessours en temps passe; purvieu que cest act du resumpcion nextend my ne soit prejudiciall a Johan evesque du Mith, Johan abb du Seint Thomas Court, Waltere abb de meason du Seint Marie juxt Divelin, Johan abb du Mellifont, Jamys Ketyng priour du Kilmaynan, Robert Preston viscount de Gormaneston', Cristofer Flemyng baron de Slane, Richard baron du Delvyn, Nicholas Seint Laurence seignur du Houth, Cristofor Bernewall seignur du Trymleteston', Edmond Plunket seignur de Killene ne a Johan Plunket seignur du Donsany ne Cristofor Bellewe ne a nule de eaux en ascun manere ne a ascun gent' pur lour enheritance et gardez du mariage qui ount sue lour liverez par patent ou aultrement

do not extend or be prejudicial to the prior and convent of the friars preachers of Drogheda or to their successors in any manner; provided also that this act of resumption do not extend or be prejudicial in any manner to the sovereign, portreeves and commons of the town of New Ross in Leinster in any grant or grants made to them or their successors by our sovereign lord the king that now is or any of his noble progenitors or predecessors in time past; provided always that this act of resumption do not extend or be prejudicial to master Richard Walsh, parson of Trim, at any time; and by the said authority that this act of resumption do not extend or be prejudicial to the prior and convent of the house of the friars preachers of Trim, or to their successors in any manner; provided that this act of resumption or any other act made do not extend or be prejudicial or hurtful to Johanet, formerly wife to Robert Douedall, knight, for any grant made to her and John Benet, formerly her husband, jointly or separately, by our sovereign lord the king that now is or by any of his progenitors or predecessors; provided always that this act of resumption do not extend or be prejudicial or hurtful to any manner of grant or grants, act or acts made to the reverend father in God, John, bishop of Meath, or any of his predecessors and to their successors or any of them; and by the said authority that this act of resumption do not extend or be prejudicial to the prior and convent of the house of the friars preachers of Dublin, or to their successors in any manner; provided always that this act of resumption or any act made do not extend or be prejudicial or hurtful in any manner to Henry, prior of the house of the Blessed Virgin Mary of Lanthony near Gloucester in England or to his brethren, deputies and proctors in the land of Ireland as to any grant or grants, act or acts made to the said prior and convent and their successors or to them or to the successor of any of them, by our sovereign lord the king that now is, under his great seal or great seals of England or of Ireland, or by any of his noble progenitors or predecessors in time past; provided that this act of resumption do not extend or be prejudicial to John, bishop of Meath, John, abbot of St Thomas Court, Walter, abbot of the house of St Mary near Dublin, John, abbot of Mellifont, James Ketyng, prior of Kilmainham, Robert Preston, viscount of Gormanston, Christopher Flemyng, baron of Slane, Richard, baron of Delvin, Nicholas St Laurence, lord of Howth, Christopher Bernewall, lord of Trimleston, Edmond Plunket, lord of Killeen, or to John Plunket, lord of Dunsany, or Christopher Bellewe, or to any of them in any manner or to any *gentilman* for their inheritance and wardships of marriage, who have sued their liveries by patent or otherwise heretofore, or to the town of Athboy; provided that this act of resumption do not extend or be prejudicial to Christopher Bellewe of Bellewstown, esquire, or to his charter of exemption by whatever name he is called in any manner; provided always that this act of resumption or any act made or to be made in this present parliament

devaunt cest temps ne al vile du Athboy; purvieu que cest act du resumpcion nextend my ne soit prejudiciall al Cristofor Bellewe du Belleweston' esquier ne a son chartre du exempcion par quelconque noun il est appelle en nule manere; purvieu toutz foitz que cest act du resumpcion ou ascun act fait ou de estre fait en cest present parlement nextend my ne soit prejudiciall ne lesion en ascun manere al Johan priour del meason du Seint Johan Baptist du Athirde ne a covent du mesme a ascun graunt ou grauntz act ou actz faitz a le dit priour et covent et lour successours ou a eaux ou al successours dascun du eaux sibien par nostre soverain seignur le roy qui or est desoubz son graund seale Dengleterre ou Dirland ou le seall de eschequer du sa dit terre Dirland come par ascun de sez noble progenitours ou predecessours en ascun temps passe; purvieu toutz foitz que cest act du resumpcion nextend my ne soit prejudiciall a Johan Danston del office de un dez justicez du le roy del chiefe place en Irland en ascun maner; purvieu que cest act nextend my ne soit prejudiciall ne lesion en nule manere a [. . .][33] Bath par quelconque noun il soit appelle; purvieu a toutz foitz que cest act du resumpcion nextend my ne soit prejudiciall a William abb del meason Nostre Dame de Trym ne a covent du mesme ne a lour successours en nule manere; purvieu que cest act du resumpcion nextend my ne en ascun manere soit prejudiciall a Richard Nangle clerk en ou du ascun graunt ou done fait a ile pur terme de sa vie par le roy nostre soverain seignur qui or est par ou desoubz ses lettrez patentz desoubz le graund seall du cest terre Dirland del office du clerc et gardeyn del hanapere du le roy du sa chauncery Dirland ne al feez et gagez grauntez a luy en lez mesme lettrez patentz par le reason du le dit office; purvieu que cest act du resumpcion ou ascun aultre act fait ou de estre fait en cest present parlement nextend my ne soit prejudiciall ne lesion en ascun maner a James priour del meason du Seint Patric du Holmpatrik et al covent du mesme en ascun graunt ou grauntz act ou actz fait as ditz priour et covent ou a ascun du lour predecessours et a loure successours ou a eaux ou a successours dascun du eaux sibien par nostre soverain seignur le roy qui or est desoubz grand seall ou sealez Dengleterre ou Dirland come par ascun de ses noblez progenitours ou predecessours ou ascun temps passe; purvieu toutz foitz que cest act du resumpcion ou ascun act fait ou de estre fait en cest present parlement nextend my ne soit prejudiciall ne lesion en ascun manere a David priour de cathedrall esglise de Seint Trinite del cite du Divelin ne a covent du mesme a ascun graunt ou grauntz act ou actz faitz al dit priour et covent et lour successours ou ascun de lour predecessours et a lour successours ou a eaux ou al successours dascun du eaux sibien par nostre soverain seignur le roy qui or est desoubz son graund seall Dengleterre ou Dirland come par ascun du sez noblez progenitours ou predecessours en temps

33 Berry's note: blank in roll.

do not extend or be prejudicial or hurtful in any manner to John, prior of the house of St John the Baptist of Ardee, or to the convent of the same, as to any grant or grants, act or acts made to the said prior and convent and their successors or to them or to the successors of any of them, by our sovereign lord the king that now is under his great seal of England or of Ireland or the seal of the exchequer of his said land of Ireland or by any of his noble progenitors or predecessors at any time past; provided always that this act of resumption do not extend or be prejudicial to John Danston as regards the office of one of the king's justices of the King's Bench in Ireland in any manner; provided that this act do not extend or be prejudicial or hurtful in any manner to [. . .] Bath, by whatever name he be called; provided always that this act of resumption do not extend or be prejudicial to William, abbot of the house of Our Lady of Trim, or to the convent of the same, or to their successors in any manner; provided that this act of resumption do not extend or in any manner be prejudicial to Richard Nangle, clerk, in or of any grant or gift made to him for term of his life by the king our sovereign lord that now is, by or under his letters patent under the great seal of this land of Ireland of the office of clerk and keeper of the king's hanaper of his chancery of Ireland, or to the fees and wages granted to him in the same letters patent by reason of the said office; provided always that this act of resumption or any other act made or to be made in this present parliament do not extend or be prejudicial or hurtful in any manner to James, prior of the house of St Patrick of Holmpatrick and to the convent of the same in any grant or grants, act or acts made to the said prior and convent or to any of their predecessors and to their successors or to them or to the successors of any of them by our sovereign lord the king that now is under the great seal or seals of England or of Ireland, or by any of his noble progenitors or predecessors at any time past; provided always that this act of resumption or any act made or to be made in this present parliament do not extend or be prejudicial or hurtful in any manner to David, prior of the cathedral church of the Holy Trinity of the city of Dublin or to the convent of the same, as to any grant or grants, act or acts made to the said prior and convent and their successors or any of their predecessors and to their successors or to them or to the successors of any of them by our sovereign lord the king that now is under his great seal of England or of Ireland, or by any of his noble progenitors or predecessors in time past; provided also that this act of resumption do not extend or in any way be prejudicial to the vicars of the cathedral church of St Patrick of Dublin, in, of or for any grant or grants made, given or granted, grant or grants made to them and to their successors by our sovereign lord the king that now is, or any of his noble progenitors or predecessors at any time before now, by their letters patent or letters patent from any of them; provided that this act do not extend or be prejudicial or hurtful in any manner to Barnaby Bernewall, by

passe; purvieu aunxi que cest act du resumpcion nextend my ou en ascun maner soit prejudiciall as vikeries del cathedrall esglise du Seint Patrik du Divelin en du ou pur ascun graunt ou grauntz faitz donez ou grauntez[34] a eaux et a lour successours par nostre soverain seignur le roy qui or est ou ascun de sez noblez progenitours ou predecessours a ascun temps devaunt ses temps par lour lettrez patentz ou lettrez patentz a ascun du eaux; purvieu que cest act nextend my ne soit prejudiciall ne lesion en nule maner a Barnabe Bernewall par quelconque noun il soit appelle; purvieu que cest act du resumpcion nextend my ne soit prejudiciall en ascun maner graunt ou grauntz faitz a luy par nostre soverain seignur le roy qui or est; purvieu que cest act du resumpcion nextend ne soit prejudiciall as portreffes burgesez et communes de vile du Trym ne a nule de eaux de ascun graunt ou grauntz faitz a eaux joint ou severell par nostre soverain seignur le roy qui or est ou ascun de sez predecessours ou progenitours en ascun maner ne a Nicholas White une dez barons del eschekir en nule maner; purvieu auxi que cest act nextend my ne soit prejudiciall al Margarete priorasse du meason du Gracedieu ne al covent du mesme en ascun maner ne que le dit act extend my ne soit prejudiciall as maire bailliffes et communes del cite de Divelin ne a lour successours en nule maner; purvieu que cest act de resumpcion nextend my ne soit prejudiciall a ascun person ou persons as queulx le tresreverend pier en Dieu Waltere archevesque du Divelin depute lieutenaunt Dirland ad fait ascun graunt ou grauntz sibien devaunt le dit act sicome aprese le dit act en ascun maner; purvieu toutz foitz que cest act nextend my ne soit prejudiciall en nule maner a Thomas Tournoure punys; purvieu toutz foitz que cest act du resumpcion nextend my ou en ascun maner soit prejudiciall de ou pur ascun act don franchez graunt ou exempcion fait ou graunte par act du parlement devaunt cest temps de a ou pur le vile appelle le Pety Cobbragh juxt Divelin et lez terrez et tenementz dez enhabitauntys du mesme.

C.21

Item al supplicacion dez communes que lou par divers treisonez feloniez mordrez robberie extorsions coyngnez lyvereez et aultrez divers infinite mysgovernauncez faitz par lez persons queux noumez ensuount cestasaver George Netervile, Harry Rochford gentilman, Gilduf Mc Gilduf, Johan Sedgre, Johan Darcy, Peter Neill', Johan Water, Ellice Watere, Robyn Nangle, Water Serle, George Drake, William Drake, Alexander Drake, Edmond Twt de Monalty, William Betagh du Monalty et son fitz et heire, Richard Ocale de Molynger, Jamys Hadsore de Dunbro, frere Philip Ocaffy, William Wellisly,

34 *graunt ou grauntez fait* repeated in transcript.

whatever name he be called; provided that this act of resumption do not extend or be prejudicial in any manner of grant or grants made to him by our sovereign lord that now is; provided that this act of resumption do not extend or be prejudicial to the portreeves, burgesses and commons of the town of Trim, or to any of them, as regards any grant or grants made to them jointly or separately by our sovereign lord the king that now is, or any of his predecessors or progenitors in any manner, or to Nicholas White, one of the barons of the exchequer in any manner; provided also that this act do not extend or be prejudicial to Margaret, prioress of the house of Gracedieu, or to the convent of the same in any manner; and that the said act do not extend or be prejudicial to the mayor, bailiffs and commons of the city of Dublin, or to their successors in any manner; provided that this act of resumption do not extend or be prejudicial to any person or persons to whom the very reverend father in God, Walter, archbishop of Dublin, deputy lieutenant of Ireland, has made any grant or grants, both before the said act and after the said act, in any manner; provided always that this act do not extend or be prejudicial in any manner to Thomas Tournoure the younger; provided always that this act of resumption do not extend or in any way be prejudicial of or for any act, gift, franchise, grant or exemption made or granted heretofore by act of parliament of, to or for the town called Little Cabragh near Dublin and the lands and tenements of the inhabitants of the same.

c.21 [George Nettervill and others to surrender to answer for treasons, robberies and other offences]

Also, at the petition of the commons, that whereas by various treasons, felonies, murders, robberies, extortions, coigns, liveries and various other infinite misdeeds committed by the persons whose names follow, that is to say, George Netervile, Harry Rochford, *gentilman*, Gilduf Mc Gilduf, John Sedgre, John Darcy, Peter Neill, John Water, Ellis Watere, Robin Nangle, Walter Serle, George Drake, William Drake, Alexander Drake, Edmond Twt of Moynalty, William Betagh of Moynalty and his son and heir, Richard O Cale of Mullingar, James Hadsore of Dunbro, brother Philip O Caffy, William Wellisly, Gerrot Wellisly, Roland Preston, Richard Dillon of Seatown, John

Gerrot Wellisly, Rouland Preston, Richard Dillon de Seton', Johan Dreynan, William Dreynan, Richard Dreynan, Nicholl fitz Roger, Johan fitz Roger, Jamys fitz Roger, Johan fitz Roger, Jamys Delahid fitz a Water Delahide chivalier, Thomas Nugent fitz a Edward Nugent, Meiler Petite chanon du Molynger, Water Tute, Gerrot Tute, Johan Dillon bastard servaunt a Wellisly, Johan Orayly, Robert Lutterell fitz a Thomas Lutterell, William Flemyng, William Feroll clerk, Hebart Mc Donagh provysour, Gilduff Mc Kevyn, Patrik Plunket du Kerriston', Johan Gernon du Killyncoull', Thomas Gernon, George Gernon, Patrik Clynton de Clyntonestoun', Larace Douedall, Stephen Douedall, Johan Douedall, Patrik Douedall, Thomas bastard Verdon, Thomas Verdon fitz al Bertilmew Verdon, William Taff, Cristofor Taff, Richard Taff, Stephen Taff bastard, Richard Tirrell de Tippersoull', Patrik Taff, James Taff, George Taff, Patrik Betagh, Water Bellewe, Henry Mc Rowlow, William Duff Okerruill', Henry Okerrull, Cormok Scally, Gilduff Mc Robry, Patrik White de Richardeston', Nicholas White, Richard Shaunysson, Johan Fele du Richardeston', William Flemyng bastard, Patrikyn Drake, Robert Bedy Ohalpyn, Walrone Wellisly, James Walsh, William Walsh, Water Walsh, Brene Mc Guyre du Scryne, Water Walsh du Novane merchaunt, Thomas Nugent fitz a Edward Nugent, William Drake, George Drake, Gerrot fitz John, Johan Verdon de Kiltalaght, Johan Verdon fitz a Bertilmew Verdon, Cristofor Nugent du Mirath', James Taff du Milotiston', Patrik Taff fitz du Thomas Taff, Edward Flemyng du Crevagh, Peter Flemyng du mesme, Meiler Husse, Patrik Husse du Neuhagard', Remond Bermyngham du Corteiston', Richard Gernon, Hugh Mc Cragh, Thomas Mc Cragh, Tirrelagh Mc Cragh, Johan Hoy du Insmoght, Alexander Drake, Johan Darcy, Water Wellisly, Perce Nangle, Robert Herfort du Shiallon', Johan fitz al Oliver Plunket, Henry fitz al mesme, Johan Hore de Swerdez, Robert Lawles home du Harroll', Patrik Mole Archboll, Johan Tirrell du Portelaman, Water Tirrell son fitz, Shaun Mc Maon de Sonnagh, Morice Dalton fitz a Thomas Dalton, Edmond fitz Symon du Hilton', sire William Walsh viker du Swerdez, Barnabe Telyn, Thomas Telyn servaunt a Larace Douedall, Johan Bron' de Rotheston', Richard Smaill de Athirde, Roger Mc Canan de Drumkessell, Richard Molkeran de Athirde, Johan Revere de Rogeston', Johan Rowe jaditz du Maynoth, Johan Serjaunt du Divelin, Thomas Plunket du Donshoghly, Thomas Talour du Divelin, Thomas Douedall du mesme, Oliver Grace du Kilkeny, William Bron' tarde bailif du Divelin, Cristofor Michell, Oliver Michell frer al dit Cristofor, Water Archer du Kilkeny, Nicholas Gilbis du mesme, Richard Burdon du Fithird husb', Johan Stephenot, Johan Smyth, Johan Bourke, James Ochamer, Symon Petit du Molynger, Philip fitz Robert tarde du Divelin, Robyn Lutterell du Luttereliston', Johan Water du Cork, William Harroll, Johan Harroll, Water Harroll, Jamys Harroll, Gilgrome Ohalpeny, Patrik Bakagh Mc Caffrey de

Dreynan, William Dreynan, Richard Dreynan, Nicholas fitz Roger, John fitz Roger, James fitz Roger, John fitz Roger, James Delahide son of Walter Delahide knight, Thomas Nugent son of Edward Nugent, Meiler Petit canon of Mullingar, Walter Tute, Gerrot Tute, John Dillon bastard, servant of Wellisly, John O Rayly, Robert Lutterell son of Thomas Lutterell, William Flemyng, William Feroll clerk, Hebart Mc Donagh provisor, Gilduff Mc Kevyn, Patrick Plunket of Kerristown,[5] John Gernon of Killincoole, Thomas Gernon, George Gernon, Patrick Clynton of Clinstown, Laurence Douedall, Stephen Douedall, John Douedall, Patrick Douedall, Thomas bastard Verdon, Thomas Verdon son of Bartholomew Verdon, William Taff, Christopher Taff, Richard Taff, Stephen Taff bastard, Richard Tirrell of Tobersool, Patrick Taff, James Taff, George Taff, Patrick Betagh, Walter Bellewe, Henry Mc Rowlow, William Duff O Kerruill, Henry O Kerrull, Cormok Scally, Gilduff Mc Robry, Patrick White of Richardstown, Nicholas White, Richard Shaunysson, John Fele of Richardstown, William Flemyng bastard, Patrikyn Drake, Robert Bedy O Halpyn, Walerand Wellisly, James Walsh, William Walsh, Walter Walsh, Brene Mc Guyre of Skreen, Walter Walsh of Navan, merchant, Thomas Nugent son of Edward Nugent, William Drake, George Drake, Gerrot fitz John, John Verdon of Kiltallaght, John Verdon son of Bartholomew Verdon, Christopher Nugent of Moyrath, James Taff of Milotiston', Patrick Taff son of Thomas Taff, Edward Flemyng of Creevagh, Peter Flemyng of the same, Meiler Husse, Patrick Husse of Newhaggard, Remond Bermyngham of Curtistown, Richard Gernon, Hugh Mc Cragh, Thomas Mc Cragh, Tirrelagh Mc Cragh, John Hoy of Inishmot, Alexander Drake, John Darcy, Walter Wellisly, Pierce Nangle, Robert Herfort of Shiallon, John son of Oliver Plunket, Henry son of the same, John Hore of Swords, Robert Lawles man of Harrold, Patrick Mole Archbold, John Tirrell of Portloman, Walter Tirrell his son, Shaun Mc Maon of Sonna, Maurice Dalton son of Thomas Dalton, Edmond fitz Symon of Hilltown, Sir William Walsh vicar of Swords, Barnaby Telyn, Thomas Telyn servant to Laurence Dowdall, John Broun of Roestown, Richard Smaill of Ardee, Roger Mc Canan of Drumcashel, Richard Molkeran of Ardee, John Revere of Rogerstown, John Rowe formerly of Maynooth, John Serjaunt of Dublin, Thomas Plunket of Donsoghly, Thomas Talour of Dublin, Thomas Douedall of the same, Oliver Grace of Kilkenny, William Broun late bailiff of Dublin, Christopher Michell, Oliver Michell brother of the said Christopher, Walter Archer of Kilkenny, Nicholas Gilbis of the same, Richard Burdon of Fethard, husbandman, John Stephenot, John Smyth, John Bourke, James O Chamer, Simon Petit of Mullingar, Philip fitz Robert late of Dublin, Robin Lutterell of Luttrelstown,

5 ? Harristown, co. Dublin.

Siddan talour, Martyn Colman de Ramlotery, Gerrot Twt, Andrew Twt son fitz, Bernabe Braynok du Lescartan, Jamys Obyrn' chanon, Thomas Dalton capteyn de sa nacion, Nicholas Dalton, William Preston de Corragh juxt Mith, Thomas Plunket fitz a Oliver Plunket, Richard Forstall chauntour de Kilkeny, Edmond Comerford deane du mesme, William Sprengan idilman, Richard Sedgre du Ballybyn, William Wolf de Kilkeny, Johan White de Clonmell, Johan Water de Cork et Philip Water son fitz et dean du Lymeryk et le chauntour du Lymeryk, James Sex du Lexlep, Johan Sex du mesme, Patrik Sex, Thomas Sex, William Sex mester du Tully, William Oge fitz Thomas du Blakanod, Edmond Harroll capteyn de sa nacion, Patrik Braynok du Lescartan, Meiler Kentagh, Tege Mc Morice Cam, Johan Mc Crevagh du Crevagh, Thomas Harroll portrief du Tasagard, Johan Seman du mesme, Richard Archeboll de Kilrodry, Water Gelouse du Trevet, Robert Hamon servaunt a Thomas Plunket, Cristofor Rochefort fitz et heire a Robert Rocheford; lez premissez considerez enacte est establie et ordeine par auctorite du cest present parlement et proclamacion fait en le mesme que toutz lez ditz malefesours et chescun de eaux par quelconque noun ils ou chescun de eulx soient appellez rendent sez corpsez en le gard du constable du chatell du roy du Divelin le xij jour du August prochein avener illeosque demorere en le gard du constable saunz baill ou maynprice sibien a respondre a roy sicome a respondre et satisfy toutz maner persons qui voilent compleyn sur eulx ou ascun du eulx et quils ne departirent dehors le dit chatell jesques ils eient licence du tresreverend pier en Dieu Watere archevesque du Divelin depute lieutenaunt Dirland et du trespuissaunt seignur James de Ormond governour Dirland; et si ils ou ascun du eaux devaunt nosmez ne rendent sez corpsez ou departent saunz licence sicome est avauntdit que adonques ils et chescun du eulx qui ensy faitz soient adjugez felonez atteintez et forfetent toutz sez terrez tenementz bienez et chatelx la moite al roy et la aultre moite al partie.

c.22

Item al supplicacion du Thomas Botiller gentilman que come nadgayrs au temps que un Gerot count de Kildare donqs eiant lestate du roy deins cest terre ovesque autres de son oppynyon associates ove luy contrarie a lour alliegeance jades coroneroun t et honoureroun t pur lour roy a Dyvelyn un garson nient conuz a le pluys graund sclaundre et abusion que unque fuit viewe deinz cel terre Dirland le quell adonques fuit bien apperceyve et conue par lavauntdit Thomas adonques esteant deinz la dit terre pur quell cause il sy hastyment

John Water of Cork, William Harroll, John Harroll, Walter Harroll, James Harroll, Gilgrome O Halpeny, Patrick Bacagh Mc Caffrey of Siddan tailor, Martin Colman of Ramlotery,[6] Gerrot Twt, Andrew Twt his son, Barnaby Braynok of Liscartan, James O Byrne canon, Thomas Dalton captain of his nation, Nicholas Dalton, William Preston of Corragh near Meath, Thomas Plunket son of Oliver Plunket, Richard Forstall precentor of Kilkenny, Edmond Comerford dean of the same, William Sprengan *idilman*, Richard Sedgre of Ballybin, William Wolf of Kilkenny, John White of Clonmel, John Water of Cork and Philip Water his son and dean of Limerick and the precentor of Limerick, James Sex of Leixlip, John Sex of the same, Patrick Sex, Thomas Sex, William Sex master of Tully, William Oge fitz Thomas of Blakanod, Edmond Harrold captain of his nation, Patrick Braynok of Liscartan, Meiler Kentagh, Teige Mc Morice Cam, John Mc Crevagh of Creevagh, Thomas Harrold, portreeve of Saggart, John Seman of the same, Richard Archbold of Kilruddery, Walter Gelouse of Trevet, Robert Hamon, servant of Thomas Plunket, Christopher Rochefort son and heir of Robert Rocheford; in consideration of the premises, it is enacted, established and ordained by authority of this present parliament and proclamation made in the same that all the said malefactors and every one of them, by whatever name they or any of them be called surrender their bodies into the custody of the constable of the king's castle of Dublin on the twelfth day of August next [12 August 1493] to remain there in the custody of the constable without bail or mainprise both to answer the king and to answer and satisfy all manner of persons who wish to make complaint against them or any of them, and that they do not depart from the said castle until they have the permission of the very reverend father in God, Walter, archbishop of Dublin, deputy lieutenant of Ireland, and of the very powerful lord James of Ormond, governor of Ireland; and if they or any of them before named do not surrender their bodies or depart without permission as is aforesaid, that then they and every of them who do so, shall be adjudged attainted felons and forfeit all their lands, tenements, goods and chattels, half to the king and the other half to the party.

c.22 [Annulment of acts against Thomas and William Botiller]

Also, at the petition of Thomas Botiller, *gentilman*, that whereas lately one Gerald, earl of Kildare, then having the king's estate in this land, with others of his opinion associated with him, contrary to their allegiance, crowned and honoured as their king in Dublin an unknown boy, to the greatest scandal and abuse that ever was seen in this land of Ireland, which was then well perceived

6 Possibly Lamboterie, near Lusk, co. Dublin.

come il puisseit estre allast al Engleterre et il accordant a son foyall alliegeaunce auxi brevement come il puissoit este disclosast a nostre seignur le roy lez graundez et abhominable tresons et insurreccions avauntditz pur quell cause et pur le departure de mesme celui Thomas le dit count adonques esteaunt pleyne de malice et displicez nadgairs commaundist cez lettres desouth son pryve seall pur prendre le corps du William Botiller clerk parsone desglis de Kilberry deins le[35] countie de Mith friar al dit Thomas Botiller allegeaunt envers le dit William hawte et graund treason destre fait a loure pretense roy corone come destre de consente et consaillant a le departure du dite Thomas et issint avaunt procede jesques al temps que le dit count avoit proclame overtment lez ditz Thomas et William Botiller ove lour freers traitours al dit pretense et illoyall roy fait issint finalment quilz fuerent atteintz traitours par parlement; et sur ceo le dit count banna et ousta hors de cele dit terre le dit William pur lez causes avaunt reherse par reason de quell toutz lez bienz chateux et le benifice du dite William Botiller fuerent prisez et seisiez en lez meyns del dit pretense roy et en lez mayns du dit count lez quex unquor remaynez; et outre ceo la mansion ou parsonage et autrez measons du dit William le dit count debrusa jesque al terre pur quell cause et auxi pur jeoppardie de mort de les meanez du dit count le dit William ne osast pas de vener al dit terre agardre residence deins son dit benefice le quell est contrariant a bone droit et reasone; pur qil est ordeigne et estable par lauctorite du cest present parlement que le dit act et chescun autre acte ou actes adevaunt faitz ou ewes en ascun parlement al damage ou prejudice du dit Thomas Botiller William Botiller loure freers ou ascun deux soient ou soiet tout oustrement reversez voidez repellez et destre de null effect en le ley; et qilz et chescun deux par auctorite avauntdit soient restorez a touz loure terrez tenementes possessions bienz et chateux en quelconques mayns deviendrount; et quil soit loiall pur eux et chescun deux dentrer en toutz lour terrez tenementz et possessions et lez mesmez daver et tener a eux et a lour heirs solonc lour auncien droit en auxi ample fourme sicome le dit acte datteindre jammes ne fuit fait; et quils et chescun deux eient lour remedie par breve ou par bille ou autrement a le comon ley en quelconque dez courtes le roy pur recoverer lour tielx biens et chateux issint come avaunt est dit presez ou amesnez; et auxi par lauctorite avaundit que le dit William Botiller soit pardone de toutz maners dettes accomptes fynes forfaitours amercimentes et toutz autrez demaundes par luy en quelconque maner duez ou apparteignauntz au roy ou ascun autre de cez progenitours ou predecessours devaunt cez heures; et que lestatut del abscentie ou ascun autre estatut fait a ascun temps avener en null maner soit al damage ne a prejudice a le dit William Botiller par reason ou occasion de son tiell absence hors del dit terre issint fait par choercion ou man-

35 *de* in transcript.

and known by the aforesaid Thomas, then being in the said land; for which reason he went as speedily as possible into England and according to his faithful allegiance as quickly as possible disclosed to our lord the king the great and abominable treasons and insurrections aforesaid; for which cause and because of the departure of the same Thomas, the said earl, then being filled with malice and displeasure, lately commanded his letters under his privy seal to take the body of William Botiller, clerk, parson of the church of Kilberry in the county of Meath, brother to the said Thomas, alleging against the said William high and great treason to have been committed against the crown of their pretended king, in that he consented to and counselled the departure of the said Thomas, and so having proceeded until the time that the said earl had openly proclaimed the said Thomas and William Botiller with their brothers traitors to the said pretended and unlawful king, and finally brought it about that they were attainted traitors by parliament; and thereupon the said earl banned and drove the said William out of this said land for the causes before rehearsed, by reason whereof all the goods and chattels and the benefice of the said William Botiller were taken and seized into the hands of the said pretended king and into the hands of the said earl and still remain there; and moreover the said earl razed to the ground the manse or parsonage and other houses of the said William, for which cause and also for peril of death at the hands of the said earl, the said William dared not come to the said land to keep residence in his said benefice which is contrary to good right and reason; wherefore, it is ordained and established by authority of this present parliament that the said act and every other act or acts heretofore made or had in any parliament to the damage or prejudice of the said Thomas Botiller, William Botiller, their brothers or any of them, be all utterly reversed, annulled, repealed and of no effect in law, and that they and each of them by the aforesaid authority be restored to all their lands, tenements, possessions, goods and chattels into whatsoever hands they shall come, and that it shall be lawful for them and each of them to enter into all their lands, tenements and possessions and to have and to hold the same to them and to their heirs according to their ancient right in as ample form as if the said act of attainder had never been made, and that they and each of them have their remedy by writ or by bill or otherwise at the common law in any of the king's courts whatsoever to recover such their goods and chattels taken or brought away as is before said; and also by the authority aforesaid that the said William Botiller be pardoned of all manners of debts, accounts, fines, forfeitures, amercements and all other demands by him in whatever manner due or belonging to the king or any other of his progenitors or predecessors heretofore; and that the statute of absentees or any other statute heretofore made shall in no wise at any time to come be to the damage or prejudice of the said William Botiller by reason or occasion of such his absence out of the said

ace come est avaunt reherce mez quil par lauctorite avauntdit soit exempt et hors du payne del dit estatute de abscentie pur le consideracione avaunt reherce et que il soit clerement en acquite et discharge envers le roy a toutz jours le dit estatut de abscentie ou ascun autre estatute adevaunt fait al contrarye nient obstauntz.

c.23

Item al supplicacion du Johan Fitzlenes prebendar' del prebend de Howth consideraunt que le dit Johan est estudent deinz lunivercitee Doxonford et ne poet pas destre present deinz cest terre saunz ceo quil puissoiet perdre son erudicion et estodye; lez premisses considerez ordeigne est enact et establie par lauctorite de cest present parlement que le dit Johan soit licence et daver pleyne libertie de absenter luy mesme hors de cest terre par le space de v ans prochein ensuant; et par mesme lauctorite que lavauntdit Johan par soy mesme cez servauntz bailliffes factours et attorneys ou ascun deux poet aver occupie et enjoier duraunt lez ditz v anes quelconques maners terrez tenementz rentz et services ovesque loure apportenau[nces] dismes fruites oblaciouns obvenciouns commoditiees et toutz autrez profities concernauntz le dit Johan saunz vexacion ou disturbaunce du nostre soveraigne seignur le roy cez heires officers ou ministrez ou ascun autre persone ou persons ascun estatute acte ordeignaunce al contrarye adevaunt fait ou ewe nyent obstaunte.

c.24

Item al supplicacion du Richard Eustace prebendar' de le prebend de Swerdes considerant que le dit Richard est estudent deinz le univercitie Doxonford et ne poet pas destre present deinz cest terre saunz ceo quil puissoit perdre son erudicion et estodye; lez premissez considerez ordeign est enacte et establie par lauctorite du cest present parlement que le dit Richard soit licence et daver pleyne libertie de absenter luy mesme hors de cest terre par lespace de v ans prochein ensuaunt; et par mesme lauctorite que lavaunt dit Richard par soy mesme cez servauntz bailliffes factours et attorneys ou ascun deux poet aver occupier et enjoier duraunt lez ditz v anes quelconques maners terrez tenementz rentz et servicz ove loure apportenauncz dismez fruytes oblaciouns obvencions commoditiees et toutz autrez profites concernauntz le dit Richard saunz ascune vexacion ou disturbaunce du nostre soveraigne seignur le roy cez heires officers ou ministreez ou ascun auter persone ou persouns ascun estatute acte ordeignaunce al contrarye adevaunt fait ou ewe nyent obstaunte.

land so caused by coercion or menace as is before rehearsed, but that, by the authority aforesaid, he be exempt altogether from the penalty of the said statute of absentees for the consideration before rehearsed, and that he be clearly acquitted and discharged thereof towards the king for ever, notwithstanding the said statute of absentees or any other statute heretofore made to the contrary.

c.23 [Licence of absence for John fitz Lenes, prebendary of Howth, studying at Oxford]

Also, at the petition of John fitz Lenes, prebendary of the prebend of Howth, considering that the said John is a student at the university of Oxford and cannot be present in this land without losing his education and study; in consideration of the premises, it is ordained, enacted and established by authority of this present parliament that the said John be licensed and have full liberty to absent himself out of this land for the space of five years next ensuing; and by the same authority, that the aforesaid John by himself, his servants, bailiffs, agents and attorneys, or any of them, may have, occupy and enjoy during the said five years whatsoever manner of lands, tenements, rents and services, with their appurtenances, tithes, fruits, oblations, obventions, commodities and all other profits concerning the said John, without vexation or disturbance by our sovereign lord the king, his heirs, officers or ministers or any other person or persons, notwithstanding any statute, act or ordinance to the contrary heretofore made or had.

c.24 [Licence of absence for Richard Eustace, prebendary of Swords, studying at Oxford]

Also, at the petition of Richard Eustace, prebendary of the prebend of Swords, considering that the said Richard is a student at the university of Oxford and cannot be present in this land without losing his education and study; in consideration of the premises, it is ordained, enacted and established by authority of this present parliament that the said Richard be licensed and have full liberty to absent himself out of this land for the space of five years next ensuing; and by the same authority, that the aforesaid Richard by himself, his servants, bailiffs, agents and attorneys, or any of them, may have, occupy and enjoy during the said five years whatsoever manner of lands, tenements, rents and services, with their appurtenances, tithes, fruits, oblations, obventions, commodities and all other profits concerning the said Richard without any vexation or disturbance by our sovereign lord the king, his heirs, officers or ministers or

Prorogacio eiusdem parliamenti ibidem tenti die lune proximo post festum Sancti Petri quod dicitur ad vincula anno regni regis supradicti supradicto[36] coram prefato deputato etc.

c.25

Item al supplicacion du James Ormond chivaler governoure et tresorer Dirland que lou il pleroit nostre soverayn seignur qui ore est du son tresnoble et habundant grace de graunter a luy lez terrez spectauntez al count del March deinz cest terre desoubthz sez lettrez patentez sicome pluis pleynement appiert par le mesme que sez ditz lettrez patentez sount demez et adjuges par auctorite du cest present parlement bonez et loials ascun act ordenaunce ou graunt fait devaunt cest temps al contrary nient obstaunt; auxi sicome que lou en lez counteez du Kilkenny et Typperary sount divers gastes terrez conqueres par lez irrois enemyez du roy queulx ils ount disturbez entre eulx sicome sez propre terrez al dishenheritaunce du verey heirez du mesme a toutz jourez et ne poient jammez par eulx de estre recoverez par nule meane quil ne soit remedie serroit par en contynuance le vit distruccion de ditz countees que Dieu ne voilloet; ordine est et consideracion de premissez est graunte et ordine par auctorite de cest dit present parlement si lez heirez de ditz terrez ne veignent et enhabitent eulx par le fest du Pask prochein avener[37] que adonques le dit James du Ormond avera et enyoia eulx et en eulx entrare et enhabiter en ensi eulx averer a luy et sez heirez a toutz jours sicome sez propre terrez et enheritaunce; et par la mesme auctorite que cest act ne extend ne soit prejudiciale a nule spirituale person ou persones pour lour enterest et droit.

c.26

Item al supplicacion du Johan Alleyn dean de esglise cathedrale du Seint Patrikis du Divelyn entaunt que le dit esglise est du fundacion nostre soverain seignur le roy et fuit roialment et notablement endowe ove suffisaunt possessiones spirituell et temporell en chescun estate dignite et degre et ensi continua plusours anez et jours en prosperite al honoure du Dieu et Seint Patric et contynuaunce du hospitalite deinz le mesme il est ensy ore que lez ditz possessions sibien en spiritualte come en temporalte sount ensi graundement et evidentment degastes et dymynusez que le dit Johan dean ne poet devoutment

36 5 August 1493. 37 30 March 1494.

any other person or persons, notwithstanding any statute, act or ordinance to the contrary heretofore made or had,.

Prorogation of the same parliament there held on Monday next after the feast of St Peter which is called ad Vincula in the aforesaid year of the reign of the aforesaid king [5 August 1493] before the aforesaid deputy etc.

c.25 [Sir James Ormond to have waste lands in cos. Kilkenny and Tipperary unless the heirs come to inhabit them]

Also, at the petition of James Ormond, knight, governor and treasurer of Ireland, that whereas it pleased our sovereign lord that now is of his very noble and abundant grace to grant to him the lands belonging to the earl of March in this land, under his letters patent as more fully appears by the same, that his said letters patent are deemed and adjudged by authority of this present parliament good and lawful, notwithstanding any act, ordinance or grant heretofore made to the contrary; also as whereas in the counties of Kilkenny and Tipperary there are various waste lands conquered by the king's Irish enemies which they have distributed among them as their own lands to the disinheritance of the true heirs of the same for ever, and cannot by any means ever be recovered by them unless it be remedied, which would be, if continued, the speedy destruction of the said counties, which God forbid; it is ordained and in consideration of the premises, is granted and ordained by authority of this said present parliament that if the heirs of the said lands do not come and dwell in them by the feast of Easter next coming [30 March 1494], that then the said James of Ormond shall have and enjoy them and shall enter into and dwell in them and so shall have them to him and his heirs for ever as his own lands and inheritance; and by the same authority, that this act do not extend or be prejudicial to any spiritual person or persons as to their interest and right.

c.26 [The dean of St Patrick's, Dublin, his successors and tenants to be exempt from payment of taxes]

Also, at the petition of John Alleyn, dean of the cathedral church of St Patrick of Dublin, inasmuch as the said church is of the foundation of our sovereign lord the king and was royally and notably endowed with sufficient possessions spiritual and temporal in every estate, dignity and degree and so continued for many years and days in prosperity, to the honour of God and St Patrick and continuance of hospitality in the same, and now the said possessions both in spirituality and in temporality are so greatly and evidently wasted and diminished, that the said John the dean cannot devoutly serve God without worldly impediment and honourably maintain hospitality and support all other ordinary

deservire Dieu saunce impediment du mounde et honestment du garder hospitalite et supporter toutz alterez ordinaries chargez et nient obstaunt le dit Johan dean est charge annuelment et de jour en aultre ove taxes tollagez et subsidiez puis et longement importablez que jammez fuit ascun de sez predecessours deanes du Divelyn entaunt que jammez ne fuit ascun dean du Divelyn ne dignite du dean en spirituale et temporale possessions ne tenauntis chargez par force ou graunt du ascun subsidy suis ou oultre le somme du xxx s. du money curraunt jesques al temps du benoit memory William evesque de Mithe et depute lieutenaunt Dirland et de cele temps a ore le dit Johan dean par force du double subsidy graunte a parlement tenuz devaunt le dit depute a le citte du Divelyn ad este et est a chescun subsidi graunte par force ou auctorite du ascun parlement charge ove iij livres al importable al dit Johan dean de supporter considerez lez evidentz gastez et dymynusions du lez possessions avauntditz lez premissez graciousment considerez et que toutz sez possessions spirituall et temporall sount en le pais du march et plus semblable al decresser que encresser de jour en aultre; in consideracion de que enacte ajuge et establie par auctorite du cest present parlement que le dit Johan dean et sez successours ils et lour tenauntis fermours et du sez et lour spirituale possessions desorenavaunt soient frankement et quite exoneratz et dischargez du toutz et chescun taxez chalangez et subsidiez ou ascun aultre temporell exaccions ou imposicions puis appres de estre grauntez et ewez queulxconques nommez ils soient nommez; et que par le mesme auctorite toutz et chescun maner proctours assessours ou collectours soient oultrement dischargez envers nostre soverain seignur le roy sez heirez ministrez et officerez pur taxacion ou assession du ascun taxez tollagis ou subsidiez deinz ou sur ascun possession ou possessions parteynauntes al dit Johan dean et que soit loyal al dit Johan dean et as sez successours lour servauntis et officerez a deforcer ascun person ou personez ou officer du quelconque degre ou condicion il ou ils sount qui voilent presumere ou attempter de prendre ascun distresse ou plegge en ou sour ascunz possessions ou parcell du mesme al dit Johan dean sez successours ou dignite en ascun maner parteynauntis pour ascun tile subsidy taxis ou tollagis sicome est devaunt reherce saunce ascun offence empechement molestacion ou grevaunce a aver envers le roy sez heirez officerez ou ministrez purvieu que nule soit charge que roy.

c.27

Item al requisicion dez communez en consideracion que le tresorer Dirland toutz foitz ad accompte un foitz chescun tierce ane pour toutz revenuz du ceste terre al entencion que dit revenuz serroient emploie sur le public profite del dit terre en tiel maner que le dit revenuz ne serroit enbeslie ne myse al singulare

charges; and notwithstanding this, the said John the dean is charged yearly and from day to day with taxes, tallages and subsidies greater and more insupportable than any of his predecessors, deans of Dublin, ever were, inasmuch as no dean of Dublin, or dignity of dean in spiritual or temporal possessions or tenants, were ever charged by force or grant of any subsidy, above or beyond the sum of thirty shillings of current money until the time of bishop William of blessed memory, now late bishop of Meath, and deputy lieutenant of Ireland; and from that time to now the said John the dean, by reason of the double subsidy granted by the parliament held before the said deputy in the city of Dublin has been and is, in every subsidy granted by force or authority of any parliament, charged with three pounds which is impossible for the said John the dean to bear, considering the evident waste and diminution of the possessions aforesaid; in gracious consideration of the premises, and the fact that all his possessions spiritual and temporal are in the country of the march and more likely to decrease than to increase from day to day, in consideration of which, it is enacted, adjudged and established by authority of this present parliament that the said John the dean and his successors they and their tenants farmers and his and their spiritual possessions from henceforth be freely and completely exonerated and discharged of all taxes, challenges and subsidies or any other temporal exactions or imposts hereafter to be granted and had by whatsoever names they be called; and by the same authority that all and every manner of proctors, assessors or collectors be altogether discharged towards our sovereign lord the king, his heirs, ministers and officers for taxation or assessment of any taxes, tallages or subsidies in or upon any possession or possessions belonging to the said John the dean, and that it be lawful for the said John the dean and for his successors, their servants and officers to deforce any person or persons or officers of whatever degree or condition he or they are, who will presume or attempt to take any distress or pledge in or upon any possessions or part of the same in any manner appertaining to the said John the dean, his successors or dignity for any such subsidy, taxes or tallages as is before rehearsed, without any offence, hindrance, molestation or grievance to be had on the part of the king, his heirs, officers or ministers, provided that it be no charge to the king.

c.27 [Sir Roland fitz Eustace, former treasurer of Ireland, to appear and account for his term of office]

Also, at the request of the commons, in consideration of the fact that the treasurer of Ireland has always accounted once every third year for all revenues of this land to the intent that the said revenues should be employed for the

profite par reason du quele lez subjectis du roy doient estre discharges du toutz maneres imposicions taxes subsidies et toutz aulterez maneres imposicions; lez premissez considerez et commaunt sire Rouland fitz Eustace chivalier fuit tresorere du cest dit terre par la space du xl annez et pluis et jammez nad compta du temps quile ad le dit office mez toutz jours ad espendu et convertz lez revenuz du cest terre a son mesme singulare profite et use ordine est enacte et establie par auctorite du cest present parlement que le dit sire Rouland veigne et appierge en sa propre person devaunt lez baronz du leschequere du roy en cest terre le xvme du Seint Michell prochen avener[38] et illeoques a demurere en le gard du mareschall del dit exchekere tanque il parclose son entiere accompt pour le dit revenuz duraunt le temps quile fuit treasorere du la dit terre et a satisfier lez arreragis de son dit accompte; et par le mesme auctorite si le dit sire Rouland ne viendra et appierge et accompta come devaunt est dit que adonques il forfetera son terre et ses bons et son corps de estre al volunte le roy.

c.28

Item al supplicacion de Symon Murghell servaunt al tresnoble et potent sire James Dormond chivalliere governoure et tresorere Dirland commaunt en le temps de esteive le dit governour en Engleterre le dit Symon duraunt le space et temps dele un ane fuit ensy vexe et spoille en son corps et bienez par un Edmond Vale et William Vale enhabitauntes en la vile du Kilkenny par maintenaunce du un Thomas Hacket et Richard Archere de le dit vile que le dit Symon fuit myse beucoupz et plusours foitz en graunde yeopardy et perile de sa vie et al lesions et perdez du xl li. et puis pour quelx il ad fete beucoups foitz pursute et chalange dount jesques a ore il ne poet jammez de estre remedie mez par maintenaunce dez amyz defende encountre tout droit en conscience et auxi en defaulte du justice et ministrez du ley a son utter anientisment sile ne soit remedie; pour que en consideracion dez premissez et de son graunde poverte par auctorite du cest parlement est enacte et ordine si lez ditz personez Edmond William Thomas et Richard ne vint pas et rend loure corpsez al gard du constabill du chatell du roy de Divelyn al xv^{e} du Seint Michell prochen avener[39] si le bill comprehend verite sour pein en la bill comprise a respoundre al premissez sicome le courte du roy du chauncery voet agarder que soit loiale al Johan Wise chief baron du eschekere du roy en Irland justice depute pour le dit counte al assigner as ditz partiez et al chescun du eulx tiell lieu et temps sicome il pensera covenable et en lez ditz materez de oiere et terminere et exe-

38 13 October 1493. 39 13 October 1493.

public profit of the said land, in such manner that the said revenues should not be embezzled nor put to private profit, by reason whereof the king's subjects should be discharged of all manners of impositions, taxes, subsidies and all other kinds of imposts; in consideration of the premises and how Sir Roland fitz Eustace, knight, was treasurer of this said land for the space of forty years and more and has never accounted in the time that he has the said office but has always expended and converted the revenues of this land to his own private profit and use, it is ordained, enacted and established by authority of this present parliament, that the said Sir Roland come and appear in person before the barons of the king's exchequer in this land on the quindene of St Michael next [13 October 1493] and remain there in the custody of the marshal of the said exchequer until he closes his entire account for the said revenues during the time that he was treasurer of the said land and satisfies the arrears of his said account; and by the same authority, if the said Sir Roland will not come and appear and account as is before said, that then he shall forfeit his land and his goods and his body shall be at the king's will.

c.28 [Edmond Vale and others to appear to answer for the attack on Simon Murghell]

Also, at the petition of Simon Murghell, servant of the very noble and powerful lord James of Ormond, knight, governor and treasurer of Ireland, that whereas at the time of the stay of the said governor in England, the said Simon during the space and term of a year was so harassed and despoiled in his person and goods by one Edmond Vale and William Vale, inhabitants of the town of Kilkenny, by the maintenance of one Thomas Hacket and Richard Archer of the said town, that the said Simon was put many and several times in great jeopardy and peril of his life and to injuries and losses of forty pounds and more, for which he has many times made suit and claim, and for which he can never get redress, but is denied by the maintenance of [their] friends, contrary to all right and conscience, and also in default of a justice and ministers of the law to his complete destruction unless he be redressed; wherefore in consideration of the premises and of his great poverty, by authority of this parliament, it is enacted and ordained that if the said persons Edmond, William, Thomas and Richard do not come and surrender their bodies to the custody of the constable of the king's castle of Dublin on the quindene of St Michael next [13 October 1493] if the bill contains truth, under the penalty contained in the bill, to answer the premises as the king's court of chancery will award, that it shall be lawful for John Wise, chief baron of the king's exchequer in Ireland, justice deputed for the said county to assign to the said parties and every of them such place and time as he shall think suitable and in the said matters to hear and

cuter ove sicome pleyn estrete poere et auctorite al executer sicome il fuit determine en le dit courte du chauncery ou en ascun courte que le roy ad devaunt ascun du sez juges par cours del comen ley.

c.29

Item al supplicacion du Patrik Dillon gentilman fitz et heire al Johan Dillon esquiere que lou Rogere Devenysh et William Hotehald chapellains furent seisez du manerez du Staffordeston' et Gilloweston' ove lez appurtenauncez en le counte du Mithe en lour demesne come du fee et ensy esteaunt seisez par son fait endente tripartiz xxix jour du octobre le xj^{m} ane du regne du roy Henry le iiij[40] dona lez ditz manerez ove lour appurtenauntis al un Johan Netervile fitz et heyre al Henry Netervile de aver et tenir a luy et lez heirez de son corps venauntis par reson du quele le dit Johan Netervile fuit dicele seise en son demesne come de fee taile par reason du dit don et ensi esteaunt seise dicele murruist seise aprese quele mort un Margaret Netervile et Jonet Netervile come fils et heirez al dit Johan Netervile entera en lez ditz manerez et seignuriez et feserent particion ewelment accordaunt al ley et le dit Margaret prist al marite le dit Johan Dillon et ount issue le dit Patrik; lez premissez considerez est ordine et enacte et establie par auctorite du cest present parlement que soit loiale al dit Patrik et sez heirez aprese le mort de sa dit mere sicome fitz et heire a ele a enter en le moite du lez ditz manerez accordaunt al dit don et particion et le mesme de aver et enyoiere accordaunt al dit don ascun feoffement estate act matere ou cause fait a contrary dicele nient obstant; et que le dit act nient extend ne soit prejudiciale al Richard Bernewall fitz et heire al dit Jonet Netervile ne al son feffe del aultre moitie del ditz manerez; et par le mesme auctorite que le cest act ne soit prejudiciale al abbe du Seint Marie abbay ne a sez successours en nule manere.

c.30

Item al supplicacion du Cristofre Bernewall chivalere seignur du Trymleteston' que lou le dit Cristofre est seise en son demesne sicome du fee del maner du Moymurdry en le counte du Mithe ove lez appurtenauncez qui est en chescun tax tollage et subsidi extent al charew du terre et pluis et est ensy que lez seignurs deins cestez iiij countees sount clerez du lour mesmez

40 29 October 1409.

determine and execute with as full strict power and authority to execute as if it were determined in the said court of chancery or in any court which the king has before any of his judges according to the course of the common law.

c.29 [Patrick Dillon to enter into possession of half of the lands of Staffordstown and Gillstown, co. Meath]

Also, at the petition of Patrick Dillon, *gentilman*, son and heir to John Dillon, esquire, that whereas Roger Devenish and William Hotehald, chaplains, were seised of the manors of Staffordstown and Gillstown with the appurtenances in the county of Meath in their demesne as of fee and so being seised by their tripartite deed indented of the twenty-ninth day of October in the eleventh year of the reign of king Henry the fourth [29 October 1409] gave the said manors with their appurtenances to one John Netervile, son and heir to Henry Netervile, to have and to hold to him and the heirs issuing of his body, by reason whereof the said John Netervile was seised thereof in his demesne as of fee tail by reason of the said gift and being so seised thereof died seised, after whose death one Margaret Netervile and Jonet Netervile as daughters and heirs to the said John Netervile entered into the said manors and lordships and made partition equally, according to law; and the said Margaret took to husband the said John Dillon and they have issue the said Patrick; in consideration of the premises, it is ordained and enacted and established by authority of this present parliament that it be lawful for the said Patrick and his heirs after the death of his said mother, as her son and heir, to enter into half of the said manors according to the said gift and partition, and to have and enjoy the same according to the said gift, notwithstanding any feoffment, estate, act, matter or cause made to the contrary thereof; and that the said act do not extend or be prejudicial to Richard Bernewall, son and heir to the said Jonet Netervile or to her feoffee of the other half of the said manors; and by the same authority that this act be not prejudicial to the abbot of St Mary's abbey or to his successors in any manner.

c.30 [Manor of Moymurdry, co. Meath, discharged from payment of coign and livery and other charges]

Also, at the petition of Christopher Bernewall, knight, lord of Trimleston, that whereas the said Christopher is seised in his demesne as of fee of the manor of Moymurdry in the county of Meath, with the appurtenances which is extended in every tax, tallage and subsidy at a ploughland and more, and that the lords in these four counties are clear as to their own demesnes; in consideration of the premises and of the good service which the said Christopher has

demainez; lez premissez considerez in consideracion del bon service que le dit Cristofre ad fait al nostre soverayn seignur le roy deinz cest sa terre ordine est enacte et establie par auctorite du cest present parlement que desorenavaunt le dit maner ove lez appurtenauncis soit clerement quitez et utterment dischargez du tout charrettaunce coigne lyvere et pay par reason du mesme; et que le dit maner ove lez appurtenaunce soit extente et prise pur nient pluis que pur le moite charew du terre en[41] chescun tax tollage et subsidy; et que soit loiale al dit Cristofre et sez heires al deforcere toutz et chescun collectour pur le surpluis saunz ascun empechement ou molestacion de estre ewe par nostre soverain seignur le roy sez officeres ou ministrez envers le dit Cristofre ou sez heires; et que par le mesme auctorite lez collectours pur le temps estauntez deins le barony du Diueleke soient allowez et discharges sur lour accompt pur taunt que vient al dit surpluis ensi dischargez.

c.31

Item al supplicacion du Robert Preston vicount du Gormaneston' que lou lez villes du Balscaddan le Ring Matte et Lideston' ove lour appurtenauncez en le counte de Divelyn sount en graunde parte gastez pur cause lez terrez parteynauntis a icell sount moilez et base terrez et auxi oppresses ensi ove subsidiez taxes et aultres imposicionez assessez sour eulx sicome iij charuez du terre et xx acrez et pur que plusours del tenauntis ount avoidez le ditz terrez et puis sount semblement de estre avoiedez; pur que en consideracion al enhabiter lez ditz terrez meulez ordine est par auctorite du cest present parlement que lez ditz villes ove lour appurtenauncez soient mysez et assessez a ij charuez du terre et nient pluis et que toutz manerez collectourez et collectour distreina nient pluis sour lez ditz villez mese pour ij charuez du terre et sils facent est loiale al dit Robert eulx a deforcer.

c.32

Item al supplicacion de James priour del meason de Holmpatrik en le counte du Divelin et le covent du mesme que lou come lez ditz priour et covent ount commensez un eopre fesaunt une pile ou porte adjunaunt al terre nosme Medlok et de ceo en le hault mier juxt le village de Skerray juxt le dit meason quell serra la preservaunce dez viez et biens du plusurs homez lou come divers batelx maryners et merchauntz ove becoupz biens en defaute de socoure ount estez aventurez et subzmergez ore en tarde jours passez sicome est outrement

41 *ou* in transcript.

rendered to our sovereign lord the king in this his land, it is ordained, enacted and established by authority of this present parliament that from henceforth the said manor, with the appurtenances be clearly acquitted and altogether discharged of all cartage, coign, livery and payment by reason of the same and that the said manor with the appurtenances be extended and taken for no more than the half of a ploughland in every tax, tallage and subsidy; and that it be lawful for the said Christopher and his heirs to deforce all and every collector for the surplus without any hindrance or molestation by our sovereign lord the king, his officers or ministers against the said Christopher or his heirs; and by the same authority that the collectors for the time being in the barony of Duleek be allowed and discharged on their account for so much as the said surplus so discharged comes to.

c.31 [Balscaddan and other lands in co. Dublin to be assessed as two ploughlands]

Also, at the petition of Robert Preston, viscount of Gormanston, that whereas the vills of Balscaddan, Ring, Matt and Lidestown with their appurtenances in the county of Dublin, are in great part waste because the lands belonging thereto are wet and low lands and also so oppressed with subsidies, taxes and other impositions assessed upon them as three ploughlands and twenty acres, and therefore many of the tenants have left the said lands and more are likely to leave; wherefore in consideration for the inhabiting of the said wet lands, it is ordained by authority of this present parliament that the said towns with their appurtenances be put and assessed at two ploughlands and no more, and that all manner of collectors and collector shall distrain on the said towns for no more than for two ploughlands and if they do so that it is lawful for the said Robert to deforce them.

c.32 [Holmpatrick priory to receive new custom on fishing vessels called poundage to enable it to complete a harbour near Skerries]

Also, at the petition of James, prior of the house of Holmpatrick in the county of Dublin, and the convent of the same, that whereas the said prior and convent have commenced a work making a mole or port adjoining the land called Medlok and from that into the high sea near the village of Skerries near the said house which will be the preservation of the lives and goods of many men, whereas in recent times various vessels, mariners and merchants with much goods have been endangered and sunk in default of succour, as is openly held, and the fact that the quay of the same is almost finished at the great costs and

tenuz et que la key du mesme est prez finisshe as graund custagez et chargez dez ditz priour et covent et ils ne purroient performer et finissher le dit eopre sicome lez chargez ordinariez et oultre ordinariez come le hospitalite sount sy graundez; en consideracion du quell et lez ditz priour et covent ne sount pas hablez de continuer le devine service de Dieu en la dit meason et de performer le dit eopre et toutz jours de repairer et garder le suys ove annuell reparacion sinon il ne voet endurer pur que il est de jour en aultre et de neet en aultre studaunt ove graundez fluviez du mayn marie et auxi consideraunt que toutz lour possessions quils ount sount sy petitz de value et ils ne sount suffisantment enduez accordaunt a lour chargz et al extent quils purroient finissher le dit eopre sy charitable commense ordeine est enacte et establie par auctorite du cest present parlement que de ceo en avaunt lez ditz priour et covent et lour successours a toutz jours ewent levent et perceyvent en pure et perpetuell almoyn le nowell custom nosme le pondage de toutz et chescun manere vessaulx ou vesshanhours venauntz al pays pur pisherie sibien pour flask pischarie merluse et harings come ascun aultre manere du nature du pisherie pour toutz maner dez merchaundisez ils ou ascun de eulx portent al dit pile ou porte et la de estre discharge et le poundage dent destre leve en semblable manere et fourme sicome est en lez poortes de Divelin et Drogheda et le dit pondage ensy leve destre emploie et expendu sur lez ditz meason porte et pile al discrecion del dit priour et covent et lour successours a toutz jours par qui le divine service de Dieu purroit estre le meultz encresse et continue en le dit meason; et par mesme lauctorite ordeine est enacte et establie que si ascun person ou persone eiauntz auctorite ou null auctoritie attempte ou presume de lever le dit pondage ou revenuz cressauntz et venauntz du mesme en prejudice dez ditz priour et covent desorenavaunt deinz le dit pile porte bay ou aultre krikke ou lieu deinz lez possessions dez ditz priour et covent ou lour successours que bien list a eulx et chescun de eulx pur le temps esteauntz de rescower et disturber eux et chescun de eulx ensy offendauntz le mesme; et oultre ceo que chescun person et persons ensy offendauntz ou attemptauntz lez premissez ou ascun dez contemptz en icest act apres ils ou ascun dils soient requirez par lez ditz priour et covent ou ascun de lour successours a toutz jours de cesser dicell a forfeter et dever as ditz priour et covent et a lour successours a toutz jours xx li. du loiall mone si tauntz de foitz com ils ou ascun du eulx offende lez premissez ou ascun du eulx; et par mesme lauctorite bien list as ditz priour et covent et lour successours a toutz jours daver et suer un accion de dett en ascun courte que le roy ad pur lez ditz xx li. ensy forfetez sibien par breve come par bille selom lordre et cours come aultres briefes et billes sount suez en ascun dez ditz courtz; et par mesme lauctorite ordeine est et enacte et establie que toutz et chescun maner don et dons graunt doffice et grauntz dez officez relessez confirmacions liberteez franchesiez courtz consuetudez customez warennez wrekks wayffz et

charges of the said prior and convent and they could not complete and finish the said work as the charges ordinary and extraordinary, such as hospitality, are so great; in consideration of which and that the said prior and convent are not able to continue the divine service of God in the said house and to complete the said work and always to repair and maintain it with annual repairs, without which it will not endure inasmuch as it is daily and nightly contending with the great tides of the main sea, and also considering that all the possessions which they have are of so little value and that they are not sufficiently endowed in proportion to their charges, and to the intent that they might be able to finish the said work so charitably commenced, it is ordained, enacted and established by authority of this present parliament that henceforth the said prior and convent and their successors for ever shall have, levy and receive in pure and perpetual alms the new custom called poundage from all and every manner of vessels or boats coming to those parts for fishing, for flask fishing, cod and herrings as well as any other kind or nature of fishing, for all manner of merchandise that they or any of them carry to the said mole or port and to be discharged there, and the poundage thereof to be levied in like manner and form as it is in the ports of Dublin and Drogheda and the said poundage so levied to be employed and expended on the said house, port and mole, at the discretion of the said prior and convent and their successors for ever, whereby the divine service of God may be best increased and continued in the said house; and by the same authority, it is ordained, enacted and established that if any person or persons, having authority or no authority, attempt or presume to levy the said poundage or revenues accruing and coming from the same, in prejudice of the said prior and convent henceforth in the said mole, port, bay or other creek or place in the possession of the said prior and convent or their successors, that it shall be lawful for them and every of them for the time being to rescue it and to disturb them and every one of them so offending the same; and moreover that every person and persons so offending or attempting the premises or any of the contempts in this act, after they or any of them shall be required by the said prior and convent or any of their successors for ever to cease therefrom, shall forfeit and owe to the said prior and convent and to their successors for ever twenty pounds of lawful money as often as they or any of them offend the premises or any of them; and by the same authority, it shall be lawful for the said prior and convent and their successors for ever to have and sue an action of debt in any court which the king has for the said twenty pounds so forfeited, by writ or by bill, according to the order and course as other writs and bills are sued in any of the said courts; and by the same authority, it is ordained and enacted and established that all and every manner of gift and gifts, grant of office and grants of offices, releases, confirmations, liberties, franchises, courts, usages, customs, warrens, wrecks, waifs and all other kinds

toutz aultrez maners possessions queuxconques dount lez ditz priour et covent et lour predecessours ount seisiez ou possessez ou ore sount come en droit de lour dit meason ove cest clause licet abusi vel non usi fuerint devaunt cestz heurs sibien donez par nostre soverain seignur le roy quorest ou ascun de sez noble progenitours ou predecessours come par ascun aultre person ou persons par mesme auctorite sount auctorisez approvez et confirmez et lez ditz priour et covent et lour successours a toutz jours a aver et enjoier eulx et chescun de eulx saunz ascun disturbaunce vexacion suite empechement molestacion ou grevaunce ewez ou destre ewez par nostre soverain seignur le roy quorest sez heirs successours officers ou ministrez en temps avener queuxconques ou par quelconques nons soient nosmez ascun graunt act ordenaunce cause ou matier contrarie a lez premissiz ewe ou destre ewe nient obstaunt; et que cest act nextend ne soit prejudiciall al ascun graunt ou grauntz faitz devaunt cestz heurs faitz as enhabitauntz del citte du Dyvelin concernauntz lour liberteez et franchesez ne a nule maner graunt ne grauntz faitz as enhabitauntz del vile de Drogheda ne a sez liberteez et francheses ne a Robert Talbot et Water fitz Symon gentilman ne a nule de eulx doffice de admiralte ne al seignur de Houth ne al abb du meason du Benoit Marie juxt Dyvelin.

[Note by Roderick Connor]: The following memorandum is upon the back of the last membrane but one of this roll. Memorandum quod sexto die Octobris anno regni regis Henrici septimi nono[42] Jacobus Colyn deliberavit hunc rotulum Thomae Botiller clerico rotulorum cancellarie.

42 6 October 1493.

of possessions whatsoever of which the said prior and convent and their predecessors have been seised or possessed or now are as in right of their said house, with this clause "although they shall have been abused or not used" heretofore given by our sovereign lord the king that now is or any of his noble progenitors or predecessors or by any other person or persons, by the same authority are authorised, approved and confirmed and the said prior and convent and their successors for ever, shall have and enjoy them and every one of them without any disturbance, vexation, suit, hindrance, molestation or grievance had or to be had by our sovereign lord the king that now is, his heirs, successors, officers or ministers, in time to come, whomsoever or by whatever names they be named, notwithstanding any grant, act, ordinance, cause or matter contrary to the premises had or to be had; and that this act do not extend or be prejudicial to any grant or grants heretofore made to the inhabitants of the city of Dublin touching their liberties and franchises or to any manner of grant or grants made to the inhabitants of the town of Drogheda or to its liberties and franchises, or to Robert Talbot and Walter fitz Simon, *gentilman*, or to either of them of the office of admiralty, or to the lord of Howth or to the abbot of the house of the Blessed Mary near Dublin.

Note: Memorandum that on the sixth day of October in the ninth year of the reign of king Henry the seventh [6 October 1493], James Colyn delivered this roll to Thomas Botiller, clerk of the rolls of chancery.

28–29 Henry VIII

[*m.1*]

[1]Statuta ordinaciones et provisiones in quod[2] perliamento illustrissimi principis et domini nostri domini Henrici octavi Dei gratia Anglie et Francie regis fidei defensoris et domini Hibernie virtute commissionis et mandati dicti domini regis sub magno sigillo suo[3] Anglie apud Dublin' die lune primo die mensis Maij anno regni eiusdem domini regis vicesimo octavo[4] coram dilecto et fideli suo domino Leonardo Gray milite domino Gray deputato ipsius domini regis ac precharissimi et dilectissimi consanguinei sui Henrici ducis Richmond et Somersett de prosapia sua orti locumtenentis sui terre et dominii sui Hibernie tento edita et abinde die mercurii videlicet ultimo die eiusdem mensis Maij tunc proxime sequente usque diem Martiris[5] videlicet vicesimum quintum diem Julij tunc proxime sequentem ad villam de Kylkenn' adiornato et ibidem tento et continuato ibidem die mercurii videlicet vicesimo sexto die Julij usque diem veneris tunc proxime sequentem videlicet vicesimo octavo die eiusdem mensis Julij tunc proxime sequentem ad villam de Casshell adiornato et ibidem tento et continuato et ibidem dicto die veneris videlicet vicesimo octavo die dicti mensis Julij usque diem mercurii tunc proxime sequentem videlicet secundo die Augusti tunc proxime sequente[6] ad civitatem Limeric' adiornato et ibidem tento et continuato et ibidem die sabati videlicet decimo nono die eiusdem mensis Augusti usque diem veneris videlicet decimo quinto die mensis Septembris tunc proxime sequentem[7] ad civitatem Dublin' predictam adiornato et ibidem tento et continuato et ibidem die Jovis videlicet vicesimo octavo die eiusdem mensis Septembris usque diem sabati videlicet vicesimo die[8] Januarii tunc proxime sequentem ad dictam civitatem Dublin' prorogato et ibidem tento et continuato et ibidem die martis videlicet quinto die Februarii tunc proxime sequente usque diem martis videlicet primo die[9] Maij tunc proxime sequentem ad dictam civitatem Dublin' prorogato et ibidem tento [et] continuato et ibidem die martis videlicet octavo die Maij tunc proxime sequent[e] usque diem veneris videlicet vicesimo die[10] Julij tunc proxime sequentem ad dictam civit[atem] Dublin' prorogato et ibidem tento et continuato et ibidem die sabati videlicet xxj die Julij tunc proxime sequente usque diem sabati videlicet xiij diem Octobris tunc proxime sequentem ad dictam civitatem Dublin' prorogato et ibidem xx die Decembris tunc proxime sequente finito et terminato.

[Statutes, ordinances and provisions made in a parliament of our most

1 The roll is damaged at the right hand edge. Editorial additions are indicated by square brackets. Dates of transmisses, where known, have been supplied from TCD MS 1739. 2 recte *quodam*. 3 *suo* inserted. 4 1 May 1536. 5 recte *martis*. 6 recte *secundum diem ,,, sequentem*. 7 recte *decimum quintum … sequentem*. 8 recte *vicesimum diem*. 9 recte *primum diem*. 10 recte *vicesimum diem*.

illustrious prince and our lord, lord Henry the eighth by the grace of God, king of England and France, defender of the faith and lord of Ireland, held, by virtue of the said lord king's commission and order under his great seal of England, at Dublin on Monday the first day of the month of May in the twenty eighth year of the reign of the same lord king [1536], before his beloved and faithful lord Leonard Gray, knight, lord Gray, deputy of the same lord king and of his very dear and beloved kinsman, Henry, duke of Richmond and Somerset, sprung from his lineage, his lieutenant of his land and dominion of Ireland, and from there on Wednesday, that is, the last day of the same month of May then next following, adjourned to Tuesday, that is, the twenty fifth day of July then next following at the town of Kilkenny, and there held and continued [and] there, on Wednesday, that is, the twenty sixth day of July adjourned to the Friday then next following, that is, the twenty eighth day of the same month of July then next following, at the town of Cashel, and there held and continued, and there, on the said Friday, that is the twenty eighth day of the said month of July adjourned to the Wednesday then next following, that is, the second day of August then next following at the city of Limerick, and there held and continued and there on Saturday, that is the nineteenth day of the same month of August, adjourned to Friday, that is, the fifteenth day of the month of September then next following at the said city of Dublin, and there on Thursday, that is, the twenty eighth day of the same month of September, prorogued to Saturday, that is, the twentieth day of January then next following at the said city of Dublin, and there held and continued, and there on Tuesday, that is, the fifth day of February then next following,[11] prorogued to Tuesday, that is, the first day of May then next following at the said city of Dublin, and there held and continued, and there on Tuesday, that is, the eighth day of May then next following prorogued to Friday, that is, the twentieth day of July then next following at the said city of Dublin, and there held and continued, and there on Saturday, that is, the twenty first day of July then next following, prorogued to Saturday, that is, the thirteenth day of October then next following at the said city of Dublin, and there on the twentieth day of December then next following, finished and terminated.]

c.1 Thact of atteyndor[12]

Prayeth the comens in this present parliament assembled that forasmoche as Gerald fitz Gerald late Erle of Kyldare amongis manifolde and diverse enormities abuses and offences contrarie his naturall dutie of allegiaunce attemptid

11 There is an error in the date as given here. The correct date is either Monday, 5 February or Tuesday, 6 February. 12 *Statutes at large* c.1. Transmiss dated 13 September 1535.

and committid against the crowne right majestie and dignitie of our naturall and moste dread souverain lorde Henry the eight by the grace of God king of England and of Fraunce defensor of the faithe and lorde of Irland and in erthe supreme heade of the churche[13] of England the xvj yere of his moste noble reigne[14] confederid and assentid to and with oon James late Erle of Desmounde being opinly proclamed and published rebell and tradictor against our said souverain lorde for that[15] he the said James shulde sende to the frenche king then enemye unto his grace and at oppin warre with hime and his dominions to excite provoke and stirre the same frenche king to sende into thes land of Iland an armie for the taaking of the same lande oute of our said souveranne lordes possession and notwithstanding that his traitours entent wolde not take effecte by reason of a pax that then immediatelie was concludid betwixt our said souverain lorde and the frenche king he sent unto the Emperour provoking and intysing him to send an armie into this said lande for the purpose aforsaid our souverain lorde the king hawing previe intelligence theirof willid secretly the said Erle of Kyldare then being his graces deputie of his said land of Iland to apprehende and taak the said James Erle of Dessmounde. The same Erle of Kyldare falsely and traitourslie admonished the said James theirof willing him to come to noo place where he the same Erle of Kyldare shulde be or have eny power upon him and being of this and diverse other offences remittid and pardonid by our said souverain lorde the king afterwarde sojourning at Newington' in the countie of Midd' within the realme of England the eight daie of Julie in the xx^ti^ yere of the reigne of our said souverain lorde[16] willid and commaundit his doughtir Elice fitz Geralde wyf to the Baron of Slane to repaire into this the kingis lande of Iland and in his name to will all his bretherne [*m.2*] O Neyle O Conour and all other his freyndes servauntis and allies to levie erect stirr and rere warre against our said souverain lordes deputie and subjectis falsely and traitoursly against his dutie of alligeaunce whiche she accomplished accordingly by occasion wherof the persons aforenamed falsely and traitrouselie[17] made insurreccion against our said souverain lorde and his deputie by invasion and burning kylling murdring and robbing his true obedient subjectis not desisting from the same their traitours actes untill they were by force repressid by the puissaunce and power of our said souverain lorde and notwithstanding his grace of mercie and pittie remitted and pardoned the said Erle of Kildare that his traitours conspiracies and offencis the same Erle the xxiiij^ti^ yere of our said souverain lorde[18] falsely and traitoursly contrarie to the lawes and statutes of this lande of Irland and his allegiaunce not onlie permittid and suffred O Neille the kingis Irishe ennemie to invade and distroie the

13 *of the churche* repeated and struck through. 14 1524–5. 15 *that* repeated and struck through. 16 1528. 17 *and traitrouselie* inserted. 18 1532–3.

countie of Uriell within the said lande withoute any resistence made therin by him silf being the kingis deputie having the governaunce custodie and charge of the same or eny other for him but having his brother Sir John in companie with the said O Neill by his commaundement to socour and guyde aide and conduct the said O Neill in that his traitours enterprise but also in his awne propir person envadid the countie of Kylkenn' their brannyng and distruing the same riffeling and robbyng the kingis subjectis aswell their as at the faire of Tristildeirmot crying havoke upon the kingis subjectis whiche thidtheir were resortid caused theme in his owne presence to be spoyled and robbid of their goodes and diverse of theym murdred moste cruelly and traitoursly our said souverain lorde having notice of this and other his treasons haynouse offences murdres and extorciouns by him committid and willing the reformacion of the said lande and the releif and comforte of his subjectis their addressid his most gracius lettres to the said erle of Kyldare then being deputie lieutenaunt of his said lande commaunding him by the same to repaire to his highnes presence into his realme of England leving such a parson for the fornature of his rowlme and gouvernaunce of the said lande in his absentie for whose doyngis he woulde aunswere that notwithstanding at his saide departure into England he admittid and institutid in his place for the governance of the kingis said lande and subjectis as vice deputie not only his son and heire namid Thomas fitz Gerald but also contrarie to the kingis expresse commaundement declared unto the said Erle by John Alen maister of the rolles and oone of the kyngis moste honorable counsaile on the presence of the busshop of Mith and the prior of Saint Johns Jerusalem in Irland he conveied oute of the kingis castell of Dublin all his graces gonnes poulder shoot bowes arrowes caltropps billes and all other the kingis artillerie and municions of warre garnishing and furnyshing his awne castels and fortresses with the same and deliveryng parte theirof to wilde Irishe me[n] being the kingis mortall enymes after whose departure into England he at his thedir commyng perceving upon the manifestacion of his offences that the kingis majestie entendit to remove him from the governaunce of the saide lande suche persons as were knowin to be cheif of counsaile with the said Erle and undir him had not oonly the governaunce of his said son servauntes and people with the custodie of his substaunce and goodes but also of all his landes manors castels and garisons aswell counsaillid the said Thomas fitz Gerald to rebell against our said souverain lorde as for the maintenaunce of h[im] therin delivered unto him the said Erles goodes substaunce manors landes castells and garisouns togidthers with the kingis said ordinaunce and artillerie. Wherupon the said Thomas fitz Gerald immediatlie being assisted and aided by his fathers bretherne kynnesmen servauntes and followers falselie and traitourslye rebellid aginst our said souverain lorde refusing and disobeing all commaundmentis of his grace and his counsaill concludid

and determyned moost cruelly to murdre put to dethe and exile all those that were resiaunt within the lande being borne within the realme of Engl[and] and to conquere and[19] take the same from the possession of our said souverain lorde and his heires reviling his grace with moste shamefull and detestable infamies and for thaccomplishment [of] his traitours purpose did send his lettirs addressid aswell to the bushopp of Rome as themperour by oon Cale Mc Granill otherwise callid Charles Reynold archedeken of Kellis for to hawe their aide against our said soverain lorde and his heires for the wynnyng of the said lande of Irland oute of the[ir] possession and he to holde the same of them for ever. And emonge other his most detestable abhominacion[s] he procured and commaunded John Teling and Nicholas Waffer of Dublin yeoman servauntes to the said Erle of Kyldare to apprehende and take the moste reverend father in God John Alen Archebusshopp of Dublin and primate of Irland and one of the kingis moste honorable counsaill and hym to kepe in prison at Tartaine within the countie of Dublin. And the said Thomas fitz Gerald the xxviijth day of Julie in the xxvj yere of the reigne of our said sovereigne lorde king Henry the eight[20] accompanied with the moste falce disloyall traytour James Delahide Sir John Fitz Gerald Olyver Fitz Gerald brethern to the said Erle and diverse other of the same Erles servauntes caused the same Archbusshop to be drauen oute of his bed and broght befor him and the same Archebushop kneling in his sherte bare foted and bare heded befor him asking of him mercie indilatelie withoute eny respite moste shamefully and traytoursly murdred and kylled oute of hande and also caused the said Archebusshopps servauntes and as many other Englishmen as he coulde finde within the lande to be murdred, and after this accompanied with the said James Delahide being principall counsaillour to him in all his dooinges John Delahide Edwarde Fitz Geralde Sir Richarde Walshe parson of Loghsewdie John Burnell of Balgriffin Edward Rowkes James Felde of Luske and other of the said Erle of Kyldares counsaillours servauntes allies and diverse others his fautors and adherentis to longe here to be expressid with weapons invasive after the maner of warre arraied and with baners displaied falselie and traitourslie envaded the kingis domynion encamping them selves within the same there robbyng ryffeling murdering and distroyng diverse the kingis subjectis constrayning all men to gyve an othe of obedience unto him and to take his parte against the king and his heires in his said falce traitours and disloiall[21] purpose and ententis and not herwith contentid but accompanied with O Nele diverse Scottes the persouns aforsaid and many others envaded brent and distroied the landes of the Erle of Ossorie and the lorde Butlers his son and of other the kingis subjectis within the countie of Kylkenn' murdred diverse of the kingis subjectis their for that the said Erle and

19 *to* struck through. 20 1534. 21 *and disloiall* inserted.

his son toke the kingis parte against him who offred unto theim to devide and give to them half the lande of Irlande to refuse the king trusting by suche his cruell persecucions to constraine theim to incline to his purpose and further emongest other his most falce traitours actes accompanied with O Conour William Bathe of Dullardeston' Christofor Ewstas of Ballycutlan' and diverse others besiegid the kingis citie and castell of Dublin entending to take the same oute of the kingis possession and to murdre the kingis subjectis within the same and theirof[22] to disenherite our said souverain lorde and his heires for ever and semblably not only fortefied and mannid diverse shipps at see for keping and letting destroing and taking the kingis deputie armie and subjectis that they shoulde not lande within the said lande but also at the arrivall of the said armie the same Thomas accompanied with the said Erles bretherne his uncles servauntes and adherentis folowers James Delahid John Delahide John Burnell of Balgriffin with diverse others too longe here to be expressid falselie and traitourslie assembled them self togidthers upon the sea coste for the keping and resisting of the kingis deputie and armie and destroing of theme and the same tyme they shamefully murdred diverse of the said armie comyng to lande and Edwarde Rowkes pyrat at the sea captaine to the said Thomas and James Felde destroied and toke manie of theym; in consideracion wherof and other abhomynable traysouns and offencis committid against our said soveraigne lorde his right crowne and majestie and dignitie by the said Geralde Erle of Kyldare Thomas Fitz Geralde James Delahide and other their aiders comfortors counsaillours and mayntenors and in detestacion of their abhominacion tirannie falshod and crueltie [*m.3*] be it enactid ordeyned and established by the king our sovereigne lorde the lordis spirituall and temporall and the commons in this present parliament assembled and by auctorite of the same that the same Geralde Fitz Geralde erle of Kyldare late deceasid from the eight daie of Julij in the xx^{ti} yere of our souverain lorde the king that now is[23] be demyd reputed convicted adjudgid and attainted traitour of high treason and that he and his heires shall lose and forfait the title stile and name of Erle of Kildare and shall also forfait to our said souverain lorde and his heires for ever all honours castells manors lordshipps letes frauncheses hundredes liberties priviledgis advousons nominacions fundacions presentacions patronages knyghtes fees landes tenementes rentis services revercions remaindours porcions annuities pensions officis and all other hereditamentes and prof[futes] whate so ever thei be wherof he the said Gerald Erle by him silf or jointly with eny other or eny other or o[thers] to his use and behof were seasid the said eight daye of Julij or eny tyme after within the lande of Irl[and] in fee simple or in fee taile or in whiche the said Geralde late Erle of Kildare or any other to his

22 *and theirof* repeated and struck through. 23 1528.

u[se had] the said eight daie of Julij or eny tyme after lawfull cause of entre within the lande of Irland and over t[hat] the said Erle lose and forfact to the king our soverain lorde aswell all maner of suche estatis of fre[hold] in use or in possession to his use and interest for yeres of all manors castells honours landes tenementes tithes oblacions and all other proffutes as all other his godes cattaills debtis duties wardes mariagis releves and [all] other profuttes whate soo ever thei be wherof the said erle or eny other or others to his use or behof were seised [or] possessid the xxvj daie of June in the[24] xxvj yere of the reigne of our sovereigne lorde[25] or eny tyme sethens of whiche goodis cattaills debtis and duties any sale gift or payment withoute eny fraude decept or collusion have not be made to or by the said Erle; provided alway and also be it enactid by the auctorite afors[aid] that all suche person or persons whiche have bene fermors occupiers tenauntes receivors baylyves stywards [servants] and other officers of the said Erle of the said honours castelles manors lordshipps landes tenementis and all o[ther] the premissis and every parcell theirof at any tyme sethens the eight daie of Julie in the xx^ti yere of our s[aid] souverain lorde[26] unto the furst daie of Februarie in the xxv yere of his gracis reigne[27] shalbe discharged and acquited against the king our said souverain lorde his heires and successours of and for all suche r[entis] yssues revenus and all other proffutes of the said manors honours castells and all other the premissis or any [part or] parcell theirof whiche they or any of theym have paied or delivered or cause to be paied or delivered unto the said [Erle] of Kyldare or any other or others by his assignement or commaundement at eny tyme befor the said first daie o[f] Februarie; and semblablie be it established ordeyned and enacted by auctoritie aforsaid that the said [Thomas] Fitz Geralde son and heire of the said erle Sir John Fitz Geralde Olyver Fitz Geralde uncles to the s[aid] Thomas James Delahide son and heire of Sir Waltier Delahide of Moyclare knyght John Delahide Ed[ward] Delahide parson of Kylberie sonnes to the said Sir Waltier John Burnell of Balgriffin esquier Sir R[ichard] Walshe parson of Loghsewdie Chale Mc Granill otherwise called Charles Reynold clerke late archedeacon [of] Kellis James Gernon son and heire of Patricke Gernon of Gernonston' Christofor Parese son and heire to Wil[liam] Parese of Aghir Piers Walshe son to Waltier Walshe Robert Walshe and Mauriche Walshe sonnes to William [Walshe] late of Tiecroghan' Edwarde Rowkes yeoman and every of theym be demyd reputed convicted adjudged and attainted traitours of high treason and that the said Thomas James De[lahide] John Delahide Edwarde Delahide John Burnell Richarde Charles James Gernon Piers Robert Maurishe and[28] Edwarde Rokes shall suffer execucion and paynes of deathe as in cases of high treasonne hath bene accustomed and that they and al[so] the said Christofor

24 *the* inserted. 25 1534. 26 1528. 27 1534. 28 *and* repeated and struck through.

Parese John Mc Gylsenan late of Ballymon' whiche ar deade and every of theym for[fait] to our souverain lorde the king his heires and successours for every all honours castells manors lordshipps us[es] hundredes letes fraunch-eses liberties priviledges advousons fundacions nominacions patronages presentacions kny[ghts] fees landes tenementis rentis services revercions remainders porcions annuities pensions offices and all other hereditamentes and proffutes whate soo ever they bee wherof they or eny of theme or eny other or others to their use and behalf or to the use and behof of any of theme were seised the xxv^{ti} daie of Julie in the xxvj^{ti} yere of the reigne of our said souverain lorde king Henry the eight[29] or any tyme after within the lande of Irland in fee simple or fe taill or into whiche any of theme had than or any tyme after lau-full cause of entre within the lande of Irland and over that they and every of theme doo forfait and lose to our said souverain lorde the king as w[ell] all maner suche estates of freholde and interest for yeres of landes tenementis tithes oblacions and all other prof[futes] as all goodes cattailles debtis duties wardes mariages and relevies and all other proffutes whate soo ever they be wherof they or eny of theme or eny other or others to their use and behof or to the use and behouf of eny of theme were seised or possessed the said xxv daie of Julie the said xxvj^{ti} yere or eny tyme sethens wherof any sale yeft or payment withoute eny fraude disceit or collusion have not be made to or by theme or eny of theme; and over that be it enacted auctorished and established by auctoritie aforsaid that after the deathe of the auncest[ors] of eny of the said persons or eny other by whome imediatly they or any of theme moght have had eny uses landes tenementes and other hereditamentes in use by discent remaindor or reverture or other wise the furst daie of Aprile in the xxv yere of our said souverain lordes reigne[30] all honours castells manors lordshipps uses hundredes fraunches libe[rties] priviledges advousons nominacions presentacions knyghtes fees landes tenementes rentes services revercions remaynders porci[ons] annuites pensions offices possessions hereditamentes and all other proffutes whate soo ever they be that they or any of theme moght have had inmediatly in use by discent remayndor reverture entre lawfull or other wise in fee simple or in fe taill the said furst daie of Aprile in the said xxv yere yf their auncetors or the auncetors of eny of theme or eny other by whome they or any of theme moght have had in use by discent remaindor reverture entre lawfull or other wise the premissis or any parte theirof then had departid this present transitorie lyf be forfait to our said souverain lorde his heires and successours for ever and that our souveraine lorde the king his heires and[31] successours immediatlie after the death of the said auncetors or anye of theme or any other by whome immediatlie they moght have any uses landes

29 1534. 30 1534. 31 *and* inserted.

tenementes and other hereditamentes in maner and forme as is aforsaid shall entre and inyoie all the said honours castels manors lordshipps landes tenementes and all other the premissis to have and to holde to our said souverain lorde his heires and successours for ever; and be it furdyr enactyd by auctoritie aforsaid that aswell all suche persons whiche sethens the feastis of all saintes in the yere of our lorde God a thousand fyve hundred xxxiiij[ti] by the course of the kingis lawes within this lande hawe bene within this lande convictid attainted of treason as all others whiche at any tyme heraftir shall chaunce within the same to be convicted or attainted of highe treason within the space of thre yeres next folowing the furst daie of this present parliament forfaite and lose to our said souveraine lorde the king and his heires all honours castells manors lordshipps letes hundredes frauncheses liberties priviledges advousons nominacions fundacions patronages presentacions knyghtes fees landes tenementes rentes services revercions remaindours porcions annui[ties] pensions offices and all other hereditamentes profictis whate soo ever they be that they or any of theme or any other or others to their use and behof or to the use and behouf of any of theme were seasid the severall daies of their severall traisons offences and trepaces by theme committid and doone or any tyme[32] aftir to be committid and done within the lande of Irland in fee simple or in fee taile or into which any of theme had than or any time after lawfull cause of entre within this lande of Irland and also loose and forfait to our said souverain lorde aswell all suche estates of freholde and interesse of yeres of landes tenementes tithes oblacions and other proffutes as all goodes cattaills debtis wardes and all other proffutes whate soo ever they be wherof thei or any of theme or any other or others to their use or to the use of any of theme were seisid or possessed at the tyme of conviccion or attainder of any suche offences [*m.4*] wherof any sale yifte or payment withoute any fraude deceit or collusion had not bene made to or by theme or any of theme sawing allwaies to every person or persons and bodies politique their heires assignes and successours and every of theme other than suche persouns their heires souccessours feoffees recoverrers conuseez and assignes and the heires successours feoffees recoverrers conuseez and assignes of every of theme which by this present acte be attainted or sethens the feaste of all saintes the yere of our lorde God a thousand five hundred xxxiiij[ti] have bene attinted or herafter within the said iij yeres shalbe attainted and their heires and successours and all other claymyng to their uses or to the use of any of theme all suche condicions rentis commens whiche thei or any of theme shall happin to hawe in or upon any suche manors landes tenementis and any other hereditamentes that hath bene or soo shall happin to be lost [or] forfait by reasoun of this acte or by reasoun of attaindre of any of the persouns

32 erasure in MS after *tyme*.

by the same attainted sethens [the] feast of all saintes the yere of our lord God a thousand fyve hundreth xxxiiij^{ti} have bene attainted for any treas[on] or other offence at any tyme befor the said treasons and offences committed and also sawing alwaies to every person and persouns their heires assignes and successors and every of theme other than suche persons their heires successors and assignes and the heires successors and assignes of every of theme whiche by this present acte be attainted or sethens the feast of all saintes the yere of our lorde God a thousand fyve hundred xxxiiij^{ti} h[ave] be attainted or herafter within the said thre yeres shalbe attainted and their heires and successours and all other clamyng to their uses or to the use of any of theme all suche right title use interest possession condi[cion] rentis chargis fees offices annuities comons whiche thei or any of theme shall happin to have in to [and] upon any suche manors landes tenementes and any other hereditamentes that soo shall happin to be loste and forf[ait] by reason of the attaindre of any person or persons at any tyme after the xx^{ti} daie of June the xxvij^{ti} yere o[f the] rayne of our said souverain lorde the king[33] within the said thre yeres other than such persouns their heires succ[essours] and assignes and the heires successours and assignes of every of theme whiche by this present acte be or s[halbe] attainted shall chaunce or fortune to be attainted for any treasoune or other offence at any tyme befor the said treasouns and offences committed; provided also and be it enactid by auctoritie aforsaid that yf the said persons or any of theme which by this present acte be attainted or sethens the said feast of all saintes befor specified have bene attainted or that hereafter within the said thre yeres shall chaunce to be attainted of highe treasoune be or within the said iij yeres chaunce to be sole seised or possessid or joinctlie seasid or possessid with any other or others to the use of any other person or persons bodie or bodies politicque other [than] any suche person or persons that by this present acte be attainted or sethens the feast of all saintes befor specified have bene attainted or that hereafter within the said iij yeres chaunce to be attainted of any manors mesuages landes tenementes and all other hereditamentes that the said manors mesuages landes tenementes and other hereditamentes be not forfait to our said souverain lorde ne his heires ne seisible ne seised in to the handes of [our] said souverain lorde ne his heires soo that the said use being in the said other person or persons and bodies polleticque be not conveied from any of the said persons attainted or to be attainted in forme aforsaid se[thens] or after the daie of the offences and that it shalbe lawfull to every suche person and persons bodie and bodies polleticque their heires successors and assignes that be not ne hereafter within the said iij yeres shalbe attainted of high treason as is aforsaid to entre and sease aswell upon the possession of the king as any ot[her] person

33 1535.

in the said manors mesuages landes tenementes and all other hereditamentes and theme to have holde occupie and enyoie the possession according to suche estate and interest as they had in the said use of the same in suche forme as yf noo suche attaindre had not bene had nor within the said iij yeres shoulde fortune to be; and moreover be it enacted and ordeined by the said auctoritie that every of the wiffes of eny of the said persons nowe leiving by this acte attainted and unabled and every suche woman such as was the wyf of any of the said persouns now deade and were convicted and attainted of treason or at any tyme hereafter shalbe attainted or convicted of treason be put to execucion for the same by this acte unhabled freely inyoie have and possesse after the death of hir husbond all hir awne enheritaunce to hir and to hir heires other than be attainted or convicted or hereafter [at] any tyme dwring the said iij yeres shalbe convicted or attainted and unhabled by this acte and all castels manors landes tenementes and all other the premisses wherof they the severall daies of their severall husbondes traisons and offences committid and doone or to be committed and done in any wise were or shalbe seised or possessid in hir awne right estate or possession or of whiche any person or persons were or shalbe seised or possessid to the use of every of the said women and hir husbond and after the forme and maner and in like estate as they or any of theme were or shalbe entitled to the same at the severall daies of their treasons and offences committed and done or at any tyme heraftir to be committed and doon soo that the said right estate possession use or enheritaunce of the said wyf or wyves laste befor rehersid be not growen to theme or any of theme by the acte or consent of any of their said husbondes sethens or after the daie of their severall treasouns doon or to be doon and that during the said estate be not seisible ne seasid by this acte in to the kingis handes nor the king to be aunswered of any yssues or proffutes of any parte theirof after the deaths of their said severall husbondes the said estate dwring and that it be lawfull to every of thee said wifes and women and every of their heires not convicted ne attainted nor at any tyme hereafter shalbe convicted or attainted and unhabled by this acte and to every other person or persons seised to the use of the said women and their husbondes and their heires to entir into the said castels manors lordshipps and other the premissis and every of theme into whose possession soo ever thei be seised or comyn aswele upon the possession of the king or upon the possession of every other person or persons by this acte not attainted nor unhabled and theme and every of theme holde and enyoie to hir and hir heires not attainted nor convicted nor at any tyme hereafter shalbe convicted or attainted ne unhabled by this acte according to hir or their title right and interest in the same in suche forme and condicion as yf this said attaindre had never bene had; and be it furder enactid by auctoritie aforsaid that noo manors measis landes tenementis rentis revercions services ne any other hereditamentes wherof

any person or persons bodie or bodies politicque or incorporate was deseasid or expulsed of at any tyme by any of the forsaid traitours or any other person or persons whate soo ever he or they be sethens the furst daie of Februarie the yere of our lorde God a thousand fyve hundred xxxiiij shalbe forfacted unto our said souveraine lorde the king his heires or successours ne seased or seisible in his or their handes ne that this acte nor any thing therin conteyned in any wise be prejudiciall or hurtefull to any suche person or persons bodie or bodies politicque or incorporate soo disseasid or expulsed ne this same acte or any thing therin conteyned extende to any suche manors mesuages landes tenementis rentis revercions services or other hereditamentes soo had by disseason or expulsement sethens the said furst daie of Februarie.

[*m.5*]

c.2 Thact of succession of the kyng and queane Anne[34]

In their moost humble wise shewen unto your majestie your moost humble and[35] obedient subjectes the lordes spirituall and temporall and the comens in this present parliament assembled in your lande of Irlande that sethens it is the naturall inclynacion of every man gladlie and willynglie to provide for the suertie of bothe his title and succession although it toucheth his oonlie privat cause we therfor moost rightfull and dreadfull souveraigne lorde reken oure selves moche more bounden to beseche and instant your highnes although we doubt not of your pryncelie herte and wisedome myxed with naturall affeccion to the same to force and provide for the perfect suertie of bothe you and your moost laufull succession and heyres upon whiche dependeth all our joye and wealthe in whom alsoo is united and knyt thoonlie mere true enheritaunce and title of this realme without any contradiccion wherfor we your saide moost humble and obedient subjectes in this present parliament assembled callyng to our remembraunce the great divisions whiche in tyme past have bene by reason of severall titles pretendet to the emperiall crowne of the realme of Englande wherunto this your land of Irland is appendyng and belongyng whiche some tymes and for the mooste parte ensued thoccasion of[36] ambiguitie and doubtes then soo perfectly declared but that men mought upon frowarde ententes expounde theme to every mans sinistre appetite and affeccion after their sence contrarie to right legalitie of the succession and posteritie of the laufull kynges and emperours of the saide realme of England and of this lande of Irlande wherof haithe ensued great effusion and destruccion of mans blode aswele of a great nombre of the nobles as of other the subjectes and speciallie inheritours of the same and the greatest occa-

34 *Statutes at large* c.2. Transmiss dated 13 September 1535. 35 *and* inserted. 36 *and* struck through and *of* inserted.

sion theirof haithe bene because noo perfict and substanciall provision haithe bene made when doubtes and questions have bene moved and proponed of the certeyntie and legalitie of the succession and posteritie of the crowne by reason wherof by the busshop of Rome and the se apostolicque contrarie to the great and inviolable grantes of jurisdiccions geven by God immediatlie to emperours kynges and prynces in succession to their heyres haithe presumed in tymes past to envest whoo shoulde please theme to enherit in other mens kyngdomes and dominions whiche thing we your moost humble subjectes bothe spirituall and temporall doo moost abhorre and detest; and some tyme other forreyn prynces and potestates of sondrie degrees myndyng rather dissencion and discorde to contynue aswele in the saide realme of England as in your saide lande of Irland to the utter desolacion theirof than charitie equitie or unitie have many tymes supported wronge titles whereby they mought the more easelie and facilie aspere to the superioritie of the same; the contynuance and suffraunce wherof depelie considered and pondered were to daungerous and perillous to be suffred any longer and to moch contrarie to the unitie peaux and tranquilitie of the saide realme of Englande and of this your saide lande of Irland beyng greatlie reprocheable and dishonourable to the saide hole realme and land; in consideracion wherof your saide moost humble and obedient subjectes the nobles and comens in this your saide lande of Irland considering that ther is a good acte made within the realme of England for the suertie of your highnes and your succession in themperiall crowne of the same and callyng further to their remembraunce that the good unitie peax and wealthe of the saide realme of England and of this lande and the succession of the same moost speciallie and principallie above all wordlie thinges consisteth and resteth in the certeyntie and suertie of the procreacion of posteritie of your highnes in whose moost roiall person at this present tyme is noo maner of doubt nor question doo therfor moche humblie beseche your highnes that it may please your majestie that it may be enacted by your highnes with thassent of the lordes spirituall and temporall and the comens in this present parliament assembled and by auctoritie of the same that the mariage heretofor solempnysed betwene your highnes and the ladie Katheryn beyng befor laufull wife to prince Arthur your elder brother whiche by hym carnallie knowen as doeth dailie appere by sufficient proffe in a laufull proces had and made befor Thomas by the suffraunce of God nowe archebusshop of Canterburie and metropolitan and primat of all the same realme of England shalbe by thauctoritie of this present parliament diffinitiffelie clerelie and absolutelie declared deamed and adjudged to be against the lawes of almyghtie God and alsoo accepted reputed and taken of noo value ne effect but utterlie voide and adnichillated and the separacion therof made by the saide archebusshop shalbe good and effectuall to all ententes and purposes any licence dispensacion or any other acte or actes goyng afor or ensuyng the same or to the

contrarie therof in any wise notwithstondyng and that every souche licence dispensacion acte or actes thing or thinges heretofor had made doone or to be doon to the contrarie therof shalbe voide and of none effect and that the said lady Katheryn from hensforthe shalbe called and reputed onelie dowrage to prynce Arthur and not queane of the saide realme of England nor lady of this lande of Irlande and that the laufull matrymony had and solempnysed betwen your highnes and your moost dere and entierlie biloved wife quean Anne shalbe establisshed and taken for undoubtfull true syncere and perfect ever hereafter accordyng to the just judgement of the saide Thomas archebusshop of Canterburie metropolitan and primat of all the saide realme of England whose groundes or judgement have bene conformed aswele by thole clergie of the same realme in bothe the convocacions and by bothe the unyversities theirof as by the unyversities of Bonony Padua Parys Orleance Tholouse Angeve and diverse others and alsoo by the privat writyng of many right excellent wele learned men whiche groundes soo confirmed and judgement of the saide archebusshop ensuyng the same with your mariage solempnysed betwen your highnes and your said laufull wife queane Anne we your saide subjectes bothe spirituall and temporall of this your lande of Irlande doo purelie playnelie constauntly and fermelie accept approve and ratifie for good and consonaunt to the lawes of almyghtie God without errour or defaulte moost humbly besechyng your majestie that it may be establisshed for ever by your moost gracious roiall assent; and further more sethens many inconvenyences have fallen aswele within this your said lande of Irland as in others by reason of marieng within the degrees of mariage prohibited by Goddes lawe that is to saie the son to marie the mother or the stepmother the brother the suster the father his sons doughter or his doughters doughter or the son to marie the doughter of his father procreat and borne by his stepmother or the son to marie his aunt beyng his father or mothers sustre or to marie his uncles wife or the father to marie his sons wife or the brother to marie the brothers wife or any man to marie his wifes doughter or his wifes sons doughter or his wifes doughters doughter or his wifes suster which mariages albeit they be playnelie prohibited and destested by the lawes of God yet nevertheles at some tymes they have proceded undre colours of dispensacions by mans power whiche is but usurped and of right ought not to be graunted admytted or alloued, for noo man of what estat degree or condicion soo ever he be haith power to dispence with Goddes lawes as all the clergie of the saide realme of England in the saide convocacions and the moste parte of all the famouse universities of Cristendom and wee alsoo doo affyrme and thynke; be it therfor enacted by auctoritie aforsaide that noo persone or persones subjectes or resiauntes of this your saide lande of Irlande of what estat degree or dignitie soo ever they be shall fromhensfurthe marie within any the saide degrees afor rehersed what pretence soo ever shalbe made to the contrarie therof, and in case

any persone or persones of what estat dignitie degree or condicion soo ever they be haithe bene heretofor maried within this your saide lande of Irland within any the degrees above expressed and by any tharchebusshops busshops or mynystres of the churche of this your saide lande of Irland be separat from the bandes of souche unlaufull mariage that then every souche separacion shalbe goode laufull ferme and permanent for ever and not by any power auctoritie or meanes to be revoked or undoon hereafter, and that the children procedyng or procreat undre souche unlaufull mariage shall not be laufull ne legittymat any forreyn lawes licences dispensacions or other thing or thinges to the contrarie therof notwithstanding, and in case ther be any persone or persons within this your said land of Irland alreddy maried within any the saide degrees above specified and not yet separat from the bandes of souche unlaufull mariage that then every souche persone soo unlaufullie maried shalbe separated by the diffynytive sentence and judgement of tharchebusshops busshops or other mynystres of the churche of this your saide lande of Irlande within the lymytes of their jurisdiccions and auctorities and by none other power or auctoritie and that all other sentences and judgementes geven and to be yeven by any archebusshop busshop or other mynystre of the churche of this your said land within the limites of their jurisdiccions and auctoritie shalbe diffinitive ferme goode and effectuall to all [*m.6*] ententis and purposes and be observed and obeied withoute swing any provocacion apels or prohibicions or other processe from the courte of Rome to the derogacion theirof; and also be it enactid by auctoritie aforsaid that all the yssue had and procreate or hereafter to be had or procreate betwne your highnes and your moste dere and entierlie beloved wife quene Anne shalbe your lawfull children and be enheritable and enherite according to the course of enheritaunce and law of the said realme of England aswele the emperiall crowne of the said realme of England as this your said lande of Irland with all dignities honours preheminences prerogatives auctorities and jurisdiccions the same annexed or belonging in as large maner as your highnes at this present tyme hathe the same as king of the said realme and lorde of this y[our] said lande of Irlande the enheritaunce theirof to be and remayne to your said children and right heires in m[aner] and forme as hereafter shalbe declared, that is to saie furst the same emperiall croune and other the premis[ses] shalbe to your majestie and to your heires of your bodie lawfully begotten that is to say the furst son of your bod[ie] betwene your highnes and your said lawfull wyf quene Anne begotten and to the heires of the bodie of the said furst son lawfully begotten and for defaulte of suche heires than to the secunde son of your bodie and of the bodie of the saide quene Anne begotten and to the heires of the bodie of the said secunde son lawfully begotten and soo to every son of your bodie and of the bodie of the said quene Anne begottin and to the heires of the bodie of every suche son begotten according to the course of enheritaunce in that behalf; and if it shall happin your

said dere and entierlie beloved wyfe quene Anne to decease withoute yssue male of the bodie of your highnes to begotten whiche God defende than the same emperiall crowne and all other the premissis to be to your majestie as is aforsaid and to the son and heire male of your bodie lawfully begotten and to the heires of the bodie of the same son and heire male lawfully begottin and for default of suche yssue than to your secunde son lawfully begotten and soo from son and heire male to son and heire male and to the heires of the severall bodies of every suche son and heire male to be gottin according to the course of enheritaunce in like maner and forme as it is aforsaid and for defaulte of suche sonnes of your bodie begotten and of the heires of the severall bodies of every suche sones laufully begotten that than the said emperiall crowne and other the premissis shalbe to the yssue female betwne your majestie and your said mooste dere and entierly belowed wyf quene Anne begottin that is to saie furst the eldiste yssue female whiche is the ladie Elisabeth now princesse and to the heires of hir bodie laufully begottin and for defaulte of suche yssue than to the secunde yssue female and to the heires of hir bodie lawfully begottin and soo from yssue female to yssue female and to the heires of their bodies oon after a nother by course of enheritaunce according to their agis as the crowne of England hath bene accustumed and ought to goo in cases whan their be heires femals to the same and for defaulte of suche yssue than the saide emperiall crowne and other the premissis shalbe to the right heires of your highnes for ever; and be it further enactid by auctoritie aforsaid that on this side the furst day of Maij next comyng proclamacions shalbe made in all shires within your lande of Irland of the tenor and contentes of this acte and if any person or persons of whate estate dignitie or condicion soo ever they be subject or resiaunt within this your said lande of Irland after the said furst daie of Maie by writing or emprenting or by any exterior acte or deade maliciuslie procure or doo or cause to be procured or done any thing or thingis to the perill of your moste roiall person or maliciuslie geve occasion by writing printe deade or acte wherby your highnes might be disturbed or interrupted of the crowne of the said realme of England or of this your said lande of Irlande or by writing print deade or acte procure or doo or cause to be procured or done any thing or thinges to the prejudice sklaunder disturbaunce or derogacion of the said lawfull matrimonie solempnised betwene your majestie and the said quene Anne or to the perill sclaunder or disherison of any the yssues and the heires of your highnes being lymitted by this acte to enherite and to be enheritable to the crowne of the saide realme[37] in suche forme as is aforsaid wherby any suche yssues or heires of your highnes might be destroied disturbed or interrupted in bodie or in title of enheritaunce to the crowne of the said realme or of the possession of this your said lande of Irland as to theme is limyted in this acte in

37 *of* struck through.

forme abowe rehersed that than every suche person or persons of whate estate degre or condicion they be of subjectis or resiauntis within this your said lande of Irlande and their aydors counsaillours maynteynors and abbettors and every of theme for every suche offence shalbe adjudged high traditors and every suche offence shalbe adjudged high treason and the offenders and their aidors counsaillours mainteynnors and abbettors and every of theme being lawfully convicte of suche offence by presentment veradict confession or proces according to the custumes and lawes of this your said lande shall suffer paynes of deathe as in cases of high treason and also that every suche offender being convict as is a forsaid shall lose and forfact to your highnes and to your heires kingis of the said realme of England and lordis of this your said lande of Irland all suche manors landes tenementis rentis annuities and hereditamentis whiche they had in possession as awners and were sole seised of by or in any right title or meanis or any other person or persons had to their use of any estate of enheritaunce at the daie of suche treasons and offences by theme committed and doone and that also every suche offendor shall loose and forfaite to your highnes and to your said heires aswell all maner suche estates of freholde and interest for yeres of landes and rentis as all other goodis cattails and debtis whiche thei had at the tyme of conviccion or attaindre of any suche offence saving alwaies to every person and persons and bodies politicque to their heirs assignes and successors and to every of theme other than suche persons as shalbe so convict and their heires and successors and all other claymyng to their uses all suche uses right title interest possession condicion rentis fees offices annuities and comons whiche thei or any of theme shall happin to hawe to or upon any suche maners landis tenementis rentis annuities or hereditamentis that soo shall happin to be lost and forfacte by reason of attaindre for any the treasons and offencis above rehersed at any tyme befor the said treasons and offencis committed; be it further enactid by auctoritie aforsaid that yf any person or persons after the said furst daie of Maie by any wordis withoute writing or any exterior deade or acte maliciuslie and obstinately publishe devulge or utter any thing or thingis to the perill of your highnes or to the sclaundre or prejudice of the said matrimonie solempnised betwne your highnes and the said quene Anne or to the sclaundre and disherison of the yssue and heires of your bodie begottin of the said quene Anne or any other your lawfull heires whiche shalbe enheritable to the crowne of the said realme of England and of this your said lande of Irland as is afor limitted by this acte that than every suche offence shalbe taken and adjudged for misprision of treason and that every person and persons of whate estate degree or condicion soo ever they be subject or resiaunt within this your said lande of Irland soo doing and offending and being theirof lawfully convict by presentment veredicte proces or confession shall suffir imprisonement of their bodies at the kingis will and shall lose aswell all their goodes catall and dettis as all suche interesses and estatis of freholde or

for yeres whiche any suche offendor shall hawe of or in any landes rentis or hereditamentes whate soo ever at the tyme of the conviction and attaindre of suche offence; and be it also enacted by auctoritie aforsaid that no person nor persons offending in any the treasouns or misprisicions conteined and limited by this acte shall in any wise have and enyoie the priviledge of immunite of any maner saintewaries within your said lande of Irland or els where within the kingis dominions but shall utterlie lose and be excluded of the same any use costume graunte prescripcion confirmacion or any other thing or thingis to the contrarie theirof in any wise notwithstonding; and be it also enacted by auctoritie aforsaid that yf your majestie sholde happen to decesse befor eny such your yssue and heire male whiche shulde enherite the crowne of the said realme of England shalbe of his age of xviij yeres or befor shuche your yssue and heire female whiche sholde enherite the crowne of the said realme shalbe maried or be of the age of xvj yeres whiche all mightie God deffende that then your yssue and heire male to the crowne soo being within the age of xviij yeres or your said yssue and heire female to the crowne being unmaried and within the said age of xvj yeres shalbe and remayne unto suche tyme as suche yssues and heires shall come to their said severall ages afor lymitted at and in the governaunce of thir naturall mother she lyving [*m.7*] with suche other counsaillours of your realme of England as your majestie in your lyfe tyme shall depute and assigne by your will or otherwise for the same withoute contradiccion of any person or persons to the contrarie theirof and if any person or persons by writing or exterior deade or acte procure or doo or cause to be procured or doon any thing or thingis to the let or disturbaunce of the same that then any suche offence shalbe high treason and the offenders being theirof convict shall suffre suche paines of deathe and losses of enheritaunce freholdes interesses for yeres goodis cattaills and debtis in suche maner and forme as is above specified in cases of traison afor mencioned; and for the more swre establishment of the succession of your moste roiall majestie according to the tenor and forme of this acte be it further enacted by auctoritie aforsaid that aswele the nobles of this your said lande of Irland spirituall and temporall as other your subjectis nowe lyving and being or that hereafter shalbe at that full ages by the commaundement of your majestie or of your heires or deputie of this your lande at all tymes hereafter from tyme to tyme when it shall please your highnes or your heires to appoint shall make corporall othe in presence of your highnes or your heires or your deputie or befor suche other as your majestie or your heires or your deputie woll depute for the same according to the tenor of the othe hereafter folowing

> Ye shall swere to bere faith trouth and obedience to the kingis majestie and to his heires of his bodie of his most dere and entierlie beloved lawfull wyf quene Anne begotten and to be gotten and further to theires of

> our said souverain lorde according to limitacion in the statute made for swirtie of his succession in the crowne of the realme of England and of this his lande of Irland mencioned and conteyned and not to any other within the said realme of England or within this lande of Irlande nor forreyne auctoritie or potentate and in case any othe be made or hath bene made by youe to any person or persons that then ye repute the same as wayne and adnichillate and that your cunnyng witt and uttermoste of your power withoute gile fraude or other undue meane ye shall observe kepe mayntein and defende the saide acte of succession and all the hoole effectis and contentis theirof and all other actis and statutes made in confirmacion or for execucion of the same or of any thing therin conteyned and this ye shall doo againste all maner persons of whate estate dignitie degre or condicion soo ever they be and in noo wise doo or attempt or to your power suffer to be done or attempted directlie or indirectlie any thing or thingis prevely or apertlie to the let hinderaunce damage or derogacion theirof or of any parte of the same by any maner of meanis or for any maner of pretence soo helpe youe God all saintis and the holie evangeliis

and that all maner your subjectis aswele spirituall as temporall swing liverey restitucions or utter le mayne oute of the handes of your highnes or of your heires or doing of any fealtie to your highnes or to your heires by reason of tenour of their landis shall swre a like corporall othe as is afore rehersed and that they nor any of theme shall hereafter hawe any lyvereis utter le mayne or restitucion out of your handes nor oute of the handes of your heires till they have made their said corporall oothe in forme above rehersed and yf any person or persons being commaunded by auctoritie of this acte to make the said othe afor lymited obstinatlie refuse that to doo in contempt of this acte that then every suche person soo doing to be takin and accepted for offendor in misprisicion of high treason and that every suche refusel shalbe demed and adjudged mesprision of high treason and the offendor therin to suffre suche paines and imprisonement losses and forfaitures and also preveledgis of saintewaries in like maner and forme as is above mencioned for the misprisions of treasons a for lymited by this acte; provided alwaies that the artecle in this acte conteined concernyng prohibicions of mariagis within the degrees afor mencioned in this acte shall alwaies be taking interpreted and expounded of suche mariagis where mariagis were solempnised and naturall knowledge had.

[*m.8*]

c.3 Thact of absentes[38]

Forasmoche as it is notorious and manyfest that[39] this the kyngis lande of Irlande heretofor beyng inhabitid and in due obedience and subjeccion unto the kyngis mooste noble progenytours kyngis of England who in those dayes in the right of the crowne of England had great possessions rentis and profictes within the same lande hathe principally growen into ruyn dissolacion rebellion and decaye by occasion that great domynyons landes and possessions within the same lande aswele by the kyngis grauntis as by course of enheritaunce and otherwise discendid to noble men of the realme of England and especially the landes and domynyons of therldomes in Ulster and Leynster who having the same bothe they and their heyres by proces of tyme demouryng within the saide realme of England and not providyng for the good ordre and suertie of the same their possessions there in their absence and by their necligences suffred those of the wylde Irishrie (beyng mortall and naturall ennemyes to the kynges of England and Englische domynyon) to entre and holde the same[40] without resistence, the conquest and wynnyng therof in the begynnyng not oonly cost the kynges said noble progenytours chargis inestymable but alsoo those to whom the saide land was yeven then and many yeres after abidyng within the said lande nobly and valiauntly defended the same against all the kynges saide ennemyes and also kepte the same in suche tranquilitie and good ordre as the kyngis of England had due subjeccion of the inhabitauntes there the lawes obeyd and of their revenues and regalitie were duely aunswerid as in any other where within the realme of England and after the gift or discent of the said landes possessions and domynyons to the persons aforsaide they and their heyres absented them selves out of the said lande of Irland demouryng within the realme of England not pondering ne regardyng the preservacion therof the townes castels and garisons appertaynyng unto theme fell in ruyne and decaye and thenglische inhabitauntes there in defaulte of defence and justice and by compulsion of those of the Irishrie were exiled wherby the kynges saide progenytours lost aswele their domynyon and subjeccion there as also all their revenues and profictes and their saide ennemyes by readoptyng or atteynyng the saide landes dominions and possessions were elevated into great dominion power streinght and puysaunce for the subpressing of the residue of the kynges subjectes of this lande whiche they dailie ever sithe have attempted wherby they from tyme to tyme usurped and encroched upon the kynges dominion whiche haithe bene the pryncipall cause of the myserable estate wherin it is at this present tyme and those landes and dominions by necligence and in defaulte of the veray enheritors after this maner lost may be good

38 *Statutes at large* c.3. 39 *that* inserted. 40 *witho* expunged and struck through.

ensample to the kynges majestie now beyng entending the reformacion of the saide lande to forsee and prevent that the like shall not ensue hererafter for where the noble prynce Thomas Hawarde duke of Norfolke and the lorde Berkley his comparcioner clayme and holde as their auncient enheritaunce the seignyories and lordships of Cathirlaugh Olde Rosse and diverse others manors and landes within the saide lande and George Talbot Erle of Waterford and Saloppe the Seigneorie of Wexforde and the heyres generall of Therle of Ormounde dyvers other possessions and landes the Abbot of Furnes the Abbot of sainct Augustynes of Brystowe the Prior of Cristchurche of Canterbury the Prior of Lanthony Prior of Cartmell the Abbot of Kentesham the Abbot or prior of Osney thabbot or Prior of Bathe and the maister of sainct Thomas of Acres everie of theme severall landes and possessions within the saide lande whiche bothe they and their antecessors and predecessours in semblable wise not regardyng the defence ne good ordre of the same dyvers tymes not onely have suffred the kynges ennemyes to encroche and entre into their domynyons and possessions soo as for the recoverie therof the kynges highnes that nowe is his father and graundfather at dyvers and severall seasons have bene put to inestymable charges and the same soo by theme attayned the said enheritors and possessioners have entred agayn into their saide landes and possessions takyng the profictes therof for a season without provision makyng for any defence or kepyng therof in good ordre but makyng leases of dyvers their holdes and manors to the late erle of Kildare whiche by occasion of the same came to the possession of Thomas Fitz Geralde his son and heyre who nowe of late like a moost false disloyall traditor with his complices rebelled agaynst oure souverain lord the kyng entendyng moost falselie and traditorslie to take the saide lande of Irland out of his possession and hym and his heyres therof to disherite for ever amonge other was ayded assisted and maynteyned agaynst our souverayn lorde in that his moost false and traditors purpose by the inhabitauntes and occupiers of the saide landes and possessions soo as for repressing aswele of the saide Thomas Fitz Geralde and other his complices as wynnyng of the castels of Catherlagh Olde Rosse Arcloo Tullagh in Offelyme Kylrushe and other fortresses of thenheritaunce and possesion of dyvers the persons aforsaide and other landes out of his and their possessions the kynges said majestie was enforced to his great charges to sende thidther and kepe there[41] an armye royall and also consideryng that the persons aforsaide havyng heretofore the same landes and possessions at their awne disposicion and ordre perceived litle profict therby and yet by their necligence and mysordre therof and especially within the counties of Catherlagh and Wexford beyng places priveledged by the kynges saide moost noble progenytours that the lordes

41 *and kepe there* inserted.

therof may kepe and holde all maner plees within the same by occasion and undre pretence and colour wherof the kynges lawes writtes or other processe be not obeid nether any other lawe or justice ther used or admynystred for the quietyng and good ordre of the kynges subjectes inhabitauntes within the same soo as in default aswele therof as of a governoure to rule ordre and guyde theme the kynges ennemyes have theme in servage all murders roberies theftes treasons and other offenses remayne ther unponyshed the kynges wardes reliefes exchetes and all other his profictes and revenues beyng withdrawen and the service streinght and assistence of the saide subjectes is greatly mynyshed and for those and diverse other hurtes and enormyties whiche bene like to ensue to the comen weale of the saide lande to the prejudice of our souveraigne lorde the kyng and his heyres by the mysordre of the landes and possessions belongyng to eny of the persons aforsaide and in respect of thinestymable charges whiche the kyng our souveraigne lord hathe susteyned and apparauntly hathe occasion to susteyne for and about the conquest and recontynuaunce of the same out of his ennemyes possession; by aucthoritie and reason wherof albeit that his grace hathe laufull and sufficient right to all the said seignyories landes and possessions and that if his grace wolde take of the inheritours and possessioners of the same the arrerages of the twoo partes of the yerelie profictes therof by reason of their absentie out of the saide lande contrary to the statutes therof provided the same woulde contervayle the purchase therof yet for coroboracion of the right and title of our saide souverayn lorde the kyng and his heyres whiche he hathe to all the same landes domynyons and possessions be it enacted establyshed and ordeyned by the king our souveraigne lorde the lordis spirituall and temporall and comens in this present parliament assembled and by aucthoritie of the same that the kyng his heyres and assignes shall have holde and enyoie as in the right of the crowne of Englande all honours manors castels seigneories hundredes franchesis liberties countie palentynes jurisdiccions auctorities knyghtisfees advousons patronages landes tenementes woddis meddowes pastures revercions remayndours rentes services parsonages vicaragis dismys tiethes oblacions obvencions pensions and all and singuler other possessions hereditamentes and all other profictes aswele spirituall as temporall what soo ever they be whiche the saide duke and his comparcioner or the saide erle of Waterford and Salopp' or the saide heyres generall of therle of Ormonde or any the abbotes priors and maister afornamed or any of theme or any person or persons to their uses or to thuse of any of theme within this lande of Irland or wherunto thei or any of theme or any to their uses or to thuse of any of theme have laufull right title possession or clause of entree savyng to all and everie persone and persons the kynges naturall subjectes dwellyng in this lande other than the duke and his saide comparcioner the saide erle and the saide heyres generall to therle of Ormonde

and the saide abbotes priors and maister and their heyres and successors and the heyres and successors of any of theme and suche as clayme to their uses or to the use of any of theme all suche right title interest use possession leases rentes annuyties offices and fees as they have in or to the premysses or any parcell therof as if this acte had never be made; provided always and be it enacted by aucthoritie of this present parliament that this forsaid acte ne any thing therin conteyned be in any wise prejudiciall or hurtfull to Thomas Houthe of Tartayn nowe secundarie justice of our souverain lorde the kynges highe benche of Irlande and Patricke Barnewall of Feldeston' their executors or assignes or any of theme in of or for any manours meses landes tenementes rentes revercions services patronages advousons chapels priories selles parsonages vicarages dismes oblacions obvencions pensions aswele spirituall as temporall or any other hereditamentes or profictes spirituall or temporall whiche the saide Thomas and Patricke have of the graunt or lease of Richarde prior of the monastery of the Blessid Lady of Cartmell' and convent of the same in ferme with the assent and consent of the saide convent but that the saide Thomas and Patricke their executors and assignes and the executor and assigne of either of theme shall occupie have possesse and enyoie all and singuler the saide manors meses landes tenementes tiethes oblacions hereditamentes and every other the premisses graunted and let duryng and for the terme of eight and thirtie yeres next ensuyng duryng the saide terme paying therfor yerelie unto our saide souveraigne lorde and to his heyres the rent reserved in the saide endenture; provided also and be it enacted by auctoritie aforsaide that the forsaid acte or any thyng therin conteyned be in any wise prejudiciall or hurtfull to Sir John Barnewall knyght lorde of Trymletteston' and Patrick Barnewall of Feldeston' their executors or assignes or any of theme in of or for the office of the stywarde senescall surveyor and receivor of the manors and lordships of Rushe Balscadan the moitie or halfyndele of the manor of Portrarne or of the manors and lordships of Woghterarde Castelwarnyng Clyntonscourte [*m.9*] or the lordship and manor of Blackecastell or any fee pencion annuitie commoditie or proficte that they or any of theme have or shuld have by [reason] or for thexercising of the saide offices but that the saide Sir John and Patricke joynctlie and severallie during the lives of the saide Sir John [and] Patricke and the longer liver of theme shall have holde exercise occupy possesse and enyoie the saide offices and any of theme by theme selves [or any] of theme or by their sufficient deputie or deputies or by the sufficient deputie or deputies of any of theme during the lives of the said Sir [John and] Patricke and the longer liver of theme havyng takyng and perceiving suche like fees wages profictes commodities casuelties and advantages as [Sir] Bartholome Dillon knight deceased late had and percei[ved] by reason and for thexercising of the saide offices or any of theme

yerelie to be perceived levied and received at the feastes of saint Michell the archangell and Ester by even porcions of the rentes services revenues and profictes of [the] saide manors lordships and other the premisses; provided alsoo that this forsaid acte ne nothing therin conteyned be in any wise prejudici[all or] hurtfull to any archbusshop busshop abbot prior deane archedeacon of this lande of Irlande beyng resident and dwelling within the saide lande [whiche] hathe any jurisdiccion within the same or to the successors of any of theme other than the saide abbotes of Furnex sainct Augustynes of [Brystowe] and of Kentshame the abbot or prior of Osney thabbot or prior of Bathe and of[42] the maister of sainct Thomas of Acres the prior of Chri[stchurche] of Canterbury the prior of Lanthony and the prior of Cartmell and the successours of any of theme in of or for their synodols visita[cions] proccies pencions porcions and annuyties of theme or any of theme whiche they or any of theme be rightfully entitled to have by comp[osicion] custume or otherwise; provyded alwayes that this acte or any thing within the same conteyned be not prejudiciall or hurtfull to [the] right reverend father in God Edwarde busshop of Methe nor to his successors in of or for synodols proccies pencions annuyties or [of any] other yssues or prouffictes due unto the saide busshop or his successors by any maner of right title or composicion whiche the said busshop had or receivid heretofore in or of the houses and graunges of Dueleke and Colpe chirches and benefices in Irland belongyng to the saide houses [and] graunges and to the house of Lanthonye in England; provided alsoo that this forsaid acte nor any thing therin conteyned in any wise [be] not prejudiciall or hurtfull to the suffrayn portreffes and comens of the towne of Rosse or to the suffrayne bailives and comens of the towne [of] Wexforde or to the suffrayne portreffes and comens of the towne of Kilkenny or to the suffrayn burgesses and comens of the towne of Clomell [or] to any of theme or to the successors of theme or any of theme in of for or concernyng any grauntes liberties previledges faunchesis corporacions prouffictes or commodities or any other thing or thinges to theme or any of theme or to their predecessours or to the predecessours of any of [theme] extending by the same grauntes to their successors and to the successors of any of theme by any maner of meane geven graunted or conf[irmed] befor the furst day of this present parliament this present acte in any wise notwithstonding; provided also and be it enacted by auc[toritie] of this present parliament that this forsaide and present acte ne any thing therin conteyned be in any wise prejudiciall or hurtfull to any persone or [persones] in of or for any and every of the cornes (tiethes oonly except) whiche they or any of theme hathe growyng or comyng out and upon the saide lan[des] tenementes and other the premisses and every parcell therof unto the feast of saint

42 *of* inserted.

Michell the archaungell next comyng but that it shalbe lau[full to] every suche persone and persones as hathe any suche cornes to rippe carie and convey the same at his and their will and pleasure this fors[aide] and present acte or any thing therin conteyned in any wise notwithstandyng; provided alsoo and be it enacted by aucthoritie of this present parliament that all obligacions bandes of the staple recognisaunces indentures and all other writinges and specialties wherin any persone or persones standeth bounden for the payment of any rentes yssues revenues and profictes for by reason or goyng oute of the [saide] lordships manors landes tenementes and other the premisses or any parcell therof by auctoritie of this present acte be demed orderid reputed and adjudged frustrat and voide and of none effect in lawe; provided alsoo that this acte ne any thing therin conteyned be in no wise prejudiciall or hurtfull to the portreffes burgesses and comens of the towne of Fethird or to the portreffes burgesses and comens of the tow[ne] of Casshell or to any of theme or to the successors of theme or any of theme in of for or concernyng any grauntes liberties previledges franchesis corporacions prouffictes or commodities or any other thing or thinges to theme or any of theme or to their predecessours or to the predec[essours] of any of theme extendyng by the same grauntes to their successors and to the successors of any of theme by any maner of meane gev[en] graunted or confirmed befor the furst day of this present parliament this present acte in any wise notwithstondyng.

c.4 The repeale of Ponynges acte[43]

For the great trust and confidence that the kynges highnes hathe in his deputie and counsaill of this his lande of Irlande and in the nob[les] spirituall and temporall and the comens his loving subjectes of the same his majestie is pleasid and contented that it be enacted by auctor[itie of] this present parliament that this present parliament sommoned begon and holden and every acte ordynaunce provision thing or thinges of what nature n[ame] condicion or qualitie it be of had done made or establisshed or hereafter to be had done made or establisshed by auctoritie thereof shalbe good and effectuell to all ententes and purposes according to the teanor and effect of the saide actes ordynaunces and provisions [the] acte made at Drogheda in the parliament there holden the Munday next after the feast of saincte Andrewe in the tenth yere of the moost noble kyng of famous memory king Henry the vijth[44] befor Sir Edwarde Ponynges knight then being deputie of this lande or any other acte or actes use

43 *Statutes at large* c.4. A rejected draft of this act (Huntingdon Library, MS EL 2564) is printed in R. Dudley Edwards, 'The Irish Reformation parliament of Henry VIII, 1536–7', *Historical Studies*, vi (1965), pp 82–4. 44 1494.

or custume heretofor had doon or made within this lande to the contrary of this present parliament or any thing made or establisshed b[y] auctoritie of the same in any wise notwithstandyng;[45] provided alway and be it enacted that by force and vertue of this present a[cte] ne any thing therin conteyned no acte ordinaunce provision thing or thinges of what nature name condicion or qualitie so ever it be fo[r] any manors lordships landes tenementes advousons abbeyes priories sellis or any other hereditamentes what so ever they be for or betwe[ne] any person or persons body or bodyes politicque or incorporat or any other particuler acte ordynaunce or provision or eny other acte ordynaunce or provision that shalbe prejudiciall hurtfull or in derogacion of any grauntes liberties franchesses usages custom[es] or any other commodities or previledges geven or graunted by our souveraigne lorde the king or his noble progenytors to any citie or borough townes within this lande of Irlande be enacted or establisshed by vertue or auctoritie of this present parliament but onely suche actes ordynaunces and provisions thing or thinges as shalbe thought expedient for our souveraigne lorde the kinges honour thencrease of his graces revenues and profict and the comen weale of this his lande and dominion of Irlande.

c.5 Thacte of supreme hedd[46]

Like as the kinges majestie justlie and rightfully is and ought to be supreame hedde of the chirche of Englande and soo is recognysed by the clergy and auctorised by an acte of parliament made and establisshed in the saide realme soo in like maner of wise forasmyche as this lande of Irland is depending and belongyng justelie and rightfullie to the emperiall crowne of England for encrea[se] of vertue in Cristes religion within the saide lande of Irlande and to represse and extyrpe all errours heresies and other ernomyties a[nd] abuses heretofor used in the same be it enacted by aucthoritie of this present parliament that the king oure souveraigne lorde [his] heyres and successors kynges of the saide realme of Englande and lordes of this sayde lande of Irlande shalbe accepted tak[en] and reputed the oonlie supreame hedde in erthe of the hole chirche of Irlande callid hibernica ecclesia and shall have and enyoie annexed and united to themperiall crowne of Englande aswele the title and stile therof as all honours dignities preemynences jurisdic[cions] previledges auctorities immunyties proufictes and commodities to the saide dignitie of supreame hedde of the same chirche belongyng [and] apperteynyng and that oure saide souveraigne lorde his heyres and successours kynges of the saide realme of Englande and lordes [of] this lande of Irland shall have full power and auctori-

45 In margin: Nota this rapell is declaryd and explanyd benethe in this roull. 46 *Statutes at large* c.5.

tie from tyme to tyme to visite represse redresse reforme ordre correct restrayne and amende all suche errours heresyes abuses offences contemptes and enormyties what so ever they be whiche by a[ny] maner spirituall auctoritie or jurisdiccion ought or may laufully be reformed respressid orderid redressed corrected restrayned or amended moost to the pleasure of almyghtie God thencrease of vertue in Cristes religion and for the conservacion of peax unitie and tranquilitie of this lande of Irlande any usage custome forreyn lawes forreyn auctoritie prescrippcion or any other thing or thing[es] to the contrarie therof notwithstonding; provided alwaye and be it enacted by auctoritie of this present parliament that if it fortune our souveraigne lorde the kyng his heyres or successors to auctorise and depute any persone or persones to visite represse redresse refourme ord[re] correct restrayne or amende by force of the present and forsaide acte that then any suche persone or persones shall go with suche compa[ny] as shalbe convenyent and necessary for the same and that according the habilitie substaunce and power of the persone house or monasterii whiche they shall so fortune to visite represse redresse reforme ordre correct restrayne or amende and that no suche persone or persones soo appoynted or aucthorised to visit represse redresse reforme ordre correct restrayne or amende shall take or cause to be taken any proccies monye or other exaccions of any suche persone house or monastery whiche they shall so fortune to visite represse redres[se] reforme ordre correct restrayne or amende but oonly convenyent meat drynke and lodging for them selves their company servau[nts] and horses and if any suche persone or persones so appoynted and auctorised as aforsaid do take or cause to be taken any proc[cies] monye or any other exaccions (other then is aforsaid) that every of theme soo offending shall forfaicte foure tymes the value of that that he receivith or cause to be receivid the one halfe therof to our souveraigne lorde the kyng his heyres and successors and thother halfe to any persone or persons that woll sue for the same by accion of debt informacion or otherwise wherin no wageor of lawe assoyne ne proteccion shall lye.

[*m.10*]

c.6 Thacte for Piers erle of Ossorie[47]

Prayth the comens at the humble supplicacion of Piers erle of Ossorie son and heyre to James the son to Edmonde the son of Richarde Butler wheras in a parliament holden at Drogheda the Thursday next after the Purificacion of oure lady the seventhe yere of the reigne of the noble prynce of famouse memorie Edwarde by the grace of God kyng of Englande and of Fraunce and lorde of this lande of Irlande the fourth[48] befor John erle of Worcetter deputie unto

47 Exemplification printed in *Cal. Ormond Deeds*, iii, pp 206–9. 48 4 February 1468.

George than duc of Clarance lieutenaunt to the said king Edwarde of this lande of Irlande amonges other actes and at the supplicacion of the saide James Butler son to Edmonde son to Richarde Butler reciting that where after affyaunce had betwixt the saide James and Sawe than his wife and befor thespousels ther was yssue had Edmonde and Theobalde it was enacted and ordeyned by auctoritie of the forsaide parliament[49] that the saide yssue Edmonde and Theobalde shulde be made reputed and adjudged muliery and hable to enherite and enyoie all maner landes possessions rentes and services as if they had bene borne within thespousels solempnised and forasmuche as the saide acte or statute was clerely against the course of the comen lawes and disherison of rightfull heyres of the saide James whose right heyre the saide Piers nowe erle of Ossorie after the matrimony solempnysed betwixt the saide James and the saide Sawe beyng borne is that therfor and in consideracion of the faithfull harte and mynde that the saide Piers hath alway in doyng the kinges grace good service and in especiall of his politicque and valiaunt attemptates usid nowe latelie against the high and proditoriouse rebellion and treason by the rebell and traditor Thomas Fitz Geralde be it enacted ordeyned and establisshed by auctoritie of this present parliament that the saide acte in every pointe concernyng the legittimacion and makyng mulier of the saide Edmunde and Theobalde and alsoo enhabling of the saide Edmond and Theobalde to enherite and enyoie all maner landes possessions rentes and services as if they were borne within thespousels solempnised be repellid adnullid revoked and utterlie adjudged voide and of none effect in lawe; and that the saide Piers and every other which by course of the kinges comen lawes ought to be right heyres and enherit as right heyre to the saide James if the saide acte made in the saide vij^th^ yere of the saide king Edwarde the fourthe had never bene made be enhabled to have inherite and enyoie all manors landes messuages tenementes and all other maner hereditamentes as rightfull heyre to the saide James by course of the comen lawes as though suche acte of legittymacion of the saide Edmonde and Theobalde had never be made or ordeyned the saide acte made in the saide seventh yere or anything therin conteyned made to the contrarie notwithstondyng; provided alway and be it enacted by auctoritie of this present parliament that this acte of adnullacion and repelle or any thing or thinges therin conteyned shall not in any wise be hurtfull or prejudiciall to the king our souveraigne lorde nor to the moost excellent princesse quene Anne his moost dere and entierly belovid wife nor to their heyres nor to the heyres of either of theme nor to the right honourable Thomas erle of Wilteshire and of Ormonde nor to dame Margaret Bulleyn mother to the saide erle nor to dame Anne Seyntleger nor to George Seyntleger knyght nor to the heires of the saide erle

49 *Stat. Ire.,1–12 Edw. IV*, p. 487.

of Wiltshire dame Margaret dame Anne and George nor to the heyres of any of theme of for or concernyng any honours titles stiles names dignities armes or preemynences or of for or concernyng any honours castels manoirs landes tenementes rentes advousons patronages possessions or other hereditamentes what soo ever they be but that our saide souveraigne lorde the king and the saide moost excellent princes the quene and their heyres and the heyres of either of theme the saide erle of Wiltshir and of Ormonde and his heyres and all and every other person afornamed in this proviso and their heyres and theyres of every of theme shall have holde kepe and enyoie all suche honours names titles stiles armes dignyties preemynences and all suche honours castels manors landes tenementes rentes advousons patronages possessions and all other heriditamentes what soo every they be whiche they or any of theme have or may laufully pretende or clayme to have or any persone or persones to their uses or to the use of any of theme hathe or ought to have in like maner forme and condicion as if the saide acte repeale and adnullacion or any thing or thinges therin conteyned to the contrarie therof notwithstonding; and alsoo be it provided and enacted by auctoritie aforsaide that this acte of repeale and adnullacion or any thing or thinges therin conteyned shall not in any wise be hurtfull or prejudiciall to the indentures tripartite bering date the xviijth day of Februarie in the xixth yere of our saide souveraigne lorde[50] made betwene our saide souveraigne lorde of thoon partie and the saide dame Anne Seyntleger vidue and dame Margaret Bullayne vidowe by the names of dame Anne Seintleger vidowe and dame Margaret Bullayne vidowe daughters and heyres of Thomas Butler knight late erle of Ormonde and the saide erle of Wiltshire and of Ormonde by the name of the right honourable Thomas vicount Rocheforde son and heyre apparaunt unto the saide dame Margaret and the saide Sir George Seyntleger knight son and heyre apparaunt of the saide dame Anne of the seconde partie and the saide Piers erle of Ossorie by the name of Sir Piers Butler knight cousyn and heyre male to the said Thomas late erle of Ormonde and James lorde Butler by the name of James Butler esquyer son and heyre apparaunt of the saide Sir Piers of the thirde partie but that the saide indentures and all and every clause article sentence covenaunt agrement and every other thing and thynges written mencioned expressed and conteyned in the same shalbe and stande in their full streinght force and effecte to all ententes and purposes according to the teanors and effectes of the same indentures and that the saide Piers erle of Ossorie nor his heyres shall not in any wise clayme chalendge or attempte to have any honour title name dignitie armes or preemynence nor any castels honours manoirs landes tenementes or hereditamentes contrary to the teanor contentes and effectes of the same indentures

50 1528.

any thing or thinges conteyned in the saide acte of repeale or adnullacion to the let or contrarie therof in any wise notwithstonding.

c.7 Thacte of apeles[51]

Where dyvers good and holsome lawes and statutes be made and establisshed within the realme of Englande for the adnullyng and utter taking away of apeles in cases spirituall from the busshop of Rome and see apostolyke and suche other as clayme by auctoritie of the same not oonlie for great spede of justice to the kinges subjectes of the saide realme but alsoo in taking away the longe delayes costes charges and expenses that the saide subjectes susteyned by reason of suche apeles and forasmuche as this lande of Irlande is the kinges proper dominion of Englande and unyted knyt and belongyng to themperiall crowne of the same realme whiche crowne of it silf and by it silfe is fullie holye intierly and rightfully endowed and garnysshed with all power auctoritie and preemynence sufficient to yelde and rendre to all and singuler subjectes of the same full and plenarie remedies in all causes of strife debate contencion or division without any suite provocacion apele or any other proces to be had made or sued to any foreyn prynce or potentate spirituall or temporall, be it therfor and for the comen weale of the subjectes of this lande ordeyned and enacted by auctoritie of this present parliament that noo person or persons subjectes or resiauntes of this lande shall from the furst daye of this present parliament pursue commence use or execute any maner of provocacions apeles or other processe to or from the busshop of Rome or from the see of Rome or to or from any other that clayme auctoritie by reason of the same for any maner of cace grefe or cause of what nature so ever it be upon the payne that thoffendors their aidors counsaillours and abbettors contrarie to this acte shall incurre and ren into suche paynes forfaicturs and penalties as be specified and conteyned in thacte of provision and premunire made in the realme of Englande in the sextenth yere of king Richard the secounde sume tyme king of England and lorde of Irland against suche as procure to the courte of Rome or elswhere to the derogacion or contrarie to the prerogative or jurisdiccion of the saide crowne of Englande and that noo maner of persone subject or resyaunt within this saide lande shall attempte procure or optayne any maner of proces of whate kinde or nature soo ever it be to or from the same busshop of Rome or courte of Rome or see apostolicque or from any other having auctoritie by the same to the let or interrupcion of this acte or any thing therin conteyned nor in any wise obey or execute within this lande suche maner of proces upon like paynes and forfaictes as bene above rehersed; and to thentent that the subjectes and

51 *Statutes at large* c.6.

resiauntes of this lande shall and may take and here the apeles in their just and laufull causes for lacke of justice within this lande be it further enacted by auctoritie of this present parliament that in and for all maner of causes greves and cases as they or any of theme were wont and accustumed to have in their provocacions apeles and other proces in cases of debat and contencion to or from the busshop of Rome or to or from the see apostolicque or courte of Rome they now beyng greved shall have take and use from the[52] furst day of this present parliament their provocacions apeles and suche like processe to the king of Englande and lorde of Irlande his heyres and successors or to his or their lieutenaunt deputie justice or other governour what soo ever he be of this lande of Irlande for the tyme being to his or their courte of chauncery within the same realme of Englande or lande of Irlande and that upon everie suche provocacion apele and processe made to the king of Englande and lorde of Irlande and to his heyres and successors the chaunceller of Englande or keeper of the great seale for the tyme beyng shall graunte a commission or delegacye to sume discreat and wele lerned persons of this lande of Irlande or els in the realme of Englande for finall determynacion of all causes and greves conteyned in the saide provocacions and apeles and in the principall matier and in all circumstaunces and dependauntes therupon and that upon every suche provocacion apele or proces made to the saide lieutenaunt deputie justice or governour the chaunceller of this saide lande of Irlande or keper of the great seale of the same for the tyme beyng by thassent of the chief justices of the kinges bench and comen place the master of the rolles and the underthesaurer of this saide lande for the tyme beyng or any twoo of theme soo as the saide underthesaurer be oon shall graunte a commyssion or delegacie to sume discrete and wele lerned persons within this lande of Irlande for fynall determynacion of all causes and greves conteyned in the saide provocacion and apeles and in the principall matier and all circumstaunces and dependauntes therupon whiche commissioners soo named shall have like power and auctoritie in all maner of thinges as commissioners assigned in apeles made to the kinges highnes in the realme of Englande have by auctoritie of their commission or by vertue of any actes made for apeles within the saide realme any forreyn lawes prohibicions inhibicions from the courte of Rome custumes usage prescripcion or any other thing or thinges to the contrarie therof notwithstonding.

52 *furst* struck through.

[*m.11*]

c.8 Thact of sclaundre[53]

Where in a parliament begonne at London in the realme of Englande the thirde day of Novembre the xxj[ti] yere of the reigne of our moost draide souveraigne lorde kyng Henry the eight king of Englande and of Fraunce defensor of the faithe lorde of Irlande and supreme hedde in erthe of the chirche of Englande[54] and from thence adjourned to Westminster and by divers prorogacions ther holden and contynued it was and is enacted emonges other thinges in maner and forme as followeth:[55]

Forasmoche as it is moost necessarie bothe for comen policie and duetie of subjectes above all thinges to prohibite[56] provide restrayne and extyncte all maner of shamefull sclaundres perils or emynent daungier or daungiers whiche myght growe happen or ryse to their souveraigne lorde the king the quene and their heyres whiche when they be harde sene or understande can not be but odible and also abhorred of all those soortes that be true and loving subjectes yf in any pointe they may doo or shall touche the king his quene their heyres and successours upon whiche dependeth the hole unytie and the unyversall weale of this realme without providing wherfor to great a stoppe of unreasonable libertie shulde be yeven to all cankerd and treators hartes workers and willers of the same and also the kynges loving subjectes shulde not declare unto their souveraigne lorde nowe beyng whiche unto theme hathe bene and is moost entierlie bothe beloved and estemed their undoubted synceritie and trouthe be it therfor enacted by the assent and consent of oure souveraigne lorde the king and the lordes spirituall and temporall and the comens in this present parliament assembled and by auctoritie of the same that if any person or persones after the furst daye of Februarii next comyng doo maliciouselie whishe will or deasire by wordes or writyng or by crafte ymagine invente practyse or attempte any bodelie harme to be doon or commytted to the kynges moost royall person the quene or their heyres aparaunte or to deprive theme or any of theme of the dignitie title or name of their royal estates or sklaunderouselye and maliciouselie publishe and pronounce by expresse writyng or wordes that the king oure souverayn lorde shulde be heretycke scismatycke tyrant infydele or usurper of the crowne or rebelliouselie dothe detayne kepe or withholde from oure saide souveraigne lorde his heyres or successors any of his or their fortresses fortylesses or holdes within this realme or in any other the kinges dominions or marches or rebelliouselie detayne kepe or witholde from the kinges saide highnes his heyres or successours any of his or their shippes ordynaunces artillerie or other munycions or fortificacions of werre

53 *Statutes at large* c.7. 54 1529. 55 26 Henry VIII c.13 (*Statutes of the realm*, iii, pp 508–9).
56 *pro* struck through.

and doo not humbly rendre and geve upp to oure saide souveraigne lorde his heyres or successours or to suche persones as shalbe deputed by theme suche castels fortresses fortilesses holdes ships ordynaunces artillerie and other munycions and fortificacions of war rebelliouselie kept or deteyned within vj dayes next after they shalbe commaunded by oure saide souveraigne lorde his heyres and successours by open proclamacions undre the great seale that than every suche person and persons soo offendyng in any of the premisses after the saide furst day of Februarii their aidors counsaillours consentours and abettors being therof laufullie convicted according to the lawes and custumes of this realme shalbe adjudged traditors and that every suche offence in any the premysses that shalbe commytted or doon after the saide furst day of Februarii shalbe reputed accepted and adjudged highe treason and thoffenders therin and their aidors consentours counsaillours and abettors beyng laufullie convict of any suche offence as is aforsaide shall have and suffre suche paynes of deathe and other penalties as is lymyted and accustumed in cases of highe treason and to the extent that all treasons shulde be the more dread hated and detested to be doon by any person or persones and alsoo because it is a great boldenes and an occasion to evill disposed persones to adventure and embrace their maliciouse ententes and interprises whiche all true subjectes ought to studye to escheue be it therfor enacted by auctoritie aforsaide that noon offendor in any kindes of highe treasons what soo ever they be their aidors consentours counsaillours and abbettors shalbe admytted to have the benefaict or priveledge of any maner of santuarie considering that matiers of treasons toucheth so nyghe bothe the suertie of the king our souveraigne lorde his person his heyres and successors; and over that be it enacted by auctoritie aforsaide that if any of the kinges subjectes denysins or other doo commyt or practyse out of the lymytes of this realme in any outwarde parties any suche offences whiche by this acte are made or heretofor have bene made treason that then suche treasons what soo ever they be that shall happen soo to be doon or commytted shalbe enquered and presented by the othes of xij good and laufull men upon good and probable evidence and witnesse in suche shire and countie of this realme befor suche persones as it shall please the kinges highnes to appointe by commission undre his great seale in like maner and forme as treasons commytted within this realme have bene usid to be enquerid of and presentid and that upon every indictement and presentement founden and made of any suche treasons and certified into the kinges benche like processe and other circumstaunces shalbe there had and made against the offendours as if the same treasons soo presented had be laufullie founde to be doon and commytted within the lymytes of this realme and that all processe of outlarie hereafter to be made and had within this realme against any offendors in treason being resyant or inhabited out of the lymytes of this realme or in any other of the

parties of beyonde the see at the tyme of outlarie pronounced against theme shalbe as good and effectuall in the lawe to all ententes and purposes as if suche offendors had bene resiaunt and dwelling within this realme at the tyme of suche processe awarded and outlarie pronunced; and be it further enacted by auctoritie aforsaide that everie offendor and offendors being laufullie convict of any maner of highe treasons by presentementes confession veredict or proces of outlarie according to the due course and custume of the comen lawe of this realme shall lose and forfaict to the kinges highnes his heyres and successors all suche landes tenementes and hereditamentes whiche any suche offendor or offendors shall have of any estate of enheritaunce in use or possession by any right title or meanes within the realme of England or elswher within any the kinges domynyons at the tyme of any suche treason commytted or any tyme after, savyng to any person or persones their heyres and successours other than thoffendors in any treasons their heyres and successors and suche persone and persones as clayme to any their uses all suche rightes titles and interesses possessions leases rentes offices and other profictes whiche they shall have at the day of commyting suche treasons or at eny tyme afor in as large and ample maner as if this acte had never be had or made.

Considering that this estatute made in the realme of Englande is moost beneficiall and expedient to have due execucion within the kinges lande and dominyon of Irlande especiallie in respecte of the highe rebellion here latelie commytted and that the odible infamyes against the king and quene in the same acte expressed and other offences abuses and abhomynacions there mencioned principallie hathe bene promulged pronounced doon and attempted within this saide lande; be it therfor establisshed ordeined and enacted by auctoritie of this present parliament that the forsaide estatut and ordynaunce and every thing and thinges therin conteyned be establisshed confirmed acceptid demed judged and taken for a good and right lawe within this the kinges lande and dominion of Irlande and to be as good effectuall and of the same streinght qualitie effect force and vertue to all intentes and purposes within the saide lande as the same is or ought to be within the realme of England; and be it further enacted by auctoritie aforsaid that the saide estatut and acte made in Englande and every thing therin conteyned shall have relacion and take effect within this lande of Irlande against all offendors contrarie to the forme therof from the xx^ti day of Maij the xxviij^ti yere of the kinges moost noble reigne[57].

57 1536.

c.9 Thact of subside[58]

Prayen the comens that where by the meane and compulsion of that false and disloyall traditor Thomas fitz Geralde son and heyre to Geralde erle of Kildare and other traditors his false adherentes the moost parte of the king our souveraigne lordes true subjectes of this lande of Irlande against their dueties of allegeaunce have rebelled and not onelie by that traditor robbed and burned but also by their intollerable oppressions and extorcions utterlie destroyed and beggered for reformacion wherof oure saide souveraigne lorde like a graciouse prince to his exceding great charges hathe sent hither his armye royall by whose powere the saide rebellion is not nowe oonlie refourmed and the saide subjectes set at rest and quietnes but alsoo the saide traditor and other his adherentes forced to flie and wheras of longe tyme there hathe bene used aswele by the kinges deputies and other his governours of this saide lande as by the lordes and gentlemen of the same manye diverse and sundrie intollerable chargeous [*m.12*] custumes and abusions as coyne and lyveraie that is to saye horsemet and mans mete for the findyng of their horsemen and footmen with other outrageous expenses to be had levied and perceived of therthe thillers fermors and inhabitauntes of the same lande without any thing payng therfor whiche be great causes of desolacion of that lande in consideracion wherof and to thentent the kinges revenues here may be the more augmented to bere the kinges charges within the same his lande for defence and reformacion of the same without takyng the saide coyne and lyveray and other the saide unlaufull imposicions wherby all rebellions and insurreccions and alsoo the forsaide intollerable abusions and lyveraye with all other extorcions and unlaufull imposicions shalbe from hensforthe escheued and forborne within the saide lande wherby the inhabitauntes of the same may the better live in peaux according to the lawe of God and the kinges; therfor be it enacted ordeyned and establisshed by auctoritie of this present parliament that our souveraigne lorde the king shall have yerelie a subsidie of xiij$^{s.}$ iiij$^{d.}$ of laufull monye of Irlande of and upon every ploughlande occupied manured or hereafter to be occupied or manured within this saide lande of Irlande from the tyme of the occupieng or manuraunce therof as longe tyme as it shalbe soo occupied or manured to pay the saide subsidie in maner and forme aforsaide unto our saide souveraigne lorde the king his heyres and successors from the xxviij^{ti} daye of Septembre in the yere of our lorde God a M^{ll} five hundred xxxvj^{ti} to thende of the terme of x yeres then next ensuyng paiable yerelie at the feast of Ester during the saide terme and that all the crosse landes on the clergie of this lande to be yerelie charged during the saide terme with like subsidie unto our saide souveraigne lorde to be levied at the feast afor-

58 *Statutes at large* c.27. Printed in D.B. Quinn, 'The Irish parliamentary subsidy in the 15th and 16th centuries', *R.I.A. Proc.* 42 C (1934–5), pp 242–4. Transmiss dated 13 September 1535.

saide in like maner and forme as the crosse landes and clergie of the shires of Dublin Methe Kildare and Louthe was charged with the last parliament wherby the last subsidie was graunted and in noon otherwise; provided alway that noo place in any shire within this lande whiche payed noo subsidie whan any subsidie was last levied in the same shire be charged with subsidie by force of this acte; provided alsoo that noo maner man spirituall ne temporall ne comens of this lande or any corporacion within the same having landes or fredome or discharge of subsidie by the king oure souveraigne lorde or any his progenytours is grauntes acte or actes of parliament be charged with subsidie by force of this present acte; provided alsoo and be it enacted by aucthoritie of this present parliament that all lordes knyghtes esquyers and gentlemen that hereafter be caused by the lorde deputie or any other governours of this lande for the tyme being to goo or sende by reason of their landes and possessions to ostynges roodes or journeys to serve oure souveraigne lorde the king and all and every lorde knyght esquier and gentleman that by reason of his or their landes or possessions is and be chargeable by the lawe custume or usage of this lande of Irlande to goo or sende to ostinges roodes or journeys to serve our souveraigne lorde the king upon their proper costes the carting and cariage to every of theme to be assigned at ostinges roodes and journays having their principall housholde and dwelling in the cuntrey out of cities and priviledgid townes forasmoche landes and tenementes as by oon of our souveraigne lorde the kinges moost honourable counsaill and twoo of every countie and shyre made ordeyned and deputed the kynges commyssioners for the same shyre or any twoo of theme soo that he of our saide souveraigne lordes counsaill be oon shalbe thought mete and competent for the saide lorde knight esquier or gentleman to manure and occupie for their awne propre ploughing and cattaill for the mayntenaunce of their housholde and hospitalitie in the cuntrey for so longe tyme as the saide lordes knyghtes esquyers and gentlemen have their principall housholde and dwelling there out of the said cities and townes shall pay noo subsidie for the same landes ne tenementes soo by theme manured or occupied ne shall not be charged with coyne lyveraie carting ne cariages to noo oostinges roodes journeys ne in any other maner and that everie of the saide lordes knyghtes esquiers and gentlemen shall pay noo subsidie coyne lyveraye carting ne cariage for asmoche landes and tenementes as every of theme dothe occupie and manure unto suche tyme as the said commyssioners doo appoynt theme as is aforsaide; and alsoo be it enacted by auctoritie of this present parliament that if it fortune our souveraigne lorde the king his graces deputie or chaunceller of this his lande of Irlande to make ordeyne and depute any commyssioner or commyssioners in any countie or shire within this lande of Irlande the[59] counties or shires of Methe Louthe Dublin and

59 *make* struck through.

Kildare oonlie excepted for thextending and making of ploughe landes wherof or upon the saide subsidie of xiij$^{s.}$ iiij$^{d.}$ shalbe rered leviable or also for the levieng rering and perceiving of the saide subsidie to the use and behoufe of our souverain the king his heyres and successors that then every persone and persones within this lande of Irlande to their power and knowledge of what estate condicion or degre so ever they be shall aide maynteyne assiste obey performe and kepe the saide commyssioners and every of theme and alsoo the ordre leveing and receiving of the saide subsidie extente made or doon by theme or any of theme concernyng the same and that upon the payne of v$^{li.}$ to every person and persones as often as he and they shall offende the same to be forfaict to our souveraigne lorde the king his heyres and successours for ever; provided alsoo that nether the citie of Dublin the citie of Waterforde the citie of Corke the citie of Lymerycke ne the townes of Drogheda Kilkenny Kynsale Rosse ne noon other citie nor towne priveledgid ne borogh towne within this lande of Irlande be charged with subsidie; provided alsoo that all the messuages landes and tenementes in Phebleiston' in the parishe of Clonesillagh within the countie of Dublin being of arrable lande but fiftie acres and nowe named and charged for halfe of oon ploughlande and alsoo all the messuages landis and tenementes in Barbieston within the saide parishe being of arrable lande but lxxj acres iij stanges and nowe named and charged for an other halfe of oon plough lande from hensfurth all the messuages landes and tenementes in Phebleiston' and Barbieston' aforsaide shall not be sessid chargid named ne taken but for the halfe of oon sole plough lande and shall pay noo subsidie ne none other charges hereafter to be sessid upon the ploughe landes but asmoche as oon sole halfe ploughlande shall doo.

c.10 Thact for the furst fructes[60]

Prayeth the comens in this present parliament assemblid that where as at a parliament holden upon a prorogacion at Westminster within the realme of Englande the thirde daye of November in the xxvj^{ti} yere of the reigne of our moost dread souveraigne lorde king Henry theight[61] amongest other was ordeyned and enacted that the kinges highnes his heyres and successours kinges of the realme of Englande shulde have and enyoie from tyme to tyme to endure for ever of every suche persone and persones whiche at eny tyme after the furst daye of Januarie next ensuyng the saide thirde daye of November shulde be nominated elected prefected presented collated or by other meanes appoynted to have any archebusshopriche busshopriche abbacie priorie colledge hospitall archedeaconrie deanrie provestshipp prebende parsonage

60 *Statutes at large* c.8. 61 1534.

vicarage chauntrie frechaple or other dignitie benefice office or promocion spirituall within the saide realme or elswher within any of the kinges dominions of what name nature or qualitie so ever they be or to whose foundacion patronage or giftes so ever they belonge the first fructes revenues and profictes for oon yere of every suche archebusshopriche busshopriche abbay monasterie priorie colledge hospitall archedeaconrie deanrie provestship prebende parsonage vicarage chauntrie frechapell or other dignytie benefice office or promocion spirituall afornamed wherunto any suche persone and persons shall after the furst day of Januarie be nominated elected prefected presented or by any other meanes appoynted as in the saide acte more at large is conteyned[62]; and considering the great decaie of the kinges revenues within this his graces lande and dominion of Irlande and what great excessive and inestimable charges his highnes hathe bene at and susteyned and alsoo dailie susteyneth for the mayntenaunce tuycion and defence of his graces subjectes and for the destruccion exile and banysshing of his ennemyes traditors and rebelles within this his lande and domynyon of Irlande and for suche causes and consideracions as appereth by the saide acte made at Westminster the thirde day of Novembre be it ordeyned enacted and establisshed by aucthoritie of this present parliament that the king oure souveraigne lorde his heyres and successours kinges of the saide realme of England and lordes of this lande and dominion of Irlande shall have and enyoie from tyme to tyme to endure for ever of every suche persone and persones whiche at any tyme after the furst day of this present parliament shalbe nominated elected prefected presented collated or by any other meanes appoynted to have any archebusshopriche busshopriche archedeaconrie deanrie prebend parsonage or vicarage within the saide lande and dominion of Irlande of what name nature or qualitie soo ever thei be or to whose foundacions patronage or gifte soo ever they belonge the annat comenly callid within this lande the ane first fructes revenues and profictes for oon yere of every suche archebusshopriche [*m.13*] busshopriche archedeaconrie deanrie prebende parsonage and vicarage afornamed wherunto any suche persone or persones shall at any tyme or tymes after the saide furst daye of this present parliament be nominated elected prefected presented collated or by any other meanes appoynted and that every suche persone and persones befor any actuall or reall possession or medeling with the profictes of any suche archebusshopriche busshopriche archedeaconrie deanrie prebend parsonage or vicarage shall satisfie content and paye compounde or agree to pay to the kinges use at reasonable dayes upon good suerties the saide annat or ane the first fructes and profictes for one yere; be it alsoo enacted by auctoritie aforsaide

62 26 Henry VIII c.3 (*Statutes of the realm*, iii, pp 493–9).

that the chaunceller of Irland the maister of the rolles and the underthesaurer for the tyme being or any twoo of theme soo as the saide underthesaurer be one of the said two or suche other persones or persone as shall please the kinges highnes his heyres or successours from tyme to tyme at his or their pleasure to name and depute by commyssion or commyssions undre the great seale shall have power and aucthoritie aswele to examyn and serche for the just and true value of the saide annat first fructes and profictes by all wayes and meanes that they can as to compounde and agre for the rate of the saide annat ane first fructes and profictes and to stall and lymyt reasonable dayes upon payment therof upon good and sufficient suerties or suertie by writinges obligatories by their discressions and if composicion or agrement be had or made for the said annat first fructes and profictes befor the saide lorde chauncellor the maister of the rolles and the underthesaurer for the tyme being or any twoo of theme soo as the saide underthesaurer be oon of the saide twoo that than the writinges obligatorie or mony taken for the same shall rest remayne and abide in the handes of the underthesaurer or in the hanaper of the kinges chauncerie in Irlande there saufelie to be kepte to the kinges use and the money to be due of suche writinges obligatorie or to be received in hande by reason of any suche composicion shalbe payed unto the saide underthesaurer or in the saide hanaper to the clerc of the hanaper for the tyme being and that the saide underthesaurer for suche writinges obligatorie and money as cometh to his handes or ought to come to his handes shall make a true and a just accompt therof and that alsoo the saide clerc of the hanaper for suche writinges and money as he receivith or ought to receive shall make a just and a true accompt therof like as he is bounde to do of the money received of the profictes of the kinges great seale and if composicion or agrement be had or made for the saide annat furst fructes and profictes afor any other persone or persones to be deputed by the kinges highnes his heyres or successors by commyssion undre his great seale that then the writinges obligatory and monye taken for the same shalbe delivered to the saide underthesaurer or elswhere to whom it please the kinges highnes his heyres and successors to geve aucthoritie by commission under his great seale to receive the same; and it is alsoo ordeyned and enacted by aucthoritie aforsaide that everie writing of acquitaunce subscribed with the hand and name of the underthesaurer clerc of the hanaper or other comissioners aforsaide or any of theme witnessing the receipt of the said annat first fructes and profictes or any part therof and all writinges obligatories to be taken for payment of the saide annat ane first fructes and profictes by and afor the saide lorde chauncellor the maister of the rolles and underthesaurer or any twoo of theme as is aforsaide or by and afor any other persone or persones to be deputed to compounde and agree for the saide annuat ane first fructes and profictes as is aforsaide shalbe of the same streinght force vertue qualitie and effecte to all ententes and

purposes within this lande and dominion[63] of Irlande as all suche writinges of acquitaunces and writinges obligatorie subscribed and taken by and afor suche persones and persone as be lymyted and appoynted by the saide acte made at Westminster the saide thirde daye of Novembre be within the realme of Englande and that upon certificat hereafter to be made into the kinges chauncerie of any suche writing obligatorie to be taken for payment of suche annat first fructes and profictes like processe and execucion shalbe therupon made and hadde against any persone spirituall or temporall as hathe bene accustumed to be made against any lay persone upon certificat of writinges obligatorie of the statut of the staple and that noo persone shalbe compellid to pay for any writing obligatorie to be made for the saide payment of the saide first fructes above eight pence nor for any acquitaunce to be made for any receipt of suche first fructes above foure pence and suche persone or persones as shalbe deputed by the kinges highnes by commission undre the great seale of England and Irland to compound and agree for the saide first fructes shall at thende of every sex monethes next after the date of their commission and so from sex monethes to sex monethes deliver or cause to be delivered unto the underthesaurer of this forsaide lande for the tyme being or elswhere to suche commissioners as shalbe appointed as is aforsaide to receive the same aswele all suche monye as all suche specialties and bandes as thei shall have taken for the payment of the saide first fructes by endenture to be made betwene theme and the saide underthesaurer or other commissioners as is aforsaide concernyng the certeintie and numbre of the somes of monye specialties and bandes by theme taken and receivid and if any persone or persons to whom any deputacion shalbe made by commission to compounde and agree for the payment of the saide first fructes their heyres executors or admynystrators cancele or imbeasill any of the saide specialties and bandes taken for the payment of the saide first fructes and do not delyver theme according to the teanor of this acte that then every suche offenders shall forfaict that office of deputacion and over that make fyne and raunsome at the kinges awne pleasure and will; and be it likewise enacted by aucthoritie aforsaide that all and every article provysion and thing what soo ever they be enacted or comprised within the saide acte made at Westminster the third day of November for the suertie of payment of the said first fructes in the saide realme of England be in the same force and streinght vertue qualitie and effect to all intentes and purposes within this lande and dominyon of Irlande as thei and every of theme be within the saide realme of England[64]; be it further enacted by aucthoritie aforsaide that annat first fructes and profictes of benefices heretofor accustumed to be taken and payed by and

63 *and dominion* inserted. 64 In margin: Before suche further order comprysed in the act in Yngland.

to thexecutors or admynystrators of thincumbentes of the saide benefices or to any other persone or persones within this lande or dominion of Irland shall from the saide first day of this present parliament sease and be extynct and noo longer be[65] payed ne taken but oonly to the kinges highnes his heires and successours in suche forme as is above mencioned in this acte; provided alway and be it enacted by auctoritie of this present parliament that in asmoche as by this present and forsaide acte our souveraigne lorde the king his heyres and successors haithe and shall have for ever among other the premisses the annat and first fructes of parsonages vicarages and suche benefices as hathe cure that our saide souveraigne lorde his heyres and successours for ever at every avoidaunce of any suche parsonage vicarage or benefice by any maner meane of thissues and profictes comyng or growing of any suche parsonages vicarages or benefices shall provide and fynde a sufficient and an hable preest to serve the cure from any suche avoidaunce till that one be admytted and instituted to the same.

c.11 Thact for Lexlep

Where kyng Henry the vijth of moost famous memorie father to our souveraigne lorde the kyng that nowe is in consideracion of a mariage had betwixt Gerald Fitz Gerald then erle of Kildare and dame Elizabeth Saint John by his lettres patentes ded yeve and graunte unto the said erle and dame Elizabeth his wife and theyres males of their twoo bodies laufully to be begotten the manor and lordshep of Leislip with thapurtenaunces being situat within the countie of Kildare in this the kinges land of Irland by force of whiche graunt the said erle and his saide wife were therof seasid accordingly. After the said erle dyed and the forsaid Elizabeth survived and therof was seasid and dyed seasid of the forsaid manor and lordship in hir demeasne as of fee taile after whose death the same discended to one Henry Fitzgerald son and heyre to the said Elizabeth by the said erle begotten by force wherof the said Henry was therof seasid and dyed seasid after whose death the said manor and lordship discendid to one Thomas Fitz Gerald as brother and heyre male to the said Henry by force wherof the said Thomas was therof seased and died seasid in his demeasne as of fee taile by force of the yefte aforsaid after whose death the said manor and lordship discended to one James Fitz Gerald as brother and heyre male to the said Thomas by force of the yefte aforsaid by force wherof the said James was and is therof seasid in his demeasne as of fee taile by force [*m.14*] of the yeft aforsaide forasmoche as the said manor and lordship of Leislep with thapurtenaunces was befor the said gifte of the kinges auncient enheritaunce and for

65 *be* inserted.

that the blood of the Geraldines is corrupted toward the crowne of England be it establisshed and enacted by auctoritie of this present parliament that the said yefte graunte and the lettres patentes therupon and every thing therin conteyned from the furst day of the cession of this present parliament be revoked repeled adnulled and demed voide in lawe and that our souveraigne lorde king Henry the eight by the grace of God king of England and of Fraunce defender of the faith lorde of Irland and in erthe supreame hed of the chirche of England and of Irland shall from the furst daie of the cession of this present parliament have and enyoie the same manor and lordship of Leislip with thapurtenaunces to hym and to his heires and successours in the right of the crowne of England for ever the said lettres patentes or any thing conteyned in the same or in any other acte or actes had made or doone to the contrary hereof notwithstanding saving to every person and persones their heyres and successours other than the saide Sir James his heyres and successours and suche persone and persones as clayme to any their uses all suche rightes titles interest possessions leases rentes offices or other profictes whiche they had at the said furst daie of the cession of this present parliament or at any tyme before in as large and ample maner as if this acte had never bene had or made.

c.12 Thact of sainct Wolstans[66]

Forasmoche as the kinges highnes hathe utterly determyned his pleasure that the priory or monasterie of chanons of saint Wolstans within the countie of Kildare be suppressed extyncte and utterly dissolved and the rentes and profictes with all thapurtenaunces therto belongyng to be at his graces disposicion and ordre be it enacted by aucthoritie of this present parliament that his majestie from the vjth daie of June last past shall have and enyoie to hym and to his heires for ever the scite ambite and precincte of the said priorie and all the meses landes tenementes mylles and other hereditamentes with their appurtenaunces in Parsoneston' wherof dan Richard Weston late prior of the said priorie toke the profictes or caused to be taken and all and singuler other the manors graynges mylles waters meses landes tenementes reversions rentes services tiethes pencions porcions chirches chapels rightes titles entrees condicions advocacions patronages annuyties and other hereditamentes goodes cattals and other profictes what soo ever thei be than or at any tyme befor appertaynyng or belongyng to the said priorie or wherof dane Richard Weston late prior there or any other his predecessour or predecessours or any other to his or their use joinctlie or severally at any tyme befor the said vjth daie of June

66 Printed in modernised form in Brendan Bradshaw, *The dissolution of the religious orders in Ireland under Henry VIII* (Cambridge, 1974), pp 254–5.

or sethens was or were seasid in the right of the said priorie of saint Wulstane or otherwise to have and to holde the premisses to his majestie his heyres and successors for ever to dispose therwith their free willes and that all and every lettres patentes to be made of the premisses or any parte or parcell therof without and befor any office or offices found and retourned of the same to any persone or persones or bodie politicque shalbe good and effectuall according the wordes and tenors of suche lettres patentes any estatut lawe usage or custome to the contrarie notwithstanding and that aswele the kinges highnes his heires and successors as every persone or persones and bodie politicque their heires succcessors and assignes whiche hereafter shall have any lettres patentes of any manors landes tenementes rentes services tiethes pencions porcions advocacions patronages or other hereditamentes whiche apperteyned or of right ought to appertayne to the saide priorie of saint Wulstans shall and may have suche accions suytes entrees and all other remedies for thoptaynyng and recoveryng of any thing or thinges conteyned in the saide lettres patentes as the said Sir Richard Weston late prior there or any other of his predecessours mought have had at any tyme befor the said vjth day of June or sethens saving to all and every persone and persones being tenaunt at will his or their cornes and alsoo they and every of theme to have laufull warnyng according the custume of the cuntrey and also saving to all maner of persone and persones lay or temporall all grauntes and leases goyng or comyng out of the saide priorie or house or any parcell of the premisses according the purporte of their grauntes and leases made without covyne or collusion befor the said vjth day of June; provided alway and be it enacted by aucthoritie of this present parliament that the said Sir Richard Weston shall have and enyoie a convenyent chambre with a chymney in the saide priorie with competent wod or other fuell to make hym fyre and that the said dane Richard shall have for hym self in the said priory sufficient meat and drynke during the said dane Richardes life and that Gerald Aylmer and Thomas Luttrell shall have and enyoie a yerelie rent of iiij$^{li.}$ of good and laufull money of Irlande goyng out of the saide priorie and other the premysses to theme and to their heyres duryng the life of the said dane Richard to the use of the said dane Richarde yerelie to be payed at the feastes of Mighelmas and Ester by even porcions and if the said iiij$^{li.}$ or any parcell therof be behinde after eny of the said feastes that then so often it shalbe laufull to the said Gerald and Thomas and their heyres to distrayne for the same in every parcell of the premisses; provided alwayes by aucthoritie of this present parliment that this acte nor nothing therin conteyned be prejudiciall nor hurtfull to the moost reverend fader in God George archebusshop of Dublin nor to his successors concernyng all suche proxies as he and his predecessours have used and of right ought to receive in the said house of saint Wulstans that is to saie iiij markes iij$^{s.}$ iiij$^{d.}$ and the saide iiij markes iij$^{s.}$ iiij$^{d.}$ to have to hym

and his successors in like maner and forme as though the house ded contynue still not suppressed nor dissolved any parte of this acte notwithstonding and as thogh no suche acte to the contrarye had bene made.

c.13 Thacte of Delahide landes in Carbrie[67]

Forasmoche as oure souveraigne lorde the king after the deathe of Sir Waltier Delahide knyght is juste and rightfullie intitled to have possess and enyoie all the manors lordships landes tenementes and other hereditamentes wherof the said Sir Waltier or eny other or others to his use was seasid or possessed the furst daye of Aprill in the yere of our souveraigne lorde the king that nowe is the xxv[ti] [68] in fee symple or fee taile to his grace his heires and successors for ever and that by reason of that wilfull and disloyall traditor James Delahide sonne and heire of the said Sir Waltier whiche was one and the chief counsaillour of that traditor and rebell Thomas Fitz Gerald in all his traitors procedinges and that it is thought that the said Thomas Fitz Gerald and James were partely ruled and counsailled by the said Sir Waltier and Jonet Eustace then his wife in all their traditors purposes and in asmoche as dyverse of the said manors lordships landes tenementes and other the premisses is in Carbrie and situat in thiese places wherby the kinges subjectes therunto adjoynyng mought be the better defended and in that that when the said Sir Waltier ded take uppon hym the rule and governaunce of the saide manors and other the premisses in Carbry by his necligence and the love and favour that he and his servauntes bare to the said James Delahid John Delahide and Sir Edward Delahide other of the sonnes of the said Sir Waltier certeyn of the castles and piles beyng buylded uppon the saide landes were burned spoiled and clerelie cast down by his said sonnes and other the adherentes of the said Thomas Fitz Gerald to the great inquyetnes and lostes of the kinges true subjectes and to thentent that his grace may have all the said landes and tenementes in Carbry wherby his grace may have the better occasion to defend his subjectes soo that the said Sir Walter shall have noo medlyng ne noo parte therof wherby by his necligence and favour no like inconvenyence as is aforsaid may ensue and that in especiall for that his grace may rightfullie be intitled to the same if he wolde put his lawes in execucion be it enacted ordeyned and establisshed by aucthoritie of this present parliament that our souveraigne lorde the kyng his heyres and successors for ever from the feast of Ester that was in the yere of our said souveraigne lorde the xxvj[ti] [69] shall have hold possesse and enyoie all the manors lordships landes tenementes and other heredytamentes with their appurtenaunces wherof the said Sir Waltier Delahide or eny other or others yoinctlie

67 *Statutes at large* c.9. 68 1534. 69 1535.

or severallie to his use was seasid or possessed in fee simple or fee taile the xx^{ti} day of Januarie in the xxv^{ti}[70] yere of our said souveraigne lorde or at eny tyme after in the barony of Carbrie with all thissues and profictes of all the said landes and tenementes and other the premisses with thapurtenaunces in Carbry from the feast of Estre aforsaid and that his grace shall have and enyoie all the goodes and cattails that at eny tyme of right did belonge or aperteyne to the said Sir Waltier whiche came to the possession of the kinges underthesaurer and generall receivor of this his lande of Irlande; and for the further suertie of the said landes and other the premisses to whiche our said souveraigne lorde is rightfullie entitled immediatly after the deathe of the said Sir Waltier be it enacted ordeyned and establisshed by aucthoritie of this present parliament that our souveraigne lorde the kyng his heyres and successors for ever from the day of the deathe of the said Sir Waltier Delahide shall have holde possesse and enyoie all other the manors lordships landes tenementes and other hereditamentes with their appurtenance wherof the said Sir Waltier Delahide or eny other or others yoynctly or severallie to his use was seasid or possessed in fee symple or fee taile the xx^{ti} daie of Januarie in the xxv^{ti} yere of our saidė souveraigne lorde or at any tyme after within the lande of Irland savyng to John Talbot of Dardyeston' and to his heyres all suche right title interest entree and possession as he or they have to eny of the premysses.

c.14 **Thact for landes in Athirde**

Forasmoche as it is thought and supposed that our souveraigne lorde the king is juste and rightfullie entitled to the custodie and wardship of the ij partes of the manor of Athirde by reason of the nonage of Edward Barnewall son and heyre male of the body of Robert Barnewall late of Dromnaghe deceassed and by reason of suche mayntenaunce bolstering and bearing out as is made oure said souveraigne lorde can have noo indifferent triall to fynde his graces title of the same by office according the due ordre of the lawe wherfor be it enacted ordeyned and establisshed by aucthoritie of this present parliament that our saide souveraigne lorde the king his heyres and successours shall have possesse[71] and enyoie from the day of the deathe of the said Robert Barnewall duryng the none age of the saide Edwarde Barnewall (if he soo longe live) the custodie and wardship of the ij partes of the saide manor with thapurtenaunces and thogh no office therof be founde and retourned or to be founde or retourned after the deathe of the saide Robert Barnewall that yet our said souveraigne lorde the kyng his heyres and successors for any intrusion takyng of profictes or any other offence doon or commytted or to be doon or commytted

70 1534. 71 *possesse* inserted in another hand.

in the ij partes of the saide manor or any parcell therof shall have like remedies as though a good and a perfict office therof were founde and retourned according to the due ordre of the lawe; saving to every persone and persones the kinges true subjectes after that the said Edward Barnewall come to his full and laufull age (if he soo longe live) all suche right title use interest and possession as they or any of theme have in or to the said ij partes of the said manor or any parcell therof as if this acte had never bene made and saving to everie persone and persones their peticion of right.

c.15 [An act how persons robbed shall be restored to their goods][72]
Be it enacted by this present parliament that if eny felone or felons hereafter do robbe or take away eny monye goodes or cattels from eny of the kinges subjectes from their persone or otherwise within this land of Irland and therof the saide felone or felons be indited and after arrayned of the same felony and found gilty therof or otherwise attaynted by reasone of evidence given by the partie soo robbed or owner of the said monye goodes or cattels or by eny other by their procurement that then the partie soo robbed or owner shalbe restored to his saide monye goodes and cattels and that aswele the justices of gaole delyver as other justices befor whom any suche felon or felons shalbe found giltie or otherwise attaynted by reason of evidence given by the partie soo robbed or owner or by eny other by their procurement have power by this present acte to adward from tyme to tyme writtes of restitucion for the said mony goodes and cattails in like maner as thoghe eny suche felone or fellons were attaynted at the suite of the partie in appele.

[*m.15*]
c.16 Thact for tributes to Irishmen[73]
Prayen the lordes spirituall and temporall and the comens in this present parliament assembled that where as the kynges Irishe ennemyes have bene heretofore of great force and strength within this lande of Irlande by reason wherof they have charged diverse the kynges townes and faithfull subjectes with tributes and exaccions for consideracion that the said Irishmen whiche do take the said tributes shoulde defend the kinges said subjectes whiche they have not done ne doo not and yet the kinges said subjectes at the charge to pay theme the said unlaufull imposicions to their utter impoverysshing wherfor and forasmoche as our souveraigne lorde the king havyng respecte to the povertie of his

72 No title is given in the margin of the roll. The title given here is taken from *Statutes at large*. *Statutes at large* c.10. 73 *Statutes at large* c.11.

said pore subjectes of this his lande of Irlande hath sent his arme royall hither for thexonerating of his graces said subjectes wherby his graces said subjectes ar highly anymated and fortified and the said Irishe ennemyes greatly enfeblisshed soo as nothing lieth in theme to do for havyng any suche tribute be it therfor by aucthoritie of this present parliament enacted establisshed and ordeyned that noo maner Irishman within this lande of Irlande shall have any tribute exaccion or any other unlaufull imposicions of or upon any the kinges townes or faithfull subjectes within the same lande but that all and every the kinges said townes and subjectes shalbe clerely from hensforth for ever more acquieted discharged and exonerated from all and every suche tributes eny lettres or commaundementes sent to theme or any of them or hereafter to be sent contrarie to this present acte in eny wise notwithstandyng.

c.17 Thacte of succession betwixt the kyng and queane Jane

In theire moost humble wise showeth unto your moost roiall majestie the lordes spirituall and temporall and all other your moost loving and obedient subjectes the comens in this your highe courte of parliament assembled that when in your last parliament begonne and holden at Dublin the furst daie of Maij in the xxviij^ti^ yere of your moost gracious reigne[74] it was made and enordynied an acte concernyng amonges many thinges aswele for ratificacion and confirmacion of your mariage then had and solempnysed betwene your highnes and the late lady Anne Boleyn marques of Pembroke as for the lymytacion of the succession of your dominyon and lordship of this lande of Irland to thissue of your bodie begotten and to be begotten of the bodie of the said lady Anne with dyverse remaynders over for defaulte of suche yssue as in the said acte pleynlie and particulerlie more at large is expressed and mencioned and wheralsoo in by the said acte it was ordeyned and establisshed that all and singuler your subjectes shuld take a corporall othe for the fulfilling maynteynyng and defendyng thoole effectes and[75] contentes of the saide acte and it was further ordeyned by the said acte amonges other thinges that if eny persone or persones subject or resiaunt within the dominion of this londe after the saide furst daie of Maij by writing print dede or acte procured ded or cause to be procured or doon eny thing or thinges to the prejudice sclaundre disturbaunce or derogacion of the said matrimonie solempnysed betwene your majestie and the said lady Anne or to the perill sclaundre or disherison of eny thissues and heyres of your highnes being lymyted by the same acte to enherit and to be enheritable to the said dominion and lordship of this lond wherby any suche yssues or heyres of your highnes myght be distroyed disturbed or interrupted in bodie or title of enheritaunce to

74 1536. Above, c.2. 75 *content* struck through.

the saide dominion and lordshipp of this londe as to theme is lymyted in the same acte that then every suche persone and persons their aidors councellours mayntenors and abettors and every of theme for every suche offence should be adjudged highe traditors and that everie suche offence should be adjudged highe treason and thoffendors and their aidors councellours mayntenors and abettors and every of theme being lawfullie convicted of suche offence by presentment veredict confession or proces according to the custume and lawes of the realme of Englond shulde suffre paynes of deathe as in cases of highe treason as in the said acte amonges many other articules clauses and provisions is more at large mencioned and specified; and albeit moost draid souveraigne lorde that the said acte were then made as it was then thought by your majestie nobles and comens upon a pure perfict and clere foundacion thinking the said mariage then had betwene your highnes and the said lady Anne in their conscience to have bene pure sincere perfect and good and soo was reputed accepted and taken in the realme of England and this land of Irland til nowe of late that God of his infynit goodnes from whom noo secrete thinges can be hidde hathe caused to be broght to light evydent and oppen knowledge aswele certein just true and laufull impedymentes unknowen at the making of the said acte and sithen that tyme confessed by the saide lady Anne befor the moost reverend father in God Thomas archebusshop of Canterburie metropolitan and primat of all Englonde sitting judicially for the same by the whiche playnelie appereth that the said mariage betwene your grace and the saide lady Anne was never good nor consonaunt to the lawes but utterlie voide and of noon effecte by reason wherof your highnes was and is laufullie deforced and separated from the bandes of the said mariage in the life of the seid ladie Anne; and this notwithstonding moost gracious souveraigne lorde the ladie Elizabeth your doughter being borne undre the saide unlaufull mariage by vertue and aucthorite of thact of your succession above remembred for lacke of heyre males of your bodie should immediatelie succede as your laufull heyre in the moste hie estate of your dominion and lordship of this lond of Irlond against all honour equitie reason and good conscience if remedie shulde not be provyded for the same and over this moost draid souveraigne lorde albeit that your majestie not knowing of eny laufull impedimentes entred into the bandes of the saide unlaufull mariage and advaunced the same lady Anne to the honour of the souverain estate of quene of this realme of Englond yet nevertheless she enflammed with pride and carnall desires of her boddy putting aparte the dread of God and excellent benefictes received of your highnes confeterated hersilf with George Bulleyn late lord Rochefourth her naturall brother Henry Nores esquyer Fraunces Weston knyght William Bruarton esquier gentlemen of your privaie chambre and Marke Smeton grome of your saide privaie chambre and soo being confederat she and they moost traditorslie commytted and perpetrated divers detestable and abhomynable treasons to the

moost ferefull perill and daungier of the distruccion of your moost royall persone and to thutter losse disherison and desolacion of this lande yf God of his goodnes had not in due tyme brought the said treasons to light for the whiche being pleynlie and manyfestly proved they were convicted and attaynted by the due course and ordre of your comen laws of the saide realme of Englond and hath suffred according to their demerites as by the recordes therof more at large may appere; and albeit moost gracious and moost draid souveraigne lorde dyverse and sondry honourable just true and reasonable clauses be conteyned and expressed in the said act made for thestablishement of your succession whiche be veray necessary and profictable for the comen wealthe of this your londe yet nevertheles bicause certein articles and clauses conteyned in the same concernyng the ratificacion of your said unlaufull mariage betwene your highnes and the said lady Anne and the limitacion of your succession to the yssues of your body had by the said lady Anne and thothe expressed and mencioned in the saide acte above remembred for the defendyng and maynteynyng thoole effectes and contentes of the saide acte which clauses and articles be nowe become of late soo dishonourable and soo farre distaunt from the due course of your comen lawes of your realme of Englande and this your lande and alsoo soo moche agaynst good reason equitie and good conscience that they can not be susteyned ne tollerated to contynue and endure without great perill of division hereafter to be had by occasion of the same amonges us your saide moost humble loving and obedient subjectes and our posterities it may therfor please your highnes of your moost excellent and accustumable goodnes and for thentier love favour and herty affeccion that your majestie hathe alwayes borne and beareth to the comen wealthe of this your lond and for the conservacion of the good peaux unytie and rest of us your moost bounden and obedyent subjectes and of our said posterities that it may be enacted by aucthoritie of this present parliament that the said acte and all clauses articles and provisions therin conteyned from the said furst day of May shalbe repelled adnulled and made frustrate and of none effecte; provided alwey that the saide repeale and adnullacion of the said acte whiche was made for thestablishement of your succession shall not be taken expounded nor understonde to discharge any persone or persons whiche have done or commytted eny offences of treasone or mesprision of treason contrarie to the same acte or eny parte therof at eny tyme afor the said furst daie of Maij but that suche offenses of treason and mesprision of treason doone and commytted by eny persone or persons contrary to the same acte afor the said furst day of Maij shalbe and remayne in the same degree and qualitie to be punyshed by aucthoritie of the same acte as if the same acte had not be repealed the repeale and adnullacion of the same acte by aucthoritie of this present parliament in eny wise notwithstonding; and that it be further enacted by aucthoritie aforsaid that the said late quene Anne, George Bulleyn late lorde Rochefourth Henry Norres esquyer

Fraunces Weston knyght William Bruarton esquyer and Marke Smeton for their abhomynable and detestable treasons by theme and every of theme moost abhominably and traditorsly commytted and doon against your majestie your realme of Englond and this your lande of Irland shalbe by aucthoritie of this present parliament convicted and attaynted of highe treason in suche maner and forme and accordingly as they by the due course and ordre of your lawes of your saide realme and that the said late quene Anne George Bulleyn late lorde Rochfourth Henry Norres esquyer Fraunces Weston knyght William Bruarton esquyer and Marke Smeton and every of theme shall lose and forfeict to your highnes and to your heyres all suche their manors meases londes tenementes rentes revercions remayndors uses possessions offices rightes condicions and all other hereditamentes of what names nature or qualities soo ever they be whiche they or eny of theme or eny other to their use or to the use of eny of theme had or ought to[76] have had of eny state of enheritaunce in fee symple or in taile in use or in possession at the dayes of their severall treasons commytted lymyted and expressed in their indictment or at eny tyme after saving to every persone and persones and bodies poleticque and to theyres assignes and successors of every of theme other then the said late quene and thother traditors afor named and their heyres and assignes and theyres assignes and successors of every of theme and all and every other persone and persones claymyng by theme or any of theme or to their uses or to the use of any of theme or to thuse of any of their heyres all suche right title use possession interest condicion fees offices rentes annuyties comens and all other commodities hereditamentes what sooever they or any of theme myght shuld or ought to have had if this acte had never bene had ne made; and over this moost gracious souveraigne lorde forasmoche as it hathe pleasid your moost royall majestie notwithstonding the great and intollerable perils and occasions whiche your highnes hathe suffred and susteyned aswele by occasion of your furst unlaufull mariage solempnysed betwene your highnes and the lady Katheryn late prynces dowager as by occasion of the said unlaufull mariage betwene your highnes and the said late quene Anne at the moost humble peticion and intercession of your nobles of your said realme of Englond for thardent love and fervent affeccion whiche your highnes bearith to the conservacion of the peaux and unytie of this same realme and of this your lande of Irland and for the good and quiet gouvernaunce therof of your moost excellent goodnes to entre into mariage ageyne and have chosen and taken a right noble vertuouse and excellent lady quene Jane to your true and laufull wife and have laufully celebrated and solempnysed mariage with her according to the lawes of holy churche who fo[r] her convenyent yeres excellent beawtie and purenes of fleshe and blood is apte God willing to conceive yssue by your highnes whiche

76 *to* inserted.

mariage is soo pure and syncere without spot doubte or ympedyment that thyssue procreated under the same (wh[en] it shall please almyghty God to send it) cannot be laufully truelie nor justely interrupted or disturbed of the right and title [and] succession of your dominyon of this lande; it may therfor nowe please your moost gracious majestie at the moost humble peticion and intercession of us your nobles and comens assembled in this present parliament aswele for the clere extynguyshement of all [*m.16*] ambiguities and doubtes as for a pure a[77] perficte unitie of us your moost humble and obedient subjectes and of all our posterities that it be enacted by your moost gracious and royall majestie by consent of us the lordes spirituall and temporall and the comens in this present parliament assembled and by auctoritie of the same in maner and forme as hereafter in articles ensueth; furst forasmoche as the mariage heretofor solempnysed betwene your highnes and the saide lady Katheryn late princes dowager decessed which afor was laufull wife to your naturall brother prynce Arthure and by hym carnally knowen as hathe duely bene proved by sufficient witnes at all tymes was is and ought to be deamed and determyned to be agaynst the lawes of almyghty God and not dispensable by eny humane aucthoritie and soo hathe bene deamed and determyned aswele by thoole clergy of this realme in bothe convocacions and by bothe thunyversities therof and by thunyversities of Bonanye Padwey Parys Orleans Tullus Angeo and dyverse other and alsoo by a great nombre of privat writynges of many right excellent wele lerned men; be it therfor enacted by auctoritie of this present parliament according as it was ordeyned and enacted in the said acte made in the last parliament for thestablishment of your succession that the said mariage heretofor had and solempnysed betwene your highnes and the saide lady Katheryn whiche was befor laufull wife to the saide prynce Arthur your elder brother and by hym carnally knowen as dothe duelie appere by sufficient prove in a laufull proces had and made befor the said moost reverend father in God Thomas by the suffraunce of God archebusshop of Canterbury metropolitane and prymat of all Englond shalbe by auctoritie of this present parliament dyffynytyvelie clerely and absolutely declared demed and adjudged to be agaynst the lawes of almyghty God and alsoo accepted reputed and taken of noo value ne effecte but utterly voide and adnychillat and that the said separacion thereof made by the said archebusshop shalbe good and effectuall to all ententes and purposes any licence dispensacion or eny other acte or actes goyng befor or ensuyng the same or to the contrarie thereof in eny wise notwithstonding and that every suche lycence dispensacion acte or actes thing or thinges had made done or to be doon to the contrarie therof shalbe to all ententes void and of noon effect and soo shalbe reputed and taken by and amonges all us your true subjectes and inhabitantes of

77 recte *and*.

and in this your lande and dominion of Irland for ever and that thyssue borne and procreated undre the same unlaufull mariage made and solempnysed betwene your highnes and the said lady Katheryn shalbe taken demed and accepted illegittimat to all ententes and purposes and shalbe utterly forclosed excluded and bard to clayme chalendge or demaunde eny enheritaunces as laufull heyre to your highnes by lynyall discent; and also forasmoche as the mariage solempnysed betwen your highnes and the saide late quene Anne uppon true and just causes was and is demed and adjudged by the said moost reverend father to be of noo value ne effecte and a devorce and separacion therof had and made by the due ordre and proces of the lawes of the churche of Englond befor the said reverend father be it therfor enacted by auctoritie of this present parliament that the same mariage betwene your highnes and the said late quene Anne shalbe taken reputed demed and adjudged to be of noo force streingth vertue nor effect and that the separacion and devorce therof had by the sentence and myndement of the said moost reverend father in God shalbe good and effectuall and soo hereafter shalbe taken and reputed for ever by all your subjectes their heyres and successors and that noon appele reapele revocacion or adnullacion therof nor eny parte of the same shall hereafter be had taken allowed or admytted in eny behalfe and that all thyssues and children borne and procreat under the same mariage betwene your highnes and the said late quene Anne shalbe taken reputed and accepted to be illegittimat to all ententes and purposes and utterlie forclosed excluded and bard to clayme chalenge or demaund eny enheritaunce as laufull heyre or heyres to your highnes by lynyall discent the saide formor acte made in the last parliament for thestablishement of your succession or eny thing therin conteyned or eny other thing or thinges to the contrarie therof notwithstondyng; and ferthermore sythens many inconveyences have fallen aswele within this lande as in others by reason of marieng within the degrees of mariage prohibited by Goddes lawes that is to saye the son to mary the mother or the stepmother carnally knowen by his father the brother the sustre the father his sonnes doghter or his doghters doghter or the sonne to mary the doghter of his father procreated and borne by his stepmother or the son to mary his awnte being his father or mothers suster or to mary his uncles wyfe carnally knowen by his uncle or the father to mary his sonnes wife carnally knowen by his son or the brother to mary his brothers wife carnally knowen by his brother or eny man maried and carnally knowing his wife to mary his wifes doghter or his wifes sonnes doghter or his wifes doghters doghter or his wifes sustre, and further to delate and declare the meanyng of thiese prohibicions it is to be undrestoud that if it chaunce any man to knowe carnally eny woman that then all and synguler persons being in any degree of consanguynytie or affynytie as is above written to eny of the parties so carnally offending shalbe demed and adjudged to be within the cases and lymytes of the seid prohibicions of mariage all whiche mariages

albeit they be pleynly prohibited and detested by the lawes of God yet nevertheles at some tymes they have proceded under colours of dispensacions by mans power whiche is but usurped and of right ought not to be granted admytted ne allowed for noo man of what estate degree or condicion soo ever he be hathe power to dispence with Goddes lawes as all the clergie of the realme of Englond in the said convocacions and the moost parte of all the unyversities of Cristendome and we alsoo doo affyrme and thinke; be it therfor enacted by auctoritie aforsaid according as is declared and conteyned in the said acte made in the last parliament for thestablishment of your succession that noo persone or persons subjectes or resiauntes of this lond of what estate degree or dignytie soo ever thei be shall from hensforth mary within the degrees afor rehersed what pretence soo ever shalbe made to the contrarie therof and in case eny persone or persons of what estat dignytie degree or condicion soo ever they be hathe bene heretofor maried within the realme of Englonde or this londe within eny degrees above rehersed and by eny thearchebusshops or mynystres of the churche of Englond or[78] of Irland be separat from the bandes of suche unlaufull mariages that then every suche separacion shalbe good laufull firme and permanent for ever and not by eny power aucthoritie or meanes to be revoked or undoon hereafter and that the children proceding or procreat under suche unlaufull mariage shall not be laufull ne legittimat eny foreyn lawes licences dispensacions or other thing or thinges to the contrarie hereof notwithstondyng and that in case ther be eny person or persons within this dominion and land alredy maryed within eny of the said degrees above specified and not yet separated from the bondes of the said unlaufull mariage that then every suche persone soo unlaufully maried shalbe separated by the diffinitive sentence and judgement of the said archebusshops busshops and other mynystres of the churche of[79] Englond or of Irland within the lymytes of their jurisdiccions and auctorities and by none other forreyn power or auctoritie and that all sentence and judgementes yeven and to be yeven by eny archbusshop busshop or other mynystre of the churche of Englond or of Irland within the lymytes of their jurisdiccions and auctoritie shalbe diffynytive ferme good and effectuall to all ententes and be observed and obeid without sewyng any provocacions appels prohibicions or other proces from or to the court of Rome to the derogacion therof or contrarie to thact made sithen the begynnyng of the last parliament for restraint of suche provocacions apels prohibicions and other proces; and alsoo be it enacted by auctoritie aforsaid that all thyssue hereafter to be had and procreated betwene your highnes and your said moost dere and entierlie biloved laufull wife quene Jane shalbe your laufull children and heyres and be enheritable and enherit according to the course of enheritaunce and lawes of the realme of Englond and this your lande

78 *or* inserted. 79 Illegible word struck through.

of Irland the dominyon and lordship of the same lond with all dignyties honours preemynences prerogatives auctorities and jurisdiccions to the same annexed or belongyng in as ample and large maner as your highnes at this present tyme hath the same as king of the realme of Englond and lorde of this dominion and lande, thenheritaunce therof to be and remayne to your said children and right heyres in maner and forme as hereafter shalbe declared, that is to saie furst the seid dominion and lordship of this lond and other the premisses shalbe to your majestie and to your heyres of your bodie laufully begotten knyt and unyted to thymperiall crowne of the realme of Englond that is to say to the furst son of your body betwene your highnes and your seid laufull wife quene Jane begotten and to theyres of the boddy of the seid furst son laufully begotten and for default of suche heyres then to the second son of your boddy and of the boddie of the said quene Jane begotten and to theyres of the body of the same second son laufully begotten as aforsaid and soo to every son of your bodie and of the body of the said quene Jane begotten and to theyres of the body of every suche son begotten according to the course of enheritaunce in that behalfe knyt and unyted to thimperiall crowne of the realme of Englond for ever and if it shall happen your said moost dere and intierly biloved wife quene Jane to deceasse without yssue male of the body of your highnes to be gotten (whiche God defend) then the same dominion and lordship and all other the premysses to be to your majestie as is aforsaid and to the son and heyre male of your body laufullie begotten by any other laufull wife and to the heyres of the body of the same son and heyre male laufully begotten and for default of suche yssue then to your second son of your body laufully begotten and to the heyres of the body of the same second son laufully begotten and soo from son and heire male to son and heyre male and to the heyres of the severall bodies of every suche son and heyre male laufully begotten according to the course of enheritaunce in like maner and forme as is above said, and for default of suche sonnes of your bodie laufully begotten and of the heyres of the severall bodies of every suche son laufully begotten that th[en] the said dominion and lordship and other the premisses shalbe to thyssue female betwene your majestie and your said moost dere and intier[ly] biloved wife quene Jane begotten and for lacke of suche yssue then to theyres femals of your bodie laufully begotten by any other laufull wife that is to saie furst to theldest yssue female and to the heyres of hir body laufully begotten and soo from yssue female to yssue female and to their heyres of their bodies one after an other by course of enheritaunce according to their ag[es] as the crowne of Englond hath bene accustumed and ought to succede and goo in case when ther is heyre female enheritable to the same; and forasmoche as it standeth at this present tyme in thoonlie will and pleasure of almyghtie God whether your majestie shall have heyres begotten and procreated betwene your highnes and your said moost dere entierlie beloved wife quene Jane or els any laufull heyres

and yssues hereafter of your owne body begotten by any other laufull wife and if [suche] heyres shuld faile (as God defende) and noo provysion made in your life who shuld rule and governe this lande for lacke of suche heyres that then this lande after your transitorie life shalbe destuted of a laufull governour or els percace encombred with suche a persone that would coveit to aspire to the same whom the subjectes of this lande shall not fynde in their hartes to love dred or obediently serve as their souveraigne lorde and if your grace (afor it may be certeinlie knowen whether ye shall have heyres or noo) shuld sodeynlie name and declare any persone or persones to succede after your deceasse for lacke of heyres of your body laufully begotten into the roiall estate of the dominyon of this lande then it is to be doubted that suche persone that shulde be soo named myght happen take great hart and courage and by presumpcion fall to inobedyence and rebellion by occasion of whiche premisses great division and dissencion may be and is verie likely to aryse and spring in this lande to the great perill and distruccion of us your moost humble and obedient subjectes and of all our posterities if remedie for the same should not be provyded; for reformacion and remedie wherof we your moost bounden and loving subjectes moost obedientlie knowledging that your majestie mooste [*m.17*] victoriouselie prudentlie poleticklie and indifferentlie haith maynteyned defended governed and rewled this your lande in good peauxe rest quietnes and obedyence during all the tyme of your moost graciouse reigne whiche we moost hertillie deasire myght contynwe for ever putting all our hole trust and confidence in your highnes and nothing doubting but that your majestie if ye shuld faile heires of your body laufully begotten whiche God defend, for the harty love and fervent affeccion that ye beare to this your dominion and lande and for avoiding all thoccasions of devision afor rehersed so ernestlie myndeth the wealthe of the same that ye can best and moost prudently provyde suche a governour for us and this your land as shall and will succede and followe in the just and right tradde of all your procedinges and maynteyn kepe and defende the same and all the lawes and ordynaunces establisshed in your moost graciouse tyme for the wealth of this dominyon and lande whiche all we desire wherby we your said moost loving and obedient subjectes and our heires and successors shall and maie live as nere as may be in as good peaux unytie and obedience after your deceasse as we have lived in the tyme of your moost gracious reigne; doo therfor moost humble beseche your highnes that it may be enacted for avoidyng of ambiguities doubtes devysions and occasions in that behalf by your moost roiall majestie by thassent of us the lordes spirituall and temporall and the comens in this your present parliament assembled and by auctoritie of the same that your highnes shall have full and plenarie power and auctoritie to yeve dispose appoint assigne declare and lymyt by your lettres patentes undre your great seale or els by your last will made in writing and assigned with your moost gracious hande at your onelie pleasure

from tyme to tyme hereafter your highe estat in and of the dominyon and lordship of this lond and all other the premisses therunto belongyng to be remayne succede and come after your deceasse and for lacke of laufull heyres of your body to be procreated and begotten as is afor lymyted by this acte to suche persone or persones in possession and remaindre as shall please your highnes and according to suche estate and after suche maner fourme facion ordre and condicion as shalbe expressed named declared and lymyted in your said lettres patentes or by your said last will; and we your moost humble and obedient subjectes doo faithfully promyse to your majestie by one comon assent that after your deceasse and for lacke of heyres of your body laufully begotten as is afor rehersed we our heyres and successors shall accepte and take love dred serve and alonely obey suche persone and persones males or females as your majestie shall give your said dominion of this lande unto by auctoritie of this said acte and to noon other and holy to stycke to theme as true and faithfull subjectes ought to doo to their regall rulers governours and supreame heddes; and for sure corroboracion therof be it further enacted by auctoritie aforsaid that suche persone and persones as to whom it shall please your majestie to dispose lymyt and assigne the said dominion of this lande and other the premisses therunto apperteynyng by your lettres patentes or by your last will as is aforsaid shall have and enyoie the same after your deceasse and for lacke of heyres of your body laufullie begotten according to suche estate and after suche maner forme facion ordre and condicion as shalbe therof expressed mencioned and conteyned in your said lettres patentes or in your said last will in as large and ample maner as if suche persone or persons had bene your laufull heyres and enheritable to the imperiall crowne of your realme of Englond and to the dominion of this lande and as if the same dominion of this lande had bene yeven and lymyted to theme playnely and particulerly by speciall names and sufficient termes and wordes by the full and immediat auctoritie of this highe court of parliament; and it is further enacted by auctoritie aforsaid that if any of your heyres or children hereafter doo usurpe the one of theme upon thother in the dominion of this lande or clayme or chalendge the said dominion of this lande in any other forme or degree of dissent or succession then is afor lymyted by this acte or if any persone or persones to whom it shall please your highnes of your moost excellent goodnes by auctoritie of this acte to give and dispose your said dominion of this lande and other the premisses therunto apperteynyng or theyres of any of theme doo at eny tyme hereafter demaund chalenge or clayme your said dominion of this lande otherwise or in any other course forme degree or condicion then the same shalbe yeven disposed and lymyted unto theme by your highnes by vertue and auctoritie of this acte, or if any suche persone or persones to whom your majestie shall hereafter give or dispose your said dominion of this land by auctoritie of this acte or any of their heyres doo interrupte or let any of the heyres of your majestie that

is or shalbe begotten borne and procreated undre your laufull pure syncere and undoubted mariage nowe had and solempnysed betwene your highnes and your said moost dere and intierlie biloved wife quene Jane or any other your laufull heyres hereafter to be begotten of your body by any other laufull wife peasiblie and quietlie to kepe have and enyoie the said dominion of this lande and other the premisses by course of enheritaunce according to the lymytacion therof expressed and declared by this acte as knyt and unyted to thimperiall crowne of the roialme of Englond that then all and singuler thoffendors in any of the premisses contrary to this acte and all their abbettors mayntenors faultors councellours and aidors therin shalbe demed and adjudged highe traditors to your roialme of Englond and this your dominion and lande; and that every such offence shalbe accepted reputed and taken to be highe treason and thoffendors therin their aidors mayntenors faultors councellours and abbettors and every of theme for every suche offence shall suffre suche judgement and paynes of death losses and forfaicturs of landes goodes and priviledges of sanctuarie as in cases of high treason; and over that aswele your said heyres and children as every such person and persones to whom your highnes shall lymyt your said dominion of this land in forme as is aforsaid and everie of their heyres for every suche offence above specified by theme or any of theme to be commytted shall loose and forfaict aswele all suche right title and interest that they may clayme or chalendge in or to the dominion of this lond as heyrs by discent or by reason of any yefte or acte that shalbe done by your highnes for his or their advauncement by auctoritie of this acte or otherwise by any maner of meanes or pretence what soo ever it be; and be it further enacted by auctoritie aforsaid that if any persone or persons of what estate degre dignytie or condicions so ever thei be at any tyme hereafter by wordes writing imprinting or by any exterior acte or dede maliciousely or willingly procure or doo or cause to be procured or done directlie or indirectly any thing or thinges to the perill of your moost roiall person or to the perill of the persone of any of your heyrs or successors havyng the roiall estat of the crowne of the realme of Englond and thestat of the dominion of this lande as knyt and unyted to the same crowne or maliciousely or willinglie give occasion by wordes writing prynt dede or acte wherby your highnes or any of your said heyrs or successors havyng thestat of the dominion of this lande might be disturbed or interrupted of the dominion of this land or any thing unto the same apperteynyng or by wordes writing print dede or acte procure or doo or cause to be procured or doon any thing or thinges to or for thinterrupcion repell or adnullacion of this acte or of anything therin conteyned or of any thing that shalbe doon by your highnes in the lymytacion and disposicion of your dominion of this lande by auctoritie of the same or by wordes writing print dede or acte procure or cause to be procured or done any thing or thinges to the prejudice sclaundre disturbaunce or derogacion of the seid laufull matrymonye

solempnysed betwene your majestie and the said quene Jane or any other your laufull wife or wyves hereafter by your highnes to be taken or to the perill sclaundre or disherison of any of thissues heyrs of your highnes being lymyt by this acte to enherit and to be enheritable to the dominion of this land in suche fourme as is aforsaid or to thinterrupcion or disherison of any suche person or persones to whom your highnes shall assigne and dispose your said dominion of this lande by auctoritie of this acte as is afor remembred wherby any suche yssues or heyrs of your highnes or such other person or persons myght be distroied disturbed or interrupted in fame body or title of enheritaunce to the dominion of this lande as to them is lymyted in this acte in forme above rehersed or as to theme shalbe lymyted and assigned by your highnes by vertue and auctoritie of this acte; or if any person or persons by wordes writing imprynting or any other exterior acte directly or indirectly accepte or take judge or beleve any of the mariages had and solempnysed betwen the kynges highnes and the said lady Kathryn or betwene the kinges highnes and the said late quene Anne to be good laufull or of any effecte or by wordes writing pryntyng or by any other exterior acte directly or indirectly sclaundre interrupte impeche gaynsaie or impugne the laufull judgementes and sentences of the said moost reverend father in God Thomas archebusshop of Canterbury and prymat of all Englond for and concernyng the devorses and separacions of the said unlaufull mariages or any of theme or by wordes writing printing or any exterior acte directly or indirectlie take accept name or call by any pretence any of the children born and procreated undre any of the said unlaufull mariages to be legittimat and laufull children of your majestie or if any person or persons craftely ymagyn invent or attempt by colour of eny pretence to deprive the kinges highnes the quene or the heyrs of their bodies laufully begotten or any other the heirs of the kinges bodie laufullie begotten or any person or persons to whom the kinges highnes shall dispose give and lymyt the dominion of this lande by auctoritie of this acte of any of their titles stiles names degrees states or power or if any person or persons at any tyme hereafter being requyred or commaunded by the kinges highnes or his heyrs or successors or by suche person or persons as shalbe auctorised by his grace or his laufull heirs or any persons or person to whom the kinges highnes shall dispose give and lymyt the dominion of this lande by auctoritie of this acte or their heyrs to make or take an othe to aunswer to suche questions and interrogatories as shalbe abjected to theme upon any clause article sentence or worde conteyned in this acte do contemptuousely or utterlie refuse to make or take suche othe or without frustratorie delaie do not make or take the same othe or after the making or taking suche othe do contemptuouselie refuse directlie to aunswer to suche questions and interrogatories as shalbe abjected concernyng the same or any parte therof that then every suche person and persons of what estat degree or condicion soo ever he or they be and their aidors councellours maynteynors

and abbettors and every of theme for every suche offence afordeclared shalbe adjudged highe traditors and that every suche offence afor especified shalbe adjudged highe treason [*m.18*] and thoffendors therin and their aidors councellours maynteynors and abbettors and every of theme beyng laufully convicted of any suche offence by presentement veredict confession or proces accordyng to the custome and lawes of the realme of Englond and this land shall suffre paynes of deathe as in cases of highe treason and that alsoo every suche offendor beyng convicted as is aforsaid shall lose and forfeict to your highnes and to your heyres or successors kynges or regall rewlers of the realme of Englond and lordes of the dominion of this londe all suche manors landes tenementes rentes annuyties and hereditamentes whiche thei had in possession as owners or owner sole seased of by or in any right title or meanes or any other persone or persones had to their use of any estate of enheritaunce at the daie of suche treasons and offences by theme commytted or doon or any tyme after and shall alsoo lose and forfeict to your highnes and to your saide heyres or successors aswele all maner of suche estates of freholde and interest for yeres of landes and rentes as all other goodes cattels and debtes whiche they had at the tyme of their conviccion or attayndor of any suche offence savyng alwaie to every suche persone and persones and bodies politicque to their heyres assignes and successors and to the heyres and successors of every of theme other then suche persones as shalbe convicted and attaynted and their heyres and successors and all other claymyng to their uses all suche right title use interest possession condicion rentes fees offices annuyties and comens whiche they or any of theme shall have in or upon any suche manors landes tenementes rentes annuyties or hereditamentes that shall soo happen to be lost and forfect by reason of any conviccion or atteynder of any the treasons or offences above rehersed at any tyme before the saide treasons and offences commytted; be it alsoo enacted by auctoritie aforsaid that noo persone or persones offending in any the treasons conteyned and lymyted by this acte or in any other treasons shall in any wise have and enyoie the priveledge of immyunitie of eny maner sainctuarie within this dominion and lande or elswher within the lymytes or precynctes therof but shall utterlie lose and be excluded of the same any use graunte custome prescripcion confirmacion or any other thing or thinges to the contrarie hereof in any wise notwithstonding; be it further alsoo enacted by auctoritie aforsaid that if your majestie shall happen to discees befor any suche your yssue and heire male of your bodie whiche shuld inherit the crowne of the realme of England and your dominion of this lande shalbe of his age of xviij yeres or befor that suche your yssue and heyre female whiche should enherit the crowne of your said realme of England and your dominion of this land shalbe maried or be of thage of xvj yeres whiche almyghtie God defend that then the said yssue and heyre male to the dominion of this land soo being within thage of xviij yeres or your said yssue and heyre female to your said dominion of

this lande soo beyng unmaried or within the said age of xvj yeres shalbe and remayne until suche tyme as suche yssue and heyrs shall come to their said severall ages afor lymyted at and in the governaunce of their naturall mother and of suche other your councellours and nobles of your realme of Englond as your highnes shall lymyt and appoynt by your last will made in writing signed with your moost graciouse hand if it shalbe thought by your highnes moost convenyent soo to be or els the said yssues and heyres shall be at and in the governaunce of suche of your councellours and nobles as your majestie shall name and appoynt by your last will made in writing and signed with your moost gracious hand as is aforsaid; and if any persone or persones by writing pryntyng or exterior dead or acte directlie or indirectly procure or doo or cause to be procured or done any thing or thinges to the let or disturbaunce of the same that then every suche offence should be highe treason and thoffendors being therof convicted shall suffre suche paynes of deathe and losse of enheritaunce priveledges of sainctuarie freholdes interestes for yeres goods cattails and debtes in suche maner and forme as is above specified in cases of treason afor mencioned; and for the more sure establishement of the succession of your moost roiall majestie according to the tenor and forme of this acte be it further enacted by auctoritie aforsaid that aswele all the nobles of this your lande spirituall and temporall as all other your subjectes now lyvyng and beyng or that hereafter shall be at their full ages by the commaundement of your majestie or of your heyres or successors at all tymes hereafter from tyme to tyme when it shall please your highnes or your heyres or successors to appoynt shall make a corporall othe in the presence of your highnes or your heyres or successors or befor suche other as your majestie or your heyres or successors will assigne for the same for the keaping observing defending avowyng and mayntenyng of this acte and of all thinges that shalbe doon by your highnes by auctoritie therof according to the tenor of an othe hereafter ensuyng that is to saie: ye shall swere to beare faith trouth and obedience alonly to the kinges majestie supreme hed in erthe undre God of the churche of Englond and of Irland duryng his life and to his heyres of his body of his moost dere and intierly welbiloved laufull wife quene Jane begotten and to be begotten and procreated and further to the heyres of our said souveraign lorde according to the limitacion aswele in the statute made for suertie of his succession in the crowne of the realme of Englond in the parliament begon and holden at Westminster in theight daie of June in the xxviij[ti] yere of the kinges moost gracious reigne[80] as in the statut made for the suertie of his succession in the dominion of this lande in the parliament holden upon prorogacion at Dublin in the xiij daie of Octobre in the xxix[ti] yere of the kinges moost gracious reigne[81] and alsoo for lacke of suche heyres to suche persone and persones

80 1536. 28 Henry VIII c.7 (*Statutes of the realm*, iii, pp 655–62). 81 1537.

as the kinges highnes shall lymyt and appoynt to succede to the crowne of the realme of Englond and to the dominion of this land by vertue and auctorite of the same actes and not to any other within the realme of Englond or this land nor forreyn auctoritie power or potentate and in case any other othe be made or hath bene made by you to any other persone or persons that then ye to reput the same as vaine and adnychillat and that to your connyng wit and uttermost of your power without gyle fraud or other undue maner ye shall observe kepe maynteyn and defend aswele the said acte of succession made in the said parliament begon and holden at Westminster in the said eight daie of June in the said xxviij^ti^ yere of the kinges moost roiall reigne as the said act of succession made in the said parliament holden upon a prorogacion at Dublin in the saide xiij day of Octobre in the said xxix^ti^ yere of the kinges moost gracious reigne and all thole effectes and contentes of every of the said actes and all thinges that shalbe doon by the kinges highnes by auctoritie of every of theme and all other actes and statutes made in confirmacion or for execucion of the same or of any thing therin conteyned and thus ye shall doo against all maner of persons of what estat dignitie degree or condicion soo ever thei be and in noo wise do or attempt nor to your power suffre to be doon or attempted directly or indirectly any thing or thinges prively or apertly to the let hyndraunce domage or derogacion therof or of any parte of the same or of any thing[82] or thinges that shalbe done by the kinges highnes by vertue or auctoritie of eny of the said actes by eny maner of meanes or for eny maner of pretence soo helpe you God all sainctes and holy evaungelistes; and it is alsoo enacted by auctoritie aforsaid that all maner your subjectes aswele spirituall as temporall suyng lyveraie or utterlemayn out of the handes of your highnes or of your heires or successors or doyng any fealtie to your highnes or to your heyres or successors by reason of the teanure of their landes shall swere the said corporall othe above mencioned and that they nor any of theme shall hereafter have any lyveraie utterlemayn or restitucion out of your handes nor out of the handes of your heyrs or successors til they shall have made the said corporall othe in forme above rehersed; and if any persone or persones being commaunded by auctoritie of this acte to make the said othe afor lymyted obstynately or wilfully refuse that to doo or will protest and saye when they shalbe examyned upon any interrogatories that shalbe objected to theme for and concernyng this acte or any thing therin conteyned that thei be not bounde to declare their thought and conscience and stiffely theron abyde that then every suche persone soo doyng for every suche offence shalbe taken and accepted for offendor in highe treason and that every suche refusell shalbe deamed and adjudged highe treason and thoffendors therin beyng as is afor lymyted laufullie convicted or attaynted therof by the lawes of the realme of Englond or of this

82 *thing* inserted.

lond shall suffre suche paynes of deathe losses and forfeicturs and also lose priv-eledges of sainctuaries in like maner and forme as is above mencioned for the treasons afor lymyted by this acte; and be it further enacted by auctoritie of this present parliament that if it shall please the kinges majestie at any tyme hereafter by his lettres patentes undre his great seale or by his last will made in writyng and signed with his moost gracious hand to avaunce any person or persones of his moost roiall blood to any title stile or name of any estat dignytie or honour what soo ever it be and to give theme or to any of theme any castle honours manors landes tenementes liberties francheses or other heredytamentes in fee symple fee taile or for term of their[83] lyves or the life of any of theme that then all and every suche lettres patentes and last will of your highnes soo to be made to any suche person or persons of your blood shalbe good and effectuall to theme and every of theme according to the teanor purportes and effectes of every suche lettres patentes and last will and that the said persone and persones and every of theme shall have and enyoie aswele all suche titles stile and names of honour dig-nitie and estate whiche shalbe conteyned and expressed in any suche lettres patentes or last will of the kynges highnes as suche castels honours manors lon-des tenementes liberties frauncheses and other hereditamentes whiche shalbe specified and mencioned in every suche lettres patentes or last will in suche maner forme facion or condicion and according to suche estate or estates in the lawe as shalbe expressed and lymyted in every suche lettres patentes or last will in as large and ample maner to all ententes and purposes as if the stiles titles and names of honour dignitie and estate and the castels honours manors landes ten-ementes liberties francheses and other hereditamentes whiche shalbe comprised in any suche lettres patentes or last will to be made were alredie given by good and sufficient lettres patentes to suche persone or persones of the kinges blood by their speciall names and surnames ratified and confirmed by auctoritie of this present parliament or as if the names of such person and persons soo being of the kinges blood and suche titles stiles names castles honours manors londes ten-ementes liberties frauncheses or other hereditamentes had bene named and expressed in this acte and gyven to suche persone and persons of the kinges blood by their proper names and surnames by sufficient wordes termes clauses and sentences immediatly by auctoritie of this present parliament saving to all and every persone and persons and bodies politicque and to their heyres assignes and successors other than to the kinges highnes his heyrs or successors all suche right title interest possession rentes annuyties fees offices comens rightes inter-estes pencions condicions and all other hereditamentes whiche they or any of theme may or myght clayme of in or to any the said titles stiles names castles honours manors landes tenementes liberties frauncheses and other heredita-

83 *their* inserted.

mentes conteyned and mencioned in any suche lettres patentes or last will in as large and ample maner as if this acte had never bene had ne made; and be it fynally enacted by auctoritie aforsaid that this present acte and every clause article and sentence comprised in the same shalbe taken and accepted according to the playne wordes and sentences therin conteyned and shall not be interpreted nor expounded by colour of any pretence or cause or by any subtill argumentes invencions or reasons to the hyndraunce disturbaunce or derogacion of this acte or any parte therof any thing or thinges acte or actes of parliament heretofor made or hereafter to be had done or made to the contrarie notwithstondyng and that every acte statute lawe provision thing or thinges heretofor had or made or hereafter to be had doon or made contrarie to theffect of this statut shalbe voide and of no value nor force.

[*m.19*]

c.18 Thact for the first fructes of abbaies[84]

Prayeth the comens in this present parliament assembled that where in a parliament holden at Dublin within this lande the furst daie of Maij in the xxviij^ti^ yere of the reigne of our moost draid souveraigne lorde king Henry theight[85] emonges other was ordeyned enacted and establisshed[86] that the kinges highnes his heyres and successors kinges of the realme of Englond and lordes of this land and dominion of Irland shuld have and enyoie to endure for ever of every suche persone and persones whiche at eny tyme hereafter the said furst daie of Maij shulde be nominated elected prefected presented collated or by any other meanes appoynted to have any archebusshopriche busshopriche archedeaconrie deanrie prebend parsonage or vicarage within this said lande or dominion of Irlande of what name nature or qualitie soo ever thei be or to whose foundacion patronage or yeft so ever thei belonge the annuat comenly called within this lande the anne furst[87] fructes that is to saie the revenues and profictes for oon hole yere of every suche archebusshopriche busshopriche archedeaconrie deanrie prebend parsonage and vicarage afor named wherunto any suche persone or persones shall at eny tyme or tymes after the said furst daie of Maij be nominated elected prefected presented collated or by any other meanes appoynted as in the said acte more at large is conteyned; and considering that for the better augmentacion of the kinges revenues within this lande whose majestie like a moost gracious prynce and souveraigne lorde hathe with thexpence of an importable some of his awne treasure defended us from the ravyn and spoile of suche rebelles and traditors as latelie attempted the utter

84 *Statutes at large* c.26. Draft bill (PRO, SP 60/5/61) printed in Quinn, 'Bills and statutes', pp 142–6. 85 1536. 86 Above, c.10. 87 *profit* struck through.

destruccion of the state of this lande and wele perceiving a gratuytie agayne in us to be our shelde against all like attemptates that it is bothe reasonable meate and convenyent that his moost excellent majestie his heyrs and successors shuld have and enyoie from tyme to tyme to endure for ever the furst fructes revenues and profictes for oon yere of every abbathie monasterie priorie colledge and hospital and of the priorie or hospitall of sainct John the Baptist of Jerusalem in Irland and the commaundrees of the same religion aswele as of the said archebusshopriche busshopriche archedeaconries deanries prebendes parsonages or vicarages and moche more the rather seyng that the said abbathies abbayes monasteries colledges and hospitals and the said priorie or hospitall of sainct Johns and the commaundrees of the same may better or aswele satisfie content and paie the said furst fructes revenues and profictes for oone yere as thother persons bound by the said estatutes; be it therfor ordeyned enacted and establisshed by auctoritie of this present parliament that the king our souveraigne lorde his heyrs and successors kinges of the said realme of Englond and lordes of this lande and dominion of Irland shall have and enyoie from tyme to tyme to endure for ever of every suche persone and persones whiche at eny tyme hereafter the furst daie of this present parliament holden at Dublin uppon prorogacion shalbe nominated elected prefected presented collated or by any other meanes appoynted to have any abbay priorie colledge hospitall the priorie or hospitall of sainct John the baptist of Jerusalem in Irlande or any commaundre of the same religion within this lande and dominion of Irland of what name nature or qualitie soo ever thei be or to whose foundacion patronage or gifte soo ever they belonge the annuat comenlie callid within this lande the anne furst fructes that is to saie the revenues and profictes for one hole yere of every suche abbaie priorie colledge hospitall the priorie or hospitall of sainct John Baptist of Jerusalem in Irland and of every the commaundrees afornamed wherunto suche persone or persones shall at eny tyme or tymes after the said furst day of prorogacion of this present parliament be nominated elected prefected presented collated or by any other meanes appoynted; and that every suche persone and persones befor any actuall or reall possession or medling with the profictes of any suche abbay priorie colledge hospitall the priorie or hospitall of saint John the baptist Jerusalem or any commaundree shall satisfie content and pay compound or agree to pay to the kinges use at reasonable daies upon good suerties the said annuat or ane first fructes and profictes for one hole yere; be it alsoo enacted by auctoritie aforsaid that the chaunceller of Irland the underthesaurer and clerc or maister of the rolles of this lande for the tyme being or any twoo of theme soo the said underthesaurer be oon of the said twoo or suche other persone or persones as shall please the kinges highnes his heyres or successors from tyme to tyme at his or their pleasure to name and depute by commyssion or commyssions undre the

great seale shall have power and auctoritie aswele to examyn and serche for the just and true value of the said annuat furst fructes and profictes by all wayes and meanes that they can as to compounde and agree for the rate of the said annuat furst fructes and profictes and to stablishe appoynt and lymyt reasonable daies for the payment therof uppon good and sufficient suerties or suertie by writinges obligatories at their discressions and if composicion or agrement be had or made for the said annuat furst fructes and profictes befor the said lorde chaunceller the underthesaurer and the maister of the rolles for the tyme beyng or any twoo of theme soo the said underthesaurer be oon of the two that then the writinges obligatories or mony taken for the same shall rest remayne and abide in the handes of the underthesaurer for the tyme being or in the hanaper of the kinges chauncerie in Irland there saulfely to be kept to the kinges use and the monye to be due of suche writinges obligatorie or to be received in hand by reason of any suche composicion shalbe paied to the said underthesaurer or in the said hanaper to the clerc of the hanaper for the tyme being and that the said underthesaurer for suche writinges obligatorie and monye as cometh to his handes or ought to come to his handes shall make a true and just[88] accompte therof at suche tymes and after suche sorte as he shall accompt for the rest of the kinges highnes revenues and that alsoo the said clerc of the hanaper for suche writynges and mony as he receiveth or ought to receive shall make a just and true accompt therof like as he is bounde to doo of the monye received of the profictes of the kinges great seale; and if composicion or agrement be had or made for the said annuat furst fructes and profictes afor any other persone or persons to be deputed by the kinges highnes his heyrs or successors by commission under his great seale that then the writinges obligatorie and mony taken for the same shalbe delyvered unto the said underthesaurer or elsewhere to whom it pleaseth the kinges highnes his heyrs and successors to geve auctoritie by commission undre his great seale to receive the same; and it is enacted alsoo by auctoritie aforsaid that every writing of acquyttaunce subscribed with the hand and name of the underthesaurer clerc of the hanaper or other commissioners aforsaid or any of theme witnessing the receiptes of the said annates furst fructes and profictes or any parte therof and all writinges obligatories to be taken for the paymentes of the said annates annee furst fructes and profictes by and afor the said lord chaunceller underthesaurer and maister of the rolles or any twoo of theme or by or afor any other persone or persones to be deputid to compound and agree for the said annates anne furst fructes and profictes shalbe of the same strenght force vertue qualitie and effecte to all ententes and purposes within this land as all suche writinges and acquytaunces and writinges obligatories subscribed and taken by

88 *and just* inserted.

and afor suche persone and persones as be lymyted and apoynted by thact made at Westminster within the realme of England the thrid daie of Novembre in the xxvj^ti yere of the reigne of our moost drad souveraigne lorde king Henry theight[89] be within the said realme of England; and that uppon certificat hereafter to be made in the kinges chauncerie of this lande for any suche writing obligatorie to be taken for the payment of any suche annuat furst fructes and profictes like proces and execucion shalbe theruppon made and had agaynst any persone spirituall or temporall as have bene accustomed to be made against any ley persone upon certificat or writinges obligatorie of the statut of the staple; and that no persones shalbe compelled to paie for any writing obligatorie to be made for the payment of the said furst fructes above viij^th pence nor for any acquyttaunce to be made for any receipt of suche first fructes above iiij pence; and suche persone or persones as shalbe deputed by the kinges highnes by commission undre the great seale of England or of this lond to compound and agree for the said furst fructes shall at the ende of every sex monethes next after the date of their commission and soo from sex monethes to sex monethes delyver or cause to be delyvered unto the underthesaurer of this land for the tyme beyng or elswher to suche commissioners as shalbe appoynted as is aforsaid to receive the same aswele all suche monye as all suche specialties and bandes as thei shall have taken for the payment of the said furst fructes by endentur to be made betwene theme and the said underthesaurer or other commyssioners as is afor said concernyng the certeintie and nombre of the somes of monye of the specialties and bandes by them taken and received; and if any persone or persones to whom any deputacion shalbe made by commission to compound and agree for the payment of the said furst fructes their heyrs executors or admynystrators concele or ymbecill any of the said especialties and bandes taken for the payment of the said furst fructes and doo not delyver theme according to the tenor of this act that thei and every suche offendor shall forfaict that office of deputacion and over that their bodies and goodes to be holie for every suche offence at the kinges will and pleasur; and be it likewise enacted by auctoritie aforsaid that all and every article provision and thing what soo ever they be enacted and comprised in and within an acte made and establisshed at a parliament holden uppon a prorogacion at Westminster within the realme of England the thrid day of Novembre in the xxvj^ti yere of the reigne of our moost drad souveraigne lorde king Henry theight[90] for the suertie and payment of the furst fructes revenues and profictes in the realme of England and serche for the due knowledge of the yerely revenue of the said abbaies and other afornamed and every other thing materiall comprised in thact be in the same force streingth vertue qualitie and effect to all intentes and

89 1534. 26 Henry VIII c. 3 (*Statutes of the realm*, iii, pp 493–9). **90** 1534.

purposes withing this land as they and every of them be within the realme of Englond.

[*m.20*]

c.19 Thact for proctors[91]

Forasmoche as at every parliament begon and holden within this land twoo proctors of every dioces within the same land have bene used and accustumed to be sommoned and warned to be at the same parliament whiche were never by thorder of the lawe usage custome or otherwise any membre or parcell of the hole bodie of the parliament nor have had of right any voice or suffrage in the same but onlie to be there as counsaillours and assistauntes to the same and upon suche thinges of lernyng as shuld happen in controversie to declare their opynyons moche like as the convocacion within the realme of Englond is comenlie at every parliament begon and holden by the kynges highnes speciall licence as his majesties judges of his said realme of Englond and dyverse other substanciall and lerned men havyng groundelie enquered and examyned the root and furst establishment of the same doo clerely determyne and yet by reason of this suffraunce and by the contynuaunce of tyme and for that most comenlie the said proctors have bene made privie to suche matiers as within this land at any tyme have bene to be enacted and establisshed and their advyses deasired and taken to the same they nowe of their ambicious myndes and presumpcion inordynatelie deasiryng to have aucthoritie and to intromeadle with everie cause or matier without any just grounde or cause reasonable to the same doo temerariouselie presume and usurpedly take upon theme selves to be parcell of the bodie in maner claymyng that without their assentes nothing can be enacted at any parliament within this lande whiche as it is thought cometh not without the procurement and mayntenaunce of some of their superiors to thoonely entent that the said proctors for the more parte being nowe their chapleyns and of meane degre should be the stoppe and let that the devillishe abuses and usurped aucthoritie and jurisdiction of the busshop of Rome (by some men callid the Pope) nor of theme selfes should not come to light or knowledge that some good and godlie reformacion therof myght be had and provyded; wherfor be it enacted ordeyned and establisshed by auctoritie of this present parliament that the saide proctors ne any of theme soo sommoned or warned to any parliament begon or holden or to be begon and holden within this lande is ne shalbe any membre ne parcell of the bodie of the same parliament ne shall give ne have any voice opynyon assent or agrement to any acte provision or ordynaunce to be regarded ne enacted in any parliament within

91 *Statutes at large* c.12. Transmiss dated 30 July 1537.

this land ne yet their voices assentes or agrements or oppynyons shall not be necessarie ne requisite to any suche act provision or ordynaunce but that by auctoritie aforsaid every acte ordynaunce provision thing or thinges made ordeyned or establisshed or to be made ordeyned or establisshed at any tyme in any parliament holden or to be holden within this lande without thassent consent or agrement of the said proctors or the more parte of theme or contrarie to the same is and shalbe good and effectuell to all ententes and purposes according to the teanor purport meanyng and effect of every suche acte provision or ordynaunce and by the same aucthoritie the said proctors ne any of theme shalbe accepted reputed deamed or taken from the furst daie of this present parliament as parcell or any membre of the said parliament or any other parliament hereafter to be holden within this land but onlie as counsaillours and assistauntes to the same any lawe usage customes prescripcion or any other cause or matier thing or thinges what soo ever it or they be in any wise to the contrarie notwithstanding.

c.20 Thact for pardons[92]

Forsmoche as the kinges moost excellent majestie our moost gracious and moost benygne souveraign lorde haith bene by his deputie and counsaill here advertised and enformed howe that diverse and many his subjectes of this land of Irlande that by any meanes were seduced in the tyme of the late moost detestable rebellion of the Geraldynes and soo trayned into the conspiracie and attemptat of the same beyng moche souroufull and repentaunt for their moost haynous and grevous offences commytted agaynst his highnes in that behalf doo not oonlie moost humbly submyttyng theme selves to his grace and mercie deasire his majesties moost gracious pardone for the same but doo alsoo as it were for an argument and token of their repentaunce offre to make fyne to his highnes for some parte of satisfaccion his majestie of his moost gracious nature moche more deasiryng the gentle reformacion and amendement of all his subjectes that have in any wise offended hym then the just punyshement of theme according to their demerites hathe not onelie at this present addressed his commission under his privaie seale of England to his right trusty and right welbeloved cousyn and counsaillour the lorde Leonard Gray deputie of his said lande to Anthony Seintleger of Ulcombe esquyer George Poulet Thomas Moile William Berners William Brabazon and Gerald Aylmer esquyers gevyng theme and twoo of theme auctoritie by the same to compound with all suche persones as will sue for his said moost gracious pardone and to cesse suche fyne and fynes uppon theme for the same as they or twoo of theme shall by their

92 Draft bill (PRO, SP 60/4/48) printed in Quinn, 'Bills and statutes', pp 146–7.

wisedomes and discressions thynke convenyent but is also contented and pleased for the moor profict and suertie of the said pardones to be thus graunted to his said subjectes it shalbe enacted ordeyned and establisshed in maner and forme followyng: furst be it enacted ordeyned and establisshed by auctorite of this present parliament that all and every bill or shedule to be made out by the commissioners befor named or by twoo of theme and subscribed with their or twoo of their handes and directed to the lord chaunceller of this lande shalbe to hym sufficient warraunt and discharge therupon to make and geve out a pardon under the great seale of this lande according to suche a mynut signed with his graces hande as his majestie haith delyvered to the said commissioners to be delyvered to the chauncellor for that purpose; and be it further enacted that all and every the said pardone or pardones made out upon the warrauntes aforsaid shalbe to the parties that shall have the same as sufficient and vaillable to all ententes and purposes as if every of the same should passe by a speciall warraunt from the kinges majestie any act statut or provision heretofor made to the contrarie in any wise notwithstondyng; provided alwaies that thauctoritie yeven by this acte aswele to the said commissioners as to the said chaunceller shall take ende and be determyned the furst daie of Julij next comyng soo as all men entendyng to enyoie the benefict of this acte must in the meane season make their fynes and composicions with the said commissioners or twoo of theme or els at their adventur abide thordre of the lawe for the due punyshement of their offences and transgressions accordinglie; provided and be it enacted by aucthoritie aforsaid that noon of thofficers or clerkes of the chauncerie shall wilfullie[93] receive and take or cause to be received and taken for the writyng and enrollyng of every suche pardone or eny other thing by theme or eny of theme to be done and executed in the said chauncerie above the some of vj s. Irishe and that the clerc of the crowne in the Kinges Benche shall not wilfullie receive or take or cause to be received and taken for thallowaunce of eny suche pardone and making up the recorde there and any other thing ther to be doon and executed above the some of xij d. Irishe upon payne to every persone or persons offending the same of the losses and forfaictur of his or their offices; provided alsoo that this acte ne any thing therin conteyned shall in noo wise extende or be beneficiall to any person or persones that be alredie attaynted by especiall name by auctoritie of parliament but that the same persons and every of theme shall remayne in the same estate and condicion they were in by force of the formor act or actes made for their said attaindor any thing or thinges herein expressed or soundyng to the contrarie notwithstonding.

93 *receiv* struck through.

c.21 Thact for Dueleke

Forasmoche as the kinges highnes utterlie determyned his moost graciouse pleasur of a certain lease to be made of the hole possessions and profictes aswele spirituall as temporall of the priorie celles and houses of Dueleke and Colpe latelie belongyng to the monasterij or house of Lanthony in England and nowe of right belongyng to his highnes and in his graces disposicion and pleasure by auctoritie of parliament payeng therfor yerelie to his highnes his heyres and successors the yerelie and usuall rent befor this tyme used and accustumed to be payed, whiche notwithstonding upon privaie and secrete suggestion to his highnes made on the behalfe of John Bathe and Edmond Gryffen his grace having then noo remembraunce of his said formor determynacion signed with his moost victorious hande a bill or warraunt of his moost gracious lettres patentes to be made unto the said John and Edmonde of the parsonages or churches of Cowloke Rathbegan' Kylmessan' and Douthe and the tiethes and profictes belongyng to theme with all the tiethes and dysmes of Moche Ryvereston' Litle Ryvereston' Scaternagh and Acarne parcell of the premisses and the moost commodious parte therof and more in value and profict than a great substaunce of the rest whiche bill or warraunt the right honourable lorde Crumwell lorde privey seale and vicegerent of the same calling to his remembraunce the kynges said formor determynat pleasure and the losses that shuld ensue to his highnes by the same and perceivyng the said bill or waraunt to be surrepticiouselie purchased by the said John and Edmond estopped the same at the signet and yet by fraudulent and indirect meane without the kinges signet or privaie seale the same passed the kynges brood seale of Englond contrarie to the teanor forme and effect of the statute therin provyded; wherfor consideryng the premisses and in especiall the great losses and hyndraunce that shall ensue to the kinges highnes in setting or lettyng the rest of the saide priorie celles or houses and the possessions and profictes belongyng to theme in dismynyshing the usuall or yerelie rent therof used and accustumed to be paied by reason that a great substaunce of the possessions belongyng to the same be in the marches adjoynyng to Irish disobeysauntes and in maner wast and alsoo the substaunce of thother residue wher any commoditie or profict doo rest is conteyned in the said bill or warraunt and in the said lettres patentes made uppon the same whiche beyng entierlie set togither may be preserved and saved to his highnes; be it enacted ordeyned and establysshed by auctoritie of this present parliament that all and every gyft lease or graunt made yeven or graunted by the kinges highnes unto the said John and Edmond or to either of theme by his gracious lettres patentes or otherwise of the said parsonages or churches of Couloke Rathbeggan' Kylmessan' and Douthe and the tiethes and profictes belongyng to theme with all the tiethes and dysmes of Moche Ryvereston' Litle Ryvereston' Scaternagh and Athcarne or of any parte or par-

cell of the said priorie celles or houses of Dwleke and Colpe or any thing or thinges that at any tyme belonged to the house of Lanthony in England within this land of Irlande and all and every lettres patentes of the same by reason of the said warraunt or bill signed made or hereafter to be made be resumed revoked and adnychillated made frustrat utterly voide and of noon effect in the lawe; and further be [*m.21*] it enacted by auctoritie aforsaid that if any suche lettres patentes come to the handes of the saide John or Edmond or into the handes of any suche persone where that the said John or Edmond may conveyentlie come to the same that then after request to theme or any of theme made or to be made by any person or persones then the said John and Edmond or one of theme within vj monethes next after that any suche lettres shall come to their handes or to the handes of any other persone or persons wher they maie convenyentilie come to it as is aforsaid shall take surrendre and delyver any suche lettres patentes of any suche lease gift or graunt into the kinges chauncerie of this his land there to be cancelled and soo entred of recorde uppon payne of forfaictur unto the said John and Edmond and either of theme soo offendyng of xl$^{li.}$ sterling to be forfaicted and recovered to the kinges use in any of his graces courtes of recorde within this his land by origynall writ or debt informacion bill or otherwise wherin noo essoyne proteccion ne wageor of lawe shalbe admytted or allowed.

c.22 Thact for marieng with Irishmen[94]

Forasmoche as by mariage alterage and fostering of the kinges subjectes of this his lande of Irlande with his graces Irishe rebels great lacke of obedience hathe growen to his highnes and his moost noble progenitours of their people within this lande and by the same dyverse enormyties myschieves and inconvenyences have ensued and comen to his said loving subjectes from tyme to tyme for the more parte during thiese CC yeres as evidentlie to every of the kinges subjectes of this his lande for the tyme beyng having knowledge or practyse playnlie ded and dothe appere and though in the tyme of the kynges moost noble progenitours the same myschiefes and inconvenyences whiche followed sethens to the utter undoyng and desolacion of his graces said subjectes was then right wele perceived and dyverse good estatutes and actes by auctoritie of parliament therfor provyded wherin is conteyned that every of the kinges subjectes offendyng the same shulde be a traditor attaynted yet notwithstonding what by the defaulte and necligence of the heddes and rulers of this lande undre the kinges highnes that the said estatutes or actes were nat duelie put in execucion as the

94 *Statutes at large* c.28.

wilfull appetyt of his said subjectes havyng noo remembraunce of their bounden dueties to their moost drad souveraigne lorde their awne commoditie quietnes and profict ne the utilitie and publicque weale of their native cuntrey ne yet the contempt or daungier of the transgressyng of the said actes ded often and many tymes aswele mary as fostre with the said Irishe rebelles and some tymes by fraude and covyne havyng then a perfect knowledge and an entent that every suche Irishe rebell with whom they entended to marie or foster wold in noo parte use hym selfe as to the kinges true and obedient subject shulde apperteigne but for their awne saulfgarde and discharge from the penaltie and daungier of the said estatutes or actes onelie to delude or defraude thordynaunce and purvey of the same ded procure to make the said Irishe rebelles with whom they entended soo to mary or foster denyzyns by the kinges moost gracious lettres patentes wher as the said Irishe rebels soo made denizins ded or doo in noo parte use theme selfe as to the kinges subjectes doo apperteyn through whiche the kinges highnes hathe lost for the moor parte thobediencie of his people of this his lande and diverse myschieves and inconvenyences to his said subjectes from tyme to tyme hathe ensued and moche more like to ensue onles that some good remedie or provision be had or provided in that behalfe; for reformacion wherof be it enacted ordeyned and establisshed by thauctoritie of this present parliament that noo persone ne persones the kinges subjectes within this his lande of what estate degree dignitie or condicion so ever he or they be shall marie or foster them selves their childer or kynsfolke within the fourthe degree or any of theme to or with any Irishe persone or persons of Irishe blood which be not the kinges true subjectes ne use theme selves accordynglie thogh any suche person or persones be made denizyns oneles that every suche persone soo to be made denizin doo his homage and feaultie befor the kynges chauncellor or keaper of the great seale for the tyme beyng to the kinges highnes swering thothe comprised in thact of succession for the fulfilling and accomplishement of theffect tenor and purport of the same and alsoo shalbe bound by recognisaunce befor the kinges chaunceller or keaper of his graces great seale of this his land for the tyme being in suche somes of monye as to the said chaunceller or keaper of the great seale shalbe thought meat and convenyent that he from the tyme that he is made denizin shalbe faithfull true and obedient to the kinges highnes his heyrs and successors and that everie persone and persones the kinges subjectes within this his lande that shall soo marie or foster theme selves their childer or kynsfolke or any of theme to or with any suche persone or persons of Irishe blood as is aforsaid without fraude or covine at the tyme of the said mariage or fostring shall have a true and unfayned intent and meanyng that the partie soo made denyzyn with whom he or they intend so to marie or foster will during his naturall life be faithfull true and obedient to the kinges highnes his heyrs and successors and if any persone

or persons nowe made or whiche herafter shalbe made denizin at any tyme or tymes herafter with whom any suche mariage or fostring shalbe had or made doo transgresse his fidelitie and faithe to the kinges highnes his heyres or successors using hym silf as the kinges rebell and proclamacion therof made by the kinges lieutenaunt or deputie or by his or their commaundement by thadvyse of the kinges consaill in the shire or oppen markettes next adyoynyng to suche offendor then every suche of the kinges subjectes whiche soo shall have fostred or maried with any suche denyzyn soo rebelling or offending contrarie his othe or duetie shall utterlie avoide any wilfull famyliaritie or company with hym or theme that soo shall offende oneles it be to reconcile suche offendor or offendors to knowledge their offences commytted to the kinges majestie or els to thentent to have restitucion of suche goodes as any suche persone or persones soo offending have taken from any the kinges subjectes; and if any of his highnes subjectes of this his lande doo offende in the premysses or in any parcell therof that then every such offence shalbe demed highe treason and that every persone and persones soo offending being therof laufullie convicted according to the due ordre and proces of the kinges lawes shalbe adjudged a traditor attaynted of highe treason and shall have and suffre suche paynes of deathe losses and forfaictur of landes tenementes goodes and cattails as in cases of highe treason; and be it alsoo enacted by auctorite aforsaid that if any suche persone or persons made or to be made denizins doo not to his and their wit knowledge and power fulfill and accomplishe the teanor purport and effecte of the said othe and of the condicion of the said recognysaunce but wilfullie transgresse and withdrawe their obedience and bounden duetie to their moste drad souveraigne lorde from his highnes that then if any suche persone or persones the kinges true subjectes their freendes or servauntes that hathe maried or fostred or at any tyme hereafter shall marie or foster theme selves their childer or kynsfolkes or eny of theme to or with any suche persone or persons made or to be made denyzins will or do aide maynteyne supporte succour counseill favour or by eny other meane encourage any suche persone or persons soo made or to be made denizins contemptuouselie offending as is aforsaide oneles it be to reconcile and bryng theme to their duetie of obedience due to their moost drad souveraigne lorde or els to have restitucion of goodes by theme taken as is aforsaid that then he or they soo offending and every of theme being therof laufully convicted according the due ordre and proces of the kinges lawes shalbe adjudged a traditor attaynted of highe treason and shall have and suffre suche paynes of deathe losses and forfaictur of landes tenementes goods and cattails as in cases of highe treason; and be it further enacted that all and every article clause and sentence comprised in any other acte or actes which be repugnaunt or contrarie to theffect tenor and purport of this acte or any thing therin conteyned shalbe voide to all ententes and purposes;

provided that this acte be not in force or take execucion befor the same be proclamed in every shire in due forme.

[*m.22*]

c.23 Thact for the Busshop of Rome[95]

Forasmoche as notwithstonding the good and holsome lawes ordynaunces and statutes heretofor made enacted and established by the kinges highnes our moost gracious souveraigne lorde and by thole consent of this highe court of parliament for the extirpacion abolicion and extinguyshement out of this lande of the pretended power and usurped auctoritie of the busshop of Rome (by some called the Pope) used within the same whiche dud obfoscat and wreste Goddes holie worde and testament a longe season from the spirituall and true meanyng therof to his wordlie and carnall affeccion as pompe glorie avarice ambicion and tiranny covering and shadowing the same with his humayn and craftie devises tradicions and invencions set forthe undre the cloke of vertue onely to promote and stablishe his dominion aswele bothe upon the sowles and bodies as alsoo upon the temporall goodes of all christen people excluding not onelie Christ out of his kingdome and rule of mannes soule as moche as they myght but alsoo other temporall kinges and princes out of their dominions whiche thei ought to have by Goddes lawe upon the bodies and goodes of their subjectes wherby he ded not onelie robbe the kinges majestie being onelie the supreame hedde of the realme of Englande and of this his lande of Irland immediatlie undre God of his honour right and preemynence dew unto hym by the lawe of God but alsoo spoiled this his lande of Irelande yerelie of unumerable treasur and besides the losses of the same disceivid the kinges lovyng and obedient subjectes perswadyng to theme by his lawes bulles and other his disceivable meanes suche dremes vanyties and fantasies as by the same many of theme were seduced and conveied unto supersticious and erronyous oppynyons soo that the kinges majestie the lordes spirituall and temporall and the comens in this his lande being over weried and fatigated with thexperience of thinfinit abhomynacions and myschief procedyng of his impostures and craftie coloured disceiptes to the great damages of soules bodies and goodes were aforced of necessitie for the publicque weale of this lande to exclude that forreyn pretended power jurisdiccion and auctoritie used and usurped within this said land and to devise suche remedies for their relief in the same as dothe not onelie redounde to the honour of God the highe praise and advauncement of the kinges majestie and of this his lande but also to the great and inestimable utilitie of the same which said good and holsome lawes

95 *Statutes at large* c.13.

notwithstonding soo made and heretofor establisshed it is common to the knowledge of the kinges highnes and alsoo to diverse and many his loving feithfull and obedient subjectes howe that dyverse sedicious and contencious persons being ymps of the said busshop of Rome and of his see and in hart membres of his pretended monarchie do incovers and elswhere as they dare whesper inculce preache and perswade and from tyme to tyme instill into the aeres and heddes of the poor simple and unlettred people thadvauncement and contynuaunce of the said busshops feyned and pretended auctoritie pretendyng the same to have his grounde and origynall of Goddes lawe wherby thoppynyons of many be suspended their judgementes corrupted and disceived and dyversitie in opynyons augmented and encreasid to the great displeasure of almyghtie God the highe discontentacion of our said moost drad souveraigne lorde and the interrupcion of the unytie love charitie concorde and agrement that ought to be in a christen region and congregacion; for avoiding wherof and of all suche sediciouse persones as be the meanes and auctours of suche inconvenyences be it enacted ordeyned and establisshed by the king our souveraigne lorde and the lordes spirituall and temporall and the comens in this present parliament assembled and by auctoritie of the same that if any persone or persones dwelling demurring inhabityng or resiaunt within this lande of what estate dignytie preemynence ordre degree or condicion soo ever he or they be after the furst daie of November which shalbe in the yere of our lord God a thousand five hundred seven and thirtie shall by writyng cifering printing preaching or teaching or by any deade or acte obstynately or maliciousely holde or stand with to extoll setforth maynteyn or defend the auctority jurisdiccion or power of the busshop of Rome or of his see heretofor claymed used or usurped within this lande or by any pretence obstynatelie or maliciousely invent any thing for thextolling advauncement setting forthe maytenaunce or defence of the same or any parte therof or by any pretence obstynatelie or maliciousely attribute any maner of jurisdiccion auctoritie or preemynence to the said see of Rome or to any busshop of the same see for the tyme beyng within this lande that then every suche persone or persons soo doyng or offendyng their aidors assistentes comfortors abbettors procurers mayntenors faultors councellours counsaillours and every of theme being therof laufully convicted according to the lawes of this lande for every suche default and offence shall incurre and ron into the daungiers penalties paynes and forfaicturs ordeyned and provided by the statut of provision and premunire made in the xvj^{ten} yere of the reigne of the noble and valiaunt prince king Richarde the second[96] agaynst suche as attempte procure or make provision to the see of Rome or

96 1393. 16 Richard II c. 5 (*Statutes of the realm,* ii, pp 84–6).

elswher by any thing or thinges to the derogacion or contrarie to the prerogative roiall or jurisdiccion of the crowne and dignitie of the reálme of England the lawes custumes and usages of this lande; and to thentent that this acte at all tymes may be wele and truely executed and thoffendors therof have and receive condigne punyshement according to their demerites it is enacted by the auctoritie aforsaid that aswele justices of assises in their circuites as justices of peaux within the lymytes of their commission and auctorities or twoo of every suche justiciars of peaux at the leste wherof oon to be of the quorum shall have full power and auctoritie to enquere of all offenses contemptes and transgressions perpetrated commytted or doone contrarie to this acte in like maner and forme as they may of other offences against the kinges peaux and shall certifie every presentment afor theme or any of theme had or made concernyng this acte or any parte therof befor the kyng in his benche of this lande within xl^{ti} dayes next after any suche presentement had or made if the terme be then oppen and if not then at the furst day of the terme next following the said xl^{ti} dayes upon payne that every of the justiciars of assise or justiciars of peaux befor whom suche presentement shalbe made making defaulte of suche certificat contrarie to this acte shall lose and forfaict fourtie poundes to the kinges highnes; and it is enacted by thauctoritie aforsaid that the justiciars of the kinges benche aswele upon every suche certificat as by enquere befor theme selves within the lymytes of their aucthorities shall have full power and auctoritie to hear ordeyn and determyn every suche offence doon or commytted contrarie to this acte according to the lawes of the realme of England and of this lande in suche like maner and forme to all ententes and purposes as if the person or persones against whom any presentement shalbe had upon this statute had be presented upon any matier or offence expressed in the said estatut made in the said xvj yere of king Richard the second; and it is alsoo enacted by thauctoritie aforsaid that all and every archebusshops busshops and archedeacons within this lande their commissaries vicars generall and other their mynystres in every their visitacions and seanes shall make diligent enserche enquere and examynacion of all and every ecclesiasticall and religiouse persons within and of their jurisdiccion which shalbe suspected accused or deamed to be a transgressor or offendor of this acte and if upon suche serche enquere and examynacion any ecclesiasticall or religiouse persone shalbe presented suspected accused or founde culpable by witnes or confession of any offence contrarie to this acte and be present at the tyme of suche presentment examynacion or accusacion that then every tharchebusshops busshops and archedeacons their commissaries vicars generall and other their mynystres afor or to whome any suche persone shalbe presented suspected accused or founde culpable as is aforsaid shall commyt every suche person soo presented accused or founde culpable (if he be presented as is aforsaid) to the

nexte common gaole of the shyre wher suche enquiere examynacion or accusacion shalbe had or made or els by good and sufficient suerties to be bounde by obligacion to the kinges use shall let every suche persone to baile by their discessions[97] to appere befor the king and his counsaill or his graces deputie of this lande in the castle of Dublin within xv daies next after suche enquere presentment or accusacion if the terme be then oppen and kept orels in the furst day of the terme next following after the said enquiere presentment or accusacion and at the said day lymyted for suche apparaunce they shall certifie into the said castle of Dublin by writing under their seales aswele the said bond and thobligacion taken for suche apparaunce as the presentement examynacion accusacion or conviccion of every suche person and all deposicions and circumstaunces therof and the name of the gaole wheunto they have commytted the said persone and if any suche ecclesiasticall or religious person being presented suspected or accused in any seane or visitacion be not present all the tyme of the said seane or visitacion as is aforsaid that then nevertheles every the said archebusshops busshops and archedeacons their commissaries vicars generall and all other their mynystres afor or to whom any suche presentment suspeccion or accusacion shalbe had or made shall certifie every suche presentment suspeccion or accusacion and all circumstaunces therof as is aforsaid unto the castle of Dublin within xv daies next after suche presentement suspeccion or accusacion had or made or in the furst day of the terme next following after such presentement suspeccion or accusacion in suche maner and forme as is afor rehersed and in case any ecclesiasticall[98] or religiouse persone being presented suspected or accused of any offence doon or attempted contrary to this statute be therof convicted by confession or witnes befor any archebusshop busshop or archedeacon or befor any the commyssaries vicars generall or other their mynystres in their seanes or visitacions or befor the kinges counsaill in the castel of Dublin that then every suche spirituall and religious persone soo being convicte shall suffre suche paynes penalties and forfaicturs as be expressed in the said estatut made in the xvj yere of king Richard the seconde; it is alsoo enacted by thauctoritie aforsaid that if any ecclesiasticall judge or visitor doo voluntarilie concele cloke hide or colour any presentement accusacion or confession that shalbe made to hym concernyng this statute and doo not certifie every suche accusacion presentement or confession befor the king or his deputie and his counsaill in the castell of Dublin in suche maner and forme as is above specified in this statut that then every suche ecclesiasticall judge and visitor soo wilfully offendyng for every suche defaulte shall forfaict xl$^{li.}$ thone halfe therof to the kinges highnes thother halfe to suche persone as will sue for the same by origynall writ bill pleynt or

97 recte *discressions*. 98 *persone* struck through.

enformacion in any of the kinges courtes in which suit noo essoyne proteccion or wageor of lawe shalbe admytted or allowed; and for stronger defence and mayntenaunce of this acte it is ordeyned and enacted by auctoritie aforsaid that all and every ecclesiasticall judge ordenary chaunceller commissarie officiall vicar generall and other ecclesiasticall officer and ministre of what dignitie pre-emynence or degree so ever they shalbe and all and every temporall judge justiciar maior bailif shirif undersherif escheator alderman [*m.23*] jurate constable hedborowe thirdborowe borsolder and every laie officer and mynystre to be made created elected or admytted within this lande of what estate ordre degree or condicion soo ever he shalbe from and after the said furst daie of November shall befor he take upon hym thexecucion of suche office make take and receive a corporall othe[99] upon the evaungelies befor suche persone or persones as have or shall have auctoritie to admyt hym that he from hensforthe shall utterlie renounce refuse relynquyshe and forsake the busshop of Rome and his auctoritie power and jurisdiccion and that he shall never consent ne agree that the busshop of Rome shall practise excercise or have any maner of auctoritie jurisdiccion or power within this lande but that he shall resist the same at all tymes to the uttermost of his power and that from hensforthe he shall accepte repute and take the kinges majestie to be onely supreame hed in erthe of the churche of Englond and of Irelande and that to his connyng wit and uttermost of his power and without gyle fraude or other undewe meane he shall observe keape maynteyne and defende thole effectes and contentes of all and synguler actes and statutes made and to be made within this lande in derogacion extirpacion and extinguyshement of the busshop of Rome and his auctoritie and all other actes and statutes made and to be made in reformacion and corroboracion of the kynges power or supreame hed in erthe of the churche of Englande and of Irlande and this he shall do against all maner of persons of what estate dignitie degree or condicion they be and in noo wise do nor attempte nor to his power suffre to be doon or attempted directly or indirectly any thing or thinges privelie or apertelie to the let hyndraunce damage or derogacion therof or of any parte therof by any maner of meanes or for any maner of pretence and in cace any othe be made or hathe bene made by hym to any person or persons in mayntenaunce defence or favour of the busshop of Rome or his auctoritie jurisdiccion or power he repute the same as vayne and adnichillat soo hym helpe God and all sainctes and the holie evaungelistes; and it is alsoo enacted by auctoritie aforsaid that all and every person and persons spirituall and temporall suyng lyveraie restitucions or any utterlemayne out of the king his heyres or successors handes or which shalbe sworne to the king his heyres or successors or that shall have any office fee or rowlme of his moost

99 In margin: juramentum contra episcopum Romanum.

gracious gifte or of his majesties heyres or successors or shalbe reteyned in service with his grace his heyres or successours shall make take and receive the seide othe and that alsoo all and every religious persone at the tyme of his or their profession or entre into religion and every other ecclesiasticall persone at the tyme of his taking of ordres and all and every other persone which shalbe promoted or preferred to any degree of lernyng in any unyversitie within this lande at the tyme of his promocion or preferment and every of theme shall make take and receive the said othe befor his or their chaunceller ordynarie or their commissarie of suche unyversitie; and it is alsoo enacted by auctoritie aforsaide that if any persone or persones lymyted or commaunded by auctoritie of this acte to make the said othe or commaunded by any other persone or persons auctorised by the kinges highnes commyssion under his great seale prevey seale or his seale ordeyned for causes ecclesiasticall to make the said othe obstynatelie refuse that to doo that then every suche offence and contempt shalbe highe treason and thoffendor therof being laufully convicted shall suffre paynes of death and other forfaicturs penalties and losses as is lymyted and accustumed in cases of highe treason by any lawes or statutes of this lande heretofor made; provided alwayes and be it enacted that this acte ne any thing or thinges in the same rehersed mencioned or comprised be in any wise prejudiciall hurtful or derogatori to the ceremonyes uses and other laudable and politicque ordynaunces for a tranquilitie disciplyn concorde devocion unitie and the decent ordre heretofor in the churche of Irland used instituted taken and accepted nor to any persone or persons accordingly using the same or any of theme; provided that notwithstanding this acte or eny other acte made for the taking away of the said busshop of Romes usurped power auctoritie preemynence and jurisdiccion or any thing or thinges in the same comprised that all and every archebusshop busshop archedeacon commyssarie and officiall and every of theme shall and may use and exercise in the name of the king onelie all suche canons constitucions ordynaunces and synadols provyncial being alredie made for the direccion and ordre of spirituall and ecclesiasticall causes which be not contrariaunt nor repugnaunt to the kinges lawes statutes and customes of this lande nor to the domage and hurte of the kinges prerogative royall in suche maner and forme as they were used and executed befor the making of this acte till suche tyme as the kinges highnes shall ordre and determyne according his lawes of Englond and suche ordre and determynacion as shalbe requisit for the same and the same to be certified hither under the kinges great seale or otherwise ordred by parliament; provided alsoo that this acte or any thing therin conteyned be not intended ne ment nor shalbe expounded nor interpretated that any dispensacions licences or confirmacions for mariages or otherwise graunted to any the kinges subjectes of this land at any tyme befor the making of this acte whiche were not repugnaunt to the lawes of God the

kinges lawes or the prerogative roiall shalbe appeyred or of any lesse value strenght force or effect then they were befor the making of this acte.

c.24 Thact for the libertie of the countie of Wexford

Where as the libertie of the countie of Wexforde otherwise called the libertie of Wexforde withe all the[100] possessions and hereditamentes lately belongyng to George nowe erle of Salop is come into the kinges highnes our moost draid souveraigne lordes handes by aucthoritie of parliament forasmoche as the same libertie is nowe cessed and in the kinges hande and that it is thought that thadmynystracion of justice there in the said countie of Wexford where every man in the said countie for the moost parte useth and speacketh thenglish tongue and language and in some parte useth thenglish habit shoulde be expedient for sondrie respectes to be used as it hathe bene til our said souveraigne lordes pleasure shalbe further determyned touching the same; be it therfor enacted and ordeyned by auctoritie aforsaide that the said libertie of Wexforde or the libertie of the countie of Wexforde from the furst day of December which shalbe in the yere of our lorde God a thousand five hundred and xxxvij[ti] shalbe contynued used and put in experience and execucion in like maner forme condicion and qualitie and in the same strenght force and effecte to all ententes and purposes as the said George or any other of his antecessors sethens the furst graunt of the said libertie had used and enyoied the same during the pleasure of the kinges majestie his heyres and successors kinges of England and till his highnes his heyres or successors shall by his or their lettres patentes or otherwise determyne the same and establish therin further ordre as shalbe thought moost expedient the teanor and purporte of whiche lettres patentes shall by vertue herof have and be in full streinght force and effect to all ententes and purposes touching thordre of the saide countie of Wexforde and that every officer by the kinges majestie his heyres or successors appoynted ordeyned or made or to be appoynted ordeyned or made of for or concerning the same libertie or any admynystracion of justice or any other thing or thinges to be doon or executed within the same libertie (the graunting of pardones to eny persone or persones for eny treason murdre felony or eny other offence or contempt onelie except) shall use execute and excercise the same and like auctoritie in the king oure souveraigne lordes name and every other thing to every entent and meanyng as the late and like officers of the said libertie then being in the saide Georges handes possession or ordre or any other of his antecessors sethens the furst graunt of the same had used or enyoied or myght have had used or enyoied the said acte of parliament or any acte of resumpcion or any

100 *liberties of* struck through.

cause of forfeyctur or seasure of the said libertie or eny other cause or matier thing or thinges what soo ever they be in eny wise notwithstanding; provided and alsoo be it enacted by auctoritie aforsaid that it shalbe laufull to any the kinges highnes justices of the comen place within this lande for the tyme being to take receive and holde plee in or upon any writ of entree in le post to be had or suffred by assent of bothe the parties of any landes or tenementes within the jurisdiccion or precynct of the said libertie and alsoo to take and receive all maner of fynes and the knowledge of the same in or upon any maner of accions wherupon any fyne may be levied by thordre of the lawe of any landes or tenementes within the libertie aforsaide in like maner forme and condicion as the said justices or any of theme may doo of any landes or tenementes within the counties of Methe and Dublin or any of theme this present acte or any thing or thinges therin conteyned notwithstonding.

c.25 Thact for the xx^ti parte[101]

And forasmoche as it is and of veray duetie ought to be the naturall inclynacion of all good people like moost faithfull lovyng and obedient subjectes sencerelie to deasire to provide not onely for the publicque weale of their native cuntrey but alsoo for the supportacion mayntenaunce and defence of the royall estate of their moost dread benygne and gracious souveraigne lorde upon whom and in whom dependeth all their joye and wealthe in whom alsoo is unyted and knyt soo pryncelie a hert and courage myxed with mercie wisedome and justice and alsoo a naturall affeccion joyned to the same as by the great inestymable and benevolent argumentes therof being moost bountefullie largely and many tymes shewed mynystred and approved towardes his loving and obedient subjectes hathe wele appered which requyreth a like correspondence of gratitude to be considered according to their moost bounden duties wherfor his said humble and obedient subjectes aswele the lordes spirituall and temporall as the comens in this present parliament assembled calling to their remembraunce not onelie the manyfolde and innumerable benifictes dailie admynystred by his highnes to theme all and to the residue of all other his subjectes of this lande but alsoo howe longe tyme his majestie hathe moost victoriouslie by his highe wisedome and policie to his inestymable charges in exhausting of his graces treasure out of his realme of England protected defended and governed this his lande and mainteyned his people and subjectes of the same in tranquilitie peaux unitie quietnes and wealthe and amongest other of late tyme from the captivitie and bondage of that late traditor Thomas Fitz Garrot and his adherentes and alsoo considering what great excessive and

101 *Statutes at large* c.14.

inestimable charges his highnes haith hertofor bene at and susteyned by the space of xxviij yeres hole and alsoo dailie susteyneth for the maytenaunce tuicion and defence of this his lande and his loving subjectes of the same whiche can not be susteyned and borne without some honourable prohibicion and remedie may be made founde provided and ordeyned for mayntenaunce therof doo therfor deasire and moost humblie pray that for the more suertie of contynuaunce and augmentacion of his highnes royall estate being not onelie nowe recognised as he alwayes indeade hertofor hathe bene the onelie supream hedde in erthe next and immediatly under God of the churche of Englond and of Irelond but alsoo their moost assured and undoubted naturall souveraigne liege lorde and king havyng the hole governaunce tuicion defence and mayntenaunce of this lande and his moost obedient and loving subjectes of the same; it may therfor be ordeyned and enacted by his highnes and the lordes spirituall and temporall and the comens in this present parliament assembled and by auctoritie of the same that the kinges majestie his heyres and successors kinges of the realme of England for more augmentacion and mayntenaunce of the roiall estate of his imperiall crowne and dignitie of supreme hed of the churche of Englond and of Irelande shall yerely have take and enyoie and receive unyted and knyt to his imperiall crowne for ever one yerely rent or pencion amounting to the value of the twentie parte of all the revenues rentes fermes tiethes offringes emolumentes and of all other profictes aswele callid spirituall as temporall nowe apperteynyng or belongyng or that hereafter shall [*m.24*] belonge to any archebusshopriche busshopriche abbacie monasterie priorie archedeaconrie diaconrie hospitall commaundre colledge house colledgiat prebende cathedrall churche colledgiat churche conventuall churche parsonage vicarage chauntrie or fre chaple or other benefice or promocion spirituall of what name nature or qualitie soo ever they be within any dioces of this lande the said pencion or annuall rent to be yerelie payed for ever to our saide souveraigne lorde to his heyrs and successors kinges of the realme of Englande at the feast of the nativitie of our lorde God and the furst payment therof to begynne at the feast of the nativitie of our lorde God a thousand five hundred and xxxvij^ti^ and to be paied yerelie by suche as shalbe appoynted to have the collection therof by this acte in suche maner and forme as shall hereafter be lymyted by this acte befor the furst daie of Aprill yerelie next following after the saide feaste of the nativitie of our lorde God; and it is ordeyned and enacted by auctoritie aforsaid that the saide yerelie rent and pencion shalbe taxed rated levied received and payed to the kinges use his heyres and successors in maner and forme hereafter to be declared by this acte that is to saye that the chaunceller or keaper of the great seale of this lande of Irlande for the tyme being shall have power and auctoritie to directe into every dioces in this lande severall commissions in the kinges name undre his great seale aswele to

tharchebusshop or busshop of every suche dioces as to suche other persone or persones as the kynges highnes shall name and appoynt commaunding and auctorising the said commissioners for to be named in every suche commission or thre of theme at the least to examyn serche and enquiere by all the wayes and meanes that they can by their discressions of and for the true and just hoole and entier yerelie values of all the manors landes tenementes hereditamentes rentes tiethes offeringes emolumentes and all other profictes aswele spirituall as temporall apperteynyng or belongyng to eny archebusshopriche busshopriche abbacie monasterie priorie archedeaconrie deanrie hospitall commaundre colledge house collegiat prebend cathedrall churche colledgiat churche conventuall churche parsonage vicarage chauntrie frechaple or to any other benefice or promocion spirituall within the lymytes of their commission withe a clause to be conteyned within every suche commission that the said commissioners or thre of theme at the least shall deducte and allowe in makyng and rating of the said yerelie values of the premisses thies deduccions following and noon other that is to say the rentes resolute to the chief lordes and all other annuall and perpetuall rentes and charges whiche any spirituall persone or persons bethe bounde yerelie to paye or keape or to give yerelie in almes by reason of any foundacion or ordynaunce and all fees for stiwardes receivors councellours bailiffes and auditors and sinodes and proxes with another clause to ba alsoo conteyned in every suche commission that the said commissioners or thre of theme at the leaste shall certifie under their seales at suche dayes as shalbe lymyted by the saide commissions into the kinges eschequier of this lande aswele thoole and entier value as the deduccions aforsaide of every archebusshopriche busshoprich abbacie monasterie priorie archedeaconrie deanrie hospitall commaundre colledge house collegiat prebende cathedrall churche colledgiat churche conventuall churche parsonage vicarage chauntrie frechapel and of all other benefices and promocions spirituall; and it is ordeyned and enacted by auctoritie aforsaide that the saide commissioners that shalbe soo appointed or thre of theme at the leaste shall have full power and auctoritie to do accomplishe and execute theffectes and contentes of their said commissions in every behalfe and that every of the said commissioners befor they shall execute their saide commission shall receive and take a corporall othe befor the lorde chanceller or keaper of the great seale or befor suche other as shalbe appointed by the said chaunceller or keaper of the great seale by the kinges writ of dedimus potestatem that they shall diligentlie and truelie without favour affeccion fraude coven meade dread or corrupcion doo fulfill and execute the hole effectes and contentes expressed in every suche commission within the lymytes therof to their connyng wittes and uttermost of their power; and it is ordeyned and enacted by auctorite aforsaide that after suche a certificat made by the saide commissioners the saide yerelie rent and pencion

of the xx^{ti} parte shalbe set taxed rated and taken justelie truelie and indifferently by the theasurer and barons of the kinges eschequier of and out of the clere yerelie value of the premisses that shalbe above the deduccions afor mencioned and none otherwise and that every archebusshopriche busshopriche abbacie monasterie priorie archedeaconry deanrie hospitall commaundre colledge house collegiat prebende cathedrall churche colledgiat churche conventuall churche parsonage vicarage chauntrie frechapell or other benefice or promocion spirituall shalbe severallie and distinctlie taxed charged and chargeable in the proper dioces wher they bene for the payment of suche porcion of the saide xx^{ti} parte as shalbe taxed and set upon theme by auctoritie of this acte that is to saie every of theme by or for theme selves shalbe taxed charged and chargeable in the proper dioces wher they bene for the xx^{ti} parte of the yerelie value of their possessions and profictes to theme belongyng wher so ever their said possessions and profictes shall happen to be or lie in any parte of this lande and that noon of theme shalbe charged nor chargeable for the payment of thothers charge or porcion; and it is alsoo enacted by auctoritie aforsaide that after such certificat made into the kinges eschequier and tax set of the xx^{ti} parte in forme above remembred every archebusshop and busshop nowe being and that hereafter shalbe charged and chargeable to levie collect and receive within their proper dioces aswele in places exempte as not exempt all suche somes of monye wherwith the dignities benefices and other promocions spirituall afor mencioned within their dioces chargeable by this acte shalbe set taxed and charged towardes the payment of the saide yerelie pencion and shall paye and content the saide somes of monye yerelie befor the said furst daie of Aprill to the kinges highnes is underthesaurer or generall receivor of this his lande for the tyme being or to any other persone or persons whom it shall please the kinges highnes his heyres or successors to appoynt to receive the same and that every of the said archebusshops and busshops their executors and admynystrators and the possessioners of their dignities and churches shall stande charged and chargeable for the sure and true payment of suche somes of monye as they shall collecte and receive of the saide yerelie rent and pencion and that the[102] thesaurer and barons of the kinges eschequier shall yerelie cause proces to be made by their discressions for none payment of the saide pencion or yerelie rent or any parcell therof against every archebusshop and busshop of this lande that is to saye against every archebusshop and busshop for somoche parte and porcion of the saide pencion and yerelie rent wherwith the dignities benefices and other promocions spirituall afor mencioned within his dioces shalbe taxed and charged soo that every of the said archebusshops and busshops shalbe charged and chargeable for the rate and porcion of the saide

102 *the* repeated.

yerelie rent and pencion set and taxed within his awne peculier dioces and none otherwise; and be it alsoo enacted by auctoritie aforsaide that every archebusshop and busshop shall have power and auctoritie to levie take and perceive by auctoritie of censures of the churche or by distres or otherwise by their discression all suche somes of monye as shalbe rated taxed and set to goo oute of the landes tenementes hereditamentes profictes and emolumentes of any dignitie benefice or other place or promocion spirituall within their dioces towardes their payment of the said yerelie rent or pencion and that noo repleven prohibicion nor supersedeas upon any excommunicacion nor any other writ or impediment shalbe sued alloued or obeyed for any persone or persons making defaulte of payment of suche parte and porcion as they shalbe rated and taxed unto by auctoritie of this acte till suche tyme as they have truelie satisfied their saide parte and porcion to theme allotted of the saide yerelie rent and pencion; and it is alsoo enacted by auctoritie aforsaide that when soo ever and as often as any of tharchebusshopriches or busshopriches happen to be voide that then the deane and chapitre of the cathedrall churche or the prior and convent or chapitre or convent of the monasterii or cathedrall churche where the see of suche archbusshopriche or busshopriche being voide shall happen to be during the tyme of the vacacion therof their executors admynystrators and possessioners shalbe charged and chargeable to do and cause to be doone all and every thing and thinges for the due execucion of this acte within the dioces of suche archebusshopriche or busshopriche as the same archebusshop or busshop of the see being voide shulde have doone according as it is lymyted and appoynted by this acte or by any thing therin conteyned; and it is ordeyned and enacted by auctoritie aforsaide that if any some of money being ones due by any incumbent of any of the dignities benefices or promocions spirituall afor specified charged to the payment of the saide yerelie pencion and annuell rent be reasonablie demaunded and required any tyme after the said feaste of the nativitie of our lorde as other dignities monasteriis priories hospitals commaundres colledges churches chauntries or houses by tharchebusshop or busshop or suche as shalbe charged with the colleccion of any parte of the saide pencion or by any other their mynystres servauntes or officers to pay suche porcion of the said pencion and yerely rent as they shalbe taxed and assessed be not truely content and payed unto suche archebusshop or busshop or their mynystres and officers or to suche other persone and persones [*m.25*] or their mynystres or servauntes as shall have the charge of colleccion therof every yere yerelie at the tyme of suche request and demaunde therof or els within xl dayes next after every suche request at the furthest that then every incumbent making suche defaulte of payment after suche defaulte therof certified into the kinges eschequier in writing under the seales of any archebusshop or busshop or of suche as be lymyted and charged to the

colleccion of the said pencion by this acte shalbe adjudged deprived ipso facto of all suche dignities benefices pencions and promocions spirituall as any suche incumbent making suche defaulte shall have at the tyme of suche certificate to be made or at eny tyme after soo that all suche dignities benefices pencions and promocions spirituall whiche any incumbent making suche defaulte of payment shall have at the tyme of any suche certificate to be made or at any tyme after shalbe clerelie voide and destitute of incumbent in the lawe to all ententes and purposes as if suche incumbent making suche defaulte of payment were deade indede; and it is ordeyned and enacted by auctoritie aforsaide that if any archebusshop or busshop or any other lymyted and charged by this acte to the colleccion and payment of the said pencion and annuall rent doo make a certificat into the kinges eschequier befor the saide furst daie of Aprill or at eny tyme within xxiiij[ti] daies next after the said furst day of Aprill that they according to this acte have reasonblie required and demaunded any incumbent of any dignitie benefice or promocion spirituall chargeable by this acte to pay suche parte and porcion of the saide pencion and annuell rent as they shall happen to be assessed unto and that suche incumbent soo being required haithe not payed his said parte and porcion according to the forme and effect of this acte that then every suche archebusshop and busshop and every other persone havyng the charge by this acte for colleccion and payment of the saide pencion and annuell rent upon every suche certificat shalbe discharged and acquited for ever against the king his heyres and successors of and for all suche somes of money as any suche incumbent against whom suche certificat shalbe made shoulde or ought to have payed by this acte and that then in every suche cace the thesaurer and barons of the kinges eschequier shall devise and directe uppon every suche certificate suche proces out of the kinges eschequier against every suche incumbent agaynst whom any suche certificat shalbe made and their executors and admynystrators or for insufficiencie of theme against the successors of every suche incumbent wherby the kinges highnes his heyres and successors shall and may be truelie aunswered payed and contented of suche porcion and parte as thincumbent against whom any suche certificate shalbe made was taxed and assessed for his dignities benefices or promocions spirituall chargeable by this acte; and it is alsoo ordeyned and enacted by auctoritie aforsaide that all maner of acquitaunce made by the kinges underthesaurer and generall receivor of this his lande or by any other suche commissioners as shalbe appoynted as is aforsaid to receive the saide pencion or any parte therof and subscribed withe the name of the saide underthesaurer and generall receivor or any other suche commissioner for the payment of the saide pencion or annuell rent or any parte therof to any suche persone or persones as be lymyted and charged with the colleccion therof shalbe as good streinght force vertue and effecte to the parties havyng the same as if they were made in the

kinges name under his great seale and soo shalbe alloued admytted and accepted in all courtes of this his lande and that the thesaurer and barons of the kinges eschequier shall by vertue and auctoritie of this acte aswele admyt and allowe suche acquitaunces as all suche certificates as shalbe made against any incumbent for defaulte of payment as is above saide uppon thaccompte of every archebusshop and busshop and of every other persone lymyted and charged by this acte for the colleccion and payment of the saide pencion and annuell rent without any writ bill or warauntie to be sued in or for that behalfe and that no maner of officer of the kinges eschequier shall take of any archebusshop or busshop or of any other persone havyng charge with the colleccion and payment of the said pencion or annuell rent any maner rewarde or thing for makyng their accompte or quietus est in the same eschequier or for any maner of thing aperteynyng to the same concernyng the saide pencion and annuell rent uppon peyne of every officer doyng contrarie this acte to lose and forfaicte his office and make fyne to the king at his will and pleasur; and for asmoche as every incumbent of the dignities benefices and promocions spirituall afor mencioned shalbe charged by this acte to the payment of the xx^ti^ parte of the value of their dignities benefices and promocions spirituall without any deduccion or allowaunce of suche pencion or pencions wherwith some of theme bene charged to paye to their predecessours during their lives or to other persons to the use of suche their predecessours during their lives it is therfor ordeyned and enacted by auctoritie aforsaide that it shalbe laufull to every incumbent charged with any such pencion paiable to any his predecessours or to any to his use to retayne and keape in his handes the xx^ti^ parte of every such pencion and that every suche incumbent and his suerties shall from hensforthe be acquited and discharged of the said xx^ti^ parte of every suche pencion by vertue and auctoritie of this present acte any decree ordynaunce or assignement of any suche ordynarie or any collaterall writing or suertie made for suche pencion to any spirituall persone or persons or to any to their uses for terme of their lives in any wise notwithstonding and that aswele every incumbent as such persons as stande bounden for him for payment of any suche pencion shall pleade this acte in every of the kinges courtes for the cleare extinguishement and discharge of the xx^ti^ parte of every suche pencion; and alsoo be it enacted by auctoritie aforsaide that whensooever any persone or persons from the furst daie of December whiche shalbe in the yere of our lorde God a thousand five hundred thirtie and seven shalbe named prefected collated or by any other meanes appointed to have any archebusshopriche busshopriche deanrie archdeaconrie prebende parsonage vicarage or any other promocions spirituall within this lande chargeable for the payment of the furst fructes of the same shall at his or their composicion agrement or entree into specialtie or specialties for the payment of the saide furst fructes have allowaunce and

deduccion of the said xx[ti] parte of the hole out of the some to be payed for the saide furst fructes for the yere wherin he or they shalbe furst nominated prefected presented collated or by any other meanes appointed to have any of the said dignities benifices offices or other promocions spirituall according to the just rate taxacion and sessement of the xx[ti] parte of every of the said archebusshopriches busshopriches deanries archdeaconries prebendes parsonages vicarages or any other promocions spirituall within this lande of what name nature or qualitie soo ever they be or to whose foundacion patronage or yefte so ever they belonge nowe being enrolled or that hereafter shalbe enrolled in the kinges eschequier or in any other the kinges courte of recorde; provided and be it enacted by auctoritie of this present parliament that all and singuler fermors and lessees of any manors lordships londes tenementes tiethes or other what soo ever profictes and commodities belonging to any archebusshop busshop or other prelate or spirituall persone or persones or bodie corporate or politicque wherof any furst fructes or yerelie pencion of the xx[ti] parte is graunted to the king our souveraigne lorde in this present cession of the said courte of parliament or otherwise shalbe discharged and not chargeable to pay to our saide souveraigne lorde of his or their proper monye cost or charge for or in discharge of the lessor or lessors owner or owners of the same by reason of any covenaunt bargayne bonde condicion clause of reentre or other thing heretofor made or concluded but that every of the saide lessors and owners and their successors shalbe charged and chargeable to pay and satisfie the same of his or their proper cost and charge to the king our souveraigne lorde his heyres and successours according to the graunte therof any covenaunt bargayne contract bonde condicion clause of reentre or other thing hertofor made or concluded to the contrarie therof in any wise notwithstonding; and forasmoche as the deane chauntor chaunceller thesaurer and archedeacon and all other the dignities and prebendes of the cathedrall churche of sainct Patrickes besides Dublin for the tyme being of their awne free willes and by their loving and obedient assent immediatelie uppon their admission institucion and induccion to any suche [*m.26*] dignities or prebendarie be chargeable by auctoritie of parliament to the payment and satisfaccion of the furst fructes that is to saie the veray yerelie value of oon hole yere of their saide dignities or promocion spirituall what soo ever it be to the kinges highnes his heyres and successors forever and also by auctoritie of this present acte be likewise chargeable to the payment and satisfaccion unto the kinges highnes his heires and successors of the xx[ti] parte of the yerelie value of their dignities and promocion spirituall what soo ever it be thannuall and perpetuall charges used and accustumed to be payed therin alloued wherby and divers other their conformable actes their loving hartes towards the kinges highnes playnelie and evidentlie maie appere and considering that the saide cathedrall churche of sainct Patrickes is of our

moost draid souveraigne lordes moost noble progenytours foundacion and that sethens the furst foundacion therof by the wisedome and pollicie of the deane of the said churche and his brethern for the tyme being have bene kepte maynteyned and supported according thastablishement of the same aswele by the daily contynuaunce and keaping of Goddes devyne service and other laudable usages and custumes establisshed uppon the foundacion therof as alsoo by the dailie and contynuall residence and keaping of hospitalie of the saide deane and others having the dignities of the saide churche to the pleasur of almightie God the honour of our moost dread souveraigne lorde and the comforte relief and supportacion of divers the kinges true and nedefull subjectes and to thentent that the deane and other his bretherne havyng the dignities and prebendes of the saide cathedrall churche being in maner thonely lanterne and light of any godlie and ecclesiasticall rule or ordre within this lande shulde not be soo exacted or charged through whiche the saide devyne service and other laudable usages and custumes and keping of hospitalities myght be decreased or in any parte dismynysshed but rather shulde be soo encouradged that they and every of theme from tyme to tyme to the uttermost of their power wit and connyng shoulde contynue encrease and augment the same according thestablishement of their furst foundacion to the pleasur of almightie God the honour and prosperitie of our moost draid souveraigne lorde his heyrs and successors and the quietnes tranquilitie and publicque comen weale of this lande be it enacted ordeyned and establisshed by auctorite of this present parliament that the deane chauntor thesaurer and archedeacon of the saide cathedrall churche of sainct Patrickes and every other persone and persones havyng any dignitie prebende or any other promocion spirituall within the saide cathedrall churche of sainct Patrickes for the tyme being shalbe quite and discharged to goo or sende to any hosting roode viage or journaie at any tyme to be had or assigned within this lande for or in consideracion of their saide dignities prebendes or promocions spirituall within the said cathedrall churche what soo ever it be soo that they ne noone of theme for not going or sending to any suche hosting viage rood or journaye shall not be amercied or otherwise assessed in any penaltie or somes of monye and if they or any of theme be amercied or assessed contrarie to the teanor of this acte and that the kinges shirif or any other persone or persons woll distrayne for the same that then by auctoritie aforsaide every suche shirif by writ commaundement or otherwise and person or persons taking any suche distres shall forfaicte for every suche tyme ten poundes thone halfe therof to our souveraigne lorde the king and thother halfe to the partie greved that will sue for the same by accion of debt bill pleynte enformacion or otherwise wherin noo essoin proteccion ne wageor of lawe shalbe admytted or allowed; and forasmoche as the purport and meanyng of this acte is whensoo-ever any persone or persons is or be chargeable at his or their admission to any

promocion spirituall to the payment of the furst fructes to the kinges highnes that upon the composicion for the payment of the saide furst fructes the saide xx^{ti} parte to be payed to the kinges highnes by auctoritie of this acte shulde be alloued in the same and for that that Edwarde Basnet nowe deane of the said cathedrall churche for this yere to be ended after the feast of Ester next ensuyng haithe compounded for the furst fructes that is to saie the yerelie value of the saide deanrie for oon hole yere endyng after the said feast of Ester havyng none allowaunce ne deduccion of the xx^{ti} parte of the yerelie revenue or profict of the saide deanrie to be due to our souveraigne lorde the king at the feast of the nativitie of our lorde which shalbe in the yere of our lorde God a thousande five hundred xxxvij^{ti} being in the saide yere for whiche he compounded for the said furst yeres fructes be it provided and alsoo enacted that this present acte or any thing therin conteyned for the payment of the said xx^{ti} parte shall extende in any wise to charge the said Sir Edwarde nowe deane of the said cathedrall churche for the payment of the said xx^{ti} parte of the yerelie profict or revenue of the said deanrie till the feast of the nativitie of our lorde whiche shalbe in the yere of our lorde God M v^{c} xxxviij^{ti} this acte or any thing therin conteyned or mencioned in any wise notwithstanding; provided and alsoo be it enacted by auctoritie aforsaide that the lorde prior of sainct Johns Jerusalem in Irlande and his successors from tyme to tyme shalbe charged and chargeable with the gathering levieng receiving and payeng of the xx^{ti} parte to be due to the kinges highnes by auctoritie of this acte in and of the priorie of sainct Johns Jerusalem in Irlande and the commaundre of the same religion in like maner forme condicion qualitie and degree as any archebusshop or busshop of this lande within his dioces is charged and chargeable by auctoritie of this acte for the collecting receiving and payeng of the xx^{ti} parte likewise to be due unto his highnes of eny spirituall promocion within any suche archebusshops or busshops diocie and that noo archebusshop ne busshop shalbe charged or chargeable for the colleccion receiving payment or satisfaccion of the sam or any parcell therof; be it provided and alsoo enacted that the clergie shall have twoo dayes of payment for the xx^{ti} parte aforsaide that is to say the moitie of the same to be payed at the feast of Ester next ensuing and the other moitie at the feast of sainct Michell tharcaungell by even porcions and so to contynue from yere to yere perpetuallie to endure.

c.26 Thact for thenglishe ordre habit and langage[103]

The kinges majestie oure moost gracious and moost redoubted souveraigne lorde perpending and wayeng by his great wisedom lernyng and experience

103 *Statutes at large* c.15. Transmiss dated 30 July 1537.

howe moche it dothe more conferre to thinduccion of rude and ignoraunt people to the knowledge of almyghtie God and of that good and vertuous obedience whiche by his moost holie preceptes and commaundementes they owe to their princes and superiors then a good enstruccion in his moost blessid lawes with a conformytie concordaunce and familiaritie in language tongue in maners ordre and apperell with theme that be civill people and doo professe and knowledge Christes religion and civill and poleticque ordres lawes and direccions as his graces subjectes of this parte of this his lande of Irlande (that is called thenglishe pale) dothe and moost graciouselie considering therwith upon the great love zeale and deasire whiche his moost excellent majestie haithe to thadvauncement of the state of this his said lande and to the conveyaunce and traynyng of his people of the same to an honest cristen civilitie and obedience whom his highnes tendreth as his membres of this politicque bodie wherof immediatelie under God he is supreme hed and governour that there is agayne nothing whiche doeth more conteyne and keape many of his subjectes of this his said lande in a certein savage and wilde kinde and maner of living then the diversitie that is betwene theme in tongue language ordre and habite whiche by the eye disceiveth the multitude and perswadeth unto theme that they shoulde be as it were of sondrie sortes or rather of sondrie cuntreis where in deade they be holly togither oon boddie wherof his highnes is thoonlie hed under God as it is aforsaide of his moost noble and princelie disposicion and fervent zeale which his highnes hathe and beareth to thadvauncement of the state of this his lande for a certein direccion and order to be had that all we his saide subjectes therof myght the better knowe God and doo that thing that myght in tyme be and redounde to our awne wealthe quiet and commoditie dothe not oonlie deasire that all suche good lawes as by wise godlie and prudent princes his moost noble progenitours have bene heretofor made for the use of thenglishe tongue habit and order within this his saide lande may be put in due execucion but alsoo that the same may be soo establisshed and in this present parliament brought to suche a perfeccion that the saide englishe tongue habite and order may be from hensfurth contynually (and without ceassing or retournyng at any tyme to Irishe habite or language) used by all men that woll knowledge theme selves according to their dueties of allegeaunce to be his highnes true and faithfull subjectes his majestie dothe hereby intymate unto all his saide subjectes of this lande of all degrees that who soo ever shall for any respecte at any tyme declyne from thorder and purpose of this lawe touching thencrease of thenglishe tongue habite and ordre or shall suffre any within his familie or rule to use the Irishe habit or not to use theme selves to thenglishe tongue his majestie woll repute theme in his moost noble herte as persons that esteme nat his moost draid lawes and commaundementes but what soo ever they shall at other tymes pretende in wordes and

countenaunce to be persons of an other sorte and inclynacion then becometh true and faithfull subjectes; wherfor be it enacted ordeyned and establisshed by auctoritie of this present parliament that noo persone ne persons the kinges subjectes within this londe being or hereafter to be from and after the frist daye of Maij which shalbe in the yere of our lorde God M v^c^ and xxxix^ti^ shalbe shorne or shawen above the eares or use the wearing of heare uppon their heddes like unto longe lockes callid glibbis or have or use any heare growing on their upper lippes callid or named a crommeall or use or weare eny shirt smocke kerchour bendell neckerchour mocket or lynnen cappe coloured or dyed with saffron ne yet use or weare in eny their shirtes or smockes above seven yardes of clothe to be measurid according to the kinges standarde; and that alsoo no woman use or weare eny kirtill or cote tucked up or embrowdred or garnysshed with sylke or couched or laid with usker after the Irishe facion; and that noo persone ne persons of what estate condicion or degre they be shall use or weare eny mantels cote or hode made after the Irishe facion; and if eny persone or persons use or weare eny shirt smocke cote hode mantyll kerchour bendel neckerchour mocket or lynnyn cappe contrarie to the forme above recited that then every persone soo offending shall forfaict the thing soo used or worne; and that it shalbe laufull to every the kinges true subjectes to sease the same; and further thoffendor in eny of the premisses shall forfaicte for every tyme soo wearing the same ageinst the forme aforsaid suche penalties and somes of monye as hereafter by this present acte is lymyted and appoynted; provided alway that this acte ne any thing therin conteyned be prejudiciall to eny woman or any herdes or horseboies for the using or wearing of eny mantell ne shall extende or be hurtfull to eny persone or persones for or by reason of wearing of eny mantels during suche tyme as he or they shalbe in goyng ridyng or abiding in any hosting journey or roode or reysing out upon a crye but that they and every of theme shall and maye liberally and frelie use and [*m.27*] weare at their pleasurs their mantels during suche hostinges journeyes or roodes or reysing out eny thing in this acte befor to the contrarie mencioned or declarid nowithstonding; and be it enacted by auctoritie aforsaide that every persone or persons the kinges true subjectes inhabityng this lande of Irlande of what estate condicion or degree he or they be or shalbe to the uttermost of their power connyng and knowledge shall use and speake comenlie thenglishe tonge and language and that every suche persone and persons havyng childe or children shall endevoir theme selfe to cause and procure his said childe and children to use and speacke thenglishe tongue and language and according to his or their habilitie connyng and power shall bring up and keape his saide childe and children in suche places wher they shall or may have occasion to lerne thenglishe tongue language ordre and condicion; and further be it enacted by auctoritie aforsaide that every the said persone and persons having

or keaping any house or housholde shall to their power knowledge and habilitie use and keape their houses and housholdes as ner as ever they can according to thenglishe ordre condicion and maner upon payne of forfaicture to every lorde spirituall and temporall that shall offende in the premisses or eny parcell therof as often as he shall soo offende the some of $vj^{li.}$ $xiij^{s.}$ $iiij^{d.}$ and upon payne of forfaictur to every knight and esquier that shall offende in the premisses or any parcell therof as often as he shall soo offende $xl^{s.}$ and upon payne of forfaictur to every gentleman or merchaunt that shall fortune to offende in the premisses or any parte therof as often as he shall soo offende $xx^{s.}$ and upon payne of forfaictur to every freholder and yeoman that shall offende in the premisses or any parcell therof as often as he shall soo offende $x^{s.}$ and upon payne of forfaictur to every husbandman that shall offende in the premisses or any parcell therof as often as he soo offende $vj^{s.}$ $viij^{d.}$ and upon payne of forfaictur to every other the kinges subjectes within this londe what soo ever he be that shall offende in the premisses or any parte therof as often as he shall soo offende $iij^{s.}$ $iiij^{d.}$ thone halfe of the whiche forfaicturs to be to our souveraigne lorde the king his heyres and successors and thother halfe of the same to the partie that will sue for the recoveraie therof by accion of debte bill pleynte enformacion or otherwise in any of the kinges courtes wherin noo essoyne proteccion ne wageor of lawe shalbe admytted ne alloued; and be it further enacted by auctoritie aforsaide that every justice of peaux sheriff maior suffrayne and portreve and every other hed officer of eny citie borowe or towne constables or keapers of castels or garisons within this lande within their lymytes auctoritie and jurisdiccions shall from the said furst daie of Maij aide and assist eny suche persone soo seasing suche saide Irishe garment or apparell used or worne against the forme of this estatute and alsoo shall take and sease the saide garment if noo other persone doo sease suche garment soo used or worne contrarie to the saide estatute and the same garment soo seased and taken to have to his or their propre use and every other persone and persons the kinges true subjectes at all tymes requisite shall aide maynteyne supporte and assist every of the saide seasors and every of the saide justices of peax sheriffes maiors suffraynes portreves and every other hed officer of cities or borowe townes constables or keapers of castels and garisons in due and full execucion of the same; be it further enacted by auctoritie aforsaide that if any persone or persons whose garment or Irishe habite is seasid or taken by force of this present acte doo make or procure or goo about to take eny distres or pledge or eny other recompence for the same of eny suche person or persons that soo did sease or take the same or of any other their servauntes or freendes or any other the kinges subjectes for the cause aforsaid shall forfaict for every suche tyme soo offending $v^{li.}$ thone halfe therof to our souveraigne lorde the king and thother parte to him that woll sue for the recoveraie therof by accion of debt

bill playnte enformacion or otherwise in any of the kinges courtes wherin noo essoyn proteccion ne wageor of lawe shalbe admytted ne allowed; and over that it shalbe laufull to the justices of peaux and every other the kinges officers and subjectes to take all and every suche persone soo offending and hym to commyt to the next pryson or gaoll there to remayne till the next generall cessions within the said countie to be kepte and further unto suche tyme as he be delyvered by the justices sittyng in the saide cessions upon suche reasonable fynes as by theme or any twoo of theme shalbe thought convenyent; and further be it enacted by auctoritie aforsaide that if any archedeaconrie deanrie provostship prebende parsonage vicarage or chauntrie or any other dignitie benefice office or promocion spirituall within this land of Irlande undre the king our souveraigne lordes obedience tuicion and governaunce leviable or chargeable with paymentes of the furst fructes to the kinges highnes doo at eny tyme after the said furst daie of Maij whiche shalbe in the yere of our lorde God M v^c^ xxxix^ti^ happen or become voide that then every persone and persones and bodies politicque the kinges true subjectes and undre his rule and governaunce havyng auctoritie power right interest and title to nominat electe present collate or yeve any suche archedeaconrie deanrie provostship prebende parsonage vicarage or chauntrie or other suche dignitie benefice office or promocion spirituall shall nominat electe presente collate or yeve as the title shall require the same archedeaconrie deanrie provostship prebend parsonage vicarage chauntrie or other dignitie benefice office and promocion spirituall soo happenyng voide to suche persone or persones as can specke englishe and to none other persone ne persones oonles ther be noo persone ne persons whiche can specke englishe that will accept and take the same; and if suche persone or persons or bodies poleticque having right title and interest to nominat electe collate present or yeve any suche archedeaconrie deanrie provostship prebende parsonage vicarage chauntrie or other dignitie benefice office or promocion spirituall as is aforsaide upon convenient serche and enquierie by him or theme made can not within iij monethes after suche archedeaconrie deanrie provostship prebende parsonage vicarage chauntrie or other dignitie benefice office or promocion spirituall shall soo happen to come and be voide have ne get eny suche persone that can specke englishe to accept and take suche archedeaconrie deanrie provostship prebend parsonage vicarage chauntrie or other diginitie benefice office or promocion spirituall soo being voide then such persone and persons to whom the right title and interest of nominacion eleccion collacion presentacion or giving of suche archedeaconrie deanrie and other dignitie benefice office or promocion spirituall aforsaid shall apperteigne or belonge shall make or cause to be mad foure solempne proclamacions openlie to be proclamed at foure severall merket daies holden in the next merket towne adyoynyng to the churche chaple or place wher suche dignitie benefice office or

promocion spirituall is then voide that if eny persone or persones whiche can specke englishe apte and convenyent to accept occupie and use the same dignitie benefice office or promocion spirituall soo then being voide will come and repayre unto hym or theme to whom the right title and interest of nominacion eleccion presentacion collacion or gifte of suche dignitie benefice office or promocion spirituall shall apperteigne or belonge and will take and occupie the same dignitie benefice office or promocion spirituall shall have the nominacion eleccion presentacion collacion or gifte of the same as the case and matier therin shall require; and if noo persone ne persons whiche can[104] englishe as is aforsaide will or doo repaier or come to him or theme that hathe the right title and interest of nominacion eleccion presentacion collacion or gifte of suche dignitie benefice office or promocion spirituall then being voide within five weckes after the frist of the same proclamacions in fourme aforsaid made to take and receive the presentacion collacion nominacion eleccion or gifte of the said dignitie benefice office or promocion spirituall soo then being voide then it shalbe laufull to every suche persone and persons havyng right title or interest to the nominacion eleccion collacion presentacion or yefte of suche dignitie benefice office or promocion spirituall then being voide to present collate nominat electe or give the same dignitie benefice office or promocion spirituall to eny honest sufficient hable persone albeit suche persone can nat specke englishe eny thing in this acte to the contrarie mencioned nowithstonding; and if eny persone or persons havyng right title interest or laufull auctoritie to nominat collate present electe or give any suche dignitie benefice office or promocion spirituall doo hereafter nominat collate electe present or give any suche dignitie benefice office or promocion spirituall soo being voide to eny persone or persones whiche can not specke englishe contrarie to the forme and maner afor recited being therof laufullie convicted according the due proces of the kinges lawes upon any enquerie or presentement befor any of the kinges judges that then the same collacion nominacion eleccion presentacion and gifte and thadmission and institucion of suche persone shalbe voide and then it shalbe laufull to the king our souverain lorde his heyres and successors to collate electe nominat present and give the same dignitie benefice office or promocion spirituall to eny persone and persons that can speake englishe and to none other; and if the kinges highnes his heyrs and successors upon suche presentacion collacion nominacion eleccion and gifte be interrupted or disturbed then he shall have his writ of quare impedit against suche disturbor and recover the presentacion therof for that tyme in like forme as his grace shoulde have doon for any other presentacion of his awne patronage; and if the kinges highnes his heyres and successors present any parson by vertue of this acte

104 *specke* omitted.

whiche can not speake englishe that then the same yefte to be voide and the patrones former yefte to stande in his first force any thing in this acte to the contrarie notwithstonding; provided alway that suche presentacion collacion nominacion or yefte soo to be made by the kinges highnes his heyres and successors shall not in eny wise be prejudiciall hurtfull or enpairement to hym or theme that at tyme of suche presentement had right title or interest to the same but that they and every of theme shall and may when suche dignitie benefice office or promocion spirituall shall next become voide present collate electe nominat or geve the same as thogh noo suche nominacion collacion or presentement had bene had by the kinges highnes[105] his heyres and successors any thing in this acte to the contrarie nowithstondyng; and further be it enacted by auctoritie aforsaide that every archebusshop busshop suffrican and every other havyng auctoritie and power to yeve ordre of preesthode deacon and subdeacon shall at suche tyme as they or any of theme do give to eny persone or persons eny of the said ordres of preesthode deacon or subdeacon yeve unto every persone taking eny of the said ordres of preesthoode deacon or subdeacon a corporall othe that he or they soo taking ordre as is aforsaide shall to the uttermost of his power wit and connyng endeavour hym silfe to lerne thenglishe tongue and language and use englishe ordre and facions if he may lerne and attayn the same by possibilitie in suche place and places wher his cure or dwelling shalbe and further shall endeavour hym silfe to move endoctryne and teache all other being under his ordre rule and governaunce to accomplishe and performe the same; and that alsoo every suche archebusshop busshop suffrican archedeacon commissionary and other havyng power and auctoritie to admyt install collat institute or inducte eny persone or persones to eny dignitie benefice office or promocion spirituall as is aforsaide shall at the tyme of thadmission institucion installacion collacion and induccion of suche persone and persons to eny dignitie benefice office or promocion spirituall[106] yeve unto the saide persone and persones soo admytted instituted installed collated or inducted a corporall othe that he and [*m.28*] they soo beyng admytted instituted installed collated or inducted shall to his wit and connyng endeavour hym selfe to lerne instruct and teache thenglishe tongue to all and[107] every being under his rule cure ordre or governaunce and in likewise shall byd the beades in thenglishe tongue and preache the worde of God in englishe (if he can preache) and alsoo for his awne parte shall use and excercise thenglishe ordre and habite and alsoo provoke as many as he may to the same and alsoo shall keape or cause to be keapte within the place territorie or paroche wher he shall have preemynence rule benefice or promocion a scole for to learne englishe if

105 *his* struck through. 106 *as is aforsaid* struck through. 107 *all and* repeated and struck through.

any children of his paroche come to hym to lerne the same taking for the keaping of the same scole suche convenient stipend or salarie as in the saide lond is accustumablie used to be taken; and if any archebusshop busshop suffrican or other havyng auctoritie or power to give ordres as is aforsaid or havyng auctorite or power to collate institute admit install or inducte any persone or persons to any dignitie benefice office or promocion spirituall as is aforsaide or eny of theme doo yeve ordres to eny persone or persons without geving thothe aforsaid or doo in any wise admyt collate institute installe or induct any persone or persones to eny dignitie benefice office or promocion spirituall without yeving to suche persone or persons soo collated admytted instituted installed or inducted suche corporall othe as is aforsaide that then every suche archebusshop busshop suffrican ordenarie and other havyng power and auctoritie to yeve ordres as is aforsaid or to collate admyt institut installe or induct any persone or persons to any dignitie benefice office or promocion spirituall as is aforsaide shall forfaict for every tyme offending against this estatute iij$^{li.}$ vj$^{s.}$ viij$^{d.}$ thoone moitie to our souveraigne lorde the king thother moitie to that persone or persons that woll sue for the same as is aforsaide; and further be it ordeyned establisshed and enacted by auctoritie aforsaide that if any persone or persons being promoted collated instituted installed or inducted in any dignitie benefice office or promocion spirituall doo not observe performe and fulfill the tenor purporte and effecte of the said othe that then suche persone and persones upon condempnacion therof by due proces of the lawe had as is aforsaide shall forfaict for the furst tyme vj$^{s.}$ viij$^{d.}$ and if suche persone or persons be eftsones laufullie condempned for like offence then he shall forfaicte xx$^{s.}$ and if the third tyme he be laufully condempned for like offence then suche dignitie benefice office or promocion spirituall whiche suche persone or persons have wher suche offence is commytted shalbe taken deamed and adjudged to be voide; and that it shalbe laufull to hym or theme to whome the right title or interest of nominacion collacion presentacion eleccion or yefte therof shall aperteigne to nominat collate present electe or yeve the same to any other sufficient and hable persone or persons in like maner and forme as thogh thencumbent had dyed any thing or thinges by hym afor then doone notwithstonding; provided and be it enacted by auctoritie aforsaide that this acte in any wise extende not or be prejudiciall to eny persone or persons whiche hereafter shalbe benificed within this lande being bounde to keape residence in any metropolitan cathedrall or collegiat churche nether to eny persone or persons soo benyficed whiche shalbe at studie in eny unyversitie either being in the kinges service or otherwise out of the lande by the kinges commaundement but that suche paroche preist or preestes whiche shall have the service of any paroche churche undre hym or theme shall during their absentie teache thenglishe tongue and keape a scole according the forme of this acte upon payne of

forfaictur to every suche paroche preest of xx$^{s.}$ for every yere that he shall omyt the same; provided alsoo that this acte shall take no effecte ne execucion untill it be oppenlie proclamed in due forme.

c.27 Thacte for suppression of abbaies[108]

Moost humblie deasire the kinges highnes his humble subjectes that it may be enacted by thauctoritie of this present parliament that his majestie shall have and enyoie to hym and to his heyres for ever the monasteries and religious houses of the Bectyf sainte Peters besides Trym Duske Dueleke Holme Patrick Baltynglas Grane Taghmolyn' Dunbrodie Tenterne the priorie of Balliboggan' and thabbaies of the Hogges and Fernes and in like maner shall have and enyoie all the scites and circuites of every suche religious house and all and singuler the manors graunges and meses londes tenementes revercions rentes services tiethes pencions porcions churches chapels advousons patronages annuyties rightes interestes condicions and other hereditamentes apperteynyng or belongyng to every of the saide monasteries or religious houses in as ample and large maner as thabbotes priors abbasses prioresses and other governours of the saide monasteries and religious houses at any tyme within thole yere next befor the making of this acte had ought or myght or have had possessed and enyoied in the right of their saide houses and alsoo that his highnes shall have to hym and to his heyres all and singuler such monasteries and religious houses not being alredy by his grace geven to any persone or persons by lettres patentes whiche at any tyme within twoo yeres next befor the making of[109] this acte haithe bene geven to his majestie by any abbote prior abbesse or prioresse undre their convent seales or by any other meane or that otherwise hathe bene suppressed or dissolved and all and singuler the manors londes tenementes rentes services revercions tiethes pencions porcions churches chapels advousons patronages rightes interestes condicions and other interestes and hereditamentes to the same monasteries or religious houses or to any of theme belongyng or apperteynyng whiche befor the making of this acte his highnes hathe not yeven and graunted to any persone or persons by his lettres patentes as is aforsaide to have and to holde all and singuler the premisses withe all their rightes profictes jurisdiccions and commodities unto the kinges majestie and to his heyres and successors for ever knyt and united to thymperiall crowne of England to doo and use therwith his and their awne willes to the pleasur of almyghtie God and to thonour and profict of this lande; and it is ordeyned and enacted by auctoritie aforsaid that all and every persone and persons and bodies poleticque whiche nowe have or hereafter shall have any lettres patentes of

108 *Statutes at large* c.16. 109 *of* repeated and struck through.

the kinges highnes of any the scites circuites manors londes tenementes rentes revercions services tiethes pencions porcions churches chapels advousons patronages tiethes interestes condicions interestes[110] and other hereditamentes which apperteignethe to ony monasteriis abbaies priories or religious houses hertofor gyven or graunted to the kinges highnes or otherwise suppressed or dissolved or whiche apperteigne to any of the said monasteriis or religious houses that is or shalbe suppressed or dissolvid by auctoritie of this present acte shall have and enyoie the said scites circuites manors landes tenementes rentes revercions services tiethes pencions porcions churches chapels advousons[111] patronages tiethes interestes and all other hereditamentes conteyned and specified in their lettres patentes nowe being therof made and to be conteyned and expressed in any lettres patentes hereafter to be made according to the teanors purportes and effectes of every suche lettres patentes and shall alsoo have all suche accions[112] suytes entrees and remedies to all intentes and purposes for any thing and thinges conteyned in any suche lettres patentes now made or to be conteyned in any suche lettres patentes hereafter to be made in like maner forme and condicion as thabbotes priors abbesses prioresses and chief governours of every religious house whiche had the same myght or ought to have had if they had not bene suppressed nor dissolved; saving to every persone and persons and bodies politicque their heirs and successors other then thabbotes priors abbesses prioresses and chief governours of the said religious houses specified in this acte and the conventes of the same and their successors and suche as pretended to be foundors patrones or donors to the said monasteriis or religious houses or of eny landes tenementes or hereditamentes belongyng to the same or their heirs and successors all suche right title interest possession leases of yeres rentes services annuyties comens fees offices liveries and livinges pencions porcions corrodies synadolles proxies[113] and all other profictes as they or any of theme have ought or myght have had in or to any of the saide monasteries or religious houses or in or by any manors landes tenementes rentes revercions services tiethes pencions porcions and other hereditamentes apperteynyng or belongyng or that aperteigneth to any of the saide monasteriis or religious houses as if the saide monasteries or religious houses had not bene suppressed by this acte or by any other meane but had contynued in their assensuall bodies and estates that they nowe be or were in; provided alwaies and be it enacted that forasmoche as divers the chief governours of the saide religious houses determynyng the utter spoileng and distruccion of their houses and dreading the suppression theirof for the mayntenaunce of their detestable lives have latelie fraudulentlie and craftelie made

110 In margin: interestes and condyssyons. 111 In margin: advowssons. 112 In margin: to have all actyons. 113 In margin: synodalles and proxies.

feofmentes yeftes estates grauntes and leases undre their convent seales or suffred recoveries of their manors landes tenementes and hereditamentes in fee symple fee taile for terme of life or lives or for yeres or chargeth the same with rentes or corrodies to the great decaie and dismynyshes of their houses that all suche craftie and fraudulent recoveries feofementes yeftes estates grauntes and leases and every of theme made by any of the saide chief governours of the said religious houses undre convent seales within twoo yeres next befor the making hereof shalbe utterlie voide and of none effecte; and it is alsoo enacted by auctoritie aforsaid that the kinges highnes shall have and enyoie to his owne proper use all suche ornamentes jewels goodes cattails and debtes which apperteigneth or belongeth to any of the chief governours of the saide monasteriis or religious houses in the right of the saide monasteries or religious [*m.29*] houses at the furst day of June in the yere of our lorde God M v^{c} xxxvj^{ti} or any tyme sithen not yeven ne graunted by the kinges majestie at any tyme befor the making of this acte to any persone or persons by his lettres patentes wher soo ever and to whos soo ever possession they shall come or be founde except oonlie suche beastes grayne and woddes and souch other like cattaill and revenues as hathe bene solde in the saide furst daie of June or sithen for the necessarie and reasonable expences or charges of any of the saide monasteries and houses; and in consideracion of whiche premisses to be had to his highnes and to his heyres as is aforsaide his majestie is pleased and contented of his moost excellent charitie to provide to every chief hed and governour of every suche religious house during their lives suche yerelie pencion or benefices as to their degree and qualities shalbe reasonable and convenient wherin his highnes will have moost tender respecte to souche of the saide chief governours as wele and truelie conserve and keape the goodes and ornamentes of their houses to the use of his grace without spoile wast or inbeasilling of the same; and for the due fulfilling and accomplisshing of the same his highnes dothe ordayne and depute his trustie and right welbiloved counsailours his graces deputie chaunceller thesaurer underthesaurer chief justices of the kinges benche and comen place and chief baron of his graces eschequier of this his lande for the tyme being or any sex five foure thre or twoo of theme at the least soo that the said underthesaurer be oon to assigne and depute to souche chief governour the certeintie of souche pencion or other livyng and that any souche pencion or livyng soo to be lymyted or yeven to any the saide chief governours shalbe as good and effectuall to all ententes and purposes as though the kinges highnes had yeven the same undre his lettres patentes and that none of the saide chief governours shall pay any thing in thanaper for thensealing of any suche pencions to be lymyted as aforsaide; and alsoo his majestie will ordeyne and provide that the conventes of every suche religious house shall have their capacities if they will to live honestly or vertuouselie abrode and some convenient charitie disposed

to theme towardes their livyng or els shalbe commytted to souche honourable great monasteries of this lande wherin good religion is observed as shalbe lymyted by his highnes or his graces saide counsailours or any vj v iiij iij or ij at the least there to live religiouselie during their lives; and it is ordeyned by auctoritie aforsaid that the chief governours and conventes of souche greate monasteries shall take and accept into their houses from tyme to tyme souch noumbre of persons of the saide conventes as shalbe assigned and appoynted by the kinges highnes or his saide counsaillours or any vj v iiij iij or ij of theme at the least and keape theme religiouselie during their lives within the saide monasteries in like maner and forme as the conventes of suche great monasteries be ordred and keapte; and alsoo the kinges majestie is pleased that it be enacted by auctoritie aforsaide that his highnes shall satisfie content and paye all and singuler souche just and true debtes whiche bene owing to any person or persons by the chief governours of any of the saide religious houses in as large and ample maner as the saide chief governour shulde or ought to have done if this acte had never bene made; provided alwaies that the kinges highnes his heyrs and successors at any tyme after the making of this acte may at their pleasurs ordeyn and declare by their lettres patentes undre their great seale that souche of the saide monasteries or religious houses not befor this tyme yeven by his grace to eny persone or persons by his lettres patentes as is aforsaid whiche his majestie shall not be disposed to have suppressed nor dissolved by auctoritie of this acte shall still contynue and be of the same boddie corporat and in the said essensuall estate qualitie and condicion aswell in possession as otherwise as they were befor the making of this acte without any suppression or dissolucion theirof or any parte of the same by auctoritie of this acte and that every souche ordynaunce and declaracion soo to be made by the kinges highnes shalbe good and effectuall to the chief governours of the saide religious houses whiche his majestie will not have suppressed and to their successors according to the teanors and purportes of the lettres patentes therof to be made ony thing or thinges conteyned in this acte to the contrarie hereof notwithstonding; savyng alwaies and reserved to every persone and persons being founders patrones or donors of any the saide monasteries or religiouse houses that is or shalbe suppressed by this acte or otherwise by any other meanes their heyres and successors all souch right title and interest possession rentes annuyties fees offices leases comens proxies pencions and synodols and all other profictes what soo ever they be whiche any of theme have or shulde have had without fraude or covyne by any maner of meanes otherwise then by reason or occasion of the dissolucion of the saide monasteries or religious houses into or uppon any the saide monasteries or religious houses whereof they be foundors patrones or donors or into or upon any the landes tenementes or other hereditamentes apperteynyng or belongyng to the same in like maner

forme and condicion as other persons and bodies politicque be saved by this acte as is befor rehersed and as if the saide monasteries or religious houses had not bene suppressed or dissolved by this acte or otherwise by any other meane but had contynued still in their assensuall bodies and estates as they be nowe or weare in any thing in this acte to the contrarie hereof notwithstonding; and ferther be it enacted ordeyned and establisshed by auctoritie aforsaide that all and singuler persons bodies politicque and corporat to whome the kinges majestie his heyrs or successors have yeven letten or dymysed or hereafter shall yeve graunte let or dymyse any scites circuites or precincte with thowses therupon buylded together with all the demaynes of eny the saide monasteries or religious houses that is or have bene or shall be desolved or yeven to the kinges highnes by this acte or otherwise by any other meanes and their successors executors and assignes of every suche persone bodie politicque and corporat shalbe bounden by auctoritie of this acte under the penaltie hereafter ensuyng to keape or cause to be kepte an honest fermors house or housholde in the same scite circuite or precincte according to the quantitie of the demaynes of the same and if any persone or persons bodies politicque or corporat that shalbe bounden by this acte doo not keape or cause to be kept suche an honest fermors house or housholde that then he or they soo offending shall forfaicte to the kinges highnes for every quarter of a yere doing the contrarie an hundred shillinges to be recovered to his use in every of his courtes of recorde; and over that it is enacted by auctoritie aforsaide that all justices of peaux in every shyre wher any souche offence shalbe commytted or done contrarie to the trewe meanyng or intent of this present acte shall in every quarter and generall cessions within the lymytes of their commission enquiere of the premisses and shall have full power and auctoritie to heare and determyne the same and to taxe and cesse noo lesse fyne for every of the saide offences then is afore lymyted for the same offences and thestreates therof to be made and certified in the kinges eschequier of this lande according and at souche tyme and forme as other estreates of fynes issues and amercymentes bene made by the saide justices; provided[114] that this acte ne any thing therin conteyned shall extende or in any wise be ment to the rectories parsonages vicarages or churches of the Norraghe and Taghmolyn Begge or to any dismes tiethes offeringes alterages landes tenementes and other profictes what soo ever they be belongyng to them or any of theme during the lives of Sir John Derthicke parson of the Norraghe aforsaide and Sir Thomas Festame parsone of Taghmolyn aforsaid; provided that this acte ne any thing therin comprised shall extende or in any wise be ment to the rectories parsonages vicarages or churches of Holywod Dullardeston' and the frechapell of Armakrenan' and Kiluskie and the par-

114 In margin: proviso for the parsonayges of Norra Tymolyn bege and Taghmollyn and other.

sonage of Uske or to any dismes tiethes offeringes alterages landes tenementes and other profictes what soo ever they be belonging to theme or any of theme during the lives of Sir Robert Luttrell parsone of Holliwod aforsaide Sir John Connyll vicare of Hollywod aforsaide Sir John Lawles vicare of Taghmolyn' Begge aforsaid Sir Alexander Baron parsone of Dullardeston' aforsaide Sir Eustace Browne maister or governour of the saide frechaple of Armacrenan' and Kiluskie and Sir Edmonde Eustace parsone of Uske but that they and every of theme shall have and enyoie their saide benefices with thyssues and profictes of the same during their lives; provided alsoo[115] by auctoritie aforsaid that any article provision matier[116] thing or thinges what soo ever it be comprised or mencioned in this present acte shall extende or in any wise be prejudicial or hurtfull to the moost reverend father in God George archebusshop of Dublin or any his successors in to or for any right possession or title that the saide moost reverende father in God or any his predecessours hathe or shall have to any advouson parsonage vicarage patronage presentacion or collacion to or of any benefice or promocion spirituall what soo ever it be latelie belongyng or in any wise apperteyning to the said house or monasterii of Taghmolyn' Begge any thing or thinges in this present acte notwithstondyng; provided that this acte neither any thing therin conteyned be prejudiciall or hurtfull to the vicars chorals of sainct Patrickes churche of Dublin neither to their successors for their right title interest possesion and entree into and for the benifice pencion and tiethes of Kynnegh within the countie of Cathirlaghe.

[*m.30*]

c.28 Thact for loding of woll and flockes[117]

Where in a parliament holden at Dublin the xiijth yere of the reigne of our souveraigne lorde king Henry the eight[118] that nowe is befor the right honourable lorde Thomas then erle of Surrey and the kinges lieutenaunt within this lande of Irlande amongest other thinges for the comen and publicque weale of the same lande it was establysshed ordeyned and enacted that noo persone ne persones shoulde lode ne convey noo maner of woll ne flockes oute of this saide lande of Irlande uppon peyne of forfaictur to the king our souveraign lorde the double value of the same that notwithstanding for because there was noo auctoritie geven by the saide estatute to any officer of the kinges or other comen persone to entre and make seasure in the saide woll and flockes to be loden contrarie to the same ordynaunce the saide good and beneficiall estatut hathe taken

115 t*ha* struck through. 116 *matier* inserted. 117 *Statutes at large* c.17. 118 1521–2. The parliament began on 24 May 1521 and was dissolved on 21 March 1522 (Quinn, 'Bills and statutes', p. 116). The act is printed in *Statutes at large* as c.2.

litle effecte but contrarie to the mynde entent and effecte of the same great plentie of woll and flockes hath contynuallie hetherto sethens the making therof bene laden and conveyed out of this saide lande to the great and ynestymable hurt decaye and ympoverishement of the kinges pore subjectes within the said lande; for redresse wherof and in consideracion that lodyng and conveyng of the wolle of the growe of this lande out of the same is oon of the greattest occasions of thidelnes of the people wast ruyn and desolacion of the kinges cities and borrowe townes and other places of his domynyon within this lande be it therfor enacted ordeyned and establisshed by thassent and consent of our saide souveraigne lord the king the lordes spirituall and temporall and the comens in this present parliament assembled and by auctoritie of the same that all licences and plackardes heretofore had made or graunted by our souveraigne lorde the king or hereafter to be hadde made or graunted by any the kinges lieutenauntes deputie or deputies of this lande to any persone or persons contrarie to the true meanyng forme and effecte of the saide statut shalbe clerelie voide and of none effecte; and alsoo that noo maner persone ne persons from hensforth doo lode ship convey or carrie in any shyp vessell or boote noo maner wolles or flockes nor convey or carrie or cause to be conveied or carried to any porte havon place or creke to thentent to ship or lode suche woll or flockes uppon payn[119] of forfaictur aswell of the saide woll and flockes soo loded shippid conveyed and caried as of the ship vessell or boot wherin the same shalbe looded if the maister owner or governour therof be in any wise privaie to the same thoon moitie of the saide forfaictur to be to the use of our saide souveraigne lorde the kyng and thother moitie to hym or theme that shal sease fynde or present the saide forfaicturs or any of theme or that woll sue therfor by accion of debte bill pleynt informacion or otherwise in any of the kinges courtes of his graces benche comen place or eschequier wherin the partie defendaunt shall in noo wise be admytted to wage his law nor in the saide accion bill pleynt or informacion any essoyn ne proteccion nor any licence pardone or plackarde graunted or to be graunted by any lieutenauntes or deputie of this lande to any person or persons whiche shalbe ympechid to have offended contrarie to the forme and effect of this or any other acte touching the prohibicion or loding of wolles or flockes shalbe allowable; and if any plees be pleded in any suite bill pleint informacion or accion not triable within this lande nor within any suche place where the kinges writ dothe ron within this lande then by auctoritie of this acte every suche[120] plee if any yssue be taken of the same shalbe tried by veredict of xij men in the shire or place wher any suche accion bill pleynt or enformacion shalbe commensed any thing to the contrarie hereof had or made notwithstonding; and it is also enacted by auc-

119 *payn* inserted. 120 *persone* struck through.

toritie aforsaide that the kinges justices of plees befor his grace to be holden within this lande for the tyme being and every of theme and his highnes barons of his graces eschequier for the tyme being and every of theme that is to saie the saide justices in the kinges benche and the saide barons in theschequier and every persones to be auctorised by the kinges commission to enquiere of thoffendors of any thing or thinges mencioned or comprised in this present acte shall have full power and auctoritie from tyme to tyme to enquere of thoffendors of every article thing or thinges provided and establisshed by auctoritie of this present acte and of the saide acte made in the saide xiij yere of our saide souveraigne lorde aswele by presentement veredicte or othes of xij men or otherwise and the same shall heare determyn and adjudge in like maner forme and condicion as they may do any other matier comyng or growing[121] befor theme wherof they within the jurisdiccion of their courtes have good auctoritie and that none of theme shall taxe any lesse fyne upon any persone or persones soo offending and being therof laufullie convicted by veredict confession or otherwise then the veray value of the forfaictur therof lymyted and appointed by this present acte or by the said acte made and establisshed in the saide xiij yere of the reigne of our saide moost draid souveraigne lorde; and be it further enacted by the same auctoritie that every searcheor whiche shall have full knowledge or be prevaie to the carieng conveyng or lading of any woll or flockes contrarie to this acte and concele the same without presenting the cause of suche forfaictur into the kinges eschequier or befor the saide justices within xiiij daies next following if the terme be then oppen and if it be not then within sex daies of the begynnyng of the terme then next following and being convicted therof by veredict confession or otherwise befor any of the saide justices barons of the saide eschequier or commyssioners that he haith otherwise offended contrarie to this acte shall forfaicte souche estate as he shall have in his saide office at the tyme of thoffence commytted and by auctoritie of this parliament unhabled and repelled from thexcercisyng receivyng or occupieng of that office for ever any lettres patentes or other yefte or graunte to hym therof made or had or to be had or made in any wise notwithstonding; and if afterwarde contrarie to the teanor of this acte he receive excercise or use the same office he shall lose for every day that he soo useth or occupieth it xl$^{s.}$ thone halfe therof to be to the use of our souveraigne lorde the king and thother halfe to be[122] to hym or theme that woll sue for the same by originall writ of debt bill pleynt informacion or otherwise in any the kinges courtes wherin the partie defendaunt shall not wage his lawe ne in the same any essoyne licence pardone plackarde or proteccion shalbe alloued; and if any searchor or searchors within this lande doo make assigne or appoynte any deputie or deputies factor or

121 *or growing* inserted. 122 *to be* inserted.

factors servaunt or servauntes for the usyng excercisyng or occupieng of his or their saide office whiche shall have knowledge or be previe to the carieng conveyeng or loding of any wolle or flockes contrarie to this acte and concele the same without presentyng the cause of suche forfaictur in the saide kinges eschequier or befor the saide justices within xiiij daies next following if the terme be then oppen and if it be not then within sex daies of the begynnyng of the terme next following and being therof convicted by veredict confession or otherwise befor any of the saide justices barons of the saide eschequier or commissioners that they or any of theme haithe otherwise offended contrarie to this acte any suche[123] searchor or searcheors that shall soo appoynt any such[124] persone or persons to be his or their deputie or deputies factor or factors servaunt or servauntes for the usyng and excercisyng of his or their office offending and concelyng as is aforsaid shall lose and forfaicte for every suche tyme that his or their deputie or deputies factor or factors servaunt or servauntes shall offende or concele as is aforsaide v$^{li.}$ thone halfe therof to the use of our soveraigne lorde the king and thother halfe to be to[125] hym or theme that woll sue for the same by originall writ of debt bill pleynt informacion or otherwise in any of the kinges courtes wherin the partie defendaunt shall not wage his lawe ne in the same noo essoyne licence pardone plackarde or proteccion shalbe alloued; be it alsoo enacted by auctoritie aforsaide that every packe or fardell laded or shipped or caried sent or conveied to any place within this lande to thentent to be laded or shipped wherin any maner of wolle or flockes shalbe set packed or inclosed shalbe seased and forfaicted wherof thoon halfe shalbe to our souveraigne lord the kinges use and thother halfe to hym or theme that shall sease or take the same or sue for the same by accion of debte bill pleynt informacion or otherwise in any of the kinges courtes wherin the partie defendaunt shall not wage his lawe ne in the same any essoyn licence pardone plackarde or proteccion shalbe alloued any thing or thinges heretofor had made or provided to the contrarie notwithstonding; provided that this acte ne any thing or thinges therin conteyned be prejudiciall or hurtfull to or for Edwarde a Becke of Manchester merchaunt but that he by hym silfe or any other to his use during his life naturall may lode or carrie yerelie at his and their pleasur into Englande flockes or wolle to the value of xl$^{li.}$ to be yerelie entred with the custumer controller and searcheor of any porte or havon wher the same shalbe shipped and loden this acte or any thing or thinges therin mencioned notwithstonding.

123 *suche* inserted. 124 *such* inserted. 125 *to* inserted.

[*m.31*]

c.29 Thacte for the profe of testamentes[126]

Forasmoche as in a parliament holden at Westminster in the xxxj^{ti} yere of the noble prynce king Edwarde the thirde[127] upon the complaynt of his people for thoutrageous and grevous fynes and somes of monye taken by the mynystres of busshops and other ordynaries of holy churche for the probate of testamentes and for thacquytaunce by the saide ordynaries of the same to be made concernyng the same the saide noble king in the same parliament openlie chargid and commaunded the archbusshop of Canterburie and other ordynaries for that tyme being that amendement therof shulde be had and if none amendement therof be had it was by auctoritie of the same parliament accorded that the king shoulde therof make enquerie by his justices of suche misdemeanours and that the same justices shoulde heare and determyne theme aswele at the suit of the king as the partie as of olde tyme haith bene used as by the same estatute more playnlier it appereth; and after for further avoiding of the same dyvers good and holsome estatutes and lawes therof was made aswele in the thrid yere of the reigne of king Henry the fifthe[128] as in the xxj^{ti} yere of our moost draid souveraigne lorde king Henry theight[129] as by the saide statutes more playnlie it appereth; and considering the great povertie that resteth amongest the kinges subjectes of this lande of Irlande by many and diverse occasions and that the taking of the said exaccions in noo parte be dismynysshed but from tyme to tyme encreased to the ympoverysshing and hyndraunce of the kynges true subjectes the saide estatutes and lawes notwithstonding; for remedie wherof be it enacted ordeyned and establisshed by auctoritie of this present parliament that from the furst daie of Februarie in the yere of our lorde God M v^{c} and xxxvij^{ti} nothing shalbe demaunded received ne taken by eny archebusshop busshop ordenarie archedeacon chaunceller commyssarie officiall or any other maner person or persons what soo ever he or they be whiche nowe have or hereafter shall have aucthoritie or power to take or receive probacion insynuacion or approbacion of testament or testamentes by hym silfe or theme selves nor by his or their registrers notaries scribes praisers sompnors apparitors or by any other of their mynystres fermors or servauntes for the probacion insynuacion and approbacion of any testament or testamentes or for the commission of admynystracion of the goodes or catailles of any persone deyng intestat or for writing sealing praising registring fynes making of inventories yeving of acquitaunces or for any costes and charges or any other maner of cause concernyng the same wher the goodes of the testator of

126 *Statutes at Large* c.18. 127 1357–8. 31 Edward III, Stat. 1 c.4 (*Statutes of the realm*, i, p. 350). 128 1415–16. 3 Henry V Stat. 2 c.8 (*Statutes of the realm*, ii, pp 195–6). 129 1529–30. 21 Henry VIII c.5 (*Statutes of the realm*, iii, pp 285–7).

the saide testament or the persone soo deyng intestat or otherwise doo not amount clerelie over and above the value of iij$^{li.}$ vj$^{s.}$ viij$^{d.}$ Irishe monye except to the scribe or notarie to have for the writing of the probate of the testament of hym deceassed whose goodes shall not be above the same clere value of iij$^{li.}$ vj$^{s.}$ viij$^{d.}$ Irishe xij$^{d.}$ Irishe and except to thordynarie his commyssarie officiall or other mynyster having the custodie of his seale usuall accustomed for the sealing of testamentes for the wax sealing and deliveraie of the probate of the testament of hym decessed whose good shall not be above the same cleare value of iij$^{li.}$ vj$^{s.}$ viij$^{d.}$ Irishe and to the scribe for the writing of the commission of admynystracion of the goodes of any man deyng or decessyng intestat not being above like value of iij$^{li.}$ vj$^{s.}$ viij$^{d.}$ xij$^{d.}$ and to thordynarie his commyssarie officiall or other mynyster havyng the custodie of his saide seale for wax sealing and delyveraie of the same commission viij$^{d.}$ Irishe; and that neverthelesse thearchebusshop busshop ordynarie or other persone or persones having power or auctoritie to take or receive the probacion insynuacion or approbacion of testamentes refuse not to approve or make any suche testament or make any suche commission being laufullie desired tended or offred to theme to be proved approved or made then wherof the goodes of the testator or persones soo deyng intestate or otherwise amount not above the value of iij$^{li.}$ vj$^{s.}$ viij$^{d.}$ Irishe soo that the saide testament or commyssion be exhibited to hym or theme in writing reddie to be sealed and that the same testament be laufullie proved befor the same ordynarie befor the sealing to be true hole and last testament of the same testator in souche forme as haith bene comenlie customed in that behalfe; and when the goodes of the testator dothe amount over and above the clere value of iij$^{li.}$ vj$^{s.}$ viij$^{d.}$ and doo not excede the some of x$^{li.}$ Irishe that then noo archbusshop busshop ordynarie nor other maner persone or persones what soo ever he or they be nowe havyng or that hereafter shall have auctoritie to take probacion or approbacion of any testament or testamentes as is aforsaide by theme selfe or any of their saide registrers scribes notaries praisers sompnors apparators nor any other their mynystres for the probacion insynuacion and approbacion of any testament or testamentes or for the commission of admynystracion of the goodes and cattails of any person deing intestat or for writing registring sealing praising making of inventories yeving of acquytaunces fynes or for any costes or charges or for any other maner of cause concernyng the same shall take or cause to be taken of any persone or persons but onelie iij$^{s.}$ iiij$^{d.}$ Irishe and not above wherof to be to thordynarie or to other person or persons havyng power or auctoritie to take eny probacion of eny testament or testamentes for hym and his mynystres ij$^{s.}$ and not above and xvj$^{d.}$ residue of the said iij$^{s.}$ iiij$^{d.}$ to be to the scribe notarie or registrer for the writyng and registring of the same; and wher the goodes of the testator or persone or persons soo deing intestate or otherwise doo amount over and above the

clere value of x$^{li.}$ Irishe and doo not excede the some of xx$^{li.}$ Irishe that then tharchebusshop busshop ordynarie nor other persone or persones now having or whiche hereafter shall have auctoritie or power to take probate of testamentes as is aforsaide by hym or theme selfe or eny of his or their saide registrers scribes notaries praisers sompnors apparators or eny other their mynystres for the probacion insynuacion and approbacion of eny testament or testamentes or for the commission of admynystracion of the goodes or cattails of any person deyng intestate or for writing registring sealing praisyng making of inventories yeving of acquitaunces fynes or for eny costes or charges or for eny maner of cause concernyng[130] the same shall take or cause to be taken of eny persone or persons but oonlie vj$^{s.}$ viij$^{d.}$ Irishe and not above wherof to be to thordynarie or to other person or persones having power or auctoritie to take any probacion of eny testament or testamentes for hym and his mynystres v$^{s.}$ Irishe and not above and xviij$^{d.}$ residue of the saide vj$^{s.}$ viij$^{d.}$ to be to the scribe notarie or regystrer for the writing and registring of the same; and when the goodes of the testator or persone or persons soo deyng intestate or otherwise doo amount to the cleare value of xx$^{li.}$ Irishe and do not excede the some of xl$^{li.}$ Irishe that then thearchbusshop busshop nor ordynarie nor other persone or persons nowe havyng or whiche hereafter shall have auctoritie or power to take probate of testamentes as is aforsaide by hym or theme silfe or eny of his or their registrers notaries praisers sompnors apparators or any other their mynystres for the probacion insynuacion and approbacion of eny testament or testamentes or for the commission of admynystracion of the goodes or cattails of eny person deyng intestate or for writing registring sealing praising making of inventories yevyng of acquytaunces fynes or for eny costes or charges or for eny maner of cause concernyng the same shall take or cause to be taken of any person or persons but onelie x$^{s.}$ Irishe and not above wherof to be to the ordynarie or to other person or persones havyng power or auctoritie to take any probacion of any testament or testamentes for hym and his mynystres viij$^{s.}$ Irishe and not above and ij$^{s.}$ residue of the saide x$^{s.}$ to be to the scribe notarie or registrer for the writing and registring of the same; and when the goodes of the testator or persone or persons soo deing intestate or otherwise doo amount to the cleare value of xl$^{li.}$ Irishe and not excede the some of a C$^{li.}$ Irishe that then tharchebusshops busshops nor ordynaries nor other person or persons nowe havyng or whiche shall have hereafter auctoritie or power to take probate of testamentes as is aforsaide by hym or theme silfe or eny of his or their registrers notaries praisers sompnors apparators or eny other their mynynstres for the probacion insynuacion and approbacion of eny testament or testamentes or for the commission of admynystracion of the goodes and cattails of eny

130 *as* (?) struck through.

persone deyng intestate or for writing registring sealing praising making of inventories yeving of acquytaunces fynes or for eny costes or charges or for eny maner of cause concernyng the same shall take or cause to be taken of eny person or persons but onelie xvj$^{s.}$ viij$^{d.}$ Irishe and not above wherof to be to thordynarie or to other persone or persons havyng power or auctoritie to take eny probacion of eny testament or testamentes for hym and his mynystres xiiij$^{s.}$ Irishe and not above and ij$^{s.}$ viij$^{d.}$ residue of the saide xvj$^{s.}$ viij$^{d.}$ to the scribe notarie or registrer for the writing and registring of the same; and when the goodes of the testator or persone or persones so deyng intestat or otherwise doo amount to the cleare value of a C$^{li.}$ Irishe and above what soo ever the some or quantitie therof be that then thearchebusshops busshops or ordynaries or other persone or persons nowe havyng or whiche hereafter shall have auctoritie or power to take probat of testament as is aforsaide by hym or theme silfe or eny of his or their registrers notaries praiseres sompnors apparators or eny other their mynystres for the probacion insynuacion and approbacion of eny testament or testamentes or for the commission of admynystracion of the goodes and cattails of eny persone deyng intestate or for writing registring sealing praising making of inventories yeving of acquytaunces fynes or for eny costes or charges or for eny other maner of cause concernyng the same probate of testament shall take or cause to be taken of eny persone or persons but onelie xx$^{s.}$ Irishe and not above wherof to thordynarie or to other persone or persons having power or auctoritie to take eny probacion of testament or testamentes for hym and his mynystres xvj$^{s.}$ viij$^{d.}$ Irishe and not above and iij$^{s.}$ iiij$^{d.}$ residue of the saide xx$^{s.}$ to be to the scribe notarie or registrer for the writing and registring of the same; and that every suche archebusshop ordynarie or other persone or persons soo having or whiche herefter shall have auctoritie or power to take or receive the probacions or approbacions of eny[131] testamente or testamentes or to make eny commission of any admynystracion of any goodes or cataills of any persone or persons deing intestate their registrers scribes notaries and mynystres shall approve ordeyne make insynuat seale and register from tyme to tyme the saide testamentes and commissions and delyver the same sealed with the seale of their office to thexecutor or executors admynystrator or admynystrators named or appoynted for the same; and that for the said some or somes above saide and in maner and forme as is above rehersed to delyver it with convenyent spede without eny frustratorie [*m.32*] delay; and in case eny dey intestate or that thexecutors soo named refuse to prove the saide testament then the saide ordynarie or other persone or persons havyng auctoritie to take probate of testamentes as is above saide shall graunte thadmynystracion of the goodes of the testator or persone dissessid to the

131 *eny* inserted.

wodou of the persone dissessid or to the next of his kynne or to bothe as by the discression of the same ordynarie shalbe thoght good taking suertie of hym or theme to whome shalbe made suche commission for true admynystracion of the goodes cattails and debtes whiche he or they shalbe soo auctorised to mynystre; and in case wher diverse persons clayme thadmynystracion as next of kyn the whiche be egall in degree of kinred to the testator or persone dissessed and where any persone onelie deasirethe thadmynystracion as next of kyn where in dede diverse persons be in equalite of kynred as is aforsaide then in every souch case thordynarie to be at his eleccion and libertie to except any one or moo making request wher diverse doo require thadmynystracion or wher but one or moo of theme and not all being of equalitie of degre doo make request then thordynarie to admyt the vidue and hym or theme onelie making request or eny one of theme at his pleasur taking nothing for the same but the saide some and that in maner and forme as is aforsaide; and that thexecutor and executors named by the testator or persone decessed or suche other persone or persons to whom suche admynystracion shalbe admytted wher eny person died intestate or by way of intestat calling or taking to hym or theme suche persone or persons twoo at the least to whom the saide person soo deing was indebted or made any legacie and upon their refusell or absence two other honest persons being next of kyn to the persone soo deing and in their default or absence twoo other honest persons and in their presence and by their discressions shall make or cause to be made a true and perfict inventorie of all the goodes cattails wares merchaundises aswele movable as not movable whatsooever that were of the saide persone soo discessed and the same shall cause to be endented wherof thone parte shalbe by the saide executor or executors admynystrator or[132] admynystrators upon his or their othe or othes to be taken befor the saide archebusshop busshop ordynaries their officiall or commissaries or other persone havyng power to take probate of testamentes upon tholie evaungelist to be good and true and the same one parte endented shalbe presented and delyvered into the keaping of the saide archebusshop busshop ordynarie or ordynaries or other persone or persons havyng power to take probate of testamentes and thother parte therof to remayne with thexecutor or executors admynystrator or admynystrators; and that noo archebusshop busshop ordynarie or other persone havyng auctoritie to take probat of testamentes as is above saide upon the peyne in this estatut hereafter conteyned refuse to take eny suche inventorie or inventories to hym or theme presented or tended to be delyvered as is aforsaide; and that they ne noon of theme shall procure or cause to be procured any other inventorie for the probacion or approbacion of eny testament or making

132 *admynystrator or* inserted.

any lettres or commyssion of admynystracion of the saide inventorie or inventories be presented to hym or theme or tended to be delyvered in maner and forme as is aforsaide; in whiche inventorie or inventories to be made in maner and forme as is aforsaide all corn and cattaill to be rated and valued to the same price and value as hath bene used and accustumed to be valued and preysid within the dioces of Methe in every inventorie befor this tyme made for the probacion of eny testament or making of eny commission of admynystracion; provided alway if the persone or persons so decessid will by his or their testamentes or last will eny landes tenementes or hereditamentes to be solde that the monye therof comyng nor the profictes of the saide landes for eny tyme to be taken shall not be accompted as any of the goodes or cattails of the saide person soo decessed; and that the saide archebusshop busshop ordynary or other persone or persons having auctoritie to take probate of testament or testamentes as is aforsaide[133] upon the delyveraie of the seale and sign of the testator doo cause the same seale to be defaced and there uppon incontynent to redeliver the saide seale unto the saide executor or executors admynystrator or admynystrators without clayme or chalendge therunto to be made; and in case any persone or persons at eny tyme hereafter requyre a copie or copies of the saide testamentes soo proved or of the saide inventory soo made that then the saide ordynarie or ordynaries and thother persons havyng auctoritie to take probat of testamentes or their mynystres shall from tyme to tyme with convenyent spede without eny frustratorie delaie deliver or cause to be delyvered a true copie or copies of the same to the saide person or persons soo demaundyng theme or any of theme taking for the searche and for the making and writing of every of the saide testamentes or inventories but onelie suche fee as is befor rehersed for the writing and registring of the same; provided alwaie that wher any person or persons having power or auctoritie to take probate of testamentes have used to take lasse somes of monye then is above saide for the probate of testamentes or commyssions of admynystracions and other cause concernyng the same shall take and receive suche some or somes of monye for the probate of testamentes and commissions of admynystracions and other cause concernyng the same as they befor the making of this acte have usid to take and not above; be it further enacted by auctoritie aforsaide that no archebusshop busshop ordynarie or other persone havyng eny power or auctoritie to prove or approve any testament shall compell the husbande or freende of any woman coverte to prove or approve any testament of hir husbandes goodes or shall take or receive or cause to be taken or receivid any monye or other thing for the probacion or approbacion of any testament of any woman covert or making of any commission of admynystracion for or concernyng the

133 *who* struck through.

pretensed goodes of any souche woman covert unles the saide woman covert be executor or admynystrator to eny testator decessid or otherwise have cause or title of accion wherof hir husbande after hir death have noo remedie by course of the comen lawe upon payne hereafter lymyted; and it is enacted that every archebusshop busshop ordenarie archedeacon chaunceller commyssarie official and other persone or persons havyng or the which herefter shall have auctoritie to take eny probat of testamentes their mynystres fermors registrers scribes praisers sompnors apparators and all other their officers or servauntes what soo ever they be that shall doo or attempt or cause to be doon or attempted against this acte or ordynaunce in eny thing shall forfaict and lose for every tyme soo offendyng to the partie greved in that behalfe soo moche monye as eny suche persone above said shall take contrarie to this present acte and over that shall forfaict $x^{li.}$ Irishe wherof thone moitie shalbe to the king our souveraigne lorde and thother moitie to be to the persone soo greved in that behalfe that woll sue by accion of debt bill pleynt informacion or otherwise in eny of the kinges courtes for the recoverie of the same in which accion noo essoyn proteccion ne wageor of lawe shalbe admytted or allowed; and that every of the saide archebusshops busshops and other persons whiche hereafter shall incurre or fall into the daungier of suche penaltie or forfaictur shalbe charged onelie for hym silfe and none of theme to be chargeable to that penaltie for other offences; provided alway that this present acte be not prejudiciall to eny ordynarie or other persone whiche nowe have or hereafter shall have auctoritie to take probate of testamentes but that every of theme shall may convent befor theme all and every persone or persons made and named executor or executors of eny testament to thentent to prove or refuse the testament or testamentes of their testator or testators and to bring inventories and to do every other thing concernyng the same as they myght doo befor the making of this acte soo that alwaies eny suche ordynarie or other persone or persons havyng souche auctoritie by theme silfe their commyssaries scribes registrers or other mynynstres aforsaide shall not in eny wise take for the same above the[134] fees lymyted by this acte ne in any wise attempte eny thing contrarie to eny parte of the same acte.

c.30 Thact for faculties[135]

Where in a parliament begon at London in the realme of Englande the third daie of Novembre in the xxj^{ti} yere of the reigne of our moost draid souveraigne lorde kyng Henry theight king of Englande and of Fraunce defendor of the

134 *the* repeated and struck through. 135 *Statutes at large* c.19. Draft bill (PRO, SP 60/5/62) printed in Quinn, 'Bills and statutes', pp 147–50. Transmiss dated 13 September 1535.

faithe lorde of Ireland and supreame hed in earthe of the churche of England[136] and from thens adjourned to Westminster and by diverse prorogacions there holden and contynued it was and is enacted amongest other thinges in maner and forme as followeth:[137]

Moost humblie besechen your moost royall majestie your obedient and faithfull subjectes the comens in this present parliament assemblid by your moost draid commaundement that wher your subjectes of this your realme and of other countreys and dominyons being undre your obeysaunce by many yeres past[138] have bene and yet be greatlie decaied and ympoverisshed by such intollerable exaccions of great somes of monye as have bene claymed and taken and yet contynuallie be claymed to be taken out of this your realme and other your saide countraies and dominyons by the busshop of Rome callid the pope and the see of Rome aswele in pencions cences petirpence procuracions fructes suites for provicions and expedicions of bulles for archebusshopriches and busshopriches and for delegacies and rescriptes in causes of contencions and apeles jurisdiccions legatine and also for dispensacions licences faculties grauntes relaxacions writtes callid per inde valere rehabilitacions abolicions and other infynyt sortes of bulles breves and instrumentes of sondrie naturs names and kyndes in great nombres heretofor practised and optayned otherwise than by the lawes laudable uses and custumes of this realme shulde be permytted the specialties wherof bene over longe large in nombre and tedious here particulerlie to be inserted wherin the busshop of Rome aforsaide haith not bene onelie to be blamed for his usurpacion in the premysses but alsoo for his abusion and begyling your subjectes pretending and perswading to theme that he hathe full power to dispence with all humayn lawes uses and custumes of all realmes in all causes whiche be callid spirituall whiche matier haithe bene usurped and practised by hym and his predecessours by many yeres in great derogacion of your ymperiall crowne and auctoritie royall contrarie to the right and conscience for wher this your graces realme recognysing noo superior under God but onelie youre grace [*m.33*] hathe bene and yet is free from subjeccion to any mans lawes but onelie to souche as have bene devysed made and ordeyned within this realme for the wealthe of the same or to souche other as by suffraunce of your grace and youre progenitours the people of this your realme have taken at their free libertie by their awne consent to be used amonges theme and have bounde theme selves by longe use and custome to thobservaunce of the same not as to the observaunce of the lawes of eny forreyn prynce potentate or prelate but as to thaccustumed and auncient lawes of this realme origynallie establysshed as lawes of the same by the saide suffraunce consentes and custumes and none otherwise; it standeth therfor with

136 1529. 137 25 Henry VIII c.21 (*Statutes of the realm*, iii, pp 464–71). 138 *past* inserted.

naturall equytie and good reason that in all and every souche lawes humayn made within this realme or induced into this realme by the said suffraunce consentes and custome your roiall majestie and your lordes spirituall and temporall and comens representing the hole state of your realme and this your moost highe courte of parliament have full power and auctoritie not onelie to dispence but also to auctorise some electe person or persons to dispence with those and all other humayne lawes of this your realme and with every one of theme as the qualitie of the persons and matieris shall requyre and alsoo the saide lawes and every of theme to abrogate adnull amplifie or dymynyshe as it shalbe seen to your majestie and the nobles and comens of your realme present in your parliament meat and convenyent for the wealthe of your realme as by dyverse good and holsome actes of parliament made and establisshed aswele in your tyme as in the tyme of your moost noble progenitours it may playnlie and evidentlie apere and because that it is nowe in thiese daies present seen that estate dignytie superioritie reputacion and auctoritie of the saide emperiall crowne of this realme by the longe suffraunce of the saide unreasonable and uncharitable usurpacions and exaccions practised in the tymes of your moost noble progenitours is moche and sore decaied and dymynyshed and the people of this realme therby empoveryshed and soo or worse be like to contynue if remedie be not therfor shortelie provided; it may therfor please your moost noble majestie for the honour of almyghtie Godde and for the tender love zeale and affeccion that ye beare and alwaies have borne to the wealthe of this your realme and subjectes of the same forasmoche as your majestie is supreame hed of the churche of Englande as the prelates and clergie of your realme representyng your saide churche in their synodes and convocacions have recognysed in whome consistith full power and auctoritie upon all souche lawes as have bene made and used within this realme to ordeyne and enacte by thassent of your lordes spirituall and temporall and the comens in this your present parliament assemblid and by auctoritie of the same that noo persone or persons of this your realme or of eny other your dominyons shall from hensforthe pay any pencions censes porcions petirpence or eny other ymposicions to the use of the saide bisshop or of the see of Rome like as heretofor they have used by usurpacion of the said busshop of Rome and his predecessours and suffraunce of your highnes and your moost noble progenitours to doo but that all souche pencions cences porcions and petirpence whiche the said busshop of Rome otherwise callid pope haith heretofor taken and perceived or caused to be taken and perceived to his use and his chaumbres whiche he callethe apostolicke by usurpacion and suffraunce as is above saide within this your realme or any other your dominyons shall frome hensforthe clearelie surceasse and never more be levied taken perceived nor payed to eny persone or persons in any maner of wise any constitucion use prescripcion or custome to the contrarie

therof notwithstanding; and be it further enacted by thauctorite aforsaide that neither your highnes your heyres nor successors kinges of this realme nor any your subjectes of this realme nor any of any other your dominyons shall from hensforthe sue to the saide busshop of Rome called the pope or to the see of Rome or to eny persone or persons havyng or pretending any auctoritie by the same for licences dispensacions imposicions faculties grauntes rescriptes delegacies or eny other instrumentes or writynges of what kynde name nature or qualitie so ever they be for any cause or matier for the whiche eny licence dispensacion composicion facultie graunte rescripte delegacie instrument or other writing heretofor haithe bene used and accustumed to be had and optayned at the see of Rome or by auctoritie therof or of eny prelate of this realme nor for eny maner of other licences dispensacions composicions faculties grauntes rescriptes delegacies or eny other instrumentes or writinges that in causes of necessitie may laufullie be graunted without offending of holy scriptures and lawes of God but that from hensforthe every souche licence dispensacion composicion facultie graunte rescripte delegacie instrument and other writing afor named and mencioned necessarie for your highnes your heyres and successours and your and their people and subjectes upon the due examynacions of the causes and qualities of the persons procuring suche dispensacions licences composicions faculties grauntes rescriptes delegacies instrumentes or other writinges shalbe graunted had and optayned from tyme to tyme within this your realme and other your dominions and not elswhere in maner and forme following and none otherwise that is to saye the archebusshop of Canterburie for the tyme being and his successors shall have power and auctoritie from tyme to tyme by their discressions to yeve graunt and dispose by an instrument under the seale of the saide archebusshop unto your majestie and to your heyres and successors kinges of this realme aswele all maner suche licences dispensacions composicions faculties grauntes rescriptes delegacies instrumentes and all other writinges for causes not being contrarie or repugnaunt to tholie scriptures and lawes of God as heretofor haithe bene used and accustumed to be had and optayned by your highnes or eny your moost noble progenitours or any of your or their subjectes at the see of Rome or any persone or persones by auctoritie of the same and all other licences dispensacions faculties composicions grauntes rescriptes delegacies instrumentes and other writinges in for and upon all souche causes and matiers as shalbe convenyent and necessarie to be had for the honour and suyrtie of your highnes your heyres and successors and the wealthe and proficte of this your roialme soo that the said archebusshop or any his successors in noo maner wise shall graunte any dispensacion licence rescripte or eny other writing afor rehersed for eny cause or matier repugnaunt to the lawes of almyghtie God; be it alsoo enacted by auctoritie aforsaide that the saide archebusshop and his successors after

good and due examynacions by theme had of the causes and qualities of the persons procuring for licences dispensacions composicions faculties delegacies rescriptes instrumentes or other writinges shall have full power and auctoritie by theme selves or by their sufficient and substanciall commyssarie or deputie by their discressions from tyme to tyme to graunt and dispose by an instrument undre the name and seale of the saide archebusshop aswele to eny of your subjectes as to the subjectes of your heyres and successors all maner licences dispensacions faculties composicions delegacies rescriptes instrumentes or other writinges for eny suche cause or matier wherof heretofor souche licences dispensacions composicions faculties delegacies rescriptes instrumentes or writinges have bene accusumed to be had at the see of Rome or by auctoritie therof or of eny prelate of this realme and that the saide archebusshop and his commyssarie shall not graunt any other licence dispensacion composicion facultie writyng or instrument in causes unwont and not accustumed to be had or optayned at the courte of Rome nor by auctoritie therof nor by any prelate of this realme untill your grace your heyres or successors or your or their counsaile shall furst be advertised therof and determyn whether souche licences dispensacions composicions faculties or other writinges in suche causes unwont and not accustumed to be dispenced withall or optayned shall comenlie passe as other dispensacions faculties or other writinges shall or may upon payne that the graunters of every such licence dispensacion or writing in souche causes unwont contrarie to this acte shall make fyne at the will and pleasur of your grace your heyres and successors and if it be thought and determyned by your grace your heyres or successors or your or their counsaill that dispensacions faculties licences or other writinges in any souche causes wnwonte shall passe then the saide archbusshop or his commyssarie havyng licence of your highnes your heyrs or successors for the same by your or their bill assigned shall dispence with theme accordinglie; provided alwaies that noo maner of dispensacions licences faculties or other rescriptes or writynges hereafter to be graunted to eny persone or persons by vertue or auctoritie of this acte by the saide archebusshop or his commyssarie being of souche ymportaunce that the taxe for thexpedicion therof at Rome extended to the some of iiij$^{li.}$ or above shall in any wise be put in execucion til the same licence dispensacion facultie rescript or other writing of what name or nature soo every it be furst confirmed by your highnes your heyres and successors kinges of this realme undre the great seale and enrollid in your chauncerie in a roll by a clerc to be appoynted for the same and that this acte shalbe sufficient waraunte to the chaunceller of Englande for the tyme being or to hym whom your grace your heyres or successors shall depute to be keaper of the great seale to conferme in your name your heyres or successors the forsaide writynges passed under the saide archebusshops seale by lettres patentes in due forme therof to be made

under your great seale remyttyng aswele the said writing under tharchebusshops seale as the saide confirmacion under the great seale to the parties from tyme to tyme procuring for the same and that all souche licences dispensacions faculties and other rescriptes and writinges for thexpedicion of the whiche the saide taxes to be payed at Rome was undre iiij$^{li.}$ whiche be matiers of noo great importaunce shall passe onelie by tharchebusshops seale and shall not of eny necessitie be confyrmed by the great seale unlesse the procurers of souche licence facultie or dispensacion deasire to have theme soo confirmed in whiche case they shall pay for the said[139] great seale to the use of your highnes your heyres and successors v$^{s.}$ sterling and not above over and beside souch taxe as shalbe hereafter lymyted for the making writing registring confirmyng and enrolling of souche licences confirmacions and writinges under the said taxe of iiij$^{li.}$ and that every souche licence dispensacion composicion facultie rescripte and writing of what name or nature soo ever it be for souche causes as the taxe was wont to be iiij$^{li.}$ or above soo [*m.34*] graunted by the archebusshop and confirmed undre the great seale and all other licences dispensacions faculties rescriptes and writinges hereafter to be graunted by tharchebusshop by vertue and auctoritie of this acte wherunto the great seale is not lymyted of necessitie to be put to by reason that the taxe of theme is undre iiij$^{li.}$ shalbe accepted approved alloued and admytted good and effectuall in the lawe in all places courtes and jurisdiccions aswele spirituall as temporall within this realme and elswher within your dominions and as beneficiall to the persons optayning the same as they shulde have bene if they had bene opteyned with all thinges requisite of the see of Rome or of eny other persone by auctoritie therof without eny revocacion or repeale hereafter to be had of eny suche licences dispensacions faculties rescriptes or writinges of what nature soo ever they be and that all children procreated after solempnyzacion of any mariages to be had or doone by vertue of suche licences or dispensacions shalbe admytted reputed and taken legittymate in all courtes aswele spirituall as temporall and in all other places and enherite thenheritaunce of their parentes and auncestors within this your realme and all other your dominions according to the lawes and custumes of the same and all actes to be doone had or executed according to the teanor of souch licences dispensacions faculties writinges or other instrumentes to be made or graunted by auctoritie of this acte shalbe ferme permanent and remayne in force any forreyn lawes constitucions decrees canons decretals inhibicions use custume prescripcion or any other thing had or hereafter to be made to the contrarie notwithstondyng; and be it further enacted that the saide archebusshop and his successors shall have power and auctoritie to ordeyne make and constitute a clerc whiche shall write

139 *said* inserted.

and register every suche licence dispensacion facultie writing or other instrument to be graunted by the saide archebusshop and shall fynde parchement wax and silken leases convenyent for the same and shall have for his peynes suche somes of monye as shalbe hereafter in this present acte to hym lymyted in that behalfe for the same; and that likewise your grace your heyres and successors shall by your lettres patentes undre your great seale ordeyne depute and constitute one sufficient clerc being lerned in the course of chauncerie whiche alwaies shalbe attendaunt upon the lorde chaunceller or the lorde keaper of the great seale for the tyme being and shall make write and enrolle the confirmacions of all souche licences dispensacions instrumentes and other writinges as shalbe thidther brought undre tharchebusshops seale there to be confirmed and enrolled[140] and shall alsoo entitle in his bokes and enrolle of recorde souche other writinges as thidther shalbe brought undre tharchbusshops seale not to be confirmed taking for his paynes souche reasonable somes of monye as hereafter by this acte to hym shalbe lymyted for the same and that aswele the said clerc apointed by the saide archebusshop as the saide clerc to be apointed by your highnes your heyres or successors shall subscribe their names to every suche licence dispensacion facultie or other writing that shall come to their handes to be written made graunted sealed confirmed registred and enrolled by auctoritie of this acte in forme as is befor rehersed; and forasmoche as the charges of the optaynyng of the said licences dispensacions faculties and other rescriptes or writinges afor named at the courte of Rome by the losses exchaunges and in conducting of currors and wageyng solicitors to sue for eny souche licences dispensacions faculties instrumentes and other rescriptes or writynges have bene grevouse and excessive to your people and many tymes greatter somes have bene demaunded for the spedie expedicion in the courte of Rome than be expressed in tholde tax lymyted to be payed for the saide expedicions wherby your people have bene brought to an uncertaintie upon the payment for expedicions of souche thinges and by reason therof have bene constrayned to pay more then they were wont to do to the great ympoverisshing of this realme as is aforsaide and some tymes the speding of suche dispensacions faculties licences and other writinges at Rome have bene soo longe differred that the parties lauboryng for the same have suffred great incommodities and losses for lacke of quycke spede whiche hereafter may be had within this your realme to the great commoditie of your people wherby the charges of makyng exchaunges conductyng of currors and solicitors for the saide dispensacions shalbe abbated and your people soo moche releved and eased to thentent that all ambiguitie and incertaintie of paymentes for dispensacions faculties licences and other rescriptes and writinges may be taken awaie

140 *and enrolled* inserted.

that noo fraude or exaccion shalbe excercised upon your people by souche officers as shalbe appoynted by this acte to take paynes in spedyng souche dispensacions faculties and licences but that your people may be suer and certayne what they be appoynted to paye for the same; be it enacted by this present parliament and by thauctoritie of the same that there shalbe ij bokes drawen and made of oon teanor in whiche shalbe conteyned the taxes of all custumable dispensacions faculties licences and other writinges wont to be sped at Rome whiche bookes and every lefe of those bokes and bothe sides of every leafe shalbe subscribed by tharchebusshop of Canterburie the lorde chaunceller of England the lorde thesaurer of Englonde and their chief justices of bothe the benches for the tyme being to the whiche bookes all suitors for dispensacions faculties licences and other writinges afor rehersed shall have recourse if they requyre it and oon of the said bookes shall remayne in the handes of hym whiche shalbe apoynted to be registrer and scribe of the saide dispensacions faculties and licences undre the saide archebusshop of Canterburie in forme as is befor saide and thother boke shall remayne with the clerc of the chauncerie whiche by your grace your heyres or successors shalbe apoynted as is befor rehersed whiche clerc of the chauncerie shall alsoo entitle and note particulerly and dailie in his boke ordeyned for that purpose the nombre and qualitie of the dispensacions faculties licences and other rescriptes and writinges whiche shalbe sealed oonlie with the seale of the said archebusshop and also which shalbe sealed withe the saide seale and confirmed wtih the great seale in forme as is aforsaide that all fraude and concelement in this behalfe may be avoided; and be it enacted by this present parliament and by thauctoritie of the same that noo man suyng for dispensacions faculties licences or other rescriptes or writinges whiche were wont to be sped at Rome shall pay noo more for their dispensacions faculties licences or rescriptes then shalbe conteyned taxed and lymyted in the saide duplicate bokes of taxes (onelie composicions excepted) of whiche being arbitrarie noo tax can be made wherfor the tax therof shalbe set and lymyted by the discression of the saide archebusshop of Canterburie and the lorde chaunceller of Englande or the lorde keaper of the great seale for the tyme being and that souche as shall exacte or receive of eny suitor more for eny dispensacion facultie or licence then shalbe conteyned in the saide bokes of taxes shall forfaicte x tymes asmoche as he shall soo extorciouselie exacte and receive thone halfe of the whiche forfaicture to be to the use of your grace your heyres or successors and thother halfe therof to be to souche of your subjectes as woll sue for the same by accion bill or playnte in any of your graces courtes wherin the defendaunt shall have no essoyne or proteccion allowed neither shalbe admytted to wage his lawe; be it alsoo enacted by this parliament and auctoritie of the same that the taxe or some apoynted to be payed for every souche dispensacion licence facultie instrument rescripte or other writing to be

graunted by auctoritie of this acte shalbe emploied and ordrid as hereafter ensueth that is to saie if the taxe extende to iiij$^{li.}$ or above by reason wherof the dispensacion licence facultie rescript or writyng whiche shall passe by the saide archebusshops seale most be confirmed by thappencion of the great seale then the saide taxe soo extending to iiij$^{li.}$ or above shalbe devided into iij partes wherof ij shalbe perceived by the saide clerc of the chauncerie to be apoynted as is aforsaide to the use of your highnes your heyres and successors and to the use of the lorde chaunceller or the keaper of the great seale for the tyme being and to the use of the said clerc in souche wise as hereafter shalbe declared and the third parte shalbe taken by the saide clerc of tharchebusshop to the use of the same archebusshop and his commyssarie and the saide clerc and registrer in souche wise as hereafter shalbe ordred and lymyted by this acte that is to saie the saide ij partes shalbe devided in iiij partes of whiche iij partes shalbe taken to thoonlie use of your highnes your heyres and successors and the iiijth parte shalbe devyded in iij partes wherof the chaunceller of England or lorde keaper of the great seale for the tyme being shall have ij partes and the saide clerc of the chauncerie the iij^{de} parte for his paynes travailes and labours that he is lymyted to write and doo by vertue of this acte and the saide iij^{de} parte of thole taxe apoynted to the saide archebusshop and his officers as is aforsaide shalbe devided in iij partes wherof thearchebusshop shall have to his use ij partes and his officers shall have the iij^{de} parte therof of whiche iij^{de} parte to be devided ij partes the saide clerc or registrer whiche shall fynde parchement wax and sylke and shall devise and write the saide [*m.35*] dispensacions licences faculties rescriptes or other writinges and register the same shall have for his saide labour and for receiving and repayeng of the somes of monye that shall come to his handes for dispensacions faculties licences and other rescriptes aforsaide the one moitie therof and the commyssarie of the saide archebusshop apoynted to seale the same dispensacions faculties licences and rescriptes shall have thother parte; and if the taxe be under iiij$^{li.}$ and not undre xl$^{s.}$ then the saide taxe shalbe devided into iij partes as is aforsaide wherof the kinges highnes his heyres and successors shall have ij partes wherof abating iij$^{s.}$ iiij$^{d.}$ whiche shalbe to the saide clerc of the chauncerie for subscribing entitling and enrolling the saide dispensacions licences faculties rescriptes and other writinges aforsaide and receiving of the kinges monye soo taxed and tharchebusshop and his officers shall have the iij^{de} parte whiche iij^{de} parte shalbe devided into ij partes wherof tharchebusshop shall have thoon intierlie to hym silf his scribe and commyssarie thother parte therof egallie to be devided amongest theme for their costes and paynes in that behalfe; and if the taxe be undre xl$^{s.}$ and not undre xxvj$^{s.}$ viij$^{d.}$ the same taxe shalbe devided into ij partes wherof thone parte shalbe unto your grace your heyres and successors deducting therof for the clerc of the chauncerie twoo shillinges for his paynes as is aforsaide and

thother parte shalbe to the saide archbusshop and his officers whiche other parte shalbe devyded into twoo partes wherof tharchebusshop shall have thooone and his commyssarie and scribe shall have thother egallie devided amongest theme; and if the taxe be undre xxvj$^{s.}$ viij$^{d.}$ and not undre xx$^{s.}$ the same shalbe devided in twoo partes wherof your grace your heyres and successors shall have thone parte intierlie abating ij$^{s.}$ therof to the saide clerc of the chauncerie and tharchebusshop and his officers shall have thother parte and the same other parte shalbe devided into iij partes wherof the archebusshop shall have one his commissarie the seconde and his scribe or registrer the iij^{de}; and in case the taxe be undre xx$^{s.}$ the same shalbe perceived to the use of the saide commissarie clerc of the saide archebisshop and clerc of the chauncerie to be egallie devided amongest theme for their paynes and labours by theme to be susteyned by auctoritie of this acte as is aforsaide; provided alwaies that this acte shall not be prejudiciall to tharchebusshop of Yorke or to eny busshop or prelate of this realme but that they may laufullie notwithstonding this acte dispence in all causes in whiche they were wont to dispence by the comen lawe or custume of this realme afor the making of this acte; provided alsoo and be it enacted by auctoritie aforsaide that if it happen the see of tharchebusshopriche of Canterburie to be voide that then all souche maner of licences dispensacions faculties instrumentes rescriptes and other writinges whiche may be graunted by vertue and auctoritie of this acte shall during the vacacion of the same see be had done and graunted undre the name and seale of the gardian of the spiritualities of the said archebusshopriche for the tyme being according to the teanor and forme of this acte and shalbe of like force value and effecte as if they had bene graunted undre the name and seale of tharchebusshop for the tyme being; and be it further enacted that if the forsaide archebusshop of Canterburie for the tyme being or the saide gardian of the spiritualities for the tyme being hereafter refuse or denaie to graunte any licences faculties dispencacions instrumentes or other writinges whiche they be auctorised to do by vertue and auctoritie of this acte in suche maner and forme as is afor remembrid to any persone or persones that hathe a good just and reasonable cause to have the same by reason wherof this present acte by their wilfulnes necligence or defaulte shulde take none effecte then the chaunceller of Englande or the lorde keaper of the great seale for the tyme beyng upon eny complaynt therof made shall directe the kinges writ to the saide archebusshop or gardiane denayeng or refusing to graunte suche licences dispensacions faculties or other writinges enyoynyng hym by the saide writ upon a certayn payne therin to be lymyted by the discression of the saide lorde chaunceller or keaper of the great seale that he shall in due forme graunt souche licence dispensacion facultie or other writing according to the request of the procurers of the same or els signifie unto youre highnes your heyres and successors in the courte of chauncerie

at a certeyne day for what occasion or cause he refused and denaied to graunte suche licences faculties or dispensacions and if it shall apere to the saide lorde chaunceller or lorde keaper of the great seale upon souche certificate that the cause of refusell or denyall of grauntyng souche licences faculties or dispensacions was reasonable juste and good that then soo being proved by due searche and examynacion of the saide chaunceller or lorde keaper of the great seale to be admytted and alloued and if it shall appere upon the saide certificate that the saide archebusshop or gardian of spiritualities for the tyme being of wilfulnes in contempnyng the due execucion of this acte without a juste and reasonable cause refused or denaied to graunte souche licences faculties or dispensacions that then your highnes your heyres and successors beyng therof enformed after due examynacion had that souche licences faculties or dispensacions may be graunted without offending the holie scriptures and lawes of God shall have power and auctoritie in every souche cause for the defaulte necligence and wilfulnes of the saide archebusshop or gardyan to sende your writ of injunccion undre your great seale oute of your saide courte of chauncerie commaunding the saide archebusshop or gardian that soo shall denaie or refuse to graunte souche licence facultie or dispensacion to make sufficient graunte therof according to the teanor and effecte of this acte by a certeyn daie and undre a certaine payne in the saide writ to be conteyned and to be lymyted by your highnes your heyres and successors kinges of this realme and if the saide archebusshop or gardian after the receipt of the saide writ refuse or denay to graunte suche licences faculties or dispensacions as shalbe enyoyned hym by vertue of the saide writ and shewe and prove befor your majestie your heyres or successors noo juste or reasonable cause why he shulde soo do then the saide archebusshop or gardiane that soo shall refuse to put this acte in execucion according to the saide writ of injunccion shall suffre lose and forfaict to your highnes your heyres or successors souche peyne and penaltie as shalbe lymyted and expressed in the saide writ of injunccion and over that it shall be laufull to your highnes your heyres and successors for every suche defaulte and wilfulnes of the saide archebusshop or gardiane for the tyme being to yeve power and auctoritie by commyssion undre your great seale to suche ij spirituall prelates or persons to be named by your highnes your heyres or successors as woll doo and graunte souche licences faculties and dispensacions refused or denaied to be graunted by the saide archebusshop or gardian in comtempte of this acte; and be it further enacted by auctorite aforsaide that the saide ij spirituall prelates or persons to whom in souche cases any souche commission shalbe directed shall have power and auctoritie to graunte every souche licence facultie dispensacion instrument and other writinges soo refused to be graunted by the saide archebusshop or gardian for the tyme being by an ynstrument under their seales taking like fees and charges for the same as is

befor rehersed and not above under the payne above remembred and that every suche licence facultie and dispensacion soo graunted for any causes or matiers wherunto any confirmacion undre the kinges great seale is appoynted by this acte to be had in maner and forme above declared shalbe had and optayned accordynglie and souche licences and confirmacions shalbe had for like fees and charges as they are above specified and not above undre the paynes above mencioned and that every souche licence facultie dispensacion and other writing to be graunted by the saide prelates or persones to be assigned by the kinges highnes his heyres and successors as is aforsaide shalbe of as good value strenght and effecte and as beneficiall and profictable to the persons procuring the same as if they had bene made graunted and optayned undre the name and seale of the saide archebusshop; provided alwaies that this acte nor any thinge or thinges therin mencioned shalbe hereafter interpreted or expounded that your grace your nobles and subjectes entende by the same to declyne or varie from the congregacion of Christes churche in any thinges concernyng the veraie articles of the catholicke faithe of Christendome or in any other thinges declarid by holie scriptures and the worde of Good necesarie for your and their salvacions but onelie to make an ordynaunce by polecies necessarie and convenyent to represse vice and for good conservacion of this realme in peaux unitie and tranquilitie from ravyne and spoile ensuyng moche tholde auncient custumes of this realme in that behalfe not mynding to seke for eny reliefes succours or remedies for eny wordlie thinges and humayne lawes in any cause of necessitie but within this realme at the handes of your highnes your heyres and successors kinges of this realme whiche have and ought to have an emperiall power and auctoritie in the same and not obliged in any worldlie causes to eny [*m.36*] other superior; provided alwaie that the saide archebusshop of Canterburie or any other persone or persones shall have noo powere or auctoritie by reason of this acte to visite or vexe any monastery abbaies priories colledges hospitals houses or other places religiouse whiche be or were exempte before the making of this acte any thing in this acte to the contrarie therof mencioned notwithstondyng but that redresse visitacion and confirmacion shalbe had by the kinges highnes his heyres and successors by commyssion undre the great seale to be directed to souche persones as shalbe apointed requisit for the same in souche monasteries colledges hospitals priories houses and places religious exempt soo that noo visitacion nor confirmacion shall from hensforthe be had or made in or at any souche monasteries colledges hospitals priories houses and places religious exempted by the said busshop of Rome nor by eny of his auctoritie ne by eny oute of the kinges dominions nor that eny persone religious or other resiaunt in any the kinges dominions shall from henseforthe departe oute of the kinges dominions to or for eny visitacion congregacion or assemble for religion but that all suche visitacions congregacions

and assemblees shalbe within the kinges dominions; provided alsoo that this present acte or eny thing therin conteyned or any licence or dispensacion hereafter to be made by vertue and auctoritie therof shall not extende to the repeale or derogacion of the late acte made sethens the begynnyng of this presente parliament for the reformacion of pluralities of benefices and for none residence of spirituall persones upon their dignities or benefices nor to eny thinges conteyned or mencioned in the saide acte nor that this acte nor any thing to be doon by auctoritie therof shall not be taken expounded nor interpreted to yeve licence to eny persone or persons to have eny more nomber of benefices then is lymyted in the saide acte and that the same acte for pluralities and none residence of benefices and every thing therin conteyned shall stonde good and effectuall in all ententes according to the true meanyng therof any thing in this present acte or any licence or dispensacion to be had by auctoritie therof in any wise notwithstondyng; and be it further enacted by auctoritie aforsaide that if eny persone or persones subjecte or resiaunt within this realme or within any the kinges domynyons at eny tyme hereafter sue to the courte of Rome or the see of Rome or to any persone claymyng to have his auctoritie by the same for eny licence facultie dispensacion or other thing or thinges contrarie to this acte or put in execucion any licence facultie or dispensacion or any other thing or thinges hereafter to be optayned from Rome or the see of Rome or from any claymyng auctoritie by the same for any of the causes above mencioned in this acte or for eny other causes that may be graunted by auctoritie of this acte or attempte or do any thing or thinges contrarie to this acte or maynteyne alloue admyt or obey any maner of censures excommunicacions interdiccions or any other proces from Rome of what name or nature soo ever it be to the derogacion or let of thexecucion of this acte or of any thing or thinges to be doon by reason of the saide acte that then every souche persone or persones soo doyng offending and being therof convicte their aidors counsaillours and abbettors shall incurre and ron into the payne losse and penaltie comprised and specified in thacte of provision and premunire made in the xvj yere of your moost noble progenitour king Richarde the seconde[141] agaynst souche as sued the courte of Rome against your crowne and dignitie roiall; provided alwaie that this acte or any thing therin conteyned shall not hereafter be taken nor expounded to the derogacion or taking away of any grauntes or confirmacions of any liberties priveledges or jurisdiccion of any monasteries abbaies priories or other houses or places exempt whiche heretofor the making of this acte haithe bene optayned at the see of Rome or by auctoritie therof but that every souche graunte and confirmacion shalbe of the same value force and effecte as they were afor the making of this acte and as if this acte had never bene made; provided alwaies

141 1393. 16 Richard II c.5 (*Statutes of the realm*, ii, pp 84–6).

that the abbotes priores and other chief rulers and governours of souche monasteries abbaies priories and other houses and places exempt shall not hereafter pay any pencion porcion or other sence to the see of Rome nor admyt nor accepte any visitacion nor any confirmacion from or by the saide see of Rome or by auctoritie therof or for eny persone to be electe named or presented to be heddes of any souche monasteries abbayes priories places or houses exempte nor shall make eny corporall othe to the busshop of Rome otherwise called the pope upon paynes lymyted in this acte but that every souche visitacion and confirmacion of suche heddes elect in any souche monasteries abbaies priories houses or places exempt where after eleccion they were bounden to have and optayne any confirmacion of their eleccion or of the persone named presentid or electe shalbe from hensforthe had made and done within this realme at and within every souche abbaies monasteries priories and other houses and places exempte by souche persone or persones as shalbe appoynted by auctoritie of the kinges commyssion from tyme to tyme as the cace shall requyre and not by the see of Rome nor by auctoritie therof any thing in this next proviso above specified to the contrarie therof notwithstonding; provided alwaies that in souche monasteries abbaies priories and houses exempt where after eleccion presentacion or nominacion of their heddes noo souche confirmacion is requisit to be had nor haithe bene used to be taken by reason of souche priviledges as they have concerning the same that in every souche monasteries abbaies priories and places exempte they shall not be bounden to optayne have or take any confirmacion for the same within this realme by auctoritie of this acte but use their priveledges therin as they have doon befor the making of this acte any thing in this acte or any the provisoes next above rehersed to the contrarie therof notwithstonding; provided alsoo and be it enacted that this acte or eny thing or thinges worde or wordes therin or in the preamble therof mencioned or conteyned is not entended or ment nor shalbe expounded nor interpreted that any dispensacions licences or confirmacions for mariages graunted to any the kinges subjectes borne undre his obeysaunce at eny tyme before the xij daye of Marche in the yere of our lorde God M v^{c} xxxiij^{ti} shalbe appeyred or of any less value strenght force or effecte then they were at the saide xij daie of Marche nor that this acte or any thing therin conteyned shall not extende to the derogacion appeyring or adnullacion of any licences dispensacions confirmacions faculties or indulgences at eny tyme before the saide xij daie of Marche in the yere of our lorde God M v^{c} xxxiij had or opteyned at the see of Rome or by auctoritie therof to or for eny subjectes borne in this realme or in any the kinges dominions or to or for the hospitall of the prior of saynct Johns Jerusalem in Englande or any commaundrees [*m.37*] or membres therof or to or for any cathedrall churches hospitals monasteries abbayes priories colleges conventuall churches parochiall churches

chapels fraternyties brotherheddes or bodies politicque within this realme or in any other the kinges dominions but that every souche licence dispensacion confirmacion faculty and indulgence graunted befor the saide xij daie of Marche to any souche subjecte or to the saide hospitall of the prior of sainct Johns Jerusalem in Englande and commaundres or membres therof or to any other cathedrall churche hospitall monasterie abbaie priorie colledge churche coventuall parochiall churche chapel fraternitie brotherhed or bodie politicque or to their predecessours or auncestors within this realme or in any other the kinges dominions shalbe of the same force strenght value and effect and may be from tyme to tyme put in execucion at all tymes hereafter by and to theme that woll have the same as they moght have bene afor the making of this acte and as if this acte had never bene had or made any thing in the said acte to the contrarie hereof notwithstonding; provided alwayes that souche licences dispensacions confirmacions or faculties heretofore opteyned at the see of Rome or by auctoritie therof contrarie to thexpresse provicions of the lawes and statutes of this realme heretofore made shall not at eny tyme hereafter be used or put in execucion in eny place to the derogacion or contrarie to the saide lawes and statutes of this realme and the provisions of the same any thing in this proviso to the contrarie therof notwithstonding; and be it enacted by auctoritie of this present parliament that the king our souveraigne lorde by thadvise of his honourable counsaill shall have power and auctoritie from tyme to tyme for the ordering redresse and[142] reformacion of all maner of indulgences and priveledges therof within this realme or within any the kinges domynyons heretofore optayned at the see of Rome or by auctoritie therof and if thabuses of souche indulgences and priveledges therof as shall seame good holsome and reasonable for thonour of God and weale of his people and that souche ordre and redresse as shalbe taken by his highnes in that behalfe shalbe observed and fermelie kepte upon the paynes lymyted in this acte for thoffendyng of the contentes of the same.

Forasmoche as it is mencioned in the saide acte that theffectes therof shoulde not onelie extend into the realme of Englande and to the commoditie therof and of the subjectes of the same but alsoo to all other the kinges dominions and his subjectes and that this the kinges lande of Irelande is his proper dominion and a membre appending and rightfullie belongyng to themperiall crowne of the saide realme of Englande and united to the same and alsoo like inconveniences hathe ensued within this lande of Irlande as haith bene within the saide realme of Englande by reason of the usurpacion of the busshop of Rome like as is mencioned in the saide acte be it therfor enacted by auctoritie of this present parliament that the saide acte and every thing and thinges therin

142 *and* inserted.

conteyned shalbe establisshed affirmed taken obeyed and accepted within this lande of Irlande as a good and perfict lawe and shalbe within the said lande of the same force effecte qualitie condicion strenght and vertue to all purposes and ententes as it is within the realme of Englande and that all subjectes and resiauntes within this saide lande of Irelande shall observe keape obey accomplishe and execute theffectes and contentes specified in the saide acte in like maner and forme as the subjectes of the saide realme of England bene bounden by auctoritie of the same acte and shall have and enyoie the profict and commoditie therof after like maner forme and condicion as the kinges subjectes of the saide realme of England use doo and have the same and upon like paynes and penalties as be comprised in the saide acte and that all maner licences dispensacions faculties or other writinges optayned by eny subject or resiaunt within this lande by auctoritie of the saide acte shalbe obeyed and executed within this lande and be good and effectuall to all ententes and purposes according to the teanor and effectes therof; provided alwaie that this acte shall not be prejudiciall to eny archebisshop busshop or prelat of this lande but that they may laufullie notwithstonding this acte dispence in all causes in whiche they were wont to dispence by reason onelie of their awne proper offices and dignities by the comen lawe or custome of this lande befor the makyng of this acte; and be it further enacted by auctoritie aforsaide that all and every persone and persones auctorised and appointed or to be hereafter auctorised and appointed by the kinges highnes his heyres and successors by commyssion undre his great seale for the using excercising and occupieng of any jurisdiccion ecclesiasticall or geving or grauntyng of any faculties licences dispensacions or other thing or thinges mencioned or comprised in this acte or eny parte therof shall have the same and like auctoritie to every purpose meanyng and entent for the using excercising occupieng yeving and grauntyng of the same and every parte therof as tharchebusshop of Canterburie and his successors for the tyme being haithe or shall have by eny maner auctoritie other within the saide realme of England or this lande of Irland and that the chaunceller of this lande for the tyme being and all other persons required and appointed by the forme of this acte to execut any thing for the perfeccion of the same shall have like and the same auctoritie that the chaunceller of England and all other persons have by auctoritie of this acte within the realme of Englonde any forreyn lawe auctoritie usage or prescripcion or any thing in this acte mencioned to the contrarie notwithstonding.

c.31 Thact declaryng the repeale of Ponynges acte[143]

Prayen the lordes spirituall and temporall and the comens in this present parliament assembled that wheras in the furst cession of this present parliament holden here at Dublin the furst daie of Maij in the xxviij^{ti} yere of our moost draid souveraigne lorde the king that nowe is[144] it was enacted by thauctorite of the same[145] that every acte ordnaunce provision thing or thinges of what nature name condicion or qualitie they were of had doon made or establisshed or after that in the same parliament to be had made or establisshed by auctoritie therof shulde be good and effectuall to all ententes and purposes according to the teanor and effecte of the forsaide actes ordynaunces and provisions thact made at Drogheda in the parliament there holden the Monday next after the feast of saynt Andrewe in the xth yere of the moost noble kyng of famous memorie king Henry the vijth[146] befor Sir Edwarde Ponynges knyght then being deputie of this lande or any other acte or actes use or custome befor the saide acte made the saide furst day of Maij the same xxviij^{ti} yere had doone or made within this lande to the contrarie of the same acte in the same xxviij yere of our souveraigne lorde the king that nowe is notwithstonding wherin it was alsoo provided and enacted that by force and vertue of that acte ne any thing therin conteyned no acte ordenaunce provision thing or thinges of what nature name condicion or qualitie so ever it were of for any maner lordships landes tenementes advousons abbaies [*m.38*] priories selles or any other hereditamentes what soo ever they were for or betwene any persone or persons bodie or bodies politicque or corporat or any other particuler acte ordenaunce or provision or any other acte ordynaunce or provision that shoulde be prejudiciall hurtfull or in derogacion of any grauntes or liberties fraunchesses usages custumes or any other commodities or priveledges geven or graunted by our souveraigne lorde the king or his noble progenytors to any citie or borrowe towne within this lande of Irlande shoulde be enacted or establisshed by vertue or auctoritie of the same parliament but onelie souche actes ordenaunces and provisions thing or thinges as shoulde be thought expedient for our souveraigne lorde the kinges honour thencrease of his graces revenues and proufict and the comen wealthe of this his lande and dominion of Irlande as at large is expressed and declarid in the saide acte and forasmoche as uppon the last clause of the saide provision in the saide acte that is to say that noo acte ne actes but onelie souche actes ordenaunces and provisions thing or thinges as shoulde be thought expedient for our souveraigne lorde the kynges honour thencrease of his graces revenues and proficit and the comen weale of this his lande and dominion of Irlande diverse and sondrie argumentes alreddie have bene moved and styrred soo that

143 *Statutes at large* c.20. 144 1536. 145 Above, c.4. 146 1494.

the same acte being in souche a copulatife every acte ordenaunce and provision had enacted and made sethens the saide acte or hereafter to be had or made in this parliament shoulde be aswele for the kinges honour and profict as alsoo for the comen wealthe or otherwise souche acte made or enacted shoulde be voide and of none effecte where as the mere trouthe is the true myndes and ententes of us thordyners devisers and makers of the same acte and provision was that all actes made or to be made in this parliament either for the kynges honour or for thencrease of his graces revenues or profictes or yet for the comen weale of this saide lande shoulde be good and effectuall and the same shoulde be expoundid ment interpretated and taken that if any parte therof or actes or provisions were made or ordeyned or shoulde be made or ordeyned in this present parliament whiche sounded and were either for the kinges honour his proficte or encrease of his graces revenues or els for the comen wealthe shoulde be accepted reputed and taken for good profictable actes ordynaunces and provisions any acte or actes to the contrarie befor theme made and ordeyned notwithstondyng; for the more playner explanacion exposicion and true declaracion of our ententes and myndes the makers of the saide acte and provision be it enacted and establisshed by auctoritie of this present parliament that the saide acte and provision shalbe taken interpetrated explaned and expounded in souche sorte and forme that every acte and actes ordynaunce and provision made and to be made in this present parliament whiche toutcheth and concerneth either the kinges highnes is honour and profict or encrease of his revenues or otherwis concerneth the comen wealthe of this his lande and dominion of Irlande shalbe good effectuall and available in the lawe according to the purporte and teanor of the same acte ordenaunce and provision any acte statute ordenaunce provision interpretacion construccion and opynyon to the contrarie befor this tyme made ordeyned or provided notwithstonding; and be it further ordeyned and enacted by auctoritie aforsaid that if any persone or persones at eny tyme hereafter arrogantlie wilfullie and obstynatelie by way of suit accion plee or aunswere in any courte within this lande after notice of this acte to hym made by any the judge or judges of any souche courte sittyng in judgement wher souche suit or accion shalbe commensed doo attempte to adnychillat or avoide this parliament or any acte ordynaunce or provision in the same parliament made or to be made whiche at the tyme of making of the same doeth or dud concerne either the kinges honour profict or encrease of his graces revenues or els the comen wealthe of this his lande and dominion of Irlande that every souche person and persones soo attempting to adnichillat avoide and make frustrat any souche acte actes ordenaunces or provisions made or to be made in this present parliament in forme aforsaide being therof laufullie convicte shalbe reputed accepted and taken as a felon and suffre souche penalties forfaicturs and losses as felons being laufullie convicte shall suffre and

lose by the course of the comen lawe[147]; and be it further enacted by auctoritie aforsaide that every souche suite accion and plee to be sued or pled befor eny justice or in any courte within this lande shall not in any wise be allowable but voide and of noon effecte in lawe; and alsoo be it enacted by like auctoritie that this acte shall extende to the corroborating and making effectuall of all actes ordenaunces and provision had or made or to be had or made sethens the furst daie of this parliament til the last daie of this cession whiche shalbe for the kinges honour or for the encrease of his graces revenues or profictes or for the comen wealthe of this lande and none otherwise any thing or thinges in this acte or in any other acte or actes to the contrarie had or provided notwithstonding.

c.32 Thact for the libertie of the towne of Wexforde

Forasmoche as by the lordes of the late libertie of Wexforde a suffrayne and two bailifes within the borrowe or towne of Wexforde was incorporated and establisshed to be and remayne in succession yerelie to be elected and chosen by the burgeses and inhabitauntes of the saide borowe or towne of Wexforde from tyme to tyme and diverse liberties and priveledges jurisdiccions custumes and other thinges and profictes was yeven and graunted by some of the lordes of the saide late libertie for the tyme being to theme by the name of suffrayn and bailives or by the name of suffrayne bailives and burgeses or by the name of suffrayn bailives burgeses and comens which by divers of the lordes of the saide late libertie was and be ratified confirmed and approved as by their grauntes or lettres patentes therof made playnlier may appere by whiche with the usage contynuaunce and enyoieng of the same the saide borrowe or towne of Wexforde was maynteyned supported and defended to the pleasur of almyghty God thonour of our moost draid souveraigne lorde and the comen weale of that quarters of this his graces lande and for that the saide libertie amongest other thinges was latelie yeven to the kynges highnes his heyres and successors by auctoritie of parliament in whiche acte of parliament any libertie priveledge jurisdiccion custome or proficte to theme graunted by any the lordes of the saide libertie was saved and provided as by the same acte more playnlier may appere and for somoche that by thacte made by the auctoritie of this present parliament in this present cessions the kinges highnesis moost gracious pleasur dothe appere that the saide libertie of the saide towne [*m.39*] of Wexforde and the libertie of the countie of Wexforde at the pleasur and will of his highnes his heyres and successors shoulde be in the same force strenght and

147 In margin: who so gothe abowt to adnychelatt this parliament after notyce geven be jugyd as a felon.

effect to all ententes as they weare befor that the saide liberties weare yeven to his highnes and as they weare in the possession and handes of any of the lordes of the saide late libertie sethens the furst establishement of the same as by the saide acte therof made more pleynlie shall and may appere and forasmoche as the corporacion of the saide suffrain and burgeses made or establisshed within the saide borrowe or towne and all and every liberties priveledges jurisdiccions custumes and other thinges and profictes to the same souveraigne and burgeses according their saide corporacion graunted and yeven by the late lordes of the saide late libertie was as to many is supposed avoided and made frustrat by reason that the saide liberties wear as is aforsaid given unto the kinges highnes albeit of trouthe they weare not; be it therfor (for the further corporacion assuraunce and suertie of the saide corporacion and liberties in the saide borrowe or towne of Wexforde hereafter to be contynued) enacted and establisshed by auctoritie of this present parliament that all and every liberties priveledges jurisdiccions custumes commodities thinges and profictes and every of theme with their appurtenaunces what soo ever it or they be graunted or given to any souche corporacion or corporacions or to the burgeses or inhabitauntes of the saide borrowe or towne of Wexford by what name or names so ever it be by any the late lordes of the said libertie or by any other meanes or auctoritie be in like force strenght and effecte to all and every purpose and entent as they and every of theme weare at souche tyme as therles of Schrewsburie weare owners and lordes of the saide countie and towne and at souch tyme as the same came to the kinges handes and that the suffrayn bailives burgeses and comens of the saide borrowe or towne of Wexforde and every of theme and their successors by auctoritie aforsaide shall holde occupie excercise possesse and enyoie all and every souche corporacion or corporacions liberties priveledges jurisdiccions custumes commodities thinges or profictes with their apurtenaunces to theme or any of theme graunted or given by any maner of name or names what soo ever it or they be in the same and like forme condicion force strenght and qualitie as if the kynges highnes had confirmed and graunted the saide liberties expressyng every article or thing particulerlie by his moost gracious lettres patentes or otherwise by auctoritie of his highnes is highe courte of parliament any acte or actes to the contrarie made or establisshed notwithstonding.

c.33 Thact for leases[148]

Where as the king our souveraigne lordes highnes haithe bene of late enformed that dyvers of his dominions landes and possessions within this his lande of Irlande aswele of his[149] highnes is olde enheritaunce as alsoo of those whiche

148 *Statutes at large* c.25. 149 *his* inserted.

of late bene comen to his highnes by reason of monasteries suppressed attaynder of traditors or otherwise by reason of any acte or actes of parliament within this his lande of Irlande made or confirmed doo lye wast unoccupied for the reformacion wherof our saide souveraign lorde the king considering that the manuraunce therof shoulde not alonely be to his[150] highnes is profict and honour but alsoo a great encrease and mayntenaunce of the comen wealthe hathe deputed and assigned Anthony Sentleger George Poulet Thomas Moyle William Berners William Brabazon Geralde Aylmer and John Alen his commissioners to vieu and survey aswele his wast landes as also all other his landes and possessions in the same his saide lande and by his highnes is commyssion signed with his graces hande and sealed with his prevaye seale haithe auctorised theme that they or any twoo of theme not oonly to dimise and let the saide landes and possessions aswele wast as occupied and every or any parte of theme for the terme of xxj yeres reservyng to his highnes the rentes therof to be reserved but also to direct their warauntes to the chaunceller of this his saide lande for the sealyng of souche leases as they or twoo of theme shall make or graunte of the premysses or any parte of theme as by the saide commyssion dated at Sonnynghill the last day of Julij in the xxix^ti^ yere of our souveraigne lordes moost noble reigne[151] more pleynlie it appereth; and forsomoche as it appereth by the saide commyssion that his graces pleasur is that the saide commyssioners shall make leases of the same and that it is a thing consonaunt to his highnes is honour and alsoo proficte tht souche leases to be made shoulde be good and vailhable to souche persones as shall take the same and that alsoo souche as shalbe occupiers perceivyng that the same leases soo to be made by the saide commissioners or twoo of theme in our saide souveraigne lordes name shalbe good and avaylable to the lesse or lesses soo that they shall and may laufullie enyoie and occupie the saide landes or possessions soo by theme to be taken during the saide terme according to the teanor of their leases woll the more gladlier endevour theme to have and take souche landes of the saide commyssioners; be it therfor enacted by auctoritie of this present parliament that all and every lease and leases made or hereafter to be made by the saide commyssioners or any twoo of theme in our saide souveraigne lorde the kinges name of any the honours manors landes tenementes or other possessions being the kinges olde enheritaunces or of any souche landes tenementes as dud apperteigne to any monasteries abbeyes religious houses scites of monasteries or abbaies milles tiethes oblacions alterages and other commodities and profictes with all their appurtenaunces or of any parte of theme whiche by reason of suppression of suche abbaies religious houses or monasteries or any of theme now being in his graces handes or possessions or of any of those landes

150 *his* inserted. **151** 1537.

tenementes possessions and profictes whiche be comen unto his highnes by reason of attayndor of any persone or persones by an acte of parliament or otherwise[152] and also whiche weare late yeven to his highnes by reason of any acte or actes of parliament made enacted or confirmed within this lande of Irlande or any other his graces revenues to any persone or persons according to the purporte teanor and effect of the saide commission[153] shalbe good effectuall and available to souche persone and persones as is aforsaide to whome souche lease or leases shalbe made and to their assignes for and during the terme mencioned [*m.40*] and conteyned in the same lease soo that the saide persone or persones and every of theme to whom suche lease or leases of eny of the premisses shalbe by the saide commissioners or ij of theme made or graunted in our saide souveraigne lordes name as is aforsaide and his and their assignes shall and maie occupie possess and enyoie the same for the terme mencioned in the saide lease or leases according to the covenauntes and condicions mencioned and expressed in souche lease to be made in souche ferme as if the saide leases had be made and graunted by the kinges highnes or as if the same had bene sealid by the chaunceller of this lande for the tyme by vertue of immediat warraunt to hym directed by the kinges highnes and signed with his graces hande albeit there be noo office ne inquisicion of the premisses taken ne retourned in the kinges chauncerie of this lande ne into the kinges eschequier of the same any acte ordenaunce or estatute made and ordeyned within this lande of Irlande or within the realme of Englande and ratified and confirmed in this lande to the contrarie notwithstonding; and further be it ordeyned and establisshed by auctoritie aforsaid that all and every warraunt signed with thandes of the saide commyssioners or ij of theme directed to the chaunceller or keaper of the great seale for the making out and sealing of souche leases shalbe good and sufficient discharge and warraunt to the saide chaunceller or keaper of the great seale for the makyng and sealing of the same in like sorte and forme as thoughe souche warraunt had bene signed with the hande of the kinges highnes any acte or actes statute ordenaunce provision use or custume made ordeyned declared or used to the contrarie notwithstondyng; provided alway that this acte or any thing or thinges therin comprised shall in any wise extende to any giftes or grauntes made by the kynges highnes not repelled in this parliament to eny persone or persones before the making of this acte neither to any lesse or lessees afor the xth daie of Decembre in the xxix^{ti} yere of our souveraigne lorde kyng Henry theight made and graunted unto any persone or persones under thexchequier seale but that souche yefte graunte lease and leases shalbe in the same streinght and effect in the lawe as the same and every of theme were the day of the makyng of this present acte any thing in

152 In margin: nota bene. 153 In margin: accordynge the tenor of the comyssyon.

this acte to the contrarie notwithstondyng; and be it further enacted by auctoritie aforsaide that every graunt or grauntes made or to be made under the kinges great seale of this lande by force of any warraunt signed with the saide commissioners handes or any twoo of theme soo the saide William Brabazon be oon of any warde of bodie or lande althoughe it be undre the teste of the saide deputie shalbe reputed and deamed in the lawe of like effecte and force as if the same warraunt had bene or wear signed with the kinges awne hande and immediatelie directed to the chaunceller or keaper of the great seale of this lande any thing in this acte or any other acte or actes to the contrarie notwithstonding.

c.34 Thact for penall statutes[154]

Where diverse and many penall statutes and ordynaunces have bene made and ordeyned some wherby the punyshementes be yeven onelie to the kyng our souveraigne lorde his heyres and successors by accion writ bill enditement or enformacion and some wherby the kyng by hym silfe and any other comen persone for the kyng or for hym silfe onelie may swe by writ bill enditement or enformacion against thoffendor or offendors in that behalfe and because of longe tracte of tyme and for sparing of the suite therof and that then after souche longe tracte of tyme diverse and many of the kinges true subjectes have bene in tyme past vexed and troubled for the penalties conteyned in the said estatutes and ordynaunces more for malice then for justice wherupon perjures have ensued to the great trouble and vexacion of the kinges true subjectes their heyres and executors beyng ignoraunt of the saide statutes and offences wherfor and for the tender love and zeale that our souveraigne lord the kyng beareth to his said loving subjectes and at their humble deasire be it enacted ordeyned and establisshed by his highnes and by thassent of the lordes spirituall and temporall and the comens in this present parliament assembled and by the auctoritie of the same that all and synguler souche accions suites billes enditementes or enformacions as from the furst day of this present parliament uppon prorogacion shalbe commenced taken sued had or made onelie for eny peyne and forfaicture by reason or streinght of any penall statute wherunto the kyng onelie his heyres or successors and none other comen persone shall or may have cause of accion or be entitled by reason of the said penall statutes or eny of theme shalbe commenced sued taken or had within iij yeres next after the offence or offences commytted or forfaicted of or for the same had or made agaynst thordynaunce and provision of eny souche acte or actes statut or statutes penall and not after the saide iij yeres and that for eny offence or

154 *Statutes at large* c.21.

forfaictur made or had or to be made or had agaynst thordynaunce and provision of eny acte or actes penall made or ordeyned or to be made and ordeyned wherby accion suit bill or enformacion popular is or shalbe yeven to any persone or persones souche as woll sue for the kyng and for hym or theme selfe or onelie for hym or theme silfe that souche accion bill suit or enformacion be commensed sued had or made by souche persone or persones other then the kyng as will sue in that behalfe within one yere next after thoffence or forfaictur had made or commytted against thordynaunce and provision of eny souche acte or actes penall and not after the saide yere ended; and that the kynges suit by writ bill playnte enditement and enformacion in that behalfe be commensed sued had or made within ij yeres next after thoffence or forfaictur made or had agaynst the provision and ordynaunce of eny acte or actes statute or statutes penall and not after the saide iij yeres; and if any accion suit bill enditement or enformacion concernyng the forsaide statutes or any of theme had or made otherwise then within the tyme or tymes lymyted as is aforsaide that the same accion suit bill enditement or enformacion and every of theme commensed sued had or made for the saide offence or offences forfeictur or forfeicturs shalbe voide and of noo force ne effect any acte or actes statute or statutes made or hereafter to be made to the contrarie notwithstondyng; provided alwaie that where any accion enformacion or enditement lymyted by any statute to be had made or taken within shorter tyme or tymes then is afor rehersed that it be had made and taken accordyng to the tyme lymyted in that estatute.

c.35 Thact for the pardons

Where as by a statute made in the xth yere of kyng Edwarde the thrid[155] amongest other thinges it was enacted by auctoritie of parliament that every persone and persones whiche after that tyme shoulde have chartor of pardone for any felonyes murdres and rapes shoulde fynde sufficient maynpernors befor the shiriff and coronors of the counties where the felonyes murdres or rapes soo was commytted and done that they and every of theme shoulde be of good aberyng from thensforthe and the same maynepernors to be retourned in the chauncerie within iij monethes after the chartor soo had or otherwise the same chartor to be voide as in the same acte more playner appereth and alsoo by the statute made in the xvj yere of kyng Richarde the seconde[156] the last chapiter that chartors of pardone shall not be alloued for murdre manslaghter by the way assaute or malice for pretensed treason nor rape if it be not specified within the saide pardone as more playner appereth in the saide statute; [*m.41*]

155 1336–7. 10 Edward III Stat. 1 c.2 &3 (*Statutes of the realm*, i, p. 275). **156** 1392–3. 16 Richard II c.6 (*Statutes of the realm*, ii, pp 86–7).

and forasmoche as it haith pleased the kynges highnes of his gracious mercy and pitie to auctorise the lorde Leonarde Gray his graces deputie in Irlande Anthony Sainct Legier George Poulet esquyers Thomas Moile and William Berners the kynges highe commyssioners in Irlande William Brabazon esquyer and Geralde Aylmer chief justice accordyng a certeyn scedule signed with his graces handes and delyvered to the lorde chaunceler of this lande to pardone all and every of his subjectes of this his highnes is lande of all treasons murdres felonyes rapes and all other offences commytted befor this tyme for corroboracion wherof sethens this cession amongest other thynges it was enacted that all and every warraunt signed with the handes of the saide commyssioners or any twoo of theme accordyng the teanor of the saide sceadule shoulde be as[157] good and as effectuall as thoughe the same had bene signed with the kynges hande and immediatelie directed to his saide chaunceller for the sealyng and delyveraie of every souche pardone wherin noo remedie is provided for the kinges pore subjectes swyng for suche pardons to discharge theme from the fyndyng of maynepernors accordyng the saide statute made the saide x^th^ yere of kyng Edwarde the thrid; in consideracion that the same in effecte at this season toucheth the disturbaunce of all the kynges subjectes of this lande and for their remedie and releif therin be it enacted by auctoritie of this present parliament that all and every chartor of pardone and pardones to be sealed graunted and dealyvered to any persone or persones yoinctlie or severallie from the furst daye of the cession of this present parliament untill the xx^ti^ day of Julie next that ensuyng by force of any warraunt signed onelie with the kynges saide deputies handes by force of eny lettres patentes to hym graunted or by hym and the commyssioners aforsaide joynctlie or any twoo of theme by vertue of the saide acte shalbe good effectuall available and allowable in lawe befor all and every of the kynges justices within this saide lande althoughe eny souche person and persons opteynyng swyng and receivyng souche chartor and chartors pardone and pardones doo or shall not fynde maynpernors for his her or their good abering and thoughe he she or they be not of good abering accordyng the forme and effect of the saide statute made the saide x^th^ yere of king Edwarde the thirde any thing in the same statute or any other statute lawe usage or other thing made ordeyned divised or used befor this tyme to the contrarie notwithstonding; and althogh that ther be noo mencion made within the saide chartors of pardone by the saide commyssioners or any twoo of theme graunted to any maner of persone and persones accordyng theffect and wordes of the saide statute as befor is specified of the saide murdres felonies manslaghter by the way assaute or malice for pretended treason or any other maner of thing conteyned in the saide statut made the saide xvj^ten^ yere or any

157 *as* inserted.

other statute or statutes made to the contrarie the saide chartors of pardone or pardones graunted to all maner of persone and persones in maner and forme aforsaide shalbe good effectuall available and allowable in lawe as is aforsaide as the mencion were made of the saide murdres manslaghter by the way treasons and other offences within the saide chartor the saide acte and actes notwithstondyng; and further the mynde of the makers of this saide statut is that this acte and every thing and thinges herin conteyned is for the kinges honour and comen wealthe.

c.36 Thact for the werres upon the Barrowe and other waters in the countie of Kilkenny[158]

Prayen the comens in this present parliament assembled that wher at all tymes necessarie bootes scowtes whurries clarans coettes and other vessels loden and bestowed with goodes merchaundises and other stuffe have bene used to passe and repasse through and in the kynges moost excellent majesties ryvers and waters of the Barowe the Noyre the Suyr and the Rie within this lande whiche Rye is in the countie of Kylkenny to and from the kynges citie of Waterforde and the townes of Kilkenny Rosse and Clomell to and from dyvers borrowe and corporate townes and other places beyng situated in the counties of Kildare Catherlaugh Wexforde Kilkenny Waterforde and Tipperary throughe whiche great commoditie and profict haithe growen and myght growe to the saide citie townes brughes and other places and to all and every the kinges true subjectes adjoynyng to the same waters and ryvers; and yet this notwithstonding nowe of late dyverse wilfull persones havyng no respecte to the premysses but more rather to their awne wilfulnes synguler commoditie and benefict havyng noo grounde ne cause reasonable to the same have in dyverse places of the saide ryvers and waters made souche werres purpresturs ingynnes streites and other like obstacles and theme and every of theme soo do kepe and maynteyne that by noo meanes any bootes scowtes whurries clarans coettes and other vessels laden and bestowed as is aforsaide can convenyentlie passe and repasse and through whiche the salmon frie bredyng in the saide waters and ryvers be clerelie destroied contrarie to theffect and purporte of the statutes therin provided and in divers sondrie places of the saide ryvers and waters alsoo doo take and procure to be taken dyvers exaccions and unlaufull custumes callid bankfees of any bote scowte whurrie claran coet and other vessel laden and bestowed as is aforsaide goyng and passyng in and through the kynges saide ryvers and waters albeit that parte of the saide borrowe townes by their liberties and chartors be frelie and quyte discharged of all maner tolles

158 *Statutes at large* c.22.

passages custumes and pondages in the saide ryvers and waters and the lande on every side of the same and that alsoo souche persone and persons as be the botemen and have the rule governaunce and conveyeng of the saide bootes scowtes whurries clarans coettes and other vessels laden and bestowed as is aforsaide at souche tymes as they be laded with wynes of their deceipt and craftie meanes doo from tyme to tyme drawe drynke and take with theme parcell of the saide wynes and some tymes puttyng in the vessell where the saide wyne was to replenyshe the same the quantite or somoche water wherby the residue of the saide wyne is clerelie destroyed to the great losses and damages of the veray owners therof throughe whiche premisses the merchauntes occupiers and dwellers of the saide citie townes and burghes and places be soo discoraged and indamaged that they be more liker to give over and withdraw theme selves from souche tradde of merchaundises then any further to use or excercise the same whiche is not onelie thympoverysshing of the saide merchauntes occupiers and dwellers but alsoo the utter decay of the saide borrowe townes and places oneles that some convenyent remedie therin be provided; wherfor be it enacted ordeyned and established by auctoritie of this present parliament that it shalbe laufull and justifiable to and for every of[159] the kynges subjectes within this lande goyng in company with any sherif or senescall of any countie afor named to prostrate and brecke and cause to be prostrated and broken from tyme to tyme all and every souche werres purpresturs ingynnes streytes and other like obstacles made or hereafter to be made in any of the said ryvers or waters and also a convenyent gappe or place where that bootes scowtes whurries clarans coettes and other vessels may passe and repasse in of upon and throwe every milponde made or hereafter to be made in [*m.42*] any of the saide ryvers and waters; and if any persone or persones doo resiste or make any defence in or for the prostratyng and breckyng or causyng to be prostrated and brocken of the saide werres purpresturs ingynnes streites and other like obstacles and milpondes in maner and forme as is aforsaide that then every souche persone and persones soo makyng resistence or defence for every souche tyme shall forfaict v$^{li.}$ thoon moitie therof to the kinges highnes his heyres and successors and thother moitie therof to the partie that woll sue for the same in any the kynges courtes by accion of debt bill playnt enformacion or otherwise wherin noo essoyne proteccion ne wageor of lawe shalbe admytted or allowed; and further be it enacted by auctoritie aforsaide that the sherif of eny countie and the senescall of eny libertie for the tyme beyng wherin any souche werres purpresturs ingynnes streytes and other like obstacles in any of the saide ryvers and waters is made or hereafter shalbe made or wher ther is or shalbe any milponde wherof ther is nor shalbe noo gappe as is aforsaide after

159 *of* inserted.

knowledge therof had by reaporte compaynt enquyrie or otherwise shall from tyme to tyme callyng and takyng with hym if he be sherif the power of the countie and if he be senescall the power of the libertie goo in proper persone to every souche place wheras eny werre purpresture ingynne streyte or other like obstacle in any of the saide ryvers and waters is or shalbe made or wher ther is or shalbe any milponde wherof ther is or shalbe eny gappe brocken as is aforsaide and the same prostrate and brecke or cause to be prostrated and brocken in maner and forme as is aforsaide upon payne to every souche shirif and senescall as often as he or they shall soo offende or refuse to prostrate and brecke or cause to be prostrated and brocken any of the saide werres purpresturs ingynnes streytes and other like obstacles and a gappe in any souche milponde of x^li.^ thone halfe to the kynges highnes his heyres and successors and thother halfe to the partie that woll sue for the same in eny of the kynges courtes by accion of debt bill pleynt enformacion or otherwise wherin noo essoyne proteccion ne wageor of lawe shalbe admytted or allowed; and if eny persone or persones dwelling or demurraunt within any souche countie doo refuse and woll not goo in aide of the shirif of the same countie and if eny persone or persones dwellyng or demurraunt within any souche libertie doo refuse and woll not goo in aide of the senescall of the same for the prostratyng and breckyng or causing to be prostrated and brocken of any the saide milpondes werres ingynnes purpresturs streytes and other like obstacles made or to be made in any of the saide ryvers or waters in maner and forme as is aforsaide beyng laufullie summoned and warned for the same for every souche tyme shall forfaict x^s.^ thoon halfe therof to the kyng his heyres and successors and thother halfe to eny souche[160] shirif or senescall that woll sue for the same in any the kynges courtes by accion of debt bill pleynte enformacion or otherwis wherin noo essoyne proteccion ne wageor of lawe shalbe admytted or allowed; be it further enacted by auctoritie aforsaide that noo persone ne persons bodies politicque ne corporate within this lande by hym or theme selves his or their constables fermors officers or servauntes shall take levie distrayne or receive or suffre permyt or cause to be taken levied distrayned or received noo custumes or for any custumes called bancfees ne any other duetie rent or custome of any bote scowte whurrie claran coet or any other vessell what soo ever it be passyng or repasssyng in or through any the saide ryvers or waters or any parcell of theme or of any boote or other vessell wherin any persone or persones doo fyshe in any of the saide ryvers or waters soo fur as the salte water dothe ebbe and flowe in any of the saide ryvers or of thowners of any goodes merchaundises victuall or stuffe then beyng in any souche bote scowte whurrie clarane or coet and other vessels as is aforsaide or of any the marryners botemen and

160 *souche* inserted.

other rulers and conveyors of the saide[161] bootes scowtes whurries clarans coettes and other vessels but that they and every of theme shall peasiblie suffre and permyt the saide botes scowtes whurries clarans coettes and other vessels as is afor specified with all the goodes merchaundises victuall fyshe and stuffe comprised and beyng in the same and thawners of the saide goodes merchaundises victuals fishe and other stuffe and their servauntes and the maryners bootmen and other rulers and conveyers of the saide bootes scowtes whurries clarans coettes and other vessels in uppon and through every the saide ryvers and every parcell of theme and the lande adjoynyng to the same and that the saide awners their servauntes maryners botemen and other rulers and conveyers and all other persones comyng in aide and helpe of them and every of theme at all souche tymes as the same maryners botemen and other rulers and conveyers shall thinke the same necessarie and nedefull shall have and occupie at every of their willes and pleasurs the space and bread of vij fote or more as neade requyre of playne grounde upon every parte of the lande of every side of every the saide ryvers and waters next adjoynyng to the said ryvers and waters and that to be where they must nedes drawe the saide botes and other vessels afor named with streinght of horses or men by lande oneles that at the making of this present acte ther be a castle fortresse orcharde or gardyng upon any souche lande soo adjoynyng to the saide ryvers of every side of the water soo fur and as longe as the saide ryvers or waters doo ronne or have their concource for the drawyng takyng lodyng and conveyeng of the saide bootes scowtes whurries clarans coettes and other vessels and every of theme without any impedyment let vexacion disturbaunce or inquietnes of any the possessioners or enheritors of the saide landes or any parte of theme or any persone or persones bodies politicque or corporate upon payne of forfaicture to every persone and persones bodies poleticque and corporate offendyng in the premisses or any parcell therof as often as he or they shall soo offende treble the valor of that thing that they or any of theme doo take to be forfaict and yeven to the partie greved and over that $x^{li.}$ thone halfe therof to the kyng his heyres successors and assignes and thother halfe to the partie that woll sue for the same in any the kynges courtes by accion of debt bill pleynt enformacion or otherwise wherin noo essoyne proteccion ne wageor of lawe shalbe admytted or allowed; and alsoo considring the trust and confidence that thowners of any wynes doo put in the saide maryners botemen rulers and conveyers of the saide botes scowtes whurries clarans coettes and other vessels what soo ever they be for the true conveyaunce and custodie of the saide wynes the deceipt and craftie handlyng of the saide maryners botemen rulers and conveyers of the saide botes scowtes whurries clarans coettes and other vessels and the losses

161 *saide* inserted.

and damages that haithe and may hereafter ensue to the owners of any souche wynes be it enacted by auctoritie aforsaide that if any maryner bootman ruler or conveyer of any the saide bootes scowtes whurries clarans coettes and other vessels have the carryeng freight or conveyeng of any wynes goodes or other merchaundises in any bote scowte whurrie claran coet or other vessel in or throughe the saide ryvers or waters or any parcell of theme or if any persone or persones take upon hym or theme the carrieng or conveyeng of eny wyne goodes or other merchaundises by lande in carte wayne or otherwise [*m.43*] and doo drawe drynke take or wilfullie perishe any caske or parcell of eny souche wynes goodes or merchaundises to theme or any of theme to be delivered at any tyme hereafter to be conveyed carried or transportid in the said ryvers or waters or in any parcell of theme or to any place or quarter of this domynyon by lande in maner and forme as is aforsaide shall forfaict and lose to the owner or owners of the saide wynes goodes or merchaundises as often as he or they shall offende the same asmoche money as he or they shoulde have for the freight conveyeng and cariage of all the wynes goodes and merchaundises to hym or theme at that tyme delyvered or appoynted to be conveyed or carried either by any of the side ryvers or waters or to any other place by lande and the treble valor of that thing or thinges that he or they doo take drawe drynke or wilfullie perishe or cause to be taken drawen dronken or wilfullie perished of the saide wynes goodes or merchaundises and over that to forfaict $v^{li.}$ thone moitie therof to oure souveraigne lorde the kyng his heyres and successors and thother moitie to the partie that woll sue for the same in any the kynges courtes by accion of debt bill pleynt enformacion or otherwise wherin noo essoyne proteccion ne wageor of lawe shalbe admytted or allowed; and further be it enacted by auctoritie aforsaide that none of the saide maryners or botemen or other persones afornamed shall take or receive or cause to be taken or received any somes of monye or any other thyng for the freight cariage or conveyng of any stuffe or merchaundises what soo ever they be other then souche like as is comprised in thextent therof made remaynyng in the custodie of the sherif of the countie of Tipperarie and in other places wher souche somes as they shoulde have is not mencioned or lymyted in the saide extente that then they and every of theme do take noo more wages ne somes of monye but souche like somes of monye and wages as they and every of theme in tyme passed have bene[162] moost comenlie used and accustumed to take or receive for the freight conveyeng transportyng and carriage of eny souch[163] stuffe goodes or merchaundises uppon payne to the taker as often as he shall offende in the same $xiij^{s.}$ $iiij^{d.}$ thone halfe therof to our souveraigne lorde the king his heyres and successors and thother halfe to the partie that woll sue for the same in any of

162 *bene* inserted. 163 *souch* inserted.

the kynges courtes or befor the kinges commissioners by accion of debt bill pleynt enformacion or otherwise wherin noo essoyne proteccion ne wageor of lawe shalbe admytted or allowed.

c.37 Thact for werres upon Boyne

Prayen the comens in this present parliament assembled that wher nowe of late diverse and sondrie werres purpresturs milpoundes ingens and other obstacles be made in the ryver of Boyne and other waters and streames in the counties of Methe and Uriell within this lande of Irlande wherby not onelie thoulde councourse of botes whurries and other like vessels contynuallie goyng and passyng at all tymes necessarie in the saide water of Boyne to and from the townes of Drogheda Trym the Novan and dyvers other places situated upon the saide ryver of Boyne is clere put oute of due frame and stopped after souche sorte that noo souche bote or other vessell at this tyme can in any wise passe in or upon the saide ryver to the greate hurte nisaunce and detryment of the comen weale and the kynges true and faithfull subjectes to the saide ryver and streames adjoynyng but alsoo the[164] salmone frie bredyng and beyng in the saide ryver and streames be likewise killed and utterlie in effect distroyed contrarie to the teanor and purport of dyvers beneficiall ordynaunces and statutes therin provided and moche more inconvenyences like to ensue oneles some convenyent remedy therin be had and provided; for reformacion wherof be it enacted ordeyned and establishd by auctoritie of this present parliament that it shalbe laufull and justifiable to and for all the kynges subjectes within this lande goyng or being in company with the sherif of eny countie afor named for the tyme beyng or of any the kynges commyssioners to be assigned in any the saide counties to prostrate and brecke or cause to be prostrated and brocken from tyme to tyme a convenyent gappe and space for bootes to passe and repasse whiche shalbe as large and as wide as any arche of any bridge being nowe upon the same water upon every warre purpresture milpound and other ingynne made or to be made in the saide ryver and water of Boyne [and] the water of the Cassan in the countie of Uriell and if eny person or persones doo resist or make any defence in or upon the prostrating and brecking or causing to be prostrated and brocken of the said gappe and space for bootes as is aforsaide to passe and repasse upon every warre and milpound as is afor specified that then every souche persone and persones soo makyng resistence and defence for every souche tyme shall forfaicte $v^{li.}$ thoon halfe therof to our souveraigne lorde the kyng his heyres and successors and thother halfe to the partie that woll sue

164 *the* inserted.

for the same in eny the kynges courtes by accion of debte bill pleynt enformacion or otherwise wherin noo essoyne proteccion ne wageor of lawe shalbe admytted or allowed; be it alsoo enacted by auctoritie aforsaide that the shirif for the tyme beyng of any countie afornamed and the maiors and shiriffes and comens of Drogheda and the portreffes and comens of the Navan and Trym for the tyme beyng upon whiche waters streames and ryvers souche werre mylpounde purpresture or ingynne is made or hereafter shalbe made wherof ther is nor shalbe eny gappe and space lefte and[165] brocken as is afore mencioned in this acte callyng and takyng with theme the power of the townes aforsaid and the maior and sheriffes portreffes and comens of the counties aforsaide goo in proper persone to every such place wheras any souche werre milpounde or purpresture in any of the saide ryvers waters and streames is or shalbe made wherof ther is nor shalbe eny gappe lefte and brocken as is aforsaid and the same prostrat and brecke or cause to be prostrated and brocken as is afor lymyted uppon payne to every souche shirif and maior shiriffes portreffes and comens as often tymes as they shall offende in the premisses or refuse to prostrate and brecke or cause to be prostrated and brocken any souche gappe and space upon every werre milpounde and other purpresture made or hereafter to be made in any ryver water and streame aforsaide of $x^{li.}$ thone halfe therof to be to the kyng our souveraigne lorde his heyres and sucessors and thother halfe to the partie that woll sue for the same in any of the kynges courtes by accion of debt bill pleynt enformacion or otherwis wherin noo essoyne proteccion ne wageor of lawe shalbe admytted or allowed; and if eny persone or persones dwellyng or demurraunt in any countie afor named doo refuse and woll not goo in aide of the sherif of the same countie the maior shiriffes portreffes and comens aforsaide for the prostratyng and brecking or causyng to be prostrated and brocken of eny souche gappe and space uppon eny werre milpounde or other ingynne or purpresture in any of the saide ryvers waters and streames in maner and forme as is aforsaid being laufullie summoned and warned for the same for every souche tyme shall forfaict $x^{s.}$ thone halfe therof to the kynges highnes his heyres and successors and thother halfe to eny souche shirif maior shiriffes portreves and comens that woll sue for the same in any of the kynges courtes by accion of debt bill pleynt enformacion or otherwise wherin noo essoyne proteccion ne wageor of lawe shalbe admytted or alloued; and further be it enacted by auctoritie aforsaid that the mareners botemen conveyers or rulers of any bote or other vessell at any tyme hereafter passyng or repassyng in upon or throughe eny ryver water or streame afore specified shall have and occupie at every of their willes and pleasurs and every persone and persones comyng in helpe and aide of theme the space and breade of vij fote or more as

165 *and* inserted.

nede shall requyre of playne grounde upon every parte of the lande of every side of the saide ryver waters and streames next adjoynyng to the saide ryver waters or streames and that to be wher they must of nede drawe the said bootes and other vessels with streinght of men or horses by lande oneles at the makyng of this present acte ther be a castle fortresse orcharde or garding upon any souche lande adjoynyng to the saide ryver waters or streames of every side of the same soo fur and as longe as the saide ryver waters and streames doo ronne or have their concourse for the drawyng takyng leding and conveying of the saide bootes and other vessels without any impedyment let vexaccion disturbaunce or inquietnes of any the possessioners or inheritors of the said landes or any parte of theme or any other persone or persones bodies politicque or corporate upon payne of forfeictur to every persone and persones bodies politicque and corporate offending in the premisses or any parte therof of $x^{li.}$ thone halfe therof to be to our souveraigne lorde the king his heyres and successors and thother moitie to eny persone or persones that woll sue for the same in eny the kynges courtes by accion of debt bill pleynt enformacion or otherwise wherin no essoyne proteccion ne wageor of lawe shalbe admytted or allowed; provided and be it enacted that this acte shall not endure above foure yeres from the furst daie of Maij next comyng oneles the same take the full entented effecte for passage of bootes accordyng the mynde of the makers of this acte and if it soo doo to endure for ever.

[*m.44*]

c.38 Thact for the parsonage of Dungarvan[166]

Forasmoche as the parsonage and churche of Dungarvan and alsoo the parsonages and churchis of Rennegennaghe Kynsalbegge Arglas Glassemore Amane White Churche Tampleavien Aviewe Kilronan Rossemore Lisgenan togither with the patronages advousons and giftes of the vicarages of the saide churches and all other churches and chapels advousons and patronages and all landes tenementes dismes oblacions profictes emolumentes and commodities to the saide parsonages churchis advousons and patronages belongyng whiche were united annexed and appropriated to the house or monasterie of Kentshame in Englande and that the abbot of the saide house or monastery for the tyme beyng was rightfullie patrone of the vicarages of the saide churches and the same long tyme after the unyon and appropriacion therof to the saide house or monasterie peasiblie ded possesse and enyoie without any interrupcion or let of any persone or persones unto souche tyme as in the rebellion of the late erles of Desmonde the saide erles presented certeyn persones to the

166 *Statutes at large* c.23.

same churches whiche by reason and force therof without eny colour right or title extorciouselie toke the profictes of the same and albeit that thabbotes of the saide house for the tyme beyng pursued here within this lande for the recovery therof yet neither the saide erles ne the saide persones by theme presented wolde in noo wise aunswer to the kynges preceptes or commaundementes to theme directed for the saide abbotes demaundes and pursuites and for that the saide parsonages of the saide churches and the patronages of the vicarages of the same was unyted and appropriated to the saide house or monasterie at the tyme of souche presentacion by the saide erles usurped and that the saide presentacions was in tyme of wer and in the rebellion of the saide erle of Desmonde and for that alsoo that presentacions made to any parsonages and churches soo beyng appropriated and united to any abbaie or monasterie albeit souche presentee be therto admytted and take therof the profictes is but onelie spoliacion and geveth noo interest or title to the presentor ne putteth thabbaie or monasterie out of possession of souche churches wherfor by the due course of the lawe the saide erles coulde wynne noo maner rightfull title or possession to the saide churches ne withe any of theme; in consideracion wherof and forasmoche as at a parliament holden at Dublin the furst day of Maij in the xxviij^ti^ yere of the reigne of our moost draid souveraigne lorde king Henry theight[167] emonges other thynges it was enacted ordeyned and established by auctoritie of the same parliament[168] that the kynges highnes his heyres and successors shoulde have possesse and enyoie as knyt and unyted to his and their emperiall crowne of England all and every the manors meses tenementes and all other hereditamentes patronages parsonages vicarages chapels tiethes oblacions alterages rightes titles and possessions with all other profictes aswele spirituall as temporall wherof thabbot then beyng of the saide house or monasterie or any other to his use as in right of the saide house or monasterie had possessed or enyoied or of right ought to have had possessed or enyoied by whiche the kynges highnes his heyres and successors be justelie entitled to the same and for that alsoo that the judgementes and determynacion of souche as be unlerned who suppose that not alonelie the said persones to whom any souche presentacions by the said erles was made but alsoo the saide erles by souche presentacions considering the contynuall possession and takyng the profictes of the saide churches by thencumbentes by the saide erles presented by soo longe tyme shoulde be therby to the possession therof laufullie entitled albeit the clere determynacion of the lawe is and alway haithe bene otherwise and to the contrarie for thexpellyng of whiche saide doubtes and cleare determynacion of the premisses from hensforthe to be had be it enacted ordeyned and establisshed by auctoritie of this present parliament

167 1536. 168 Above, c.3.

that every presentacion made by any of the late erles of Desmonde or any persone or persons to the parsonages of the saide churches and the vicarages of the same or any of theme and every admission institucion and induccion of theme and every of theme to the saide churches parsonages and vicarages or any of theme be reputed accepted and taken frustrate and voide and of none effect in lawe and that by souche presentacion the saide erles ne any of theme to wynne any interest or possession in the premisses and that by auctoritie aforsaid the kynges highnes his heyres and successors shall have possesse and enyoie as knyt annexed and united to his and their emperiall crowne of England the saide parsonages of Dungarvan and other parsonages aforsaid and churches and alsoo all and synguler patronages presentacions and advousons of every the said vicarages and churches togidther with all the manors meses landes tenementes tiethes porcions pencions oblacions alterages profictes commodities emolumentes and all other hereditamentes aswell spirituall as temporall with all and singuler their apurtenaunces belongyng atteynyng or in any wise apperteynyng to the saide parsonages or churches or any of theme any presentacion or presentacions heretofor made by any of the saide erles of Desmonde or any other persone or persons or any admission institucion or induccion of theme or any of theme to any of the saide parsonages churches or vicarages in any wise notwithstondyng; provided that this acte ne any thing therin conteyned shall in any wise be hurtfull or prejudiciall to Sir Maurice Connell vicare of Dungarvan or any other vicare pereptuall in any of the saide churches but that they and every of theme shall have and enyoie their vicarages during their naturall lives any thing in this acte to the contrarie notwithstonding.

c.39 Thact confermyng thordres to be made by the commyssioners and others

Be it enacted by auctoritie of this present parliament with thassent of the lordes spirituall and temporall and the comens of the same that all souche ordynaunces decrees and ordres as shalbe made and decreed by Anthony Sayntleger George Poulet Thomas Moyle and William Berners the kynges highe commissioners within this his lande of Irlande or thre of theme[169] with thassent and consent of the lorde chaunceller tharchebusshop of Dublin the prior of Kilmaynam the busshop of Methe thabbottes of sainct Thomas courte and sainct Mary abbay and the lorde of Houthe or foure of theme the maister of the rolles the recordors of Dublin and Drogheda Thomas Cusake of Cousyngeston' Thomas Agarde and Nicholas Bellewe or iiij of theme the thre chief judges and the underthesaurer or ij of theme toutching and concernyng

169 In margin: the orders follow in thys roull.

thoonlie billes exhibited in this parliament to have passed as actes for the reformacion and inhabityng of the marches and the merchauntes called gray merchauntes and the confirmacion and establishement of thacte of pluralities none residence and takyng of fermes by spirituall persones and every thing and thinges comprised in the saide billes and every of theme shalbe of like force strenght and effecte to all and every ententes and purposes as though the same and every of theme had bene made enacted and establisshed by thauctoritie of this present parliament and soo to contynue in the same streinght force and effect unto the next parliament to be holden within this saide lande of Irland; and be it further enacted by auctoritie aforsaide that the lordes spirituall and temporall and the comens in that parliament to be assembled shall have auctoritie and full power to make further establishement of the saide actes and every of theme if it shalbe so seen to theme requisit thacte of Ponnynges made at Drogheda the xth yere of kyng Henry the vij^th^[170] in a parliament there holden etc. or any other acte or actes to the contrarie notwithstonding.

c.40 Thact for leasers of corne[171]

Prayeth the comens in this present parliament assembled that wheras leasyng of corne in harvest season is a great cause of idelnes dearthe of reppyng of corne and stelling of the same whiche befor this tyme haithe bene remedied by auctoritie of parliament whiche toke none effect nor was put in execucion because the possessioners and occupiers in the country doo not endevoire theme selves therunto wherfor be it enacted and establisshed by auctoritie of this present parliament that from hensforth every persone and persons whiche hereafter shall lease in the harvest tyme in any felde or feldes within this lande as longe as the corne shalbe there in reake or otherwise shall not oonlie lose all the corne that they or any of theme shall lease to any persone or persones that will take or sease the same but alsoo shall forfeict for every tyme that they shall soo lease xij^d.^ whiche forfeictur shalbe to the lorde of the soile and to be presented and enquerid of in the saide lordes courte; and if he have no courte then the saide forfeictur to be to the kyng our souveraigne lorde and all his justices in every of his courtes [*m.45*] to enquiere therof in like forme and sorte as they doo all other estatutes penall and to see the same duely punysshed and put in execucion; and further be it enacted by thauctoritie aforsaide that every occupier or occupiers of souche feldes wherin any corne shalbe whiche willynglie shall permyt or suffre any souche persone or persones to lease contrarie to the forme aforsaide shall forfaicte to our souveraigne lorde the kyng for every tyme soo offendyng xij^d.^ of whiche offences every of the kynges justices shall

170 1494. 171 *Statutes at large* c.24.

enquier and execut in maner and forme aforsaide; and further be it enacted by auctoritie aforsaide that every persone or persones enhabityng within this lande whiche in the hervest season receive or keape in his or their houses or habitacions any persone or persones calles ynmakes whiche shall so lease contrarie to the forme of this acte shall forfeict for every souche ynmake vj$^{s.}$ viij$^{d.}$ whiche forfeictur shalbe to the lorde of the soill if it be enquered or presented in his courte or leit and in necligence or default therof to be enquered and presented in the kinges courte in maner aforsaide; and further be it enacted that every persone and persones whiche be not hable to keape their children to scoule at thage of ten yeres shall put theme to handcraftes or husbandrie upon payne of vj$^{s.}$ viij$^{d.}$ to be forfeict in maner aforsaid and to be enquered of in maner and forme aforsaide; provided that this acte ne any thing or thinges therin conteyned shall extend or be ment to any owner or owners of cornes but that they and every of theme may lease by theme selves or servauntes their awne corne any thing in this acte mencioned to the contrarie notwithstondyng.

c.41 The declaracion of thact of subsidie

And forasmoche as in the furst cession of this present parliament holden here at Dublin the furst day of Maij in the xxviij^{ti} yere of the reigne of our moost draid souveraigne lorde the kyng that nowe is[172] a subsidie of xiij$^{s.}$ iiij$^{d.}$ of laufull monye of Irlande of and upon every ploughe lande occupied or manured or hereafter to be occupied or manured within this land of Irlande from the tyme of thoccupieng or manuraunce therof as longe tyme as it shoulde be soo occupied or manured by auctoritie of the saide parliament was given unto our saide souveraigne lorde his heyres and successors from the xxviij^{ti} day of Septembre in the yere of our lorde God M v^{c} xxvj to thende of the terme of x yeres then next ensuyng in whiche acte the same subsidie is lymyted to be payed yerelie at the feast of Ester during the saide terme as more at large is expressed in the saide acte[173] wheras the mear truthe is that the true myndes and ententes of us thordynors devisors and makers of the same acte and provision was that the saide subsidie of xiij$^{s.}$ iiij$^{d.}$ shoulde be yerelie payed unto our said souveraigne lorde the kyng his heyres and successors at the feast of sainct Michaell tharchaungell during the saide terme and not at the said feast of Ester and for that diverse and sondrie argumentes alreddie have bene movid and styrred for the payment of the saide yerelie subsidie yerelie to be payed at the feast of Ester and that thonelie writyng therof uppon thengrossing of the saide acte was throughe the mesprision and necligence of the clerc contrarie to our true meanyng and entent we the lordes spirituall and temporall and the comens

172 1536. 173 Above, c.9.

in this present cession of parliament assembled and thole body of the same doo publishe expounde and declare that our hole assentes consentes agrementes ententes and myndes uppon thestablishement of the saide acte wherby the saide subsidy of xiij$^{s.}$ iiij$^{d.}$ was yeven and graunted to our saide souveraigne lorde the kyng his heyres and successors was that the same subsidie of xiij$^{s.}$ iiij$^{d.}$ and all and every other subsidy graunted and geven by the saide acte unto our said souveraigne lorde shoulde be yerelie levyable and payable at the feast of sainct Michaell tharchaungell during the saide terme and in noo wise at the saide feast of Ester soo that the writyng therof in the saide acte to be paied at the saide feast of Ester was by thoonlie mesprision and necligence of the clerc or writer of the same and that contrarie to all our assentes agrementes and ententes.

c.42 Thordres taken by the commyssioners and others

Where as in a parliament holden upon prorogacion the xiij day of October in the xxix^{ti} yere of kyng Henry theight[174] it was enacted ordeyned and establisshed by the lordes spirituall and temporall and the comens of the same[175] that all souche ordynaunces decrees and ordres as shoulde be made and decreed by Anthony Sentleger Goerge Poulet Thomas Moyle and William Berners the kynges highe[176] commyssioners within this his lande of Irlande or iij of theme with thassent and consent of the lorde chaunceller tharchebusshop of Dublin the prior of Kilmaynam the busshop of Meth the abbotes of sainct Thomas courte and sainct Mary abbay and the lorde of Houthe or foure of theme the maister of the rolles the recordors of Dublin and Drogheda Thomas Cusake of Cousyngeston' Thomas Agarde and Nicholas Bellewe or foure of theme the thre chief judges and the underthesaurer or ij of theme toutching and concernyng thoonlie billes exhibited in this parliament to have passed as actes for the reformacion and inhabityng of the marches and the merchauntes called gray merchauntes and the confirmacion and establishement of thacte of pluralities none residence and takyng of fermes by spirituall persones and every thing and thynges comprised in the saide billes and every of theme shoulde be of like force streinght and effect to all and every ententes and purposes as thogh the same and every of theme had bene made enacted and establisshed by auctoritie of that present parliament and soo to contynue in the same streinght force and effect unto the next parliament to be holden within this saide land of Irland; and it was further enacted by thauctoritie aforsaid that the lordes spirituall and temporall and the comens in that parliament to be assembled shoulde have auctoritie and full power to make further establishement of the saide actes

174 1537. 175 Above c. 39. 176 Erasure following *highe*.

and every of theme if it shoulde be soo seen to theme requisite thacte of Ponynges made at Drogheda the xth yere of kyng Henry the vijth[177] in a parliament there holden etc. or any other acte or actes to the contrarie notwithstondyng[178]; in consideracion wherof and for a perfect ordre and establishement of the same be it ordred ordeyned and decreed by us Anthony Sentleger George Poulet Thomas Moyle and William Berners the kynges saide commyssioners with thassent and consent of John Bernewall knyght lorde chaunceller of Irlande George archebusshop of Dublin John prior of Kilmaynam Edward busshop of Methe Henry abbot of sainct Thomas courte William abbot of sainct Mary abbaie Christofor lorde of Houthe John Alen maister of the rolles Thomas fitz Symonde recordor of Dublin James Bathe recordor of Drogheda Thomas Cusake of Cousyngeston' Thomas Agarde Nicholas Bellewe Gerald Ailmer chief justice of the kynges benche Thomas Luttrell chief justice of the comen place Richard Delahide chief baron of thexchequier and William Brabazon underthesaurer that every persone and persons bodies politicque and corporal that nowe have or that hereafter shall have in possession to his or their awne use or uses or in use any landes meses or houses in marches of this lande[179] in fee symple fee taile for terme of life or[180] in warde or in execucion by reason of any statut merchaunt statut of the staple or elegit shall from the feast of Ester whiche shalbe in the yere of our lorde God M v^{c} xxxix^{ti} personallie dwell and be resident in and upon their landes meses or houses or els shall assigne and appoynt souche hable persone or persons whiche shall dwell and be resident in his or their stead or place upon the same as shalbe thought meat ther to enhabit the same by the lorde chaunceller the vicethesaurer the chief and second justices of the kinges bench and comen place the chief baron of the kynges eschequier and the maister of the rolles of this lande for the tyme beyng or any foure of theme from tyme to tyme and that all and every persone and persones or bodies politicque nowe having any landes meses or houses for terme of yeres in any the saide marches shall in like wise duryng their interest be inhabityng and resident upon the same landes meses or houses or els depute and assigne souche persone or persons to enhabit and be resident upon the same as the said lorde chaunceler the vicethesaurer the chief and second justices of the kynges bench and comen place the chief baron of the kynges eschequier [*m.46*] and the maister of the rolles of this lande for the tyme beyng shall thinke hable and meate and noo persone ne persones ne bodies politicque or corporat havyng souche landes meses or houses in possessions or use in the saide marches in fee symple fee

177 1494. 178 In margin: notwithstandynge Ponynges act. 179 In margin: for owners ['inhabitants' crossed out] in [repeated] marchelandes to dwell there or sett hable persons. 180 *or* inserted.

taile for terme of life for terme of yeres in warde or execucion shall at any tyme hereafter make any lease for terme of yeres of any the saide meses landes or houses to any persone or persones but to souche as shalbe admytted and thought hable by the saide lorde chaunceller the vicethesaurer the chief and second justices of the kynges bench and comen place the chief baron of the kynges eschequier and the maister of the rolles of this lande for the tyme beyng or any foure of theme; and further it is ordered ordeyned and decreed by auctoritie aforsaid that if any persone or persones bodies politicque or corporat soo havyng or whiche hereafter shall have any maner of landes meses or houses in fee symple fee taile[181] for terme of life or for terme of yeres or in warde or in execucion by reason of any of the saide statutes of the staple merchaunt or elegit as befor is saide in the saide marches be not befor or at the saide feast of Ester the yere aforsaid resident or doo not fynde some other persone or persons to be thought meate as is beforsaid to be resident in and upon the saide possessions as is aforsaide and that duelie proved before the justices of peaux of the saide shyre or shyres or any ij of theme at the least wher any souche marche lande lieth by the veredict of an enquest and the same by any ij of the said justices certified into the kinges benche or into any other of the kynges courtes of this lande the whiche justices of peaux of every of the saide shyres and every ij of theme shall have full power and auctoritie by this present ordynaunce order and decree to enquier of the same at all and every their cessions and to certifie the same as is beforsaide and after certificat made by the saide justices of peaux or any ij of theme in maner and forme as befor is saide that then it shalbe lefull by auctoritie of this ordynaunce order and decree unto the saide lorde chaunceller vicethesaurer justices chief baron and maister of the rolles of this lande for the tyme being or any foure of theme to make a lease or leases by deade endented of all and every parte and parcell of souche landes meses and houses or any parcell therof soo presented in the name of thowner or owners possessor or possessors of the same as is aforsaide for the terme of ix yeres then next followyng at oon or severall tymes to any persone or persones joynctlie or severallie beyng thought meate by the saide lorde chaunceller vicethesaurer justices chief baron and maister of the rolles of this lande for the tyme beyng or any iiij of theme whiche shall enhabit and dwell upon the same as is aforsaide reservyng to thowner or owners possessor or possessours therof their heyres successors or assignaies and unto souche persone or persones bodies politicque or corporat their heyres or successors as the revercion or revercions remayndre or remayndres therof shall belonge or appertaigne hereafter souche rent and other profict as shalbe thought by the saide lorde chaunceller vicethesaurer justices chief baron and maister of the rolles of this

181 *fee taile* inserted.

lande for the tyme beyng or any foure of theme to be reasonable for the same thoon parte of whiche dead endented to be delyvered to the saide owner or owners possessor or possessors therof; and if it soo be that the saide owner or owners possessor or possessors at thende of the saide nyne yeres or within oon halfe yere then next ensuyng the said nyne yeres doo not eftsones by hym silf or by some other persone or persones to be thought meat as befor is saide inhabit and dwell in and upon the same his landes meses or houses than and as often it shalbe laufull unto the saide chaunceller vicethesaurer justices chief baron and maister of the rolles of this lande for the tyme beyng or any iiij of theme in the name of the saide owner or owners possessor or possessors by deade endented thone parte therof as is aforsaid to be delyvered to make a newe lease or leases of the same landes meses or houses and any parte therof soo not enhabited by the awner or awners possessor or possessors of the same or by some other persone or persones as is beforsaid to be thought meat for other nyne yeres and soo from nyne yeres to nyne yeres as often as the saide owner and awners possessor or possessors dothe after souche nyne yeres determyned by the space of oon quarter of a yere as is aforsaide absent hym silfe or not inhabite the same by theme selves or by souche other persone or persones as soo shalbe thought meat as is beforsaide reservyng souche reasonable rent and other profict as is beforsaide; and it is further ordeyned ordred and decreed by auctoritie aforsaide that it shalbe laufull for every souche awner or awners possessor or possessors their heyres successors or assignaies and to all souche persone or persones bodies politicque and corporat their heyres successors and assignaies unto whom the revercion or revercions remayndre or remayndres therof by any maner meane hereafter shall belonge or aperteigne to distreyne or to have his or their accion or accions of debt for their saide rent or other profict reserved at all souche tyme and tymes as the same rent or other profict or any parte or parcell thereof shalbe behynde unto hym or theme unpaied and to have his or their accion or accions of wast and all other laufull suites accions defenses avauntages and remedies as any leassor makyng a lease for yeres of landes in fee symple or any heire beyng in warde moght have by thordre of the kynges lawes; provided alway and alsoo be it ordeyned ordred and decreed by auctoritie aforsaid that this ordynaunce decree or ordre or any thyng therin conteyned be in noo wise prejudiciall or hurtfull or shall extende for thenhabityng or dwellyng upon the marches as is aforsaide to any persone or persones bodies politicque or corporat whiche nowe have or whiche hereafter shall have in possession as is aforsaide or in use any landes meses or houses in the said marches or in any of theme whiche now be or hereafter shalbe be at any tyme in thandes of eny persone or persones bodies politicque or corporat by reason of eny lease or leases or by reason of eny execucion by statute of the staple statut merchaunt or elegit or by reason of any wardship; provided alsoo and be

it ordeyned ordred and decreed that if any persone or persones bodies politicque or corporat whiche now have or hereafter shall have eny landes meses or houses in the saide marches by reason of any lease or leases for yeres wardship or in execucion as is aforsaide for fewer yeres than nyne yeres and doo not enhabit the same as is aforsaide that yet the saide lord chaunceller vicethesaurer justices chief baron and maister of the rolles of this land for the tyme beyng ne any iiij of theme shall not make any lease or leases of any souche landes meses or houses as is afor saide to contynue any longer then during thinterest or interestes of the saide persone or persones bodies politicque or corporat whiche nowe have or hereafter shall have souche landes meses or houses in lease or leases wardship or in execucion as is aforsaide but that every lease and leases to be made as is aforsaide of souche landes meses or houses by the saide lorde chaunceller vicethesaurer justices chief baron and maister of the rolles of this lande for the tyme beyng or any iiij of them during thenterest or interestes of the said persone and persones bodies politicque and corporat shalbe good and effectuall in lawe by the auctoritie aforsaide; and be it further by thauctoritie aforsaid ordeyned ordred and decreed that if at eny tyme hereafter any doubt or ambiguytie shall ryse where and howe fer the saide marches dothe or shall extende and what landes or tenementes be within the saide marches or whiche not the saide lorde chaunceller tharchebusshops of Dublin and Ardmaghe the busshop of Methe the prior of Kylmaynam the vicethesaurer justices chief baron and maister of the rolles of this lande for the tyme beyng or any sex of theme have auctoritie to declare and lymyt the same from tyme to tyme and that souche declaracion and lymytacion therof shall stonde and be soo taken from thensfurthe till souche tyme as it be otherwise ordred by the saide lorde chaunceller vicethesaurer justices chief baron and maister of the rolles of this lande for the tyme beyng or any iiij of theme and soo from tyme to tyme as often as any souche doubt or ambiguitie shall and dothe aryse.

Anthony Sentleger[182]
George Poulet
Thomas Moile
William Berners
Georgius Dublin'
Edwardus Miden'
Johannes Rawson prior de Kilmaynam
Henry abbot of sainct Thomas courte

182 The names are written in three columns beginning respectively 'Anthony Sentleger', 'Georgius Dublin' and 'Johannes Barnwall'. The right side of the membrane is rubbed.

William abbot of s.M. abbay
Cristofor lorde of Houthe
Johannes Barnwell [. . .]
William Brabazon [. . .]
Gerald Ailmer just[. . .]
John Alen maister of [. . .]
Thomas Luttrell [. . .]
Richard Delahid baron [. . .]
Thomas Cusake [. . .]
Thomas fitz Symon [. . .]
James Bathe [. . .]
Thomas Agard [. . .]
Nicholas Belle[. . .]

Glossary

Ad quod dampnum — A writ ordering the holding of an inquisition to determine whether anyone would suffer damage as a result of land being granted to an individual or a religious body.

Allocate — A writ to the treasurer and barons of the exchequer ordering them to give a person accountable at the exchequer allowance in his account of a specified sum of money.

Inspeximus — An official copy of a grant, appointment or other document, certified in the chancery under the great seal.

Kerde — A goldsmith or worker in other precious metals (modern Irish *ceard*).

Liberate — A writ to the treasurer and chamberlains of the exchequer, ordering them to make a payment out of the treasury.

Personate — Enabled to hold plea in court.

Saute — According to the *Oxford English Dictionary*, 'a ransom for murder or manslaughter'.

Scire facias — A judicial writ calling on a person to show cause why a judgement should not be executed.

Stuff — Materials or requisites necessary for a piece of work.

Sub poena — A judicial writ calling on a person to appear in court and specifying a penalty for non-appearance.

APPENDIX I

Exemplifications of unenrolled statutes from the reign of Edward IV

Not all acts passed in the Irish parliament were enrolled on the statute rolls, though the reason for non-enrolment of an act is not clear. Those which were not enrolled included enactments which had originated in commons' petitions as well as those based on petitions from private individuals. The text of many unenrolled statutes is known to us from other official sources such as the records of the Irish exchequer and chancery. These resulted from the process of exemplification, or issuing of certified copies of the text of an enactment, usually at the request of a party who stood to benefit from the act.

An exemplification of a statute took the form of letters patent under the Irish great seal, in which the king informed all those to whom the letters should come that he had inspected a certain act passed in a certain parliament, the text of which followed. Normally the text of the act was taken from the statute roll, but in the case of unenrolled statutes, it appears that the source used may have been either a draft, or the original petition as presented in parliament, which would have formed the basis for the legislation. Copies of exemplifications were often recorded on the patent rolls of the Irish chancery, none of which survived the fire of 1922. If the king's financial interests were involved, it would obviously be to the benefit of the person requesting the exemplification to have a copy of it enrolled for future reference on the memoranda rolls of the Irish exchequer, and the statutes printed below are all taken from this source.

The memoranda rolls themselves were destroyed in 1922, as were the Irish Record Commission's transcripts of statutes enrolled on them. However, the Record Commission's volume of translations of the statutes from the reign of Edward IV which they had discovered on the memoranda rolls has survived (NAI, RC 8/42). Those enactments which were not included in the printed volumes of Irish statutes for the reign of Edward IV are printed here. In the absence of the original acts it has been thought best to keep editorial changes to a minimum, although some alterations in word order and in the translation of certain words have been made to make the text more intelligible.

[1] 1 Edward IV [1461][1] [Remission of part of the fee farm of the city of Dublin]

Edward etc. We have seen a certain act or ordinance in our parliament held at Naas on the Friday next after the feast of St Barnabas the apostle in the first year of our reign [12 June 1461] before our beloved and faithful Thomas fitz Maurice, earl of Kildare, our justiciar of our land of Ireland, and there finished and ended, [which was] passed in these words:

Also, at the request of the commons, whereas the noble predecessor of our sovereign lord the king, Henry the sixth, late king of England, by his letters patent made at Dublin bearing date the first day of April in the fifth year of his reign [1427] under the attestation of James Butler, at that time earl of Ormond and justiciar of the said late king of his land of Ireland,[2] reciting by the said letters patent how the mayor, bailiffs and commons of the city of Dublin at that time held the said city of him by a fee farm of 200 marks yearly and how both by pestilence and invasions of the Irish enemies and in resisting the said Irish enemies in his said time they have borne, sustained and defended [themselves] and still do so at their own costs by reason of which the said mayor, bailiffs and commons cannot pay that said fee farm without great tallages being put upon the commonalty of the said city, on account of which, divers of the said commons aforesaid at this time have left the said city and others refused to come and dwell within the said city to the great damage and desolation of the said city; which premises considered, the said late king by his said letters patent with the assent of the said justiciar, granted to the said mayor, bailiffs and commons that they and their successors should be acquitted and discharged towards him and his heirs of twenty pounds yearly of the said fee farm of 200 marks during the term of 20 years then next ensuing; and afterwards, whereas the said late king by his other letters patent bearing date at Dublin the twenty-seventh day of September in the twenty-fifth year of his reign [1446],[3] with the assent of Richard, archbishop of Dublin, at that time justiciar of the said late king of the said land of Ireland, having consideration how the walls and fortresses of the said city had much greater need of repair that they had before that time, granted that the said mayor, bailiffs and commons should be discharged and acquitted against him, his heirs and successors of twenty pounds of their said fee farm of two hundred marks yearly to the end of twenty years next following the said years from the first day of April in the fifth year of his reign [1427]; and afterwards, whereas the late king by his other letters patent bearing date at Dublin the twenty-second day

1 From memoranda roll 1 Richard III (RC 8/42 pp 1–19). 2 The patent roll for 5 Henry VI is calendared in *Rot. pat. Hib.*, pp 241–2, but there is no entry corresponding to the letters patent cited here. 3 No patent roll for 25 Henry VI is calendared in *Rot. pat. Hib.*

of January in the thirty-third year of his reign [1455],[4] with the assent of Thomas fitz Maurice, earl of Kildare, then justiciar of the said late king of his land of Ireland, having consideration of the premises, granted to the said mayor, bailiffs and commons that they should be discharged and acquitted against him, his heirs and successors of the twenty pounds of their said fee farm of two hundred marks yearly to the end of forty years following the twenty years from the twenty-seventh day of September in the twenty-fifth year of his said reign [1446], as by the said letters patent fully appears, the tenor of which letters patent follows in this form:

> Henry, by the grace of God king of England and of France and lord of Ireland, to all to whom these present letters shall come, greeting. Know that we, considering how the mayor, bailiffs and commons of our city of Dublin have lately prayed us that whereas we by our letters patent made at Dublin on the first day of April in the fifth year of our reign [1427] under the attestation of James Butler, then earl of Ormond, then justiciar of our land of Ireland, reciting by our same letters how the then mayor, bailiffs and commons of the said city held the said city of us at the fee farm rent of two hundred marks a year and both by reason of pestilences and invasions of our Irish enemies and by divers other intolerable burdens which they had sustained and continued to sustain, in resistance of our said enemies both in the times of our noble progenitors late kings of England as in our time, so that they could in no manner then pay the said fee farm without great tallages being made upon the commonalty of the said city, on account of which many of the commons aforesaid had then left and quitted and others then declined and refused to come the said city and dwell there to the heavy damage and manifest desolation of the said city; and the walls, fortresses and towers around the aforesaid city in various places were then so weak and ruinous as manifestly appeared, so that it was necessary for the then mayor, bailiffs and commons to put themselves to various great expenses and costs about the works and fortification of the said city and other necessary burdens for the defence of the said city and resistance of the malice of the said enemies in this behalf; wherefore they then prayed us that we would consider the matters aforesaid and graciously grant that they, the then mayor, bailiffs and commons, should be acquitted and discharged against us and our heirs from twenty pounds yearly of the said fee farm of two hundred marks a year to the end of twenty years then next coming for the quiet of our liege people and in aid of

4 No patent roll for 33 Henry VI is calendared in *Rot. pat. Hib.*

repairing, fortifying and mending the walls and fortresses of the said city; and we then, considering the premises and the grateful and laudable services which the aforesaid then mayor, bailiffs and commons have heretofore performed to us in resistance of our said Irish enemies in divers parts of our said land and from thenceforward would perform, of our special grace, with the assent of our late justiciar aforesaid and our then council in our said land, and at the special request of the lords spiritual and temporal and commons of the said land present in our last parliament held at Dublin, have granted to the aforesaid mayor, bailiffs and commons that they and their successors should be acquitted and discharged against us and our heirs of twenty pounds yearly of the said fee farm of two hundred marks a year to the end of twenty years then next to come, for the quiet of our liege people and in aid of repairing, fortifying and mending the walls and fortresses of the said city; provided always that no person should by reason of our said grant be precluded from the payment of annuities or rewards to be received yearly out of the said fee farm as is more fully is contained in our letters aforesaid enrolled and existing of record in the rolls of our chancery of Ireland; [they prayed also that], the premises being considered, we would then be pleased further to consider the good and laudable services and great labours, costs and expenses which the said then mayor, bailiffs and commons of the said city continually from year to year expend and intend to expend for us against our Irish enemies and English rebels in our said land in defence of our liege people in divers parts of our lands aforesaid and that the profits, receipts, returns of courts, customs and other revenues of the said city then in all respects were of less value than they were in the time of the making of our said letters patent and that the walls and towers of the said city then were in greater need of being supported and repaired than [they had been] at that time, by reason of the greater weakness of our liege people in all our said land and about the country there, and graciously to grant that they, the then mayor bailiffs and commons of the said city, and their successors after the end of the said twenty years in our said letters patent should be acquitted and discharged against us and our successors of twenty pounds yearly of the said fee farm of two hundred marks a year specified in our said letters patent to the end of twenty years fully to be completed next following the said twenty years; we then, considering all and singular the premises, of our special grace with the assent of Richard, late archbishop of Dublin, our late justiciar of our land aforesaid, by our other letters patent made at Dublin on the twenty-seventh day of September in the twenty-fifth year of our reign [1446] granted to

the said then mayor bailiffs and commons of the said city and their successors that at the end of the said twenty years specified in our said letters patent, they, their heirs and successors should be acquitted and discharged against us, our heirs and successors of the said twenty pounds yearly in every year of the said fee farm of the said two hundred marks a year specified in the said letters patent to the end of twenty years then next ensuing fully to be completed; provided always that no person should be precluded by pretext of our said grant as is aforesaid from the payment of annuities or rewards out of the said fee farm yearly to be received, notwithstanding that express mention of other gifts and rewards to the then mayor, bailiffs and commons of the said city before the said twenty-seventh day of September by us our ancestors and progenitors is not made in these presents, as in our said letters patent made under the attestation of the aforesaid late archbishop, our late justiciar, is more fully contained, that we would be pleased to consider all and singular the premises and also to consider the good and laudable service and great labours costs and expenses which the now mayor, bailiffs and commons of the said city continually from year to year expend and intend to expend for us against our Irish enemies and English rebels in our said land in the defence of our liege people in various parts of our said land and that the profits, receipts, returns of courts, customs and other revenues of the said city now in all things are of less value than they were at the time of the making of our said letters patent made under the attestation of the aforesaid late archbishop, our late justiciar of our aforesaid land, and that the walls and towers of the said city are now in greater need of being supported and repaired than then on account of the greater weakness of our liege people throughout our entire said land and around the country there and graciously to grant that they the mayor, bailiffs and commons of the said city and their successors, at the end of the said twenty years specified in the said letters patent made on the said twenty-seventh day of September may be acquitted against us, our heirs and successors of the aforesaid twenty pounds yearly in every year of the said fee farm of two hundred marks a year specified in our said letters patent made on the said twenty-seventh day of September; and we, considering all and singular the premises of our special grace with the assent of our beloved and faithful Thomas fitz Maurice, earl of Kildare, our justiciar of our land of Ireland, have granted to the now mayor, bailiffs and commons of the said city and their successors that from the end of the said twenty years specified in our said letters patent made on the said twenty-seventh day of September, they, their heirs and successors shall be acquitted and

> discharged against us, our heirs and successors of twenty pounds yearly in every year of the said fee farm of the said two hundred marks; provided always that no person shall be precluded under pretext of our said grant as is aforesaid from the payment of annuities or rewards out of the said fee farm yearly to be perceived; notwithstanding that express mention does not exist in these presents of other gifts and rewards aforesaid to the late mayor, bailiffs and commons of the said city or to the said now mayor, bailiffs and commons of the said city heretofore made by us our progenitors or ancestors. In witness whereof we have caused these our letters patents to be made. Witness our aforesaid justiciar at Dublin on the twenty-second of January in the thirty-third year of our reign [1455].

Whereupon the premises being considered, it is ordained and granted by authority of the said parliament that the said letters patent and all things contained in them be accepted, ratified and confirmed and shall be as effectual as if they were granted anew to the mayor, bailiffs and commons aforesaid by our sovereign lord the king that now is under his great seal of England, and that the said mayor, bailiffs and commons by the same authority shall be acquitted and discharged against our said sovereign lord the king, his heirs and successors of the said twenty pounds yearly according to the said letters patent in all points, any grant or grants of the said twenty pounds to any person or person made notwithstanding.

[2] 5 Edward IV [1465][5] [Pardon of fee farm and grant of custom and cocket of the city of Cork to the mayor and commons there]

Recites letters patent which the king in his parliament held at Trim on the Monday next after the feast of St Laurence the martyr in the fifth year of his reign [12 August 1465] before his beloved and faithful cousin Thomas Desmond, earl of Desmond, deputy of the well-beloved brother of the said lord the king, George, duke of Clarence, lieutenant of the said lord the king of his land of Ireland, by authority of the said parliament accepted, ratified, adjudged and confirmed, the tenor of which act follows in these words:

Also, at the prayer of the mayor and commons of the city of Cork that, by authority of the said parliament, the letters patent, the tenor of which hereafter follows, [and every] matter and article contained in them, be accepted, approved, ratified and confirmed good and effectual in law in every point, notwithstanding any default in the said letters patent:

5 From memoranda roll 7 Edward IV m. 3 (RC 8/42 pp 21–5).

> Edward, by the grace of God king of England [and] France and lord of Ireland, to all to whom the present letters may come, greeting. Know that we, understanding how the mayor and commons of our city of Cork in our land of Ireland have had eleven parochial churches belonging to our city of the space and length of one mile on either part of the said city for which the said mayor [and commons] yearly paid eighty marks of fee farm to our crown of England as long as the said suburbs were preserved undestroyed, but now, as we are informed, the churches and suburbs by reason of the war stirred up by the Irish enemies and English rebels are altogether laid waste, thrown down and destroyed and [have remained] so for the term of fifty years, by reason whereof the said mayor and commonalty at no time within that term have ever [been able to pay] the said fee farm or any parcel thereof but [were acquitted] of the said fee farm by our most beloved lord and father when he was last in those parts [...]. We therefore, having consideration and respect both to the premisses and the insufficiency [and] poverty which our aforesaid city in these days sustained by reason of the said enemies [and rebels as] we have understood, and to the fidelity of hearts towards our aforesaid [father and to ourselves born and] to be born by them, of our special grace have pardoned the aforesaid mayor and commons the said fee farm in future [and] also have given and granted to the said mayor and commons the cocket of the aforesaid city [and the custom] of the same to increase the building of the walls of the said city for [the security and] safe [keeping] of the same and for the assistance, succour and relief of the said mayor and commons, to have, occupy and enjoy the said cocket until they are enabled to go outside the walls of the said city for one mile [...]. In witness whereof we have caused these our letters patent to be made. Witness [myself] at Bustella the first day of December in the second year of our reign [1462].[6]

And further it is ordained by the said authority that the mayor and commons that now are and for the time to come shall be, may receive the cocket of the said city [and the] custom of the same for repairing the walls of the said city until the said mayor [and commons] or any of them may peaceably from day to day go and do their business duly in any road outside the walls of the said city without the protection of any person or persons; and that by the said authority it is ordained and established that the mayor and commons shall be entirely discharged of any account to be returned into the exchequer of our sovereign lord the king in Ireland for the receipt of the said custom and cocket or for any

6 Calendared in *Cal. Pat. Rolls, 1461–7*, p. 214.

issues or profits pertaining to the same during the time aforesaid, [and] shall not be molested, vexed or grieved; provided that they shall not have custom of any man inhabiting in any city or town outside the franchise of the said city of Cork.

[3] 8 Edward IV [1469][7] [Confirmation of remissions and pardons previously made to Ismay Barnewall, now wife of Robert Bold]

And afterwards, in a parliament of the said lord the king at Drogheda on the Friday next after the feast of the conversion of St Paul in the eighth year of present reign [27 January 1469], before the most beloved cousin of the said lord the king, John, earl of Worcester, deputy of the most beloved brother of the said lord the king, George, duke of Clarence, lieutenant of the said lord the king of his land of Ireland, held and thence adjourned and continued to the city of Dublin, and then in like manner adjourned to the said city of Dublin, [and] there at divers times prorogued and continued, set forth etc., it was ordained and established etc. as etc. which statute follows in these words:

Also at the prayer of Robert Bold, knight, lord of Rathouth and Ismay, his wife, [late] the wife of Sir Nicholl Bernewall, knight, whereas our sovereign lord the king that [now is by] his letters patent made at Dublin the twelfth day of July in the seventh year of his reign [1467],[8] remitted and released to the said Ismay jointly with Christopher Bernewall, [son and] heir to the said Sir Nicholl, divers matters, things and articles as is expressed more fully in the [said letters] patent; whereupon, the premises being considered, [it is enacted], ordained and established by authority of the said parliament that the said letters [patent and] every article contained in them shall be adjudged and deemed [effective and good] in law and beneficial to the said Robert and Ismay in every point, [any statute], act or ordinance, resumption or restriction to the contrary made [notwithstanding. And] also, whereas our said sovereign lord by his said letters patent pardoned [the said Ismay] in like manner jointly with the aforesaid Christopher all [debts, accounts] and arrears of accounts, fines, issues, amercements [...] of the same as more fully appears [... it is enacted], ordained and established by authority of the said parliament that every [...] from answering to the king of any debt of which the said Ismay [and Christopher], as it is aforesaid,shall be quit and discharged against our said [sovereign lord the king his] officers and ministers whatsoever at all times.

7 From memoranda roll 9 Edward IV m. 23d. (RC 8/42 pp 29–37). 8 The patent roll for 7 Edward IV was too damaged to be calendared in *Rot. pat. Hib.* (p. 269)

[4] 8–9 Edward IV [1469–70][9] [Confirmation of grants of land made by kings Henry II and John to St Mary's abbey, Dublin]

Recites that in a parliament of our lord the king held at Drogheda on the Friday next after the feast of the conversion of St Paul in the eighth year of his reign [27 January 1469] before John, earl of Worcester, deputy of George, duke of Clarence, lieutenant of the said lord the king of his land of Ireland, and thence adjourned to the city of the said lord the king of Dublin and finished there on the Monday next before the feast of the nativity of St John Baptist last past [18 June 1470],[10] in which was passed a statute, the tenor of which follows in these words:

Also, at the prayer of Walter, abbot of the house of the Blessed Virgin Mary near Dublin, whereas king Henry the first,[11] formerly king of England, by his charter made at Fallis[12] in Normandy granted to Redmond [the] abbot, formerly governor of the said house, and to his successors, the lordship of Clonliff, Dryshok, Portmernok, Clonsagh, Karickbrenan, Balmacheylmere [and] Culmyn with various other lands, tenements, rents and services with the appurtenances, to wit, churches and chapels, in wood and in plains, with all manner of wrecks that come upon their lands, in meadows, in pastures, in waters, in mills, in lakes and rivers, in ways and paths, in fisheries and fishings, in harbours and towns as by the charter of the said late king more fully appears,[13] and after that, the said king Henry by his letters patent made at Fecham in his county of Louth in Ireland,[14] gave, granted and confirmed in pure and perpetual alms to God and to the church of Our Lady near Dublin and the abbot and monks there serving God, all the said lands with the said appurtenances; also Richard Strongbow, formerly governor of Ireland, before the grant made by the said Henry formerly king, granted to God and to the monks of the said house various lands, tenements, rents and services with their appurtenances as more fully [appears] by the said letters patent of the said Richard;[15] also John, formerly lord of Ireland, by his letters patent granted to the monks of the said house various tenements, rents and services as more fully appears by the letters patent of the said John, formerly lord of Ireland;[16] and after this, the said John, being king of England, gave and granted by his letters patent to the said house and to the monks there serving God various lands tenements, rents and services, with their appurtenances, as more fully appears by the letters patent of the said king John,[17] of which lands, tenements, rents and services, with their appurtenances, the abbots and monks of the said house

9 From memoranda roll 10 Edward IV m. 12 (RC 8/42 pp 33–7). 10 For the year of this parliament, see no. 6 below. 11 recte *second*. 12 Falaise. 13 *Chartul. St Mary's, Dublin*, i, pp 81–2. 14 Ibid., pp 79–81. The letters were dated at Feckenham, Worcestershire, not at Termonfeckin as the act supposes. 15 Ibid., pp 78–9. 16 Ibid., pp 84–7. 17 Ibid., pp 88–9.

have been possessed beyond the time of which there is any memory to the contrary; whereupon the premises being considered, it is ordained by authority of the said parliament that all the lands, tenements, rents and services, with their appurtenances, with every other thing contained in any of the said letters patent, be given granted and confirmed to to the said Walter, now abbot, and to his successors for ever; and that if the said Walter, now abbot of the monastery of St Mary, be impeached now or if any of his successors be impeached by our sovereign lord the king, his heirs or ministers in time to come for any manner of thing contained in any of the said letters patent, both now and in time to come, that then the said Walter, now abbot, or any of his successors may have the writs of our sovereign lord the king directed to all of his ministers or officers, commanding them to supersede the said matter; provided that this act shall extend to all manors, lands, tenements, rents and services with all manner of wreck, meadows. woods and pastures with the appurtenances, churches and chapels of which the said abbot is now seised and possessed.

[5] 8–10 Edward IV [1469–70][18] [St Mary's abbey, Dublin discharged from payment of rents in co. Dublin]

Recites that in a parliament of our lord the king held at Drogheda on the Friday next after the feast of the conversion of St Paul in the eighth year of his reign [27 January 1469] before John, earl of Worcester, deputy of George, duke of Clarence, lieutenant of the said lord the king of his land of Ireland, and thence adjourned to the city of the said lord the king of Dublin, and thence in like manner adjourned to the town of Bray, also thence adjourned to the aforesaid city in like manner and there at various times prorogued and continued, finished and ended, it was ordained and established that etc. the tenor of which statute follows in these words:

Also, at the prayer of Walter, abbot of the house of the Blessed Virgin our Lady St. Mary near Dublin and the monks there serving God, whereas the said abbot and monks yield and pay six shillings and eight pence of a certain rent yearly issuing out of a mill called Douildayismill and six shillings and eight pence of a rent issuing out of the Cappagh in the county of Dublin to our sovereign lord the king as more fully appears by the records of our said sovereign lord the king in his exchequer in Ireland, and because the said mill is often broken down and burned both by the Irish enemies of the king and by English rebels, and the said abbot and monks do not in any manner know where the said

18 From memoranda roll 10 Edward IV m. 13 (RC 8/42 pp 41–5).

Cappagh is nor do they take in any manner any profits of the said Cappagh by that name, and also whereas their lands and tenements, possessions of the said abbots and monks, in the borders of the marches are greatly wasted and destroyed both by the Irish enemies of the king and by coign, livery, oppression and extortion committed by the marchmen and English rebels of the king, so that the said abbot and monks and their successors are unlikely to maintain hospitality or continually to pray for our said lord the king his children and his noble progenitors in such number of persons as they used to do in ancient times; whereupon, the premises being considered, and how hospitality and prayer in the said house may be continued in time to come, it is ordained, enacted and established by authority of the said parliament that the said abbot and monks and their successors shall be quitclaimed, released and utterly discharged from henceforth against our said sovereign lord the king, his heirs or successors in time to come, of the said yearly rents issuing out of the said mill and Cappagh, any statute, act, ordinance, farm, deed or grant to any person or persons of the said rents or any other matter [or] cause in any manner notwithstanding.

[6] 8–10 Edward IV [1469–70][19] [Pardon to Barnaby Barnewall of all debts and accounts]

That the lord Edward the fourth, late king of England, predecessor of our lord the king that now is, in a certain parliament of his held at Drogheda on the Friday next after the feast of the conversion of St Paul in the eighth year of the reign of the said late king [27 January 1469], before John, earl of Worcester, deputy of George, duke of Clarence, lieutenant of the said lord the late king of his land of Ireland, and thence adjourned to the city of the said late king of Dublin, and thence adjourned in like manner to the town of Bray, and also again adjourned and continued in like manner to the said city, and there on the Monday next before the feast of the Nativity of St John the Baptist in the tenth year of the reign of the said late king [18 June 1470] set forth, it is ordained etc. the tenor of which act follows in these words:

Also at the prayer of Barnaby Barnewall, esquire, whereas he is lawfully seised of all the lands and tenements in Cokestown near Scryne in his demesne as of fee, which lands and tenements were in former times seized into the king's hands and valued at a certain sum and afterwards, by legal means, the hands of the king were removed, nevertheless, the said seizure was not removed from or taken out of the great roll of the exchequer, by reason of which a certain debt is incurred upon the said lands and tenements and upon the said Barnaby, and

19 From memoranda roll 13 Henry VII m. 8 (RC 8/42 pp 49–51).

also upon the tenant of the said lands and tenements, by reason of which the said Barnaby is greatly harassed at the king's suit and has lost issues without knowing anything of this; whereupon the premises being considered, it is ordained, established and enacted by authority of the said parliament that the said seizure shall be taken out of the great roll and out of every other place where it is of record in the said exchequer, as often as the said Barnaby requires the same; and that by the said authority the said Barnaby be pardoned all debts and accounts and clearly discharged against the king and his ministers and against every person both by way of distress or otherwise.

[7] 18 Edward IV [1478][20] [Lands in Slane, co. Meath to be restored to John Boys and Genet Palmer]

Also, at the prayer of John Boys and Genet Palmer his wife, whereas in an inquisition taken before the barons of the king's exchequer in Ireland at Dublin on the Tuesday next before the feast of the conversion of St Paul in the fifteenth year of the reign of the king our sovereign lord that now is [23 January 1476], it was found that one Henry Palmer of Callan was seised in his demesne as of fee on the day that he died of two messuages and ten acres of land with the appurtenances in Slane, which are of the yearly value of forty pence, which messuages and land the said Henry held of Thomas Fleming then baron of Slane by knight service, the said baron then being under age and in the wardship of the king, and also it was found by the said inquest that the said Henry was seised in his demesne as of fee on the day that he died of eighty acres of land in Fynnor which are of the yearly value of 26s. and 8d., and held the same of Christopher Bernewall of Crikestown as of his manor of Fynnor by the service of a penny for all manner of services, and that the said Henry died on the Monday next after the feast of St Michael the archangel in the seventh year of the reign of our said sovereign lord [5 October 1467], and that one Thomas Palmer was his son and heir and of the age of ten years and unmarried, and for the said reasons the said messuages and land were taken and seized into the hands of the king our sovereign lord aforesaid as more fully appears by the copy of the said inquest which was ready to be shown; and after that, the said Thomas Flemyng died, being under age and in the wardship of the king, and after that, the said Thomas Palmer died, being also in the wardship of our said sovereign lord as a wardship within a wardship, after whose death the said messuages and lands have passed to the said Genet as cousin and heir to the said Thomas, [to wit] as daughter to Thomas Palmer of Cullane the elder, father to the said Henry, father to the said Thomas mentioned in the said inquest; and

20 From memoranda roll 19 Edward IV m. 9 (RC 8/42 pp 57–61).

inasmuch as the said John and Genet are poor and powerless and have no goods or chattels except such as people give them for the love of God, so that they have not the power and are unable to sue livery of the said messuages and lands according to the form of the common law; in consideration of which, it is ordained, enacted and established by authority of the said parliament that the hands of the king our said sovereign lord shall be removed from the said messuages and lands and that it shall be lawful for the said John and Genet, as in right of the said Genet, to enter into the said messuages and lands with the appurtenances and to possess and enjoy the same, and to take, levy and receive the issues and profits thereof without any hindrance on the part of the king our said sovereign lord, his heirs, officers or ministers, saving to every man his right and title by way of action.

[8] 18 Edward IV [1478][21] [Licence for grant of property in Dublin city to the proctors of St Werburgh's church, Dublin]

Also, at the request of the commons, whereas Walter Baldewyne and William Cornell are seised in their demesne as of fee of one messuage with the appurtenances in the city of Dublin in the parish of St Werburgh, which messuage is called the Corryngham's Innes, and the said Walter and William, being thus seised, have intended to give the said messuage with the appurtenances to Patrick Burnell and Patrick Gerrote, now proctors of the said church, and to their successors, proctors of the said church, for ever, to the intent that the said Patrick and Patrick should ordain, constitute and find a priest yearly for ever to sing in the chapel of St Marome in the church aforesaid for all Christian souls; and also, Martin Broun, chaplain, is seised in his demesne as of fee of one other messuage in the same city and in the same parish in which messuage one John Duff now dwells, and it is intended to give the said messuage with the appurtenances to the said Patrick and Patrick and to their successors, proctors of the said church, in aid and support of the exhibition of the said priest, and because the yearly value of the said two messuages does not amount to the sum for which a chaplain may be yearly found and kept, and also because the repair of messuages within the said city is so expensive and costly, it is ordained and established by authority of the said parliament that the said Patrick and Patrick, now proctors of the said church, and their successors in time to come may purchase other lands and tenements to the yearly value of ten pounds and that the said Walter, William and Martin, now being seised of the said messuages, may give and grant the said messuages with their appurtenances to the said Patrick and Patrick, now proctors of the said church, to have and to hold

21 From memoranda roll 19 Edward IV m. 10 (RC 8/42 pp 61–7).

to them and to their successors, proctors of the said church, for ever, to the intent aforesaid. without prosecution of the king's writ called *ad quod damnum* or without any hindrance on the part of the king, his heirs, officers or ministers; and that by the same authority, they and their successors, proctors of the church, may be made and called proctors of the said church; and that the parishioners of the church shall have full power every year, at whatever time they please, to elect two from among themselves to be proctors of the said church, which proctors so elected, and especially the said Patrick and Patrick now proctors of the said church, or their successors proctors of the said church, shall have full authority and power to purchase the said two messuages with the other lands and tenements to the value of ten pounds, to have and enjoy them to them and to their successors for ever to the aforesaid intent, and that the said proctors who now are or in time to come shall be, shall have full power to sue assizes and all other manner of actions, real and personal and mixed, concerning the said messuages and lands and tenements as their matter and case is, lies and requires in like manner as any other person may sue, and that the said Patrick and Patrick and their successors, proctors of the said church, may have and enjoy the said messuages with their appurtenances with the other [lands] and tenements aforesaid to them and to their successors aforesaid, as against our sovereign lord the king his heirs and successors without any hindrance on the part of our said sovereign lord, his heirs, successors, officers or ministers and without any hindrance or impediment by any other persons, any thing or matter to the contrary had or to be had notwithstanding, saving to every common person their action, if they have any, according to the course of the common law, to demand the messuages or any parcel of them by any title accruing to them before any purchase thereof in fact in the form aforesaid.

[9] 18 Edward IV [1478][22] [Walter Mareward to be permitted to enter into his inheritance in cos. Dublin and Meath]

Also, at the prayer of Walter Marward, cousin and heir to Richard Marward, knight, late baron of Scryne, whereas the said Richard was seised in his demesne as of fee of the manors of Scryne and Kilcarne in the county of Meath, with their appurtenances except Ballymolghane, and also of two thirds of the manor of Sauntrefe with the appurtenances except Sturmynestown and Balincore with their appurtenances, in the county of Dublin, which manors and two thirds of the manor of Sauntreff the said Richard held of our sovereign lord the king by knight service, and being thereof seised, died seised; and also the said Richard was seised of one messuage and one ploughland with the

22 From memoranda roll 19 Edward IV m. 16 (RC 8/42 pp 67–71).

appurtenances in Braknanestown, one messuage and one ploughland in Colwellestown, one messuage and one ploughland in Ashbornrath the greater and Ashbornrath the lesser in the county of Dublin in his demesne as of freehold as tenant by the courtesy of England, by reason of Joan Ashborne his wife, because the said Richard and the said Joan had issue between them, William Marward, which William had issue the said Walter, and after the death of the said Richard, the said manors and two thirds of the manor of Sauntreff with all the lands and tenements aforesaid, with the appurtenances, have descended to the said Walter as cousin and heir of the said Richard, to wit, son and heir to William, son and heir to the said Richard, by reason of which our sovereign lord the king has given him full livery of the said manors, two thirds of the manor of Sauntreff and all the lands and tenements aforesaid with their appurtenances, out of the chancery in Ireland, because the said Walter was and is of the age of twenty-one years; whereupon the premises being considered, it is adjudged by authority of the said parliament that the said livery be ratified, confirmed, approved and adjudged good and effectual in law, and by the said authority it shall be lawful for the said Walter to enter into the said two thirds of Sauntreff with the appurtenances and into all the messuages, lands and tenements aforesaid, with their appurtenances, and to receive, levy and take yearly the issues, profits and commodities thereof pertaining to his said inheritance, without any hindrance, impediment, molestation or grievance from our said sovereign lord the king, his heirs, successors, officers or ministers; and, that by the said authority, the said Walter shall be acquitted, pardoned and clearly discharged of his homage to be made to our said sovereign lord the king, his heirs, successors, officers or ministers; provided always that this act shall not extend nor be prejudicial in any manner to Walter Cusake in and in respect of all of the messuages, lands and tenements in Balimolhane in the county of Meath, nor to Richard Stanyhurst in and in respect of all the lands and tenements in Balimore in the county of Dublin; also, by the said authority, it shall be lawful for the said Walter to receive, levy and take all manner of rents, revenues and commodities from the term of St Michael last past and so henceforward, without any hindrance on the part of our sovereign lord the king, his heirs and successors or any other person, [and] without giving any account to our said sovereign lord the king, his heirs or successors or any of his judges, officers or ministers; excepting always that this act shall not extend nor be prejudicial in any manner to Walter, abbot of the house of the Blessed Virgin Mary near Dublin, or to his successors, concerning the advowson of the vicarage of the church of St Colme of Scryne.

[10] 18 Edward IV [1478][23] [Confirmation of appointment of Thomas Archbold, *alias* Thomas Galmole, as master of the mint in Ireland]

Also, at the prayer of Thomas Archebold, otherwise called Thomas Galmole, whereas it has pleased our sovereign lord the king of his most benign and abundant grace by his letters patent made at Drogheda on the fifteenth day of December in the eighteenth year of his most noble reign [1478],[24] to ordain and constitute the said Thomas by the name of Thomas Archebold otherwise called Thomas Galmole, master of all his mints of money or monies to be made or coined within this land of Ireland, to have and to hold the said office and therein to receive yearly fees, wages and rewards according as it is specified more fully in the tenor of the said letters patent; whereupon the premises being considered, it is ordained, enacted and established by authority of the said parliament that the said letters patent and the said office, ordinance and appointment, with the wages and rewards specified in the same letters patent, by authority of this said act and ordinance, be ratified, confirmed, given, granted and ordained to the said Thomas Archebold otherwise called Thomas Galmole, to have, hold and enjoy the said office with the wages and rewards aforesaid to the said Thomas for the term of his life; provided that this act shall not extend nor be prejudicial to Walter Marchall otherwise called Marshall, master of the mint of the city of Waterford.

[11] 18 Edward IV [1478][25] [Confirmation of grant to Holy Trinity, Dublin, of £20 yearly out of the fee farm of the city of Dublin]

Also, at the prayer of Thomas, prior of the cathedral church of the Holy Trinity in the city of Dublin, and the convent of the same, whereas they, by letters patent lately made to them by Henry the sixth, late in fact and not in right king of England, by the assent of the most excellent prince Richard, late duke of York, then being his lieutenant of Ireland and at other times thereafter by the assent of Thomas fitz Morice, late earl of Kildare, then being justiciar of this land of Ireland, gave and granted to the said prior and convent of the said cathedral church and their successors twenty pounds yearly to be received out of the fee farm of the city of Dublin for a term of years, of which term eighteen years remain,[26] and, for the more ample aid and consideration of the divine

23 From memoranda roll 19 Edward IV m. 18. Exemplification dated 11 June 1479 (RC 8/42 pp 71–3). **24** No patent roll for 18 Edward IV is calendared in *Rot. pat. Hib.* **25** From memoranda roll 19 Edward IV m. 39 (RC 8/42 pp 77–81). **26** The original grant of £20 p.a. for 20 years was made on 16 June 1444; on 8 February 1455 the grant was renewed for a further 20 years after the expiry of the first term. The text of these grants has not survived, but an inspeximus and confirmation of both, dated 14 October 1461, is calendared in *Rot. pat. Hib.* p. 269 no. 70. No similar grant from the time of the lieutenancy of Richard, duke of York has been

service from day to day administered in the said church, they have been provided and kept in possession of the same and at all times in every parliament by the gracious consideration of every governor of this land for the time being; whereupon the premises being considered, it is ordained, enacted and established by authority of the said parliament that the gift and grant of the said twenty pounds yearly during the said eighteen years following the day of this present act and ordinance, by authority of this present act and ordinance, be ratified, confirmed, given and granted to the said prior and convent and to their successors, and they shall have, take, levy and receive the said twenty pounds yearly during the said term out of the said fee farm by the hands of the mayor and bailiffs of the said city for the time being at two feasts in the year, to wit, the feasts of St Michael and Easter, by equal portions, with the arrears of the same for the terms of Easter and St Michael last past before the day of the making of this present act and ordinance; and by the same authority, the mayor and bailiffs now being, and others who in time to come shall be found for the time being, upon showing sufficient acquittances made to them as for the time being by the said prior and convent or their successors for the payments during the said term thereof to be made in form aforesaid, shall receive allowance for the same in the making of their account of the said fee farm before the barons of the king's exchequer in Ireland, and that by the said authority, the act of resumption in this said parliament or parliaments made or to be made shall not extend nor be effectual in law to injure, annul or be in any manner prejudicial to this present act and ordinance nor to the said prior and convent concerning the ratification, confirmation, gift and grant before specified.

[12] 18 Edward IV [1478][27] [Discharge of the convent of Odder from payment of all subsidies and other impositions]

Edward etc. We have seen a certain act or ordinance in our parliament held at Trym on the Friday next after the feast of All Saints last past [6 November 1478] before our beloved Henry Grey, deputy of our dear and most beloved son George, our lieutenant of our land of Ireland, and thence adjourned to our town of Drogheda, and there on the Thursday next before the feast of St Katherine the virgin then next following [19 November 1478] set forth in these words:

Also at the prayer of Elizabeth, abbess of the house of Oddre and the convent of the same, whereas the said abbess and convent have no more possessions nor

traced. The reference to the 18 remaining years of the term does not fit with the dates of either of the known grants. **27** From memoranda roll 17 Henry VIII m. 31 (RC 8/42 pp 85–7).

support in spirituality or temporality than one ploughland, by which divine service and hospitality are kept continually in the said house as far as is in their power according to the said possessions, and now the said abbess and convent are so oppressed, molested and grievously harassed by coygn and livery and various other oppressions and subsidies and tallages both the king's subsidies and others, that unless a remedy be tenderly shown to them in this behalf, the said service and hospitality are [likely to be] entirely withdrawn and diminished; whereupon the premises being considered, it is ordained and established by authority of the said parliament that the said abbess and convent and their successors from henceforward shall be discharged of all manner of coign or livery, subsidies and tallages and all other oppressions, and that it shall be lawful for the said abbess and convent to deforce all manner of persons acting contrary to this act or ordinance without any hindrance or impediment from our sovereign lord the king or any of his officers [or] ministers in time to come, provided that they do not unlawfully receive William Oneley or any of the king's enemies or rebels by day or by night and that the receivers and collectors for the time being shall have due allowance thereof in their accounts.

Now we etc. have caused to be exemplified etc. the tenth day of December in the eighteenth year of our reign [1478].

[13] 19 Edward IV [1479–80][28] [Confirmation of appointment of John Estrete as king's sergeant at law in Ireland and arrangements for yearly payment to him]

Be it remembered that John Estrete, serjeant at laws of the lord king etc., exhibited to the court here a certain exemplification of a certain act etc. in these words: Edward etc. We have seen a certain act or ordinance in our parliament held at Dublin on the Friday next after the feast of the Conception of the Blessed Virgin Mary in the nineteenth year of our reign [10 December 1479] before our most beloved cousin Gerald, earl of Kildare, deputy of our beloved and most dear son, Richard of Shrewsbury, duke of York, our lieutenant of our land of Ireland, and there prorogued and thence adjourned to the town of Naas, and there in like manner prorogued and continued, and also on the Monday next after the feast of St. Hilary the bishop last past [17 January 1480] at the humble prayer of John Estrete set forth in these words:

Also, at the prayer of John Estrete, whereas it pleased our sovereign lord the king of his benign and most abundant grace, by his letters patent made at Dublin the eighteenth day of December in the eighteenth year of his most

28 From memoranda roll 19 Edward IV m. 11d. (RC 8/42 pp 89–99).

noble reign [1478] under his great seal of this his land of Ireland,[29] to give and grant to the said John the office of king's serjeant at his laws in his said land of Ireland to have, hold, occupy and exercise the said office according to the tenor and effect of the said letters patent and to receive in the said office yearly ten pounds of money at the feasts of Easter and St Michael the archangel out of the issues and profits yearly arising in the king's mints specified in the same, or out of the issues and profits arising from the king's custom yearly to be received in the port of his city of Dublin in manner as it is more fully specified in the said letters patent, together with all manner of other rewards, profits and commodities due and accustomed to the said office of ancient times, as more fully appears by the said letters patent; whereupon the premises being considered, and how also that the said mints are damaged, wherein the said John is now uncertain of his satisfaction of his said fee in this behalf, it is ordained, enacted and established by authority of the said parliament that the said letters patent and office, gift, grants and all other things specified and contained in them, by authority of this said parliament be ratified, approved and confirmed, and also by the same authority, the said John Estrete shall be given and granted in all and every manner, according to the tenor of the gifts, grants, clauses, sentences and words in the same letters patent specified and contained, and by the same authority he shall have, hold and enjoy the said office and all and every of the said gifts and together with the said yearly ten pounds of money and the yearly payments of the same at the feasts aforesaid by equal portions out of the said issues and profits of the said custom in manner as it is specified in the said letters patent, with fifty shillings thereof to be received yearly from the issues and profits yearly arising from the manor or villages of Stepultown in the county of Meath at the terms aforesaid by equal portions by the hands of the receivers, farmers or tenants thereof, [and fifty shillings][30] to be received yearly [from the issues and profits][31] arising from the king's custom heretofore received in the haven and port of his town of Drogheda at the terms aforesaid by equal portions by the hands of the customer, collector, farmer or any other manner of occupier or occupier of the same for the time being, and that by the same authority the other five pounds, residue of the said ten pounds, shall be received yearly at the terms aforesaid of the issues, profits and revenues of the king yearly arising out of this his land by the hands of the treasurer of this his said land of Ireland and the chamberlains of his exchequer in the same for the time being, or any of their deputy or deputies, with all other rewards and wages specified in the said letters patent of the said John Estrete in and of all and every manner of thing according to the purport, tenor and effect of the said

29 No patent roll for 18 Edward IV is calendared in *Rot. pat. Hib.* 30 Words omitted in text.
31 Words omitted in text.

letters patent or of this present act and ordinance for term of the life of the said John Estrete; and by the same authority no manner of act, statute or ordinance or acts, statutes or ordinances made or to be made in this said parliament or in any other manner of parliament or parliaments in this land held or to be held shall extend or be of effect in law to injure, annul or in any manner to be prejudicial to the said John Estrete or to revoke this present act and ordinance; and that it shall be lawful for the said receivers, farmers or tenants of the said manor or village for the time being, [as to] the said fifty shillings in form aforesaid to be received out of the said manor or village, and also for the said customer, collector, farmer and for every other manner of occupier of the said custom of the said town of Drogheda and for every of their deputies or deputy for the time being [as to] the other fifty shillings, to make payment thereof in form aforesaid to the said John Estrete or to his assign or assigns, receiving acquittances of the payments thereof as it is required, and that upon the delivery and showing of such acquittances thereof to be made as often as it shall be lawful, for the barons of the king's exchequer for the time being to allow all such acquittances and every of them, and by the same authority they shall be allowed in quit discharge of the payers thereof and each one of them against the king, his officers and ministers for the time being, any manner of acts, statutes, grants, gifts or any other thing to the contrary made notwithstanding; and that by the said authority the said John Estrete shall be pardoned, acquitted and to every intent discharged in every manner of things from the feast of the Epiphany of our Lord next coming [6 January] from the custom called poundage and all other manner of customs due and to be paid to our sovereign lord the king, and so reputed and taken free of custom, any act or grants to the contrary made notwithstanding; provided that this act shall not be prejudicial to the mayor and bailiffs of the city of Dublin, the mayor [and] sheriffs of the town of Drogheda, who now are or shall be, nor to their liberties, or to Thomas Plunket, chief baron of the king's exchequer in Ireland; provided also at all times that this said act shall not extend nor be prejudicial to William, bishop of Meath, or to Sir Rowland Eustace, knight, lord of Portlester, treasurer of Ireland, or to Robert St Laurence, knight, lord of Howth, or Philip Bermyngham, chief justice of Ireland, or to Barnaby Bernewall, second justice of the chief bench of the king, or to Robert Rochford, esquire, or to Roger Rocheford, gentleman, or to any of them in any manner.

[14] 19 Edward IV [1479–80][32] [Mayor, bailiffs and commons of Dublin to be permitted to distrain on all lands within the city, although they may be in the hands of the king or other persons]
Edward etc. We have seen a certain act or ordinance in our parliament held at Dublin on the Friday next after the feast of the [Conception of the] Blessed Virgin Mary last past [10 December 1479] before our most beloved cousin, Gerald earl of Kildare, deputy to our beloved and very dear son, Richard of Shrewsbury, duke of York, our lieutenant of our land of Ireland, and prorogued and thence adjourned to the town of Naas, and there in like manner prorogued and thence also [adjourned] and continued to our city of Dublin aforesaid on the Monday next after the feast of St Luke the evangelist then next following [22 October 1480], passed in these words:

Also, at the prayer of the mayor, bailiffs and commons of the city of Dublin, that whereas both by the confirmation of our sovereign lord the king that now is and by gift and grant by his noble progenitors, kings of England and lords of Ireland, they and their successors ought to have and receive [the services due to them] from all manner of lands and tenements within the franchise of the same which were held of them in chief by any manner of services in the same, of whatsoever persons they be, and also by the same gift and grant, that all manner of free persons dwelling within the franchise of the said city after the death of their ancestors should not be in wardship to any person by reason of any foreign tenure which they hold of any other person, and they and their predecessors have used from the time of the said grant until now of late, that by the death of Richard Fitzwilliam, freeman dwelling within the franchise of the said city, who died seised of the lordship of Bagotrath, his son and heir being under the age of twenty-one years and in the wardship of the king by reason of his foreign tenancy which he held of our said sovereign lord in chief, whereby our said sovereign lord and others his committees have claimed to have the wardship of the said Bagotrath, being within the franchise of the said city and held of them by the service of twenty marks by the year of the said mayor, bailiffs and commons, by reason whereof they should be put from their distress for the said twenty marks unless a remedy for them be provided; whereupon the premises being considered, and how they are daily ready to meet the wars of the said land at their own costs and charges, it is ordained, enacted and established by authority of the said parliament that it shall be lawful for the said mayor, bailiffs and commons that now are, and for their successors and for every of them for ever, to enter and distrain on all the lands and tenements which are held of them within the said franchise or of any of

32 From memoranda roll 22 Edward IV m. 33 (RC 8/42 pp 101–7).

them as in right of the said city, notwithstanding that the said lands and tenements so being within the said franchise be in the hands of our said sovereign lord the king or in those of any other person, the statute *de prerogativa regis* or any other act, ordinance or statute made to the contrary notwithstanding; and that by the same authority all free persons dwelling within the said city shall never be in wardship to any person by reason of their foreign tenancy, according to the grants made to them by our sovereign lord the king that now is and by his noble progenitors, kings of England and lords of Ireland, notwithstanding the fact that they hold any lands, tenements, rents or service of our sovereign lord the king; provided that the said mayor and bailiffs of the said city who now are or hereafter shall be, shall not distrain within the said lordship of Bagotrath for more than ten pounds during the minority of the son and heir of the said Richard, now being under the age of twenty-one years, and the other five marks to be had for the repair of the chief place, and that the said mayor and bailiffs shall be discharged of the said five marks upon their account in the king's exchequer in Ireland and that this act shall not take place until after the feast of Easter next.

We also the act etc. have caused to be exemplified. In witness whereof etc. Witness etc. the fifth day of November the twentieth year of our reign [5 November 1480].

[The full text of this act is preserved in an *inspeximus* under the Irish great seal, dated 5 November 1480, and reads:

> Item al supplicacion del maier bailliefs et comunes del cite de Dyvelyn, que sibien par confirmacion de nostre soveraine seignur le Roy qorest come par le done et graunte par sez nobles progenitours Roies dengleterre et seignurs dirlande qils et lour successours devoient avere et percevere de touts maneres terres et tenementz deins la franchesie del meisme lez queux furent tenuz de eaux en chief par ascune manere service en lez maines de quelconque person qils sount, et auxi par mesmez les done et graunte qe toute manere dez franqes gents demorauntez deins la franchesie del dit cite apres la morte de lour auncestres ne serroient my en garde a nule person par reisoun de ascune foren tenure quele ils tenoient de ascune aultre person le quele ils et lour predecessours ount usez del temps du dit graunte jesqes a ore de tarde qe par la morte de Richard fitz William franqe home et demorant dans la franchesie del dit cite le quel morust seisie del seignurie de Bagot Rath soun fitz et heire esteauntez deins le age de xxj anes et le garde du dit Roy par reisoun de soun foren tenauncie le quel il tenoit de nostre dit souveraine seignur et aultres sez committees ount clamez de avere le garde del dit

Bagot Rath esteaunt deins la franchesie del dit cite et tenuz de eaux par le service de xx marces par le ane de lez ditz maier bailliefs et comunes par reisoun de quele ils serrount misez de lour distresse pur lez ditz xx marces saunz remedie soit a eaux provide. Sur que lez premisses considerez et coment ils sount de jour en aultre prestez a respoundre lez guerres del mesme la terre sur lour proprez custages de mesmez et charges, ordene est enacte et establie par auctorite du dit parliament qe bien luist as dit maier bailliefs et comunes queux ore sount et a lour successours et a chescun de eaux pur toutz jours a enterer et distreigner en touts terres et tenementz queux issint sount tenuz de eaux deins la dit franchesie ou de ascun de eaux come en droite del dit cite nient obstaunt qe lez ditz terres et tenementz issint esteauntz deins la dit franchesie sount en lez maines de nostre dit souveraine seignur le Roy ou en ascun aultre person, lestatute de prerogativa Regis acte ordenaunce ou ascun aultre estatute fait au contrarie nient obstaunt. Et qe par mesme lauctorite toutz franqes gents demorauntez deins la dit cite ne soient my en garde a nule person par reisoun de lour foren tenauncie accordaunt a lour grauntes sibien par nostre souveraine seignur le Roy quorest come par sez nobles progenitours Royes dengleterre et seignurs dirland nient obstaunt qils teignount ascunz terres et tenementes rentes ou service de nostre souveraine seignur le Roy, purveu qe lez ditz maier et bailliefs del dit cite queux ore sount ou en temps avenire serrount ne distreignent my deins le dit seignurie de Bagot Rath sinon taunt soulment pur x livres duraunt le non age del fitz et heire du dit Richard ore esteaunt deins le age de xxj anes et les aultres v marces de estre ewez al reparacioun del chief lieu et que les ditz maier et bailliefs soient dischargez de lez ditz v marces sur lour accompte en leschequier le Roy en Irland et qe cest acte ne preigne lieu jesqes apres le fest de Pasqz proschien avenaunt.[33]]

[15] 21 Edward IV [1481–2][34] [Confirmation of office of sergeant at law to John Estrete and licence for him to leave the country whenever necessary]

Edward etc. We have seen certain acts or ordinances in our parliament held [at] Dublin on the Friday next after the feast of St Luke the evangelist in the twenty-first year of our reign [19 October 1481] before our most beloved

33 Dublin City Archives: Royal Charter to City of Dublin, no. 61 [ref: C1/1/61]. The text is reproduced here by permission of Dublin City Archives. 34 From memoranda roll 23 Edward IV m. 3 (RC 8/42 pp 109–17)

cousin Gerald, earl of Kildare, deputy of our beloved and very dear son Richard of Shrewsbury, duke of York, our lieutenant of our land of Ireland, and at various times prorogued and continued there on the Thursday next after the feast of St Luke the evangelist last past [24 October 1482] set forth in these words:

Also, at the prayer of John Estrete, serjeant of our sovereign lord the king at his laws in Ireland, whereas our said sovereign lord the king by his letters patent made at Dublin the sixth day of July in the twenty-first year of his most noble reign [1481][35] under the attestation of his well beloved cousin, Gerald, earl of Kildare, deputy of his well beloved son, Richard of Shrewsbury, duke of York, lieutenant of our said sovereign lord the king of his land of Ireland, reciting by the same letters patent how he, before that time, by other letters patent and by authority of parliament, of [his] abundant grace had given to the said John the office of his serjeant at his laws in the said land [to] hold and exercise the said office according to the tenor and effect of the said letters patent, [receiving] yearly the annual sum of ten pounds at the feasts of Easter and St Michael the archangel by equal portions, and that hereupon, of his most ample and especial grace, by the assent of his said well beloved cousin and deputy as it is aforesaid, for the greater surety of the payment of the said annual sum of ten pounds by [means] of the said letters patent as it is aforesaid made the sixth day of July in the year aforesaid, has given and granted to the said John five pounds yearly, as part of the said annual sum of ten pounds, to have and receive the said annual sum of five pounds to the said John during his life in the office aforesaid [out of the] rents, issues, profits, commodities and revenues yearly proceeding or accruing out of the [fee farm of the] said sovereign lord the king of his town of Drogheda, by the hands of the sheriffs of his [said town for the time] being, to be paid at the feasts of St Michael and Easter by equal portions, as is contained in the said letters patent; whereupon the premises being considered, it is ordained, enacted and established by authority of this parliament that the said letters patent as is aforesaid made the said sixth day of July in the year aforesaid and the said gift and grant of the said annual sum of five pounds and all other manner of things appertaining to his said office specified and contained in them, by authority of this said parliament, be ratified, confirmed and adjudged good and effectual in law, and by the same authority shall be given and granted to the said John [the said offi]ce, these and the arrears of the same to have, hold and receive for the term of his life and according to the tenor and effect of the same; and that by the same authority it

35 The patent roll for 21 Edward IV was too damaged to be calendared in *Rot. pat. Hib.*

shall be lawful for the said John at his pleasure, as often as he requires, to sue and have his actions of debt for default of payment of his fee appertaining to his said office against all and every such manner of person or persons who is or shall be chargeable with the dues and arrears thereof or any part thereof in any court that the king has in this his said land, and process thereon to be made for the interest of the said John in the same, such as lies in an action of trespass at common law. Also at the prayer of John Estrete, serjeant to our sovereign lord the king at his laws in Ireland, whereas the said John, under the licence of the benign and benevolent favours of the most noble lord Gerald, earl of Kildare, deputy lieu[tenant of Ireland], of the lords spiritual and temporal, proctors and commons in this said parliament assembled, intends to pass from this land into England and the parts of the same, to visit and see his friends in the said parts and to accomp[lish] other business which he has to do for his interest in the same; where[upon the] premises being considered, it is enacted, ordained and established by authority of the said parliament that it shall be lawful for the [said John] at any time in the future, and as often as it shall please him, to depart and be absent out of this [land of Ireland in the] said parts of England and, as often as may be requisite, to return into this land of Ireland [and the parts] of the same, and every manner of act, ordinance, statute and other manner of thing do[ne ordained or] had, or in any manner to be done, ordained or had, by which the said John in a[ny manner] might be prejudiced or injured in his office or otherwise, by authority of this said parliament shall be [adjudged] not to extend or also to be of such effect in law in any manner as to injure or prejudice [the said] John in office, or in any other manner of thing which shall be appertaining to his right title and interest in [the said] land, but that by the same authority it shall be lawful at all times for the said John to resort to and to have, [enjoy] and exercise all such things according to his right and interest in the same, any manner of [statute] in any manner to the contrary made and ordained, or to be made and ordained, notwithstanding; and if any person shall do any manner of thing by prosecution or otherwise to put the said John out of the said office or [shall accept] and occupy any office appertaining to him in any time to come. he who shall so prosecute or [put the] said John out of office and also he who shall accept or occupy the same, by the same authority shall be adjudged [to] pay to the said John ten times as much as the fees and the wages of the said office with the rewards [appertaining shall be] worth yearly.

[16] 21–22 Edward IV [1481–2][36] [Confirmation of grant of reversion of an annuity out of the fee farm of the city of Dublin made by Robert Dowdall to his son Thomas]

Edward etc. We have seen a certain [act or] ordinance in our parliament held at Dublin on the Friday next after the feast of St Luke the evangelist in the twenty-first year of our reign [19 October 1481], before our most beloved cousin Gerald, earl of Kildare, deputy of our beloved and very dear son, Richard of Shrewsbury, duke of York, our lieutenant of our land of Ireland,[37] on the Monday next after the feast of the Purification of the blessed virgin Mary then next following [4 February 1482], in these words:

Also at the prayer of Thomas Douedall of Dublin, gentleman, son to Robert Douedall, knight, chief justice of the common place of the king in Ireland, whereas the said Robert has granted to the said Thomas the reversion of ten marks of an annuity appertaining to the said Robert after the death of one John, to have and receive the said ten marks yearly to Thomas and to the heirs from his body issuing by the hands of the mayor and bailiffs of the city of Dublin for the time being, at the feasts of Easter and St Michael by equal portions as in the said deed more fully appears, the tenor of which follows in the following form:

> To all the faithful in Christ to whom the present letters may come, Robert Douedall, knight, chief justice of the lord the king of his common bench of Ireland, greeting. Know you that whereas Henry IV late king of England by his letters patent made had granted to Edward Perers and his heirs twenty marks of the fee farm of the city of Dublin to be received yearly by the hands of the mayor and bailiffs of the city aforesaid and of their successors who for the time being should be,[38] in recompense of twenty marks which the said Edward and his heirs were held to pay to the said mayor and bailiffs and their successors aforesaid for certain lands and tenements in Bagotrath within the franchise of the aforesaid city, to have and to hold the said twenty marks of the fee farm of the aforesaid city to the aforesaid Edward, his heirs and assigns for ever, which letters patent and all things contained in the same Henry V, lately king of England, by his letters patent confirmed, ratified and approved to the said Edward and his heirs aforesaid,[39] and also Henry

36 From memoranda roll 2 Richard III m. 15 (RC 8/42 pp 121–33). 37 Words relating to the adjournment of the parliament missing here? 38 The grant was dated at Dublin, 14 January 1408. It is not included in the patent roll of 9 Henry IV calendared in *Rot. pat. Hib.* pp 186–88, but is referred to in a confirmation made under the English great seal on 13 June 1413 (*Cal. Pat. Rolls, 1413–16*, p. 45). 39 *Ibid.*

the sixth, late king of England, granted, confirmed and ratified the said twenty marks to John Hall, cousin and heir of the said Edward, by his letters patent under the great seal of England and his own attestation, as is plainly manifest by the said letters patent;[40] and afterwards, in a certain parliament held at Dublin before Edward fitz Eustace, lately deputy of Richard, duke of York, lieutenant of the said Henry the sixth of his land aforesaid, it was ordained and established that the said John should have power to grant the said twenty marks of yearly rent to me, the said Robert Douedall, and William Sutton, then one of the barons of the said lord the king of his exchequer of Ireland, to have to us our heirs and assigns for ever, and that we, the said Robert and William, should have power to grant again twenty marks of yearly rent to the said John to have for the term of his life, the reversion thereof after the death of the said John Hall to belong to me, the said Robert, and to William, our heirs and assigns for ever, and that we, the said Robert and William, might separately inherit the said twenty marks to wit, ten marks thereof to me, the said Robert, my heirs and assigns and ten marks to the aforesaid William, his heirs and assigns, as in the aforesaid statute more fully appears;[41] and [that] afterwards, the aforesaid John Hall by authority of the parliament and statute aforesaid gave and granted to me, the said Robert, and to William, our heirs and assigns, the said twenty marks of yearly rent to be taken and received yearly out of the fee farm of the city aforesaid, by the hands of the mayor and bailiffs of the said city for the time being, at two terms of the year, to wit, at the feasts of Easter and St Michael by equal portions, to have and to hold to me, the aforesaid Robert, and to William, our heirs and assigns for ever, whereupon the aforesaid Robert and William, by authority of the said parliament and statute, gave and granted to the said John Hall the said twenty marks of yearly rent to be taken and received yearly out of the fee farm of the aforesaid city by the hands of the mayor and sheriffs of the said city, who then were or for the time should be, at two terms of the year, to wit, at the feasts of Easter and St Michael the archangel by equal portions, to have and to hold the said twenty marks to the aforesaid John for the term of the life of the said John, so that after the death of the said John ten marks of the twenty marks should remain and revert separately by authority of the said parliament and statute to me, the aforesaid Robert, my heirs and assigns for ever, and the other ten marks of the said twenty

40 The grant to Perers was confirmed by Henry VI on 25 April 1423 (*Cal. Pat. Rolls, 1422–9*, p. 95), but no subsequent confirmation to John Hall has been located. 41 The text of this statute has not survived. For a seventeeth century note of the enactment, see *Stat. Ire., Henry VI*, p. 296. The parliament was held at Dublin on 5 July 1454 (ibid., p. 348).

> marks after the death of the said John should remain and revert separately, by authority of the said parliament and statute, to the aforesaid William, his heirs and assigns for ever, as in our said deed made thereof to the said John more fully appears; know you that I, the aforesaid Robert Douedall, have given and granted and by this my present writing have confirmed and assigned to Thomas Douedall, my son, my said reversion or remainder of the aforesaid ten marks, part of the aforesaid twenty marks of yearly rent, which, as aforesaid, by authority of the said parliament and statute aforesaid, remains and reverts to me the aforesaid Robert my heirs and assigns after the death of the aforesaid John Hall, when that should happen, to have and to hold and receive my said reversion or remainder of the aforesaid ten marks by the hands of the mayor and bailiffs of the said city and their successors, who for the time shall be, yearly at two terms of the year, to wit, at the feasts of Easter and St Michael the archangel by equal portions, and if it shall happen that the aforesaid Thomas shall die without an heir issuing from his body, then I will that the aforesaid ten marks shall remain and revert to Joan Douedall, my daughter, and the heirs issuing from her body, and if it shall happen that the aforesaid Joan shall die without an heir issuing from her body, that then the aforesaid ten marks shall remain and revert to Margaret Douedall, my daughter, and the heirs issuing from her body, and if it shall happen that the aforesaid Margaret shall die without an heir issuing from her body, that then the aforesaid ten marks shall remain or revert to my right heirs, to have receive and take the aforesaid ten marks at the feasts of Easter and St Michael the archangel by equal portions yearly by the hands of the mayor and bailiffs of the said city for the time being. In witness whereof to this my present writing I have affixed my seal. Given the tenth day of January in the twenty-first year of the reign of king Edward the fourth [1482].

Whereupon the premises being considered, it is ordained, established and enacted by authority of the said parliament that the said grant of reversion made to the said Thomas and all and every thing contained in the deed of the said grant and every other grant in law of any lands made, given or granted in any manner to the said Thomas Douedall be authorised, ratified, approved, confirmed and adjudged good and effectual in law to the purport, tenor and effect of the same in all points, and that by the said authority [it be] decreed, granted and ordained that the said Thomas and his heirs from his body issuing and all the others contained in the said grant of reversion shall have, receive and enjoy the said ten marks of the annuity yearly to be received at the hands of the mayor and bailiffs of the said city for the time being at the feasts of

Easter and St Michael by equal portions, immediately after the death of the said John successively, to have and to hold to the said Thomas and to the heirs of his body issuing according to the tenor and purport of the said grant of reversion with all such power and authority to receive and sue for the said annuity yearly or any arrears of the same as is contained in an act of parliament made in the days of the said Henry the sixth before Edward fitz Eustace, knight, then being deputy lieutenant of this his land of Ireland, any statute, matter, title or cause done or alleged in defeasance of the payment or in avoidance of the said ten marks of annuity to be pa[id in] any of the grants made to the said Thomas contrary to the grants of the same in any manner notwithstanding.

And we etc. have caused to be exemplified etc. Witness etc. the twentieth day of November in the twenty-second year of our reign [1482].

[17] 21 Edward IV [1481–2][42] [Confirmation of all grants made to Holy Trinity, Dublin]

Edward etc. We have seen a certain act or ordinance in our parliament held at Dublin on the Friday next after the feast of St Luke the evangelist last past [19 October 1481] before our most beloved cousin [Gerald], earl of Kildare, deputy of our beloved and very dear son, Richard of Shrewsbury, duke of York, our lieutenant of our land of Ireland, and at various times prorogued also there on the Monday next after the feast of the Holy Trinity then next following [3 June 1482] at the request etc. and set forth in these words:

Also at the prayer of Thomas, prior of the Holy Trinity, being within the city of Dublin, and the canons and convent of the same there serving the Holy Trinity, in consideration of the fact that various of their deeds and muniments concerning their foundation from their antiquity are failing, ruinous and in decay, it is ordained by authority of this parliament that where any manner of person or persons, by his or their gracious dispositions inspired into them by virtue of the Holy Trinity, have founded or endowed or have given, granted, let or in any manner demised or leased to the said prior or convent, or to any of their predecessors, or in any manner in time to come will endow, give or grant, let or in any manner demise or lease to the said prior and convent, or to any of their successors, any manner of manors, lordships, messuages, lands, tenements, rents, annuities, reversions or services or any other manner of possessions whatsoever, that by authority of this present act and ordinance it shall be lawful for the said prior and convent and for their successors to retain

42 From memoranda roll 2–3 Richard III m. 7d. (RC 8/42 pp 137–43).

in their possession and to enjoy, accept, receive and to enter into all the said manors, lordships, messuages, lands, tenements, rents, grants, annuities, reversions and services, and into every and all other manner of possessions whatsoever in form aforesaid demised or leased to them and their predecessors, or to be endowed, given, granted, let or in any manner demised or leased in any time to come by any manner of person or persons to them and their successors, or solely to their successors, as to the said church or house, to have and hold, retain and enjoy to them and to their successors in pure free and perpetual alms, quit for ever, saving to the chief lords thereof their services due and accustomed of right, and this without any suit of any writ of *ad quod damnum* or any other manner of suit in this behalf to be made to them or their successors, and by the same authority that the statute made for the restraint of alienation, gifts and grants of lands and tenements and of any of the premises in mortmain, and all and every other manner of statute, act [or] ordinance in any manner to the contrary made or to be made, and also all and every manner of restraint, use, custom or any other matter or thing to the contrary had or used shall be restricted and not extend in any manner of effect in law to be prejudicial to or to injure the said prior and convent or any of their successors of, for or in any of the premises; and that by the same authority it shall be lawful for every manner of person and persons to give, grant and demise lands, tenements and [so] of every such thing that is specified in the premises and to make alienation of them and of every part thereof jointly and severally to the said prior and convent and to their successors at all times at their pleasure, and this without any manner of licence to be sued and fine to be made for the same, and for one only fee of six shillings and eight pence to be paid into the hanaper of the king in his chancery of Ireland; and that this present act shall not extend nor be prejudicial to Patrick Burnell and Anne his wife, or to Walter, abbot of the house of the monastery of St Mary near Dublin and the convent of the same, or their successors, or to Thomas Sharp, or to the proctors of the church of Warbrooke in Dublin, or to their successors, or to any of them in any manner, or to such possession and entry of the mayor, bailiffs and commons of the city of Dublin in any manner for the premises so given; except always that this act shall not extend or be prejudicial to the right reverend father in God, John, archbishop of Dublin or to John, abbot of the house of St Thomas the martyr near Dublin, or to Sir Rowland Eustace, knight, lord of Portlester, or to [the prior] of Kilmainham, or to James Flemyng, knight, baron of Slane, or to Robert St Laurence, knight, lord of Howth, or to the heirs of Nicholas White, late of Killester, esquire, or to any of them.

And we etc. have thought fit to have exemplified etc. Witness etc. the eighth day of June in the twenty-second year of our reign [1482].

[18] 21 Edward IV [1481–2][43] [Licence for William, bishop of Meath, chancellor of Ireland, to go on pilgrimage to England and to appoint a deputy]

Edward etc. We have seen a certain act or ordinance in our parliament held at Dublin on the Friday next after the feast of St Luke the evangelist last past [19 October 1481] before our most beloved cousin Gerald, earl of Kildare, deputy of our dear and well beloved son, Richard of Shrewsbury, duke of York, our lieutenant of our land of Ireland. also there to the Monday next after the feast of the blessed virgin Mary then next following [4 February 1482] passed and remaining of record in the rolls of our chancery of Ireland, in these words:

Also, at the prayer of William, bishop of Meath and chancellor of Ireland, whereas of late in his great infirmity he vowed certain pilgrimages to be made in person to St William of York, Our Lady of Lancaster, Walsingham and various other places within the kingdom of England, if God of his infinite grace would send him the relief of health out of his infirmity, in consideration of which vow it is ordained, enacted and established, and given and granted to the said bishop by authority of the said parliament that it shall be lawful for himself to absent himself out of this land of Ireland from the day of his departure out of this land to his said pilgrimage for or during the term of one entire year next ensuing and fully completed and that during the said year, he, or his proctors, attorneys, bailiffs and servants may have, collect and receive all manner of procurations, taxes, pensions, fees, wages, rents, profits, issues, commodities, oblations, tithes and emoluments whatsoever, both in and of the said office of chancellor of Ireland, and of the said bishopric of Meath, and all other manner of things in any manner belonging or appertaining to him and from time to time may send, convey and carry them and every part of them to England or elsewhere to him, and for and to his use, any statute or statutes, ordinance or provision made or ordained within the kingdom of England or this land of Ireland to the contrary notwithstanding; it is also ordained, enacted and established by the said authority that it shall be lawful for the said William, bishop of Meath, chancellor of Ireland, to make, and he may make, a deputy for whom he will answer, to have, occupy and exercise as his deputy therein the office of the deputy chancellorship in his absence within this land of Ireland, and that by the said authority the said deputy chancellor so deputed, ordained, assigned and made by the said William, bishop of Meath, shall have as full power and authority to have, occupy and exercise the said office of deputy chancellor of Ireland in all and every point as if he were named in this present act, any statute, act, ordinance or custom to the contrary made or used notwithstand-

43 From memoranda roll 22 Edward IV m. 10 (RC 8/42 pp 145–51).

ing; and that the day of the departure of the said bishop out of this said land shall be entered of record in the chancery, and if it should happen that the said deputy made by the said chancellor dies during the absence of the said chancellor, that then, by the authority aforesaid, it is ordained, enacted and established that there shall not be a vacancy in the person of the said chancellor, either by the death of the said deputy or by the absence of the said chancellor, but that the letters patent of the king made to the said chancellor of the office aforesaid and every other grant, ratification or confirmation made to the said chancellor of this office aforesaid shall be of as great force and effect as if the said bishop chancellor were present continually within the said land and not absent out of the same, the death of the said deputy and the absence of the chancellor notwithstanding; and that by the said authority it is ordained, enacted and established that the said chancellor immediately after his arrival within this land of Ireland and continually thereafter shall have, occupy, exercise and enjoy the said office of chancellor in manner and form as he now occupies the said office, his said office and the death of the said deputy notwithstanding; and that by the said authority it is ordained, enacted and established that every person spiritual and temporal being in service with the said chancellor out of this land of Ireland during the said absence shall have licence and authority to be absent out of this said land during the time of the absence of the said bishop, and shall have, receive, occupy and enjoy peaceably and freely all the issues and profits of both spiritual and temporal possessions pertaining to them and to each one of them, both in spiritualities and in temporalities, in person or by their servants, without any impediment or hindrance on the part of our sovereign lord the king, his heirs, officers or ministers whomsoever in time to come, any statute, act or ordinance to the contrary made notwithstanding; and that the said chancellor shall enter the names of his said servants who shall go along with him and who shall take advantage or benefit by this said act in the said chancery at his said departure.

Exemplified 12 April 22 Edward IV [1482]

[19] 21 Edward IV [1481–2][44] [Edward Bordon to surrender himself and make restitution to the prior of Athassel for robberies and unlawful imprisonment]

Be it remembered that our lord the king sent to his justices of the common bench of Ireland the tenor of a certain act or ordinance in his parliament held at Dublin on the Friday next after the feast of St Luke the evangelist in the

44 From memoranda roll 22 Edward IV m. 19 (RC 8/42 pp 153–9).

twenty-first year of his reign [19 October 1481] before his most beloved cousin, Gerald, earl of Kildare, deputy of his beloved and very dear son, Richard of Shrewsbury, duke of York, his lieutenant of his land of Ireland, and at various times prorogued and continued also there on the Monday next after the feast of St Luke the evangelist last past [21 October 1482] set forth etc. the tenor of which writ and act follows in these words:

Edward etc. Witness etc. the twelfth day of November in the twenty-second year of our reign [1482].

Also at the prayer of David Hakett, prior of the house of St Edward of Hassell in the county of Tipperary and the convent of the same, whereas a certain Edward Bordon of Fydyrth within the same county, gentleman, on the sixteenth day of May in the twentieth year of the reign of king Edward the fourth [1480] with various Irish enemies and English rebels came to the said place of the prior of Hassell within the said county of Tipperary and there despoiled the said prior of one hundred cows, one hundred heifers with various other goods and chattels found there to the value of one hundred pounds, against law, right and conscience, to the final destruction and desolation of the lands of the said prior; and also the said Edward Bordon with various Irish enemies and English rebels took the said prior in the king's highway with force and arms, and unjustly detained him in prison until of necessity he was obliged to await judgment of the brehons, by which he was compelled to pay forty pounds against the king's jurisdiction and reduced the aforesaid prior and his convent into such subjection that they cannot celebrate divine service there now or in the future unless a gracious remedy be provided for them in this behalf; whereupon the premises being considered, and the fact that Edward Bordon is not amenable to common law, it is ordained, enacted and established by authority of the said parliament, that proclamation be made in the same that the aforesaid Edward Bordon shall come and appear in person before the justices of the lord the king of his common bench of Ireland on the quindene of St Hilary next [27 January] within the castle of Dublin and remain there in the custody of the marshal of the said common bench without bail or mainprise until he make restitution and due satisfaction for the aforesaid injuries; and if the aforesaid Edward Bordon do not come or appear in person before the aforesaid justices on the aforesaid day and make restitution and due satisfaction in the premises, that then he shall be attainted a felon, and further, by the authority aforesaid, that all arbitrary judgments given before this time against the aforesaid prior shall be void and of no effect in law; and by the authority aforesaid it shall be lawful for the aforesaid prior and his assigns to enter into all the messuages, lands and tenements which the aforesaid Edward Bordon has within the land of Ireland, or which any person or persons have to the use of the said

Edward, and to receive the issues and profits thereof and retain them in the hands of the said prior and his assigns until the aforesaid prior be satisfied of his damages and injuries aforesaid.

[20] 21–22 Edward IV [1481–2][45] [Privileges and customs granted to the town of Ardee, co. Louth]

Edward etc. We have seen a certain act or ordinance in our parliament held at Dublin on the Friday next after the feast of St Luke the evangelist last past [19 October 1481] before our most beloved cousin, Gerald, earl of Kildare, deputy of our well beloved and very dear son Richard of Shrewsbury, duke of York, our lieutenant of our land of Ireland, and at various times prorogued also there on the Monday next after the feast of the Holy Trinity then next following [3 June 1482] set forth in these words:

Also, at the request of the portreeves, burgesses and commons of the town of Athyrd in the county of Louth, whereas the said town is situated in the borders of the march and daily in danger of the Irish enemies of the king, in consideration thereof it is ordained, established and enacted by authority of this parliament that the said portreeves, burgesses and commons shall have to them and to their successors the privileges and customs here following: first, that the said portreeves of the said town and their successors shall be coroners for the time being in the franchise, and that, by the said authority, the portreeves and burgesses of the said town for the time being shall have full power to them and to their successors to make laws, acts and ordinances in their judgment for the common benefit of the said town, except only that they shall not make laws which shall be against the king's regality; and by the same authority it is ordained and enacted that no man shall practise to buy nor sell by a weight called *ancell* upon pain of the forfeiture of their *ancells* and their bodies to be [put] in prison and to make fine according to the discretion of the said portreeves and their successors; and that the said portreeves, burgesses and commons shall have and enjoy to them and to their successors custom of all manner of merchandise issuing out of the said town in like manner and form as they have had and used to receive of all manner of merchandise coming to their town and sold in the said town or in the franchise; and that the portreeves of the said town for the time being shall have full power to have their maces carried before them and that every of them shall have a mace carried before him within their franchise; and by the said authority it is ordained that all manner of heaps of dung between the Bridgegate and the Northgate of

45 From memoranda roll 19 Henry VII m. 6d. (RC 8/42 pp 169–73).

the said town shall be sent away and displaced between this and the feast of All Saints next coming [1 November] and if they are not sent away by that time, that then it shall be lawful by the said authority for the said portreeves and burgesses and their successors to have and distrain in every house which is between the said Bridgegate and Northgate of the said town in the high street for 40d. yearly, the same to be had and paid from the rent of the said houses and to be expended upon the common works of the said town until the said heaps of dung are clearly sent away and displaced; and by the said authority all manner of grants, customs, patents of the king or by authority of parliament or by any other person shall be authorised, approved and confirmed so that this act shall not extend nor be prejudicial to any free men of the city of Dublin, or to the town of Drogheda, or to their attorney in any manner, or to Nicholas Taff, or to Robert Taff or to any of them; also that this act shall not be prejudicial to Alianore Faunt, her heirs and assigns or to any other person or persons to the use of the said Elianor, her heirs and assigns.

And we have caused to be exemplified etc. Witness etc. the fourteenth day of June in the twenty-second year of our reign [1482]

[21] 22 Edward IV [1483][46] [No assignments to be paid out of the customs and cocket of Dublin until payment has been made out of those revenues to John Estrete]

Edward etc. We have seen a certain act or ordinance in our parliament held at Limerick on the Friday next before Ash Wednesday last past [7 February 1483] before our most beloved cousin, Gerald, earl of Kildare, deputy of our well beloved and very dear son, Richard of Shrewsbury, duke of York, our lieutenant of our land of Ireland, set forth in these words:

Also, at the prayer of John Estrete, serjeant at the laws of the king in Ireland, whereas the said John, both by virtue of the king's letters patent and by authority of [an act ?] in parliament made and ordained on behalf of the said John,[47] is entitled to receive payment of his yearly fee by the hands of the customer, occupier or receiver, occupiers or receivers out of the customs and cockets of the king yearly received by and pertaining to the king of wool, leather, hides, lead, tin and of all other manner of merchandise customable and cockettable in the harbour and port of the city of Dublin, as more fully appears both by the said letters patent and by the said act; in consideration of the premises it is ordained and established that it shall not be lawful for any manner of customer, occupier, receiver, occupiers or receivers of the said customs in any time to

46 From memoranda roll 23 Edward IV m. 4 (RC 8/42 pp 161–5). **47** See above, no. 13.

come to make any manner of payments of the said customs to any manner of persons for their fees assigned or to be assigned upon the same, except such fees as are assigned upon them to Philip Bermyngham, chief justice of the chief place of the king in Ireland, and Thomas Plunket, chief justice of his common pleas in the same, until the said John be fully, yearly and from term to term, paid the hundred shillings thereof as part of his fees by virtue of the letters patent and not aforesaid assigned upon the same at two terms of the year, to wit at the feasts of Easter and St Michael the archangel yearly from henceforward by equal portions; and if any such customer, occupier or receiver, occupiers or receivers of the said custom and cocket aforesaid at any future time do contrary to this present act and ordinance, that then, by the same authority, he or they who shall be found so doing shall be adjudged debtor or debtors to the said John of all manner of such sums of money as shall happen to be unpaid and in arrear to the said John; and by the same authority it shall be lawful for the said John to sue his action or actions of debt as often as he requires it in any court the king has for the recovery of the same.

And we have caused to be exemplified etc. Witness etc. the tenth day of April in the twenty-third year of our reign [1483].

An unenrolled act passed in the 1493 parliament

In addition to the 32 enactments enrolled on the statute roll for 8 Henry VII and printed above, the parliament of that year also passed an act for the protection of pilgrims visiting the church of the Holy Trinity in Dublin (also known as Christ Church). This act does not appear on the roll as transcribed by the Irish Record Commission, but the reason for this is not apparent. It is possible, however, that it was originally enrolled on a membrane which is now lost. There are several indications that there may have been a membrane preceding the text as it now exists. The heading of the roll does not begin in the usual form 'Statutes, acts and ordinances ...', and the three customary acts confirming the liberties of the church, the land of Ireland and the cities and corporate towns, which usually appeared as the first three enactments of any parliament, are missing. The present first chapter begins 'Also ...', implying that there was at least one preceding act. It is possible that the first membrane may have been lost at an early stage and the present heading added to the top of the first surviving membrane.

The text of the act is known to us from an exemplification under the Irish great seal dated 26 August 1493, which is preserved in two formats:

(1) The exemplification copied into the *Liber Albus* or White Book of Christ Church, compiled between 1505 and 1517.[1] In this version, the text of the letters patent exemplifying the act is in Latin, but the wording of the act itself is given in English.[2]

(2) A confirmation, dated 10 July 1495, of the act by archbishop Octavian of Armagh and the bishops of that province in a provincial council held at Drogheda on 6 July 1495. The clergy of the province were ordered to excommunicate all those transgressing the act. The text of this confirmation survives in the register of archbishop Octavian and embodies the full text of the letters of exemplification of 26 August 1493.[3] The text of the

1 Representative Church Body Library, MS C 6.1.2, ff 34v–35r. H.J. Lawlor, 'A calendar of the Liber Niger and Liber Albus of Christ Church, Dublin', *R.I.A. Proc.*, 27 C (1908), p. 2. The version in the Registrum Novum of Christ Church (RCB Library, MS 270 p. 890) was copied either from this or from the original letter among the Christ Church deeds. 2 Printed in J.H. Todd (ed.), *The Book of Obits and Martyrology of the Cathedral Church of the Holy Trinity* (Irish Archaeological Society, 1845), xxiii–xxv. This edition has been reprinted in Raymond Refaussé (ed.), *The registers of Christ Church Cathedral* (Dublin, 1998). 3 Mario Alberto Sughi (ed.), *Registrum Octaviani: the register of Octavian de Palatio, archbishop of Armagh, 1478–1513*

> act is given in Latin. A copy of this confirmation, together with a similar confirmation by a provincial council of the province of Dublin, dated 30 April 1495, was among the collection of Christ Church deeds destroyed in 1922, and was also copied into the *Liber Albus*.[4]

The fact that the text exists in both Latin and English versions gives rise to the question of the original language of the act. Exemplifications usually quoted the text as it was enacted, irrespective of the language used. In the case of an act passed in 1486 in favour of Robert Lawless, the exemplification (dated 5 January 1487) states that the text has been translated from French into Latin, and then quotes the Latin version.[5] One may assume that where no such statement is made, the original version is quoted. Exemplifications of two other acts of the 1486 parliament give the text of the acts in French, while a fourth gives the text in English.[6]

Of the 32 acts passed in the 1493 parliament and enrolled on the statute roll, 30 are in French, and the remaining two (relating to St Mary's abbey, Dublin), are in Latin. Although the use of English in enactments before 1494 is rare, two instance are known – the 1486 act mentioned above, and an act passed in 1491 freeing the tenants of Glasnevin from the payment of coign and livery, an exemplification of which is also contained in the *Liber Albus*.[7] It is possible that the language of the 1493 act under discussion was English, and that the exemplification contained the original text. The Latin version in Octavian's register may represent a translation from the original English made because Latin was the normal language used in ecclesiastical administration.

(Dublin, 1999), ii, pp 692–3. 4 M.J. McEnery and Raymond Refaussé (ed.), *Christ Church Deeds* (Dublin, 2000), nos. 361–2; RCB Library, Ms 6.1.2 ff 43r–47r . 5 '… quem quidem actum sive ordinacionem de gallico in latinum transferri fecimus in hec verba …' (Quinn, 'Bills and statutes', p. 79). 6 *Ibid.*, pp 78–9, 81–3. 7 ff 34v–34r, printed in Quinn, 'Bills and statutes', pp 85–6.

The fate of the Irish statute rolls, Richard III–Henry VIII

The following list is an attempt to establish when, and if possible why, the statute rolls of the Irish parliament for the reigns of Richard III, Henry VII and Henry VIII ceased to be in official custody. It is based on the following sources: (1) a list of existing statutes compiled in 1543 (PRO, SP 60/10 p. 46); (2) a copy of certified extracts from Irish statute rolls made by the clerk of parliament in 1617 (BL, Add. MS 4801); (3) the list of surviving rolls made by the Irish Record Commission in 1819 (*Supplement to the Eighth Report of the Irish Record Commission*, p. 356); (4) NAI, Chancery Detailed Index, prepared in PROI before 1922, vol. 1, p. 208 ; (5) sources quoted in D.B. Quinn, 'The bills and statutes of the Irish parliaments of Henry VII and Henry VIII', *Analecta Hibernica* 10 (1941), pp. 71–169, and in S.G. Ellis, 'Parliaments and great councils, 1483–99: addenda and corrigenda', *Analecta Hibernica* 29 (1980) pp 96–111. The footnotes to this list indicate when notes or exemplifications of enactments were made, though it should be remembered that these may have been made from the annotated bills or petitions and not from the statute rolls themselves.

year	*regnal year*	*fate*
1484	1 Ric. III	destroyed in 1922
1485	2–3 Ric. III	destroyed in 1922
1486	1 Henry VII	lost before 1617[1]
1487	[1 Ed VI][2]	annulled 1494–5 (10 Henry VII c.14) possibly destroyed officially
1488	3 Henry VII	lost before 1617[3]
1489	4 Henry VII	lost before 1617[4]
1490	5 Henry VII	lost before 1617
1491	6 Henry VII	lost before 1617[5]
1492	7 Henry VII	lost before 1617
1493	8 Henry VII	destroyed in 1922

1 Exemplification on memoranda roll 9 Henry VIII (1517–18) (NAI, Ferguson Coll., iv, f. 48). 2 Parliament held in the name of Edward VI (Lambert Simnel). 3 Note of enactment made c.1560 (NLI Ms 2507 f. 57v.). 4 Exemplification on memoranda roll 15 Henry VIII (1523–4) (NAI, Ferguson Coll., iv, ff 78–9). 5 Exemplification on memoranda roll 24 Henry VII (1508–9) (NAI, Ferguson Coll., iii, f.365; RC 8/43 pp 281–2).

1494	10 Henry VII	annulled 1494–5 (10 Henry VII c.40) possibly destroyed officially
1494–5	10 Henry VII	destroyed in 1922
1499	14 Henry VII	'embezzled' before 1527 ? in existence 1617, lost before 1819
1508–9	24 Henry VII	destroyed in 1922
1516	7 Henry VIII	mutilated 1520 destroyed in 1922
1521–2	13 Henry VIII	lost between 1617 and 1819
1531	23 Henry VIII	lost before 1543
1533	25 Henry VIII	destroyed in 1922
1536–7	28–29 Henry VIII	in NAI
1541–3	33–35 Henry VIII	destroyed in 1922

Index

The following abbreviations have been used:

CB	common bench	CJ	chief justice	DL	deputy lieutenant
exch.	exchequer	J	justice	KB	king's bench